AN INSTITUTIONAL INVESTOR PUBLICATION

# FIXED INCOME ANALYTICS

STATE-OF-THE-ART
DEBT ANALYSIS AND VALUATION MODELING

## RAVI E. DATTATREYA
EDITOR

PROBUS PUBLISHING COMPANY
Chicago, Illinois

ISBN 1-55738-163-1

Printed in the United States of America

KP

1  2  3  4  5  6  7  8  9  0

*To my mother,*
*Srimati Lokamata Sundararajan*

# Additional Institutional Investor Titles Available from Probus Publishing

*Asset/Liability Management: Investment Strategies, Liquidity Requirements and Risk Controls for Banks and Thrifts*, Atsuo Konishi and Frank Fabozzi, Editors

*Distressed Securities: Analyzing and Evaluating Market Potential and Investment Risk*, Edward Altman

*Eurodollar Futures and Options: Controlling Money Market Risk*, Galen Burghardt, Morton Lane, Terry Belton, Richard McVey and Geoffrey Luce

*Handbook of Derivative Instruments: Investment Research, Analysis and Portfolio Applications*, Atsuo Konishi and Ravi Dattatreya, Editors

*Margins and Market Integrity: State-of-the-Art Research on the Impact of Margins in Stocks & Futures Markets*, Mid America Institute

*Strategic Investment Management: How Global Corporations Manage Financial Risk for Competitive Advantage*, Mark Ahn and William Falloon

# Forthcoming Titles from Probus Publishing

*Investing: The Collected Works of Martin L. Leibowitz*, Frank Fabozzi, Editor

*Real Estate Portfolio Management: Analysis & Evaluation for Fund Mangers, Sponsors and Consultants*, Brian Bruce, Editor

# Contents

# Preface

The major objective of *Fixed Income Analytics* is to provide insight into the ways in which the various forces in the financial markets exert their influence. More specifically, we are referring to the influence of interest rates on bond prices or of volatility, or perceived volatility, on option values. Our goal is to understand the workings of the market by focusing on ideas and concepts and by developing our own wisdom. Knowledge is advanced and wisdom is created through thorough examination of a variety of different views of the same entity, some seemingly in conflict with others. We have, therefore, provided a platform to discuss disparate ideas. A mere collection of assorted numerical and contractual details and arcane mathematical techniques tends to create black boxes. With this in mind, we have eschewed complexity for its own sake. We believe that (mathematical) details are necessary only to the extent that they help to fix and clarify our understanding. We have resisted the temptation to endlessly parade unfamiliar Greek letters representing obscure properties of dubious significance. Display of mathematical rigor[1] is not our aim, and it is used only where necessary. We urge the reader to actively seek

---

1. We confess, however, that accurate mathematical representations and modeling more often than not lead the way to the insight that we seek. The point is simply to keep our aim on the end and not get lost in the means.

and mentally form patterns, and to look for intuitive and conceptual understanding of the financial processes. Such understanding is more valuable than the knowledge of the latest algorithm running on the newest model of supercomputer.

## Acknowledgements

I wish to thank Mr. Akira Kondoh and Mr. John Copenhaver of Sumitomo Bank Capital Markets, Inc., and Mr. Atsuo Konishi of S.B.C.M. (UK) for providing assistance and for their encouragement throughout this project. I also thank Debbie Hooper for editorial assistance and Kimberly Maharaj for help in the preparation of the manuscript.

*Ravi E. Dattatreya*
Summit, New Jersey

# Chapter 1

# Introduction

Ravi E. Dattatreya
Sumitomo Bank Capital Markets

Almost all financial transactions can be viewed as trading (i.e., buying and selling) activities. For example, borrowing is the sale of a promise to pay, and lending is simply the purchase of the right to receive those payments. As traders, the most essential requirement for all participants in the financial markets is to discover a way to determine the value of things traded.

In the case of many non-financial goods, several external indicators of value exist, for example, the cost of production. These are useful indicators because the value, or at least the perceived value, is relatively stable, and does not change too frequently. Typically, large numbers of buyers and sellers of these goods often create an environment for the law of supply and demand to work uninhibitedly. Financial instruments, on the other hand, do not always have clear external indicators of value. Their perceived value can change from minute to minute so that any one indicator, such as the initial cost, can become obsolete very quickly. Many instruments are one-of-a-kind. Often, a participant can find himself the only source of demand (or supply) for that instrument. Therefore, he cannot depend upon the forces of supply and demand to determine the value of the instrument.

As a consequence of these and other factors, we need a procedure or methodology for determining the value of financial instruments. This is because the raw contractual details of the instrument, such as coupon rate and maturity, are not sufficient to determine value without further processing.

In the fixed income markets, the use of yield and maturity as representations of reward and risk represented the first attempt at the development of a methodology for relative valuation. The idea was that even though the coupon rates of two bonds are not directly comparable, the yields are. The later substitution of duration for maturity as a better measure of risk was an advancement in this direction. The popularization of convexity as an additional factor in the measurement of risk brought computer and mathematical technology to the fixed income markets.

The duration, convexity, and yield of a bond are its analytical parameters. These parameters form the mathematical description of the bond. The beauty of the parametric representation of a bond or even that of a portfolio is that it is simple, compact, and highly intuitive. We should be careful, however, that this very desirable property of parametric analysis does not entice us into attributing greater precision to it than is warranted.[1] The inclusion of convexity in the analysis is an acknowledgement of the fact that the market parameters are not static. Yet convexity itself is a static number. To make the analysis more complete, we need a way to model the dynamics of the market, that is, the dynamics of the interest rate movements.

Another way to reach the same conclusion is to see that if the value of an instrument keeps changing, we need to know the manner in which it will respond to determinant market parameters, and we need to know how these market parameters themselves will change. Since we cannot know the future, we will have to make some assumptions regarding the future behavior of the market parameters.

---

1. For detailed illustrations, see Dattatreya, Ravi E. and Fabozzi, Frank, *Active Total Return Management of Fixed Income Portfolios.* Chicago: Probus Publishing, 1989.

## Essential Characteristics of a Framework

The whole valuation procedure depends upon the assumptions that we make. As such, they are of critical importance. A framework is the collection of the assumptions, the procedures, and the methodologies of valuation. The assumptions, in a way, are our opinion about the future. Naturally, the results will reflect our assumptions.

But is there a set of objective or neutral assumptions that will not color or bias the results? Fortunately, it is possible to state two simple conditions that every acceptable framework must satisfy. The first, internal consistency, guarantees that the framework is not self-contradictory. The second, external consistency, is a practical condition that dictates that the parameters of the framework be consistent with the market. The former addresses the values of securities and establishes the basic structure. The latter connects the framework to the market prices and calibrates it.

The internal consistency or the no-arbitrage condition requires that no riskless profitable arbitrage exists among fairly priced securities. This condition is usually employed in the valuation of options and was first used in the derivation of the Black-Scholes formula for options on stocks. As a consequence of the no-arbitrage condition, we normally do not have the freedom to arbitrarily assume the way yields and prices of different securities move. They have to maintain a proper relationship among themselves in order to satisfy the condition. For example, we cannot assume that the yield curve shifts are parallel without violating this condition.[2]

In a framework, the assumptions made about the movements of interest rates imply the values of many securities. The prices of these securities in the market may not be equal to the implied values. The external consistency condition requires that the model be tuned or calibrated so that actual market prices and implied values are in agreement. Usually, the framework has certain parameters,

---

2. Note, however, that simple assumptions, such as parallel yield curve movements, do not always produce useless results. Simple assumptions often do provide valuable insight, though we would not use the results for making actual investment decisions.

such as interest rate volatility and drift, that can be varied to bring about the desired agreement. This calibration process can be modified by our view that only a subset of the market is fairly priced; that is, we can assume that the value-price equality holds only for a selected group of securities. For example, only current-coupon Treasury bonds could be used for calibration. Another valid approach is to postulate that the market, on the average, is fairly priced, though individual securities may not be. In this case, we would first determine our idea of the average, perhaps a statistical fit to the market data, and then use it to calibrate the model. Without calibration, a model can be internally consistent. However, its cheapness/richness conclusions may not be correct in the context of prevailing market conditions. Other desirable properties of an acceptable framework are as follows:

**Tractable:** The framework should not be so complex that it is very difficult to obtain any useful results. It should be analytically and computationally tractable.

**Realistic:** The assumptions forming the basis of the framework should be realistic and supported by data analysis. The corresponding distributions and results, for example, the shapes of the yield curves generated, should be plausible.

**Complete:** The framework should be complete in that it should not ignore any necessary factors or assume away the effect of one or more critical market parameters. It should also be complete in the sense that it should be able to value and analyze all types of financial instruments in which we are interested. For example, the framework should include a representation of volatility if options or instruments with option-like characteristics are to be evaluated. If a framework is not complete, we will be forced to make independent sets of assumptions to evaluate different classes of instruments, resulting in a potential consistency problem.

**Simple:** The framework should be simple so that the effect of various assumptions and parameters can be easily grasped. Often, the insight provided by a framework is more valuable than the numerical results obtained. The simpler the framework, the greater the chance of acquiring useful insight. Of course, simplicity has to be balanced with the need for the framework to be complete.

## Making Assumption versus Predicting Interest Rates

It is important to distinguish between making assumptions about interest rate movements and forecasting or predicting interest rates. Within a proper framework, assumptions are made to determine the prevailing values of securities. We might have specific views on the market, but they do not change the values of the securities we wish to examine. They merely influence our preferences for them. In the valuation of securities, it is best to keep bullish or bearish views external to the framework. For example, when considering the purchase of a long-duration bond, we would not pay more than it is worth simply because our outlook is bullish.

Intuitively, assumptions about interest rates can imply a certain amount of forecasting. Most often, the existence of such a predictive element is latent or hidden. For example, a parallel-shift assumption predicts high volatility, thereby inadvertently making dumbbells more attractive than bullets. By enforcing the internal and external consistency conditions, we can guarantee that the predictive element is completely eliminated. Thus, we ensure the objectivity of the framework. The logic of this statement is easy to see: if the assumptions imply a prediction, we could then establish an arbitrage that could exploit the prediction. Since consistent assumptions are made so as not to create any arbitrage opportunity, it follows that there are no implied predictions in such a framework.

Thus, the consistency conditions help to create an impartial, objective framework in which to analyze all fixed-income securities. Within such a framework, we can make assumptions about the future without the need to know it. We can postulate interest rate movements without making specific predictions. We believe that this quality of the framework makes the details of implementation, such as the actual statistical distributions chosen, much less important than its major characteristic: internal and external consistency.

## Return to Parametrics

We stated that static parameters such as duration, convexity, and yield do not form a complete framework. The implication is not that the parameters themselves are unimportant. On the contrary, the parameters, being summary attributes, provide succinct information about bonds and portfolios. The fact remains that longer-duration bonds can be considered more volatile, and higher-convexity portfolios still do better when interest rate volatility is higher. In other words, it is better to buy a bond at a higher yield and sell it at a lower yield.

On the average, the market seems to know that the parameters do not describe a security completely. That is why we find differences in price and yield among securities and portfolios that are parametrically similar. These differences produce the illusion of profitable trades when completeness is attributed to the parameters.

Duration, convexity, and yield are mathematical concepts and, as such, are factual. It is in the popular interpretation of these numbers, for example, duration as risk and yield as reward, that we find the weakness. Our measurements are more precise than the ideas and interpretations that they represent. Problems occur when we attribute more precision to these parameters than is merited. There is no point, for example, in computing duration to several decimal places; the resulting precision is purely academic. In many cases, it is not even worth distinguishing between Macaulay duration and modified duration. We would not do dumbbell-bullet swaps just to pick up a few basis points in yield.

Parameters can still be used, however, to set broad strategic goals and to implement specific objectives. Since the parameters are summary measures, they can be powerful and necessary tools in situations in which simple characterizations of portfolios are necessary. Two immediate applications are hedging applications and asset/liability management. When used properly, the parameters can provide an excellent handle on portfolio strategy, especially in the selection of appropriate securities.

Parametric approach has its greatest contribution in this context. It shows concern for suitability of investment that the currently fashionable, arcane techniques tend to ignore totally. This property of parametric analysis is a significant one because, in many situations, the valuation exercise must take a second place to the prudent determination of suitability.

## An Analogy

It may be useful to compare a framework to the colored lenses in a pair of sunglasses. Sunglasses make the scenery look a little strange with regard to color. Yet, we can see more clearly with them on than without them. The color distortion is, to an extent, acceptable to us. If the lenses were warped so that the shapes of things were not faithfully transmitted, then the glasses would not be acceptable to anyone.

After a few minutes, though, the eyes adjust to the new color scheme, and objects no longer look unusual. The brain is lulled into believing that colors of the objects are as the eye sees them. Other people around us can see that we are looking through colored glasses, but we are oblivious to that fact.

Only when we look at something the color of which we know very well, such as a fluorescent lamp, are we reminded of the colored nature of the lenses through which we see. With this knowledge we are able to make any required adjustment in the visual information that the eyes receive in those contexts where color perception is important.

Frameworks, in a way, all have colored lenses in the form of simplifying assumptions. They are unable to reveal the true nature and value of investments, yet without them we can hardly see the financial landscape clearly. Without them, we can be blinded by the intense complexity of the financial instruments.

A framework has to be internally consistent. Otherwise, it is like a warped lens that can cause distortions which can be dangerous if the eye adapts to them. The only way we can avoid the contradictory information coming in through a distorted lens is to close our eyes and ignore it. The only way an internally inconsistent framework is acceptable is if we are blind to its defects.

A framework can also be adjusted or calibrated for external consistency, by looking at objects whose properties are known; that is, by applying the framework to financial instruments whose values we know or are willing to assume that we know. For example, Treasury securities in the fixed-income markets are like the fluorescent lamps that reveal the color of the lenses. By using treasuries, we can make appropriate adjustments to the framework and/or to the results obtained from the framework. A framework can also be tuned to emphasize or downplay one or more of the characteristics of the instruments under analysis.

Internal consistency is a fundamental requirement in a framework. Without it, the framework is basically useless. External consistency makes the framework a good relative value indicator, relative to the standard, e.g., treasuries, used to adjust the framework.

## A Road Map

This book is broadly divided into three parts. The first part is devoted to the development of a framework for portfolio management. It begins with a discussion of the yield curve, which is historically perhaps the first attempt at valuation of fixed-income securities. Previously, investors computed the yield on a security and simply compared this yield to the yield curve at some maturity. The yield spread was a measure of value. To some, this procedure might seem to be too simple when viewed in light of today's level of computer-aided numerical complexity and the popularity of arcane measures whose representation requires the entire Greek alphabet. Yet, the yield curve is still the first fundamental data structure from which all valuation techniques emanate. It still represents the core of fixed income analysis. A good understanding of the structure of the curve and its implications is an absolute necessity before the actual valuation process can begin. Stanley Diller takes a fresh look at the yield curve by taking the view that the curve reflects people's outlook rather than the relative supplies of bonds with different maturities. He proposes a model in which relative preferences are determined by the comparing expected rates of return over short holding periods.

The next chapter, also by Stanley Diller, on the parametric analysis of fixed income securities, is an updated version of perhaps the most famous of all contributions in this area. The original work acknowledged the numerous assumptions in fixed income analysis, and popularized the concept of a framework for valuation. It also made the then arcane concept of convexity a household word. The major contribution of this work was that, for the first time, a single set of measures was described to compare and value virtually all types of fixed income securities.

The traditional yield curve only uses two properties of securities: yield and maturity or duration. In order to represent securities more fully, and to represent derivative produces, Diller's most recent analysis extends the list of properties to include higher order parameters such as convexity. Looking beyond parametrics, this analysis also correctly points out that horizon-return analysis is the proper way to value securities. Additionally, the idea of return profiles is introduced.

Some of the numerical techniques used in this chapter have been improved upon. For example, new computational methodol-

ogies are currently available for the valuation of fixed income options. Prepayment behavior of mortgage-backed securities can now
be empirically modeled given the ready availability of vast
amounts of historical data. Yet, the concepts discussed in this
chapter, and the insight developed therein still represent the state-
of-the-art, and we believe that this chapter should be required
reading for all students of fixed income analysis.

In the next chapter, "The Yield Surface," Stanley Diller takes
us one step futher. He combines the idea of a yield curve, which
represents yields or returns as a function of maturity (duration) or
risk, with the concepts developed in the parametric model of securities. This results in a three-dimensional yield curve, two dimensions representing duration and convexity and the third
representing yield. Yield, in this context, actually represents the
return over a short horizon.

Part II deals mainly with the modeling and analysis of securities with option-like features. The goal in putting together this set
of chapters is not mathematical exhibitionism; rather, the objective
is to provide an opportunity to express disparate views and diverse methodologies of looking at complex securities. The aim
here is to strengthen the concept of a framework developed in Part
I and to plunge the reader into deep thought and force him to
select the elements necessary to build a framework. It has been
said that human knowledge advances by creating conflicts and resolving them in turn. The chapters in this section are in line with
this philosophy.

In the last two decades, revolutionary advances have been
made in the valuation of contingent cash flows. Valuation began in
the early 1970s with the Black-Scholes-Merton pricing model of
options on stocks. In the 1980s, the arbitrage argument used in this
model was widely applied to the modeling of debt options. The
modeling of mortgage-backed securities, still popular today, devi-
ated from the traditional path in two ways. First, an empirical prepayment model using historical data to estimate cash flows has
been incorporated. Second, option value has been represented in

terms of a spread number rather than a dollar figure. The so called option-adjusted spread (OAS) is now quoted widely for mortgage-backed securities. Yet, it can still be an elusive number. The reader should consider whether it is always clear that a given security is a better buy than another just because the former has a larger option-adjusted spread. Wide acceptance of the OAS concept means a corresponding requirement for all participants to understand how this is computed and interpreted. David Sykes in "Introduction to Option Adjusted Spread Analysis" provides us with an compact introduction to OAS which is a popular and generally accepted tool with which to trade mortgages.

David Gordon and Michael Zaretsky, on the other hand, find popularly available return measures not totally satisfactory. They propose a different measure, the Risk Adjusted Measure (RAM),[3] for yield. They provide various examples and arguments to conclude that the RAM is more complete than other available measures.

The OAS approach, so popular in the mortgage-backed securities area, is not as widely used in the corporate and municipal bond areas. Dennis Adler correctly points out that the call option and the sinking fund options in corporate bonds are similar to the prepayment option in mortgages and, therefore, the OAS approach is equally applicable to corporates as well. Using numerous examples, this chapter illustrates the current technology in the analysis of corporate and municipal securities. Note that if we are willing to assume rational exercise of the optional rights in corporate bonds, numerical aggregation procedures are available as efficient alternatives to simulation methods.

The exercise of the prepayment option in mortgage-backed securities is generally accepted to be "irrational." More precisely, in addition to the general level of interest rates, the exercise appears to be influenced by non-economic factors. Empirical research has found that prepayment behavior has memory; that is, it not only

---

3. Perhaps a better nomenclature would be Risk-Adjusted Value Indicator.

depends upon the current level of rates, but also upon the actual course taken by interest rates to date. Because of this complexity, the option is very difficult to model analytically. One of the ways the OAS model addresses this problem is to arrive at a numerical solution (rather than an algebraic formula) by means of simulation runs. Richard Bookstaber in "Using Simulation Models to Value Option-Like Features" discusses the general concept of using simulation models to value option-like features in financial instruments.

The concept of duration applied to fixed income securities is not new. Originally, research discovered that this concept also had a temporal interpretation: if the duration of a portfolio was set equal to the time to horizon, then the portfolio would attain some qualities that make the rate of return to the horizon less sensitive (or immune) to the interest rate changes. In "Immunization-Based Duration: A New Concept for Mortgage-Backed Securities," Rajiv Sobti uses this fact to develop an immunization-based duration concept for mortgage-backed securities. The standard simulation technology of OAS analysis is used. This concept stimulates thought of suitability of investment, a key factor that appears to be ignored by the typical analysis in the mortgage-backed securities area.

Part II concludes with the discussion of the optional qualities in the bond and note futures contracts by Stanley Jonas.

In Part III, Peter Noris applies the concept of duration to several different risk factors. He shows how to implement a process of multi-factor immunization that will simultaneously control these risks.

In the 1980s, the investment community began using highly sophisticated techniques to measure the risks and rewards of investments. However, it is rare that such portfolio management techniques are applied by corporate issuers, the forgotten children of the recent quantitative revolution in finance. This situation can be justified partly by the myriad accounting, legal, regulatory and tax constraints under which they operate, not to mention the influence of the all-powerful quarterly numbers. Eileen Baecher and Laurie Goodman conclude Part III with a discussion of how corporate issuers can begin to apply derivative products in the hedging of debt issuance within exiting constraints.

# Chapter 2

# The Yield Curve

**Stanley Diller**
**Bear, Stearns & Co. Inc.**

## Introduction

As the core of fixed income analysis, the yield curve has received more attention than any other area of research. But until now, there has not been a lot to show for this work. It seems that technology has outrun theory and that complex algorithms have displaced lucid lines of inquiry. This paper tries to redress this imbalance by returning to the principles, now well accepted, nominally underlying much of the current work—namely, that the yield curve reflects people's *outlook* rather than the relative supplies of bonds with different terms of maturity.

The question is: the outlook for what? Many find it hard to believe that forecasts of future interest rates are the stuff of which yield curves are made. The proposed model assumes that people choose between a five- and ten-year bond not by forecasting the five-year interest rate five years in the future, as implied in prevailing studies, but by comparing the rates of return they expect on these bonds in the near future. Though not everyone has this near-term outlook, the general market does, particularly with the leverage available for short periods.

This approach is more consistent with the main thrust of fixed income analysis, which increasingly revolves around near term performance. With turnover costs added, the proposed model explains why the yield curves are not the same in all sectors—why, for example, tax exempt yield curves slope upward even when the Treasury curve is sharply inverted. Above all, it leads to a way of fitting smooth and accurate yield curves. Even people well versed in yield curve doctrine substitute number crunching for clear thinking when it comes to fitting the curves. Often, the resulting curves twist and turn in defiance of any plausible outlook. In these and other ways, the proposed model represents an effort to move the subject onto new ground.

The model draws on the work of the English economist John Hicks, whose *Value and Capital*[1] broke new ground in this, as in many other areas of economics. Hicks considered the yield curve to be the bridge between monetary policy and economic activity. Though monetary policy mainly influences short-term interest rates, investment (and through it economic activity) depends on long-term rates. For monetary policy to be effective, there must be a reason for long-term rates to change when short-term rates change.

Hicks argued that the market expects a change in short-term rates, perhaps brought about by monetary policy, to continue, at least in part. He defined the *coefficient of expectation* as the fraction expected to persist of the original change. The larger this coefficient, the greater are the expected changes in relation to the current change. These expected changes in short rates affect the current long rate, which Hicks defined as the average of the expected short rates (with a little added to compensate for greater risk). The *change* in the current long rate, therefore, is the average of the expected *changes* in the future short rates. In other words, monetary policy causes a change in short rates, which people extrapolate to expected changes in future short rates, which then change the current long rate.

It is well known that long rates change less than short rates. The reason, in Hicksian terms, is that expectations of changes in short yields fade with time because the coefficient of expectation is less than one since long yield changes are averages of expected

---

1. Hicks, John R. Value and Capital. London: Oxford University Press, 1939.

short yield changes, they get smaller with increasing maturity averaged in.

They become more remote or, as more of this dampened
shorter yield changes are that the coefficient shorten yield changes
are less than more of the dampened expectations are averaged into
long rates.

### Short-Term Changes in Long-Term Rates

In the following calculations, the parameter K represents Hicks'
coefficient of expectation. Each expected short-term yield change is
K times the preceding one (K being less than one). The second
change is K times the first; the third, K times the second or $K^2$
times the first; and the Nth change, $K^{N-1}$ times the first. The expected change in the one period rate N periods in the future
$(\Delta Y_{1,N})$ is:

$$\Delta Y1,N = KN\text{-}1 \times \Delta Y1,1 \qquad\qquad (1)$$

These successive changes in *expected* future short rates translate into short-term changes in longer rates. In theory, as described
above, the one-period change in the N-term rate corresponds to
the average of the consecutive forecast changes of the first N one-
period rates. For example, the one-period change in the five-period
rate is the average of the expected changes in the one-period rate
between the first and second periods, the second and third, and so
on. Calling the first of this series $\Delta Y_{1,1}$, each successive change is
$K \times \Delta Y_{1,1}$; $K^2 \times \Delta Y_{1,1}$; ... $K^4 \times \Delta Y_{1,1}$.

The average of these changes is:

$$\frac{(1 + K + K^2 + K^3 + K^4)}{5} \times \Delta Y_{1,1} \text{ or}$$

$$W_5 \times \Delta Y_{1,1}$$

Where $W_5$ is the average of the five future one-period yield changes relative to the nearest one. Hence, the one-period change in the five-period rate is given by:

$$\Delta Y_{5,1} = W_5 \times \Delta Y_{1,1}$$

More generally, for the N-term long rate:

$$\Delta Y_{N,1} = W_N \times \Delta Y_{1,1} \tag{2}$$

where

$$W_N = \frac{1 + K + K^2 + \ldots + K^{N-1}}{N} \tag{3}$$

Applying the formula for the sum of a geometric progression:

$$W_N = \frac{1 - K^N}{N \times (1 - K)} \tag{4}$$

As N gets larger, $W_N$ gets smaller, and $\Delta Y_{N,1}$ falls relative to $\Delta Y_{1,1}$. (Hereafter, the second subscript, signifying the period of change, will be dropped, since only one-period changes of the long rates will be considered.)

### Breakeven Yield Change

One expression for the rate of return (ROR) for a period spanning six months or less is:

$$ROR_N = Y_N + \Delta P_N \times \frac{12}{H} \tag{5}$$

where $Y_N$ is the starting yield to maturity, $\Delta P$ is the percent change in price *associated with a yield change,* N the term of the bond, and

H is the holding period in months. This equation says that the ROR on a bond within a single compounding period is equal to the sum of its starting yield to maturity and its *annualized* percentage price change *resulting from a yield change*. (The last phase excludes aging toward par.)

The price change may be represented (and is generally thought of) as the product of a yield change $(\Delta Y_N)$ and a factor $(D_N)$ that is the bond's duration divided by $(1 + \frac{Y_N}{2})$ (hereafter called duration).

$$\Delta P_N = D_N \times \Delta Y_N \tag{6}$$

Substituting Equation 6 into Equation 5 gives:

$$ROR_N = Y_N + [D_N \times \Delta Y_N] \times \frac{12}{H} \tag{7}$$

A reasonable condition for buying the bond at risk is that its expected ROR *at least* equal the yield $(Y_B)$ one can lock in with a security maturing at the horizon—for example, a bill. Substituting $Y_B$ for ROR in Equation 7 gives:

$$Y_B = Y_N + [D_N \times \Delta Y_{N]} \times \frac{12}{H} \tag{8}$$

The value of $\Delta Y_N$ that makes this equation true for the N-term bond is called the breakeven yield change $(BYC_N)$:

$$Y_B = Y_N + [D_N \times BYC_N] \times \frac{12}{H} \tag{8A}$$

Rearranging the terms gives the formula for the breakeven yield change:

$$BYC_N = \frac{(Y_N - Y_B) \times \dfrac{H}{12}}{D_N} \tag{9}$$

which translates into the deannualized spread between the bond and bill rates divided by the bond's duration.

### Fitting Yield Curves by Smoothing BYCs

Exhibit 1 lists the BYCs on a given day for most Treasury bonds and several horizons. The top of each column gives the horizon for the BYCs below, as well as the bill yield for the period against which the bonds break even. By definition, this yield is the same as the ROR on each bond brought about by the BYC shown for it. For this reason, an apt title for the column would be "equal return yield changes."

Equating the BYCs with *forecast* changes implies the market would accept the same returns on securities with different risk. Based on this assumption, the *expectation* of a return that could be higher or lower is as good as locking it in. While that assumption may not be appropriate for any one investor, it could be a working hypothesis for the overall market; each investor perceives maturity risk in light of his own circumstances, a short rate being riskier for one and a long rate for another. As long as investors are uniformly distributed with regard to their perception of maturity risk, the assumption of risk neutrality in this context is reasonable.

The method for smoothing the BYCs makes use of the fact, noted above and shown in Exhibit 1, that being *expected* yield changes, their absolute values fall as their terms rise. Substituting $BYC_N$ for $\Delta Y_N$ in Equation 2 gives:

$$BYC_N = W_N \times BYC \tag{10}$$

and substituting equation four into Equation 10 gives:

## Exhibit 1. Breakeven Yield Changes—Bonds versus Bills (Basis Points)

Report Date: 11/06/80
Delivery Date: 11/10/80

| | | | Bill Maturities | | | | |
|---|---|---|---|---|---|---|---|
| | | | 1-Month | 3-Month | 6-Month | 1-Year | 2-Year |
| Bond Equivalent Yields—> | | | 11.75 | 14.15 | 14.49 | 14.13 | 13.59 |
| Coupon | Maturity | Yield | | | | | |
| 7.375 | 05/15/81 | 14.150 | 27.0 | -35..0 | -526.5 | | |
| 7.500 | 05/15/81 | 14.144 | 26.9 | -35.5 | -538.2 | | |
| 9.750 | 05/31/81 | 14.324 | 30.5 | -24.8 | -141.6 | | |
| 6.750 | 06/30/81 | 14.334 | 25.7 | -17.4 | -71.0 | | |
| 9.125 | 06/30/81 | 14.366 | 26.3 | -16.0 | -60.8 | | |
| 9.375 | 07/31/81 | 14.300 | 22.2 | -12.8 | -65.7 | | |
| 7.625 | 08/15/81 | 14.459 | 22.2 | -3.5 | -32.9 | | |
| 8.375 | 08/15/81 | 14.491 | 22.6 | -2.0 | -27.6 | | |
| 9.625 | 08/31/81 | 14.335 | 22.3 | 2.1 | -41.3 | | |
| 10.125 | 09/30/81 | 14.112 | 17.4 | -9.9 | -58.2 | | |
| 6.750 | 09/30/81 | 14.319 | 19.0 | -1.9 | -31.6 | | |
| 12.625 | 10/31/81 | 13.961 | 15.3 | -11.2 | -48.7 | | |
| 7.750 | 11/15/81 | 13.779 | 12.9 | -16.7 | -58.7 | -1215.4 | |
| 7.000 | 11/15/81 | 13.779 | 12.9 | -16.7 | -58.5 | -1216.8 | |
| 12.125 | 11/30/81 | 13.979 | 13.7 | -13.4 | -44.3 | -231.5 | |
| 11.375 | 12/31/81 | 13.972 | 12.0 | -14.2 | -38.0 | -124.8 | |
| 7.250 | 12/31/81 | 13.740 | 10.2 | -19.8 | -55.4 | -273.0 | |
| 11.500 | 01/31/82 | 13.980 | 11.1 | -14.2 | -36.3 | -82.9 | |
| 6.125 | 02/15/82 | 13.535 | 7.8 | -24.0 | -63.8 | -229.5 | |
| 13.875 | 02/28/82 | 13.774 | 10.6 | -12.8 | -46.2 | -132.4 | |
| 15.000 | 03/31/82 | 13.715 | 9.2 | -14.9 | -47.1 | -119.8 | |
| 7.875 | 03/31/82 | 13.775 | 9.2 | -13.0 | -41.2 | -110.2 | |
| 11.375 | 04/30/82 | 13.686 | 8.7 | -12.6 | -38.5 | -97.4 | |
| 8.000 | 05/15/82 | 13.649 | 8.0 | -13.0 | -37.3 | -92.6 | |
| 7.000 | 05/15/82 | 13.437 | 6.9 | -17.0 | -47.7 | -133.7 | |
| 9.250 | 05/15/82 | 13.675 | 8.2 | -12.5 | -36.2 | -87.8 | |
| 9.375 | 05/31/82 | 13.686 | 7.8 | -14.0 | -38.2 | -80.0 | |
| 8.625 | 06/30/82 | 13.694 | 7.0 | -14.1 | -34.1 | -68.5 | |
| 8.250 | 06/30/82 | 13.669 | 6.8 | -14.5 | -35.4 | -72.3 | |
| 8.975 | 07/31/82 | 13.718 | 6.7 | -14.0 | -33.0 | -57.8 | |
| 9.000 | 08/15/82 | 13.701 | 6.5 | -14.1 | -33.7 | -57.7 | |
| 8.125 | 08/15/82 | 13.560 | 5.8 | -16.3 | -39.2 | -76.4 | |
| 11.125 | 08/31/82 | 13.529 | 6.6 | -12.9 | -36.9 | -79.3 | |
| 8.375 | 09/30/82 | 13.577 | 6.1 | -12.4 | -34.6 | -65.6 | |
| 11.875 | 09/30/82 | 13.574 | 6.2 | -12.8 | -36.0 | -67.9 | |
| 12.125 | 10/31/82 | 13.588 | 6.3 | -10.8 | -30.0 | -60.2 | |
| 7.875 | 11/15/82 | 13.412 | 5.2 | -12.9 | -33.8 | -73.0 | -925.8 |
| 7.125 | 11/15/82 | 13.390 | 5.1 | -13.2 | -34.4 | -74.9 | -1040.8 |
| 9.375 | 12/31/82 | 13.150 | 3.5 | -18.2 | -42.4 | -90.9 | -572.8 |
| 8.000 | 02/15/83 | 13.275 | 3.7 | -16.2 | -37.3 | -71.5 | -249.3 |
| 9.250 | 03/31/83 | 13.156 | 3.6 | -15.0 | -38.4 | -76.5 | -238.1 |
| 11.625 | 05/15/83 | 13.061 | 3.3 | -14.9 | -36.7 | -77.8 | -218.7 |
| 7.875 | 05/15/83 | 13.122 | 3.4 | -13.6 | -33.8 | -70.8 | -189.8 |
| 8.875 | 06/30/83 | 13.031 | 2.5 | -16.0 | -36.2 | -72.7 | -185.6 |
| 11.875 | 08/15/83 | 13.156 | 2.8 | -15.2 | -34.1 | -62.5 | -125.7 |
| 9.250 | 08/15/83 | 13.257 | 3.0 | -13.7 | -30.7 | -54.5 | -95.4 |
| 9.750 | 09/30/83 | 13.214 | 3.2 | -12.0 | -30.0 | -54.7 | -94.9 |
| 7.000 | 11/15/83 | 12.964 | 2.4 | -12.8 | -30.8 | -62.5 | -133.5 |
| 9.875 | 11/15/83 | 13.393 | 3.6 | -9.0 | -22.2 | -40.6 | -42.9 |
| 10.500 | 12/31/83 | 13.182 | 2.6 | -12.5 | -27.4 | -50.2 | -90.6 |

**Exhibit 1.   (continued)**

| Bond Equivalent Yields——> | | | 1-Month 11.75 | 3-Month 14.15 | 6-Month 14.49 | 1-Year 14.13 | 2-Year 13.59 |
|---|---|---|---|---|---|---|---|
| Coupon | Maturity | Yield | | | | | |
| 7.250 | 02/15/84 | 13.349 | 2.8 | -10.6 | -23.2 | -37.9 | -43.2 |
| 14.250 | 03/31/84 | 13.480 | 3.6 | -8.4 | -21.5 | -33.5 | -18.9 |
| 9.250 | 05/15/84 | 13.217 | 2.8 | -9.3 | -22.2 | -41.2 | -56.2 |
| 13.250 | 05/15/84 | 13.454 | 3.5 | -7.6 | -18.6 | -31.8 | -20.1 |
| 8.875 | 06/30/84 | 13.213 | 2.3 | -10.4 | -22.6 | -39.6 | -52.7 |
| 7.250 | 08.15/84 | 13.300 | 2.4 | -9.7 | -21.0 | -33.8 | -38.0 |
| 12.125 | 09/30/84 | 13.382 | 2.9 | -8.1 | -20.1 | -32.0 | -27.2 |
| 8.000 | 02/15/85 | 12.952 | 1.5 | -11.2 | -24.2 | -42.1 | -66.3 |
| 10.375 | 05/15/85 | 13.076 | 2.0 | -8.6 | -20.0 | -36.5 | -50.1 |
| 14.375 | 05/15/85 | 13.317 | 2.6 | -7.3 | -17.3 | -29.7 | -27.4 |
| 8.250 | 08/15/85 | 12.874 | 1.2 | -10.8 | -23.0 | -40.0 | -62.7 |
| 9.625 | 08/15/85 | 13.156 | 1.8 | -9.2 | -19.6 | -31.6 | -39.0 |
| 11.750 | 11/15/85 | 13.196 | 2.1 | -7.3 | -17.0 | -29.7 | -33.5 |
| 7.875 | 05/15/86 | 13.040 | 1.6 | -7.2 | -16.6 | -29.6 | -38.9 |
| 8.000 | 08/15/86 | 12.926 | 1.1 | -8.9 | -18.9 | -31.7 | -44.7 |
| 9.000 | 02/15/87 | 12.897 | 1.1 | -8.7 | -18.4 | -30.7 | -43.1 |
| 12.000 | 05/15/87 | 12.971 | 1.4 | -7.2 | -16.5 | -29.4 | -38.7 |
| 7.625 | 11/15/87 | 12.965 | 1.2 | -6.3 | -14.4 | -25.4 | -33.1 |
| 8.250 | 05/15/88 | 12.879 | 1.1 | -6.5 | -14.7 | -26.2 | -35.6 |
| 8.750 | 11/15/88 | 12.963 | 1.2 | -6.0 | -13.5 | -23.5 | -29.9 |
| 9.250 | 05/15/89 | 12.906 | 1.1 | -6.0 | -13.6 | -23.9 | -31.2 |
| 10.750 | 11/15/89 | 13.013 | 1.2 | -5.6 | -12.6 | -21.7 | -26.0 |
| 8.250 | 05/15/90 | 12.508 | 0.6 | -7.1 | -15.6 | -28.5 | -43.6 |
| 10.750 | 08/15/90 | 12.967 | 0.9 | -6.5 | -13.6 | -21.7 | -26.6 |
| 13.000 | 11/15/90 | 13.121 | 1.3 | -5.1 | -11.4 | -19.2 | -20.3 |
| 7.250 | 08/15/92 | 12.967 | 0.8 | -5.5 | -11.3 | -17.8 | -21.3 |
| 7.875 | 02/15/93 | 13.032 | 0.8 | -5.3 | -10.8 | -16.8 | -19.0 |
| 8.625 | 08/15/93 | 13.011 | 0.8 | -5.3 | -11.0 | -17.2 | -19.7 |
| 8.625 | 11/15/93 | 13.013 | 1.0 | -4.5 | -10.0 | -16.9 | -19.3 |
| 9.000 | 02/15/94 | 12.997 | 0.8 | -5.4 | -11.1 | -17.3 | -20.0 |
| 8.750 | 08/15/94 | 13.010 | 0.8 | -5.2 | -10.8 | -16.7 | -19.1 |
| 10.125 | 11/15/94 | 13.053 | 1.0 | -4.4 | -9.8 | -16.3 | -18.0 |
| 10.500 | 02/15/95 | 13.030 | 0.8 | -5.3 | -10.9 | -16.9 | -18.9 |
| 10.375 | 50/15/95 | 13.042 | 1.0 | -4.4 | -9.8 | -16.4 | -18.1 |
| 12.625 | 05/15/95 | 13.151 | 1.1 | -4.2 | -9.4 | -15.4 | -15.2 |
| 11.500 | 11/15/95 | 13.075 | 1.0 | -4.3 | -9.6 | -16.0 | -17.2 |
| 8.500 | 05/15/99 | 12.902 | 0.8 | -4.3 | -9.6 | -16.4 | -19.9 |
| 7.875 | 02/15/00 | 12.879 | 0.6 | -5.1 | -10.4 | -16.4 | -20.1 |
| 8.375 | 08/15/00 | 12.872 | 0.6 | -5.1 | -10.5 | -16.6 | -20.5 |
| 8.000 | 08/15/01 | 12.889 | 0.6 | -5.0 | -10.2 | -16.1 | -19.6 |
| 8.250 | 05/15/05 | 12.732 | 0.6 | -4.6 | -10.2 | -17.6 | -23.2 |
| 7.625 | 02/15/07 | 12.517 | 0.3 | -5.8 | -11.9 | -19.9 | -28.2 |
| 7.875 | 11/15/07 | 12.480 | 0.4 | -5.2 | -11.4 | -20.2 | -29.1 |
| 8.375 | 08/15/08 | 12.589 | 0.3 | -5.7 | -11.7 | -19.3 | -26.7 |
| 8.750 | 11/15/08 | 12.634 | 0.5 | -4.9 | -10.7 | -18.7 | -25.6 |
| 9.125 | 05/15/09 | 12.667 | 0.5 | -4.8 | -10.6 | -18.4 | -24.9 |
| 10.375 | 11/15/09 | 12.751 | 0.6 | -4.6 | -10.2 | -17.7 | -23.0 |
| 11.750 | 02/15/10 | 12.867 | 0.6 | -5.1 | -10.5 | -16.6 | -20.4 |
| 10.000 | 05/15/10 | 12.687 | 0.6 | -4.8 | -10.5 | -18.3 | -24.6 |

$$BYC_N = \left[\frac{(1-K^N)}{N \times (1-K)}\right] \times BYC_1 \tag{10A}$$

The bracketed term is the reduced expression for $W_N$, the ratio between the Nth and first BYC, and K is the counterpart of Hicks' coefficient of expectation. The algorithm for fitting the yield curve finds the values of three parameters that minimize the squared deviations of the $BYC_n$s from their smoothed counterparts. The three parameters are K; $BYC_1$ (the BYC on the shortest bond); and $Y_B$, the locked-in rate. The last two parameters are discussed below.

Exhibit 2 shows the fitted BYCs for a particular day. Since the pattern of the raw data is quite smooth (and remarkably similar under various market conditions), no special art or complexity is needed to fit it. Clearly, it is easier to fit the BYCs and from their fitted values infer the "fitted" yields than to fit the yields directly, as in conventional methods.

The indirect fit is achieved by reversing the terms $Y_B$ and $Y_N$ in Equation A:

$$Y_N = Y_B - [D_N \times BYC_N] \times \frac{12}{H} \tag{11}$$

which expresses the bond yield as the sum of the risk-free yield and the annualized product of duration and its BYC. (When the bond yield $[Y_N]$ is greater than the bill yield $[Y_B]$, the sign on the BYC is positive; when it is less, the sign is negative. Duration is always positive.) This equation is a tautology that gains substance when the fitted BYCs replace the actual ones:

$$Y_N = Y_B - [D_N \times BYC_N] \times \frac{12}{H} \tag{12}$$

where the "hats" signify fitted rather than actual data.

Exhibit 3 shows the yield curve that results from the fitted BYC curve in Exhibit 2. Even more remarkable than the quality of fit is the curve's ability to change direction, despite its derivation from a fitted BYC curve forced to go in one direction. Many peo-

**Exhibit 2.   Fitted Breakeven Values—04/28/80**

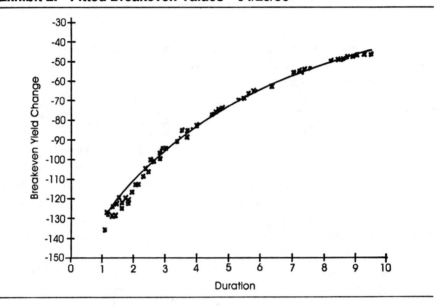

**Exhibit 3.   Yield Curve Implied by Breakeven Fit—04/28/80**

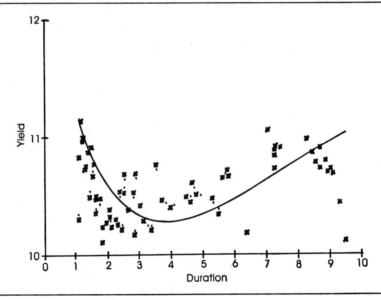

ple think a theoretically sound yield curve must go in one direction, on the grounds that it embodies remote forecasts that are unlikely to change direction. But, although the model assumes one directional forecasting, the yield curves fitted with it *can* change direction for reasons that are made clearer when Equation 10 is substituted into Equation 12:

$$Y_N = Y_B - [[D_N \times W_N] \times BYC_1] \times \frac{12}{H} \tag{12}$$

Usually, D rises faster than W falls, making D × W rise as N gets larger. In that case, the yield curve rises when BYC is positive and falls when it is negative. But in some cases, D rises first more quickly, then more slowly than W falls, making D × W first rise, and then fall. The result is a "humped" or a "U"-shaped curve for positive and negative BYCs, respectively.

Exhibit 4 shows the Ws for different values of duration and K. The terms are in years of duration, one through ten. Using the label duration instead of maturity has no effect on the computation, but only on how one interprets the results (see "Relative Yield Volatility," below). Using years *is* important, because it signifies the exponent on the *weekly* Ks needed for each W, according to Equation 4. For example, with K at 0.99, the W for the third year would be computed as follows:

$$W_3 = \frac{1 - (0.99)^{156}}{(156)(0.01)} = 0.507$$

Thus, the average expected one-week change in the one-week rate over the next three years is 0.507 times as large as the expected change in this rate next week. However, it appears that some of the curves are easier to fit when the starting point for exponentiating K is put off beyond the first week. In this paper, the exponential starts working at six months. Thus, in the above example, at the end of three years, the exponent on K is 130, the number of weeks in 2.5 years, instead of 156, giving:

## Exhibit 4.  Values of W for Various Values of K and Duration

| | | | | | Weights | | | | | |
| | | | | | Duration | | | | | |
| K | 1.0 | 2.0 | 3.0 | 4.0 | 5.0 | 6.0 | 7.0 | 8.0 | 9.0 | 10.0 |
|---|---|---|---|---|---|---|---|---|---|---|
| 0.9996 | 0.995 | 0.985 | 0.975 | 0.965 | 0.955 | 0.945 | 0.935 | 0.926 | 0.917 | 0.907 |
| 0.9992 | 0.990 | 0.970 | 0.950 | 0.931 | 0.912 | 0.894 | 0.876 | 0.859 | 0.842 | 0.826 |
| 0.9988 | 0.985 | 0.955 | 0.926 | 0.899 | 0.872 | 0.846 | 0.822 | 0.799 | 0.776 | 0.754 |
| 0.9984 | 0.980 | 0.941 | 0.904 | 0.868 | 0.834 | 0.802 | 0.772 | 0.744 | 0.717 | 0.691 |
| 0.9980 | 0.975 | 0.927 | 0.881 | 0.839 | 0.798 | 0.761 | 0.727 | 0.494 | 0.664 | 0.635 |
| 0.9976 | 0.971 | 0.913 | 0.860 | 0.811 | 0.765 | 0.723 | 0.685 | 0.649 | 0.616 | 0.585 |
| 0.9972 | 0.966 | 0.899 | 0.839 | 0.784 | 0.733 | 0.688 | 0.646 | 0.608 | 0.573 | 0.541 |
| 0.9968 | 0.961 | 0.886 | 0.819 | 0.759 | 0.704 | 0.655 | 0.611 | 0.571 | 0.535 | 0.502 |
| 0.9964 | 0.956 | 0.873 | 0.800 | 0.735 | 0.676 | 0.624 | 0.578 | 0.537 | 0.500 | 0.467 |
| 0.9960 | 0.952 | 0.860 | 0.781 | 0.711 | 0.649 | 0.595 | 0.548 | 0.506 | 0.469 | 0.436 |
| 0.9956 | 0.947 | 0.848 | 0.763 | 0.689 | 0.624 | 0.568 | 0.520 | 0.470 | 0.440 | 0.407 |
| 0.9952 | 0.942 | 0.836 | 0.745 | 0.668 | 0.600 | 0.543 | 0.494 | 0.452 | 0.414 | 0.382 |
| 0.9948 | 0.938 | 0.824 | 0.728 | 0.647 | 0.578 | 0.520 | 0.470 | 0.428 | 0.391 | 0.359 |
| 0.9944 | 0.933 | 0.812 | 0.712 | 0.628 | 0.557 | 0.498 | 0.448 | 0.406 | 0.370 | 0.338 |
| 0.9940 | 0.928 | 0.800 | 0.696 | 0.609 | 0.537 | 0.477 | 0.428 | 0.386 | 0.350 | 0.320 |
| 0.9936 | 0.924 | 0.789 | 0.680 | 0.592 | 0.510 | 0.458 | 0.409 | 0.367 | 0.333 | 0.302 |
| 0.9932 | 0.919 | 0.778 | 0.665 | 0.575 | 0.500 | 0.440 | 0.391 | 0.350 | 0.316 | 0.287 |
| 0.9928 | 0.915 | 0.767 | 0.651 | 0.558 | 0.483 | 0.423 | 0.374 | 0.334 | 0.301 | 0.273 |
| 0.9924 | 0.911 | 0.757 | 0.637 | 0.543 | 0.467 | 0.407 | 0.359 | 0.319 | 0.287 | 0.260 |
| 0.9920 | 0.906 | 0.746 | 0.623 | 0.528 | 0.451 | 0.392 | 0.344 | 0.306 | 0.274 | 0.248 |
| 0.9916 | 0.902 | 0.736 | 0.610 | 0.513 | 0.437 | 0.378 | 0.331 | 0.293 | 0.262 | 0.237 |
| 0.9912 | 0.897 | 0.726 | 0.597 | 0.499 | 0.423 | 0.365 | 0.318 | 0.281 | 0.251 | 0.227 |
| 0.9908 | 0.893 | 0.716 | 0.585 | 0.486 | 0.410 | 0.352 | 0.307 | 0.270 | 0.241 | 0.217 |
| 0.9904 | 0.889 | 0.706 | 0.573 | 0.473 | 0.397 | 0.340 | 0.296 | 0.260 | 0.232 | 0.209 |
| 0.9900 | 0.884 | 0.697 | 0.561 | 0.461 | 0.385 | 0.329 | 0.285 | 0.251 | 0.223 | 0.201 |
| 0.9896 | 0.880 | 0.687 | 0.550 | 0.449 | 0.374 | 0.318 | 0.275 | 0.242 | 0.215 | 0.193 |
| 0.9892 | 0.876 | 0.678 | 0.539 | 0.438 | 0.363 | 0.308 | 0.266 | 0.233 | 0.207 | 0.186 |
| 0.9888 | 0.872 | 0.669 | 0.528 | 0.427 | 0.353 | 0.299 | 0.258 | 0.226 | 0.200 | 0.180 |
| 0.9884 | 0.868 | 0.660 | 0.518 | 0.417 | 0.343 | 0.290 | 0.249 | 0.218 | 0.193 | 0.174 |
| 0.9880 | 0.863 | 0.652 | 0.500 | 0.407 | 0.334 | 0.281 | 0.242 | 0.211 | 0.187 | 0.168 |
| 0.9876 | 0.859 | 0.643 | 0.498 | 0.397 | 0.325 | 0.273 | 0.234 | 0.205 | 0.181 | 0.163 |
| 0.9872 | 0.855 | 0.635 | 0.488 | 0.388 | 0.316 | 0.265 | 0.227 | 0.198 | 0.176 | 0.158 |
| 0.9868 | 0.851 | 0.627 | 0.479 | 0.379 | 0.308 | 0.258 | 0.221 | 0.193 | 0.171 | 0.153 |
| 0.9864 | 0.847 | 0.619 | 0.470 | 0.371 | 0.300 | 0.251 | 0.215 | 0.187 | 0.166 | 0.148 |
| 0.9860 | 0.843 | 0.611 | 0.462 | 0.362 | 0.293 | 0.244 | 0.209 | 0.182 | 0.161 | 0.144 |
| 0.9856 | 0.839 | 0.603 | 0.453 | 0.354 | 0.286 | 0.238 | 0.203 | 0.177 | 0.156 | 0.140 |
| 0.9852 | 0.835 | 0.595 | 0.445 | 0.347 | 0.279 | 0.232 | 0.198 | 0.172 | 0.153 | 0.136 |
| 0.9848 | 0.831 | 0.588 | 0.437 | 0.339 | 0.272 | 0.226 | 0.193 | 0.168 | 0.148 | 0.133 |
| 0.9844 | 0.827 | 0.581 | 0.429 | 0.332 | 0.266 | 0.221 | 0.188 | 0.164 | 0.145 | 0.129 |
| 0.9840 | 0.823 | 0.574 | 0.422 | 0.325 | 0.260 | 0.216 | 0.184 | 0.160 | 0.141 | 0.126 |
| 0.9836 | 0.820 | 0.566 | 0.414 | 0.318 | 0.254 | 0.211 | 0.179 | 0.156 | 0.138 | 0.123 |
| 0.9832 | 0.016 | 0.560 | 0.407 | 0.312 | 0.249 | 0.206 | 0.175 | 0.152 | 0.134 | 0.120 |
| 0.9828 | 0.812 | 0.553 | 0.400 | 0.306 | 0.243 | 0.201 | 0.171 | 0.149 | 0.131 | 0.117 |
| 0.9824 | 0.808 | 8.546 | 0.394 | 0.300 | 0.238 | 0.197 | 0.167 | 0.145 | 0.129 | 0.115 |
| 0.9820 | 0.804 | 0.539 | 0.387 | 0.294 | 0.233 | 0.192 | 0.164 | 0.142 | 0.125 | 0.112 |
| 0.9816 | 0.801 | 0.533 | 0.381 | 0.288 | 0.228 | 0.188 | 0.160 | 0.139 | 0.123 | 0.110 |
| 0.9812 | 0.797 | 0.527 | 0.374 | 0.283 | 0.224 | 0.185 | 0.157 | 0.136 | 0.120 | 0.107 |
| 0.9808 | 0.793 | 0.520 | 0.368 | 0.278 | 0.219 | 0.181 | 0.153 | 0.133 | 0.118 | 0.105 |
| 0.9804 | 0.789 | 0.514 | 0.362 | 0.273 | 0.215 | 0.177 | 0.150 | 0.130 | 0.115 | 0.103 |
| 0.9800 | 0.786 | 0.508 | 0.357 | 0.268 | 0.211 | 0.174 | 0.147 | 0.128 | 0.113 | 0.101 |

Note: The formula for computing the figures in this table is as follows:

$$W_N = \frac{1 - K^{52(N-5)}}{52(N-5)(1-K)}$$

where N is years of duration.

$$W_3 = \frac{1 - (0.99)^{130}}{(130)(0.01)} = 0.561$$

which is the number shown in Exhibit 4 for a duration of three and a K of 0.99. A weekly K gives much better yield curves than monthly, quarterly, or annual Ks. For this reason, the holding period is assumed to be a week, and the risk-free rates are for a week. A by-product of using such short intervals is that the resulting curve is continuous, without any need for interpolation.

Exhibit 5 shows $D_N \times W_N$, the active part of Equation 13. Whereas the sign on BYC determines whether the curve is positive or inverted, $D_N \times W_N$ determines the rate at which it rises or falls or rises *and* falls. For high values of K, this product declines uniformly, giving either a positive or inverse yield curve. But for lower Ks, for example, 0.9848, it rises and then falls, giving a "U"-shaped or humped yield curve for negative and positive values of BYC, respectively. Exhibits 6-8 illustrate the variety of yield curves that can be fitted with this method. In each case, the BYC curve has an exponential shape; yet, the yield curves are quite different. Exhibit 6 is a fairly typical inverted yield curve; Exhibit 7 is a "U"-shaped curve; Exhibit 8 is a positive curve.

### Measuring Time with Duration

Time enters the model both as conventional calendar time, through which interest rates change, as well as the terms of outstanding bonds. The model works much better when both senses of time are measured in units of duration instead of linear calendar time. Duration comes closer than calendar time to the ideal of making an additional unit worth the same whether between 2 and 3 or 7 and 8. Its advantages for demonstrating bond terms are well known and widely accepted. But for some purposes it can provide a useful telescopic effect, in which one duration unit is worth a greater number of later than of earlier calendar years. That mirrors the perception that adjacent periods are more alike in the far than in the near future. Current expectations do not differ much

## Exhibit 5. Product of Duration and W for Various Values of K and Duration

Weight·Duration

Duration

| K | 1.0 | 2.0 | 3.0 | 4.0 | 5.0 | 6.0 | 7.0 | 8.0 | 9.0 | 10.0 |
|---|---|---|---|---|---|---|---|---|---|---|
| 0.9996 | 0.995 | 1.970 | 2.924 | 3.859 | 4.774 | 5.670 | 6.548 | 7.408 | 8.250 | 9.075 |
| 0.9992 | 0.990 | 1.940 | 2.050 | 3.724 | 4.560 | 5.363 | 6.133 | 6.872 | 7.581 | 8.260 |
| 0.9988 | 0.985 | 1.910 | 2.779 | 3.595 | 4.359 | 5.070 | 5.754 | 6.388 | 6.984 | 7.543 |
| 0.9984 | 0.980 | 1.882 | 2.711 | 3.473 | 4.170 | 4.814 | 5.406 | 5.950 | 6.451 | 6.911 |
| 0.9980 | 0.975 | 1.854 | 2.644 | 3.356 | 3.992 | 4.568 | 5.087 | 5.553 | 5.973 | 6.351 |
| 0.9976 | 0.971 | 1.826 | 2.580 | 3.244 | 3.825 | 4.340 | 4.794 | 5.193 | 5.545 | 5.855 |
| 0.9972 | 0.966 | 1.799 | 2.518 | 3.137 | 3.667 | 4.127 | 4.524 | 4.866 | 5.160 | 5.414 |
| 0.9968 | 0.961 | 1.772 | 2.457 | 3.035 | 3.518 | 3.929 | 4.275 | 4.568 | 4.814 | 5.021 |
| 0.9964 | 0.956 | 1.746 | 2.399 | 2.938 | 3.370 | 3.744 | 4.047 | 4.296 | 4.501 | 4.670 |
| 0.9960 | 0.952 | 1.721 | 2.343 | 2.845 | 3.245 | 1.572 | 3.835 | 4.047 | 4.218 | 4.355 |
| 0.9956 | 0.947 | 1.696 | 2.288 | 2.756 | 3.120 | 3.411 | 3.640 | 3.821 | 3.962 | 4.073 |
| 0.9952 | 0.942 | 1.672 | 2.236 | 2.671 | 3.002 | 3.260 | 3.460 | 3.613 | 3.730 | 3.819 |
| 0.9948 | 0.938 | 1.648 | 2.184 | 2.590 | 2.890 | 3.120 | 3.292 | 3.422 | 3.519 | 3.590 |
| 0.9944 | 0.933 | 1.624 | 2.135 | 2.512 | 2.784 | 2.988 | 3.138 | 3.247 | 3.326 | 3.383 |
| 0.9940 | 0.928 | 1.601 | 2.087 | 2.438 | 2.684 | 2.865 | 2.994 | 3.085 | 3.150 | 3.195 |
| 0.9936 | 0.924 | 1.578 | 2.041 | 2.367 | 2.589 | 2.749 | 2.860 | 2.937 | 2.969 | 3.025 |
| 0.9932 | 0.919 | 1.556 | 1.996 | 2.298 | 2.499 | 2.640 | 2.736 | 2.800 | 2.842 | 2.869 |
| 0.9928 | 0.915 | 1.534 | 1.952 | 2.233 | 2.414 | 2.538 | 2.620 | 2.673 | 2.706 | 2.727 |
| 0.9924 | 0.911 | 1.513 | 1.910 | 2.170 | 2.333 | 2.442 | 2.512 | 2.555 | 2.582 | 2.597 |
| 0.9920 | 0.906 | 1.492 | 1.869 | 2.110 | 2.257 | 2.352 | 2.411 | 2.447 | 2.467 | 2.477 |
| 0.9916 | 0.902 | 1.472 | 1.830 | 2.053 | 2.184 | 2.267 | 2.317 | 2.345 | 2.361 | 2.368 |
| 0.9912 | 0.897 | 1.451 | 1.791 | 1.997 | 2.115 | 2.187 | 2.229 | 2.251 | 2.262 | 2.266 |
| 0.9908 | 0.893 | 1.432 | 1.754 | 1.944 | 2.049 | 2.112 | 2.146 | 2.164 | 2.171 | 2.173 |
| 0.9904 | 0.889 | 1.412 | 1.718 | 1.894 | 1.986 | 2.041 | 2.069 | 2.082 | 2.086 | 2.086 |
| 0.9900 | 0.884 | 1.393 | 1.683 | 1.845 | 1.927 | 1.973 | 1.996 | 2.006 | 2.008 | 2.006 |
| 0.9896 | 0.880 | 1.375 | 1.649 | 1.798 | 1.870 | 1.910 | 1.928 | 1.934 | 1.934 | 1.931 |
| 0.9892 | 0.876 | 1.356 | 1.616 | 1.753 | 1.816 | 1.850 | 1.863 | 1.867 | 1.865 | 1.862 |
| 0.9888 | 0.872 | 1.338 | 1.584 | 1.709 | 1.765 | 1.793 | 1.803 | 1.804 | 1.801 | 1.797 |
| 0.9884 | 0.868 | 1.321 | 1.553 | 1.668 | 1.716 | 1.739 | 1.746 | 1.745 | 1.741 | 1.736 |
| 0.9880 | 0.863 | 1.303 | 1.523 | 1.628 | 1.669 | 1.687 | 1.692 | 1.690 | 1.685 | 1.679 |
| 0.9876 | 0.859 | 1.286 | 1.493 | 1.589 | 1.624 | 1.639 | 1.641 | 1.637 | 1.632 | 1.626 |
| 0.9872 | 0.855 | 1.270 | 1.465 | 1.552 | 1.581 | 1.593 | 1.592 | 1.588 | 1.582 | 1.575 |
| 0.9868 | 0.851 | 1.253 | 1.437 | 1.517 | 1.541 | 1.549 | 1.547 | 1.541 | 1.535 | 1.528 |
| 0.9864 | 0.847 | 1.237 | 1.411 | 1.482 | 1.502 | 1.507 | 1.503 | 1.497 | 1.490 | 1.484 |
| 0.9860 | 0.843 | 1.222 | 1.385 | 1.449 | 1.464 | 1.467 | 1.462 | 1.455 | 1.448 | 1.441 |
| 0.9856 | 0.839 | 1.206 | 1.359 | 1.417 | 1.428 | 1.429 | 1.423 | 1.416 | 1.408 | 1.402 |
| 0.9852 | 0.835 | 1.191 | 1.335 | 1.386 | 1.394 | 1.393 | 1.386 | 1.378 | 1.371 | 1.364 |
| 0.9848 | 0.831 | 1.176 | 1.311 | 1.357 | 1.361 | 1.358 | 1.351 | 1.342 | 1.335 | 1.328 |
| 0.9844 | 0.827 | 1.161 | 1.288 | 1.328 | 1.330 | 1.325 | 1.317 | 1.309 | 1.301 | 1.294 |
| 0.9840 | 0.823 | 1.147 | 1.265 | 1.301 | 1.300 | 1.294 | 1.285 | 1.276 | 1.269 | 1.262 |
| 0.9836 | 0.820 | 1.133 | 1.243 | 1.274 | 1.271 | 1.263 | 1.254 | 1.245 | 1.238 | 1.231 |
| 0.9832 | 0.016 | 1.119 | 1.222 | 1.248 | 1.243 | 1.235 | 1.225 | 1.216 | 1.208 | 1.202 |
| 0.9828 | 0.812 | 1.105 | 1.201 | 1.223 | 1.216 | 1.207 | 1.197 | 1.188 | 1.180 | 1.174 |
| 0.9824 | 0.808 | 1.092 | 1.181 | 1.199 | 1.190 | 1.180 | 1.170 | 1.161 | 1.154 | 1.147 |
| 0.9820 | 0.804 | 1.079 | 1.161 | 1.176 | 1.165 | 1.155 | 1.145 | 1.136 | 1.120 | 1.122 |
| 0.9816 | 0.801 | 1.066 | 1.142 | 1.154 | 1.141 | 1.131 | 1.120 | 1.111 | 1.104 | 1.098 |
| 0.9812 | 0.797 | 1.053 | 1.123 | 1.132 | 1.118 | 1.107 | 1.096 | 1.087 | 1.080 | 1.074 |
| 0.9808 | 0.793 | 1.041 | 1.105 | 1.111 | 1.096 | 1.085 | 1.074 | 1.065 | 1.058 | 1.052 |
| 0.9804 | 0.789 | 1.029 | 1.087 | 1.091 | 1.075 | 1.063 | 1.052 | 1.043 | 1.036 | 1.030 |
| 0.9800 | 0.786 | 1.017 | 1.070 | 1.071 | 1.054 | 1.042 | 1.031 | 1.022 | 1.016 | 1.010 |

**Exhibit 6.**

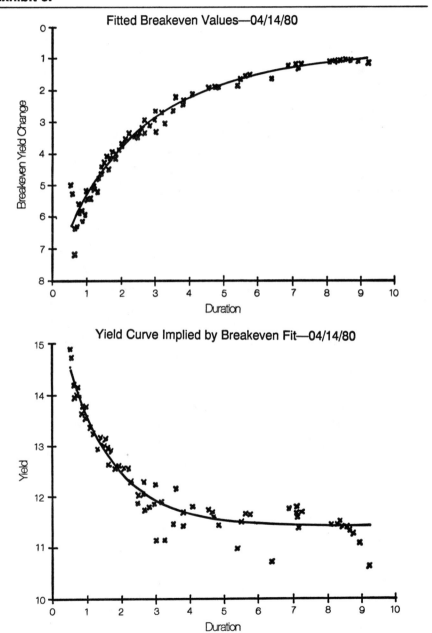

**Exhibit 7.**

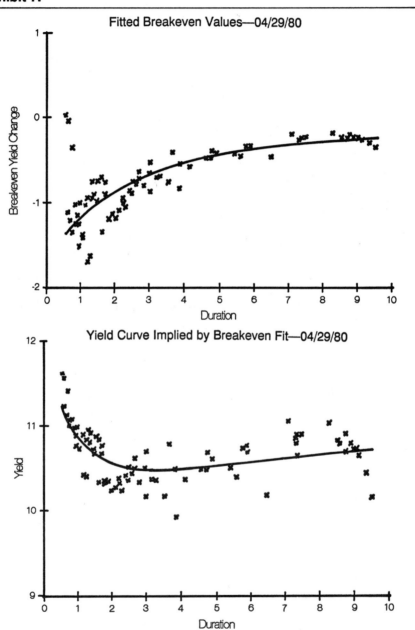

Fitted Breakeven Values—04/29/80

Yield Curve Implied by Breakeven Fit—04/29/80

**Exhibit 8.**

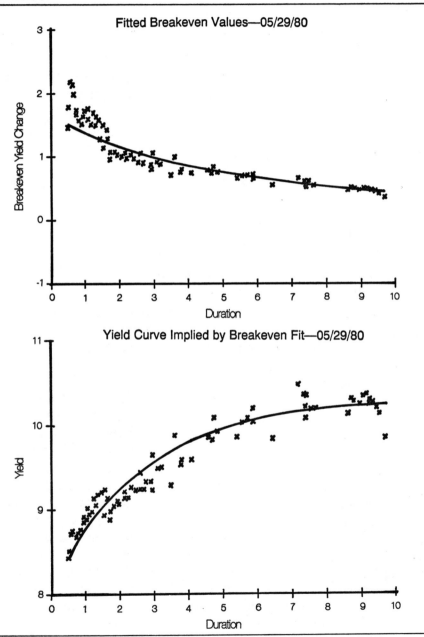

whether they are directed at 20 or at 21 years in the future. But closer in, a year could make a lot of difference. Put another way, the units of future time among which people draw sharp distinctions get much larger as one looks further into the future. In looking backward, people also tend to block out larger chunks of time the further back they go. Duration gives the same effect; there are more calendar years between durations 9 and 10 than between durations 1 and 2.

## *The Integrity of the Yield Curve*

The yield curve derived from the model depends on three variables:

- R, the one-period rate with which the bond returns are compared,
- K, the decay rate of forecast yield changes for one-period intervals in the future, and
- $\Delta R_1$, the forecast change of the one-period rate for one period.

Exhibit 9 shows the yield curve in relation to the one-week rate.

The curve starts at the half-year rate because the shorter rates are influenced by money market pressures that are not accounted for in the model (see "Liquidity Premium"). Although not part of the yield curve, the short rate is uniquely related to it, and influences the pattern of BYCs. One part of the fitting process finds the short rate whose BYCs give the best fit. The search usually converges on a rate that is quite close to the federal funds rate which, itself, plays no role in the fit. Exhibit 10 plots the two rates daily since the beginning of 1980. The correlation between the two short rates, one real and the other hypothetical, is quite remarkable in view of the way the hypothetical rate is obtained. It suggests a strong linkage between the shape of the total yield curve and the short term rate which, as noted, is not part of the curve.

The shape of the curve should be viewed as a single concept, not as a concatenation of smaller segments. That way it can be

**Exhibit 9.   The Yield Curve and the One-Week Rate**

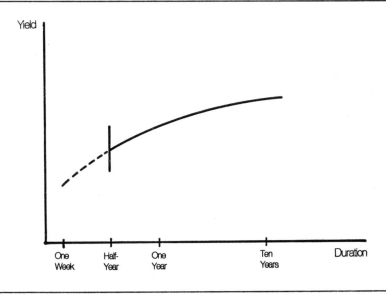

described by a few parameters that determine the particular curve from a family that is consistent with the theory. In principle, these parameters are not merely best fitting statistics but actual measures of market opinion. In contrast, the purely statistical approaches such as polynomials and splines merely describe the data without implying any explanation for them.

The plot of the Ks in Exhibit 11 covers a period when some of the most violent shifts of the yield curve occurred. Yet the Ks (estimates of the Hicksian coefficient) make a fairly smooth curve except for the spikes in April, when it was in transition between the earlier inverted and later positive slopes.

### Relative Yield Volatility

Exhibit 12 shows the correlation and regression coefficients of various long yields in relation to the one-year yield. Both coefficients are lower for the longer yields, the second much more so than the first, which makes sense within the framework of the model. Fur-

**Exhibit 10. Federal Funds versus Fitted Breakeven Short Rate**

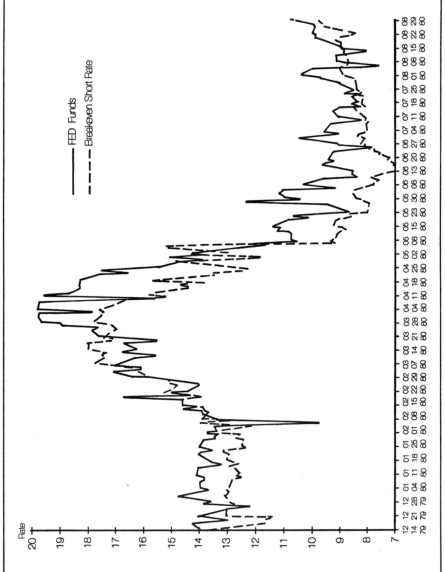

# Exhibit 11. Values of K versus Time

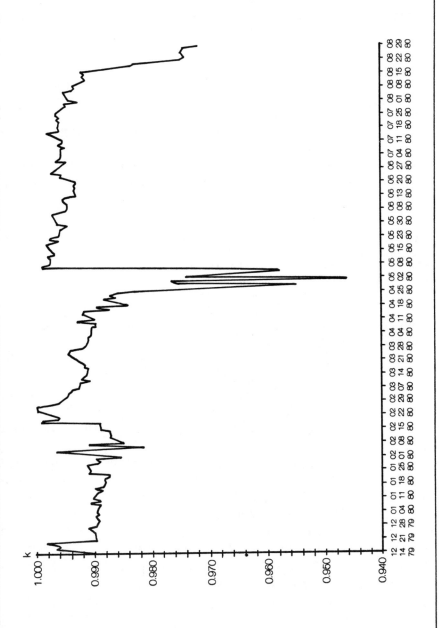

**Exhibit 12. Correlation and Regression Coefficients of Various Long Yields in Relation to the One-Year Yield(a)**

| On 1-Year | Correlation Coefficients | | | Regression Coefficients | | |
|---|---|---|---|---|---|---|
| | Weekly Change | Monthly Change | Quarterly Change | Weekly Change | Monthly Change | Quarterly Change |
| 5-Year | 0.901 | 0.942 | 0.960 | 0.625 | 0.598 | 0.591 |
| 10-Year | 0.841 | 0.884 | 0.911 | 0.451 | 0.426 | 0.430 |
| 20-Year | 0.795 | 0.847 | 0.887 | 0.369 | 0.359 | 0.371 |

(a) Constant maturity data from January 1975 through August 1980. The regressions have the following forms: $\Delta Y_L = a + b\Delta Y_1 + e$, where $\Delta Y_L$ is the respective change in the 5-, 10-, or 20-year yield; $\Delta Y_1$ is the change in the one-year yield; and b is the regression coefficient; a and e, the intercept and residual, are not shown.

ther, the correlation coefficients are larger for longer changes, for example, quarterly instead of weekly.

Exhibit 13 shows schematically how the same expected changes in future short-term yields make up the overlapping parts of expected changes in long yields. The expected yield changes over the first five years determine all of the expected change in the five-year yield, as well as the first five years' worth of the longer yields.

This year's expected one-period change in the one period yield is denoted by the box marked "O." The next four expected one-period changes in the one-period yields are denoted by S1 through S4. The average of these five expected changes equals the expected one-period change of the five period yield, S + O. The remaining expected changes, L1 and L2, merge with the first five for the expected change in the seven-year period rate, O + S + L. This is a major reason why the correlations in Table 4 remain high as terms increase. The five-year (O + S) part of the change in the seven-year yield (O + S + L) is perfectly correlated with the change in the five-year yield.

**Exhibit 13. Expected Changes in Short Yields over Time and Near-Term Changes in Different Long Yields**

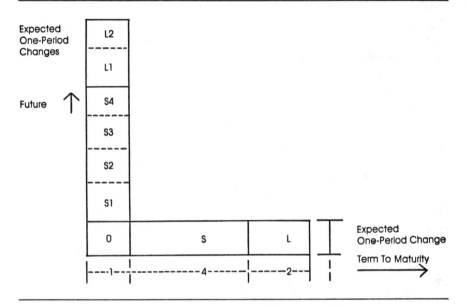

In addition, the remaining part, L, is correlated with O + S because of the way L1 and L2 depend on the first five one-period changes. According to the model, $S1 = O \times K$; $S2 = O \times K^2$; and $L2 = O \times K^6$ (K being the coefficient of expectation). If K were the same every day, $K^6$ also would be the same, and L2 would be a constant multiple of and, while smaller, perfectly correlated with it. In this case, the yield changes on bonds with different terms would be perfectly correlated, differing by a constant multiple. In contrast, the regression coefficients would be smaller on longer bonds since the exponent on K would be larger. But K is not constant from day to day, and as it changes, $K^2$, $K^3$, and so on, all change by different amounts, the differences growing with the size of the exponent. For example, if K changes from 0.7 to 0.8, $K^2$ changes from 0.49 to 0.64, and $K^{10}$ from 0.028 to 0.107. A regression over time cuts across yield curves with different Ks, each of which implies a relative change in the long versus the short rate. The regression captures roughly the average K.

The correlations are higher for quarterly changes than for monthly or weekly ones and similarily higher for monthly than for weekly changes because the market does not move as smoothly as the theory assumes. Over short periods, market imbalances get in the way of logical relationships. Over longer periods, they wash out. This effect is much stronger when it is a question of things moving together (correlation), where random shocks make it seem as if they do not, than when it concerns how much one thing moves relative to another (regression). In this case, the shocks can be on either side of the true number and roughly wash out, leaving the regression coefficient more or less intact. In any case, the errors in the measured relationship are not helped much by allowing time for them to wash out.

The most interesting part of Exhibit 12 is the fall in the regression coefficients as the terms of the yield changes rise. In a rough way, these figures coincide with the relative Ws shown in Table 5, obtained by dividing the Ws in Exhibit 4 by those for unit duration. The comparison is rough for several reasons. First, whereas the Ws are given for units of duration, the regression coefficients in Table 4 are computed with yields denominated in term to maturity. Second, dividing the Ws in Exhibit 4 by one (for unit duration) makes the resulting ratios in Exhibit 14 comparable to the regression coefficients, since they denote the volatility of yields at a given term relative to those with unit term. Each row of Exhibit 14 estimates the regression coefficient of each duration on unit duration *for a given* K. But since K changes over time, there is no stable W for the regression coefficients to estimate except, in a very rough way, the one representing the average K over the regression period. Third, the actual data published by the Federal Reserve Board comes from less than perfectly-fitted yield curves. The regression coefficients obtained with these data inherit some of their errors.

Notwithstanding these problems, the regression coefficients in Exhibit 13, roughly transformed to correspond with units of duration, are remarkably similar to the relative Ws in Exhibit 14. (The durations were computed at the average yield of each term over the regression period.) The comparison is shown in Exhibit 15.

## Exhibit 14. Ratio of the Ws for Each Duration and the W for Unit Duration

| | Duration | | | | | | | | | |
|---|---|---|---|---|---|---|---|---|---|---|
| K | 1.0 | 2.0 | 3.0 | 4.0 | 5.0 | 6.0 | 7.0 | 8.0 | 9.0 | 10.0 |
| 0.9996 | 1.000 | 0.985 | 0.975 | 0.965 | 0.955 | 0.945 | 0.935 | 0.926 | 0.917 | 0.907 |
| 0.9992 | 1.000 | 0.970 | 0.950 | 0.931 | 0.912 | 0.894 | 0.876 | 0.859 | 0.842 | 0.826 |
| 0.9988 | 1.000 | 0.955 | 0.926 | 0.899 | 0.872 | 0.846 | 0.822 | 0.799 | 0.776 | 0.754 |
| 0.9984 | 1.000 | 0.941 | 0.904 | 0.868 | 0.834 | 0.802 | 0.772 | 0.744 | 0.717 | 0.691 |
| 0.9980 | 1.000 | 0.927 | 0.881 | 0.839 | 0.798 | 0.761 | 0.727 | 0.494 | 0.664 | 0.635 |
| 0.9976 | 1.000 | 0.913 | 0.860 | 0.811 | 0.765 | 0.723 | 0.685 | 0.649 | 0.616 | 0.585 |
| 0.9972 | 1.000 | 0.899 | 0.839 | 0.784 | 0.733 | 0.688 | 0.646 | 0.608 | 0.573 | 0.541 |
| 0.9968 | 1.000 | 0.886 | 0.819 | 0.759 | 0.704 | 0.655 | 0.611 | 0.571 | 0.535 | 0.502 |
| 0.9964 | 1.000 | 0.873 | 0.800 | 0.735 | 0.676 | 0.624 | 0.578 | 0.537 | 0.500 | 0.467 |
| 0.9960 | 1.000 | 0.860 | 0.781 | 0.711 | 0.649 | 0.595 | 0.548 | 0.506 | 0.469 | 0.436 |
| 0.9956 | 1.000 | 0.848 | 0.763 | 0.689 | 0.624 | 0.568 | 0.520 | 0.470 | 0.440 | 0.407 |
| 0.9952 | 1.000 | 0.836 | 0.745 | 0.668 | 0.600 | 0.543 | 0.494 | 0.452 | 0.414 | 0.382 |
| 0.9948 | 1.000 | 0.824 | 0.728 | 0.647 | 0.578 | 0.520 | 0.470 | 0.428 | 0.391 | 0.359 |
| 0.9944 | 1.000 | 0.812 | 0.712 | 0.628 | 0.557 | 0.498 | 0.448 | 0.406 | 0.370 | 0.338 |
| 0.9940 | 1.000 | 0.800 | 0.696 | 0.609 | 0.537 | 0.477 | 0.428 | 0.386 | 0.350 | 0.320 |
| 0.9936 | 1.000 | 0.789 | 0.680 | 0.592 | 0.510 | 0.458 | 0.409 | 0.367 | 0.333 | 0.302 |
| 0.9932 | 1.000 | 0.778 | 0.665 | 0.575 | 0.500 | 0.440 | 0.391 | 0.350 | 0.316 | 0.287 |
| 0.9928 | 1.000 | 0.767 | 0.651 | 0.558 | 0.483 | 0.423 | 0.374 | 0.334 | 0.301 | 0.273 |
| 0.9924 | 1.000 | 0.757 | 0.637 | 0.543 | 0.467 | 0.407 | 0.359 | 0.319 | 0.287 | 0.260 |
| 0.9920 | 1.000 | 0.746 | 0.623 | 0.528 | 0.451 | 0.392 | 0.344 | 0.306 | 0.274 | 0.248 |
| 0.9916 | 1.000 | 0.736 | 0.610 | 0.513 | 0.437 | 0.378 | 0.331 | 0.293 | 0.262 | 0.237 |
| 0.9912 | 1.000 | 0.726 | 0.597 | 0.499 | 0.423 | 0.365 | 0.318 | 0.281 | 0.251 | 0.227 |
| 0.9908 | 1.000 | 0.716 | 0.585 | 0.486 | 0.410 | 0.352 | 0.307 | 0.270 | 0.241 | 0.217 |
| 0.9904 | 1.000 | 0.706 | 0.573 | 0.473 | 0.397 | 0.340 | 0.296 | 0.260 | 0.232 | 0.209 |
| 0.9900 | 1.000 | 0.697 | 0.561 | 0.461 | 0.385 | 0.329 | 0.285 | 0.251 | 0.223 | 0.201 |
| 0.9896 | 1.000 | 0.687 | 0.550 | 0.449 | 0.374 | 0.318 | 0.275 | 0.242 | 0.215 | 0.193 |
| 0.9892 | 1.000 | 0.678 | 0.539 | 0.438 | 0.363 | 0.308 | 0.266 | 0.233 | 0.207 | 0.186 |
| 0.9888 | 1.000 | 0.669 | 0.528 | 0.427 | 0.353 | 0.299 | 0.258 | 0.226 | 0.200 | 0.180 |
| 0.9884 | 1.000 | 0.660 | 0.518 | 0.417 | 0.343 | 0.290 | 0.249 | 0.218 | 0.193 | 0.174 |
| 0.9880 | 1.000 | 0.652 | 0.500 | 0.407 | 0.334 | 0.281 | 0.242 | 0.211 | 0.187 | 0.168 |
| 0.9876 | 1.000 | 0.643 | 0.498 | 0.397 | 0.325 | 0.273 | 0.234 | 0.205 | 0.181 | 0.163 |
| 0.9872 | 1.000 | 0.635 | 0.488 | 0.388 | 0.316 | 0.265 | 0.227 | 0.198 | 0.176 | 0.158 |
| 0.9868 | 1.000 | 0.627 | 0.479 | 0.379 | 0.308 | 0.258 | 0.221 | 0.193 | 0.171 | 0.153 |
| 0.9864 | 1.000 | 0.619 | 0.470 | 0.371 | 0.300 | 0.251 | 0.215 | 0.187 | 0.166 | 0.148 |
| 0.9860 | 1.000 | 0.611 | 0.462 | 0.362 | 0.293 | 0.244 | 0.209 | 0.182 | 0.161 | 0.144 |
| 0.9856 | 1.000 | 0.603 | 0.453 | 0.354 | 0.286 | 0.238 | 0.203 | 0.177 | 0.156 | 0.140 |
| 0.9852 | 1.000 | 0.595 | 0.445 | 0.347 | 0.279 | 0.232 | 0.198 | 0.172 | 0.153 | 0.136 |
| 0.9848 | 1.000 | 0.588 | 0.437 | 0.339 | 0.272 | 0.226 | 0.193 | 0.168 | 0.148 | 0.133 |
| 0.9844 | 1.000 | 0.581 | 0.429 | 0.332 | 0.266 | 0.221 | 0.188 | 0.164 | 0.145 | 0.129 |
| 0.9840 | 1.000 | 0.574 | 0.422 | 0.325 | 0.260 | 0.216 | 0.184 | 0.160 | 0.141 | 0.126 |
| 0.9836 | 1.000 | 0.566 | 0.414 | 0.318 | 0.254 | 0.211 | 0.179 | 0.156 | 0.138 | 0.123 |
| 0.9832 | 1.000 | 0.560 | 0.407 | 0.312 | 0.249 | 0.206 | 0.175 | 0.152 | 0.134 | 0.120 |
| 0.9828 | 1.000 | 0.553 | 0.400 | 0.306 | 0.243 | 0.201 | 0.171 | 0.149 | 0.131 | 0.117 |
| 0.9824 | 1.000 | 8.546 | 0.394 | 0.300 | 0.238 | 0.197 | 0.167 | 0.145 | 0.129 | 0.115 |
| 0.9820 | 1.000 | 0.539 | 0.387 | 0.294 | 0.233 | 0.192 | 0.164 | 0.142 | 0.125 | 0.112 |
| 0.9816 | 1.000 | 0.533 | 0.381 | 0.288 | 0.228 | 0.188 | 0.160 | 0.139 | 0.123 | 0.110 |
| 0.9812 | 1.000 | 0.527 | 0.374 | 0.283 | 0.224 | 0.185 | 0.157 | 0.136 | 0.120 | 0.107 |
| 0.9808 | 1.000 | 0.520 | 0.368 | 0.278 | 0.219 | 0.181 | 0.153 | 0.133 | 0.118 | 0.105 |
| 0.9804 | 1.000 | 0.514 | 0.362 | 0.273 | 0.215 | 0.177 | 0.150 | 0.130 | 0.115 | 0.103 |
| 0.9800 | 1.000 | 0.508 | 0.357 | 0.268 | 0.211 | 0.174 | 0.147 | 0.128 | 0.113 | 0.101 |

**Exhibit 15. Comparison Between Past Volatility of Long Yields versus Short Yields and Their Counterparts Predicted by the Model(a)**

| Term (years) | Average Yields 1975-1980 | Estimated Average Duration | Regression Coefficients | $W_D/W_1$ (K = 0.9920) |
|---|---|---|---|---|
| (1) | (2) | (3) | (4) | (5) |
| 2 | 8.14 | 1.80 | 0.840 | 0.867 |
| 3 | 8.21 | 2.60 | 0.735 | 0.753 |
| 5 | 8.36 | 4.00 | 0.598 | 0.596 |
| 7 | 8.46 | 5.20 | 0.494 | 0.501 |
| 10 | 8.55 | 6.65 | 0.426 | 0.416 |
| 20 | 8.67 | 9.45 | 0.359 | 0.305 |

(a) The regression coefficients (column 4) were obtained by regressing each long-term yield on the one-year yield, using constant maturity data for the period January 1975–August 1980, published by the Federal Reserve Board. Column 5 gives the predicted coefficients interpolated from Table 5 (for K = 0.9920) after translating the terms to maturity (column 1) into duration (column 3) at the average yields shown in Column 2.

Clearly, the orders of magnitude of the Ws and the regression coefficients are the same, a remarkable thing in itself in view of the statistical problems described above.

This result in no way depends on the arbitrarily-chosen regression period, since the coefficients are remarkably stable over various fit periods. Exhibit 16 compares the regression coefficients for periods of two, five, and ten years. In part, but only in part, this stability might reflect constraints put on the curves used to obtain the constant maturity data.

*Sectoral Yield Spreads*

Turnover costs, ignored until now, are part of the comparison between the returns on a bond and the locked-in yield on a bill. Buy-

**Exhibit 16. Regression Coefficients of Longer Yields Regressed on One-Year Yields Over Periods of Varying Length(a)**

| Term to Maturity (years) | Jan 1975- Aug 1980 | Sept 1978- Sept 1980 | Jan 1970- Sept 1980 |
|---|---|---|---|
| 2 | 0.840 | 0.833 | 0.839 |
| 3 | 0.735 | 0.725 | 0.732 |
| 5 | 0.598 | 0.597 | 0.599 |
| 7 | 0.494 | 0.492 | 0.491 |
| 10 | 0.426 | 0.421 | 0.415 |
| 20 | 0.359 | 0.358 | 0.345 |

(a)Constant maturity data of Federal Reserve Board.

ing the bond at the offer and selling it at the bid price lowers its expected round-trip return in relation to that of the bill and makes people look for compensatory yield up front. The wider the dealer spread and the more problematic the market at the time of sale, the less appealing the bond over the bill, and the greater compensatory bond yield required. For the arbitrageur, as distinct from the cash buyer, the cost of carrying the bond also affects this decision. Being able to carry treasuries on repo while having to finance corporate bonds with bank loans lowers the relative size of the sweetener on the former.

According to the proposed model, the market sets bond yields at levels where their expected round-trip returns equal the bill yield. Turnover costs and the risk of dealer spreads' widening bear on the size and variation of intersectoral spreads. For example, in the tax-exempt markets, the yield curve slopes upward virtually all of the time, even when the Treasury curve is inverted. When both curves are positive, the tax-exempt one is steeper. One important reason for the difference is turnover costs. Buying a long tax-exempt bond for a short holding period can be an expensive alternative to locking in a short rate.

Another example is the variation in the spreads between U.S. agencies and treasuries in different market environments. A few years ago, the average spread between the two sectors was roughly 15–20 basis points. At the peak yields early this year, it had widened to about 75 basis points (see Exhibit 17). Some ascribe this change to a decline in the quality of agency bonds or to increased aversion to the original quality, but neither explanation makes sense. Instead, the larger spread was probably due to the wider spread between bid and asked prices and to generally thinner markets. It is harder to do a round trip with agencies than with treasuries in any market—an important source of even their normal spread—but harder still in a bear market. The problem is liquidity, not credit quality.

Similar examples abound with Euro and Yankee bonds whose spreads against treasuries also opened during the bear market—again, a result of liquidity rather than quality. In fact, as Exhibit 18 shows, these bonds were harder hit during the bear market than comparable quality, but more liquid, industrials. The spread between representative Yankee and corporate bonds, having risen almost 100 basis points by early spring 1980, the nadir of the market, returned to earlier levels when the market came back. It would be very hard to ascribe this swing to perceived quality.

It may seem out of place to consider the spread between two long bonds in a study of the yield curve. But both belong to some yield curve and have to break even against some short-term yield. A fall-off in liquidity raises the starting yield needed to equate expected return with the short yield in the same sector or with whatever short yield the bond buyer considers an alternative. Much of what passes for changing risk differentials is really this liquidity effect.

### Liquidity Premium

Over the last several years the yield curve has as often as not been inverted over its full length, starting with the six-month term. Below this point, it is almost always positive. As shown in Exhibit 19, the three-month bill rate was below the six-month rate even when the latter exceeded the one-year rate. Exhibit 20 shows the same for CDs, except for a brief inversion early this year. This

**Exhibit 17. Two-Bond Spread History**

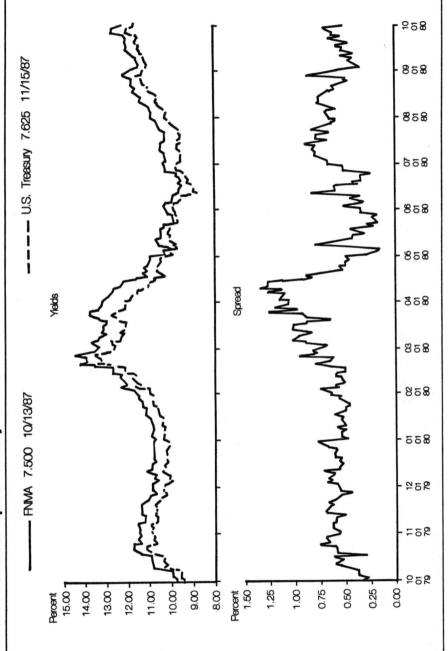

# Exhibit 18. Two-Bond Spread History

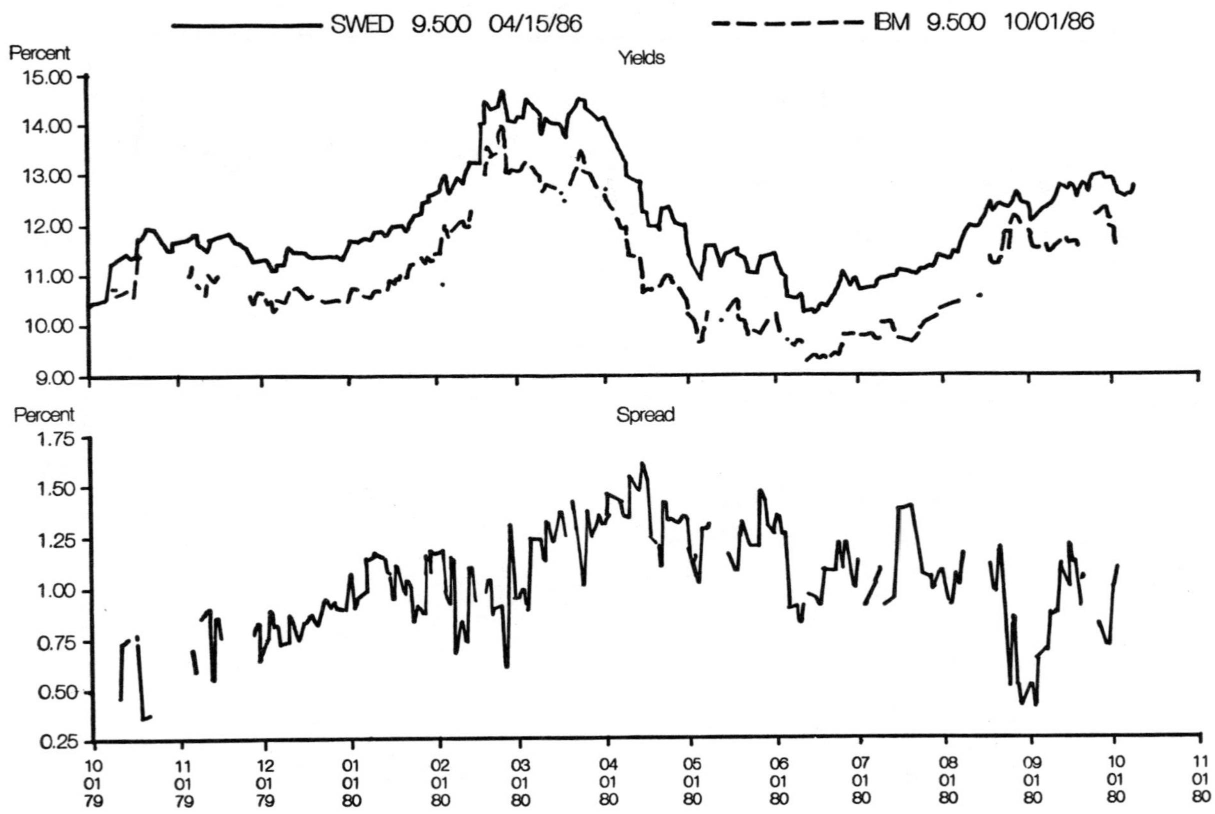

———— SWED 9.500 04/15/86

– – – – BM 9.500 10/01/86

Yields

Spread

**Exhibit 19. Yield Spreads between the 12-month and 6-month T-bills and between the 6-month and 3-month T-bills, January 1978—October 1980**

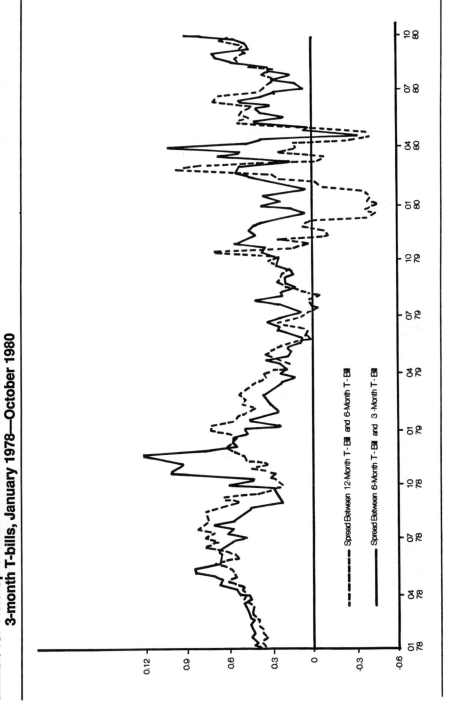

**Exhibit 20. Yield Spreads between the 12-month and 6-month CD's and between the 6-month and 1-month CD's from January 1978—October 1980**

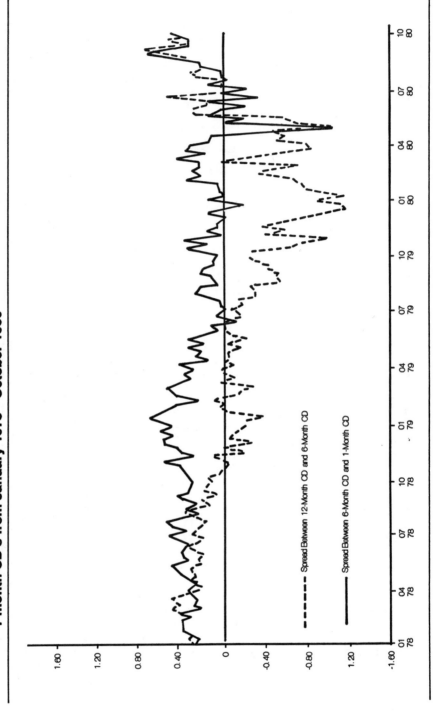

strong positive bias at the short end of the curve is due to a form of liquidity preference that is unrelated to the greater price volatility of longer bonds. In fact, the longer short-term securities—bills, CDs, and BAs—for which there are broad public markets, tend to be *more* liquid than the shorter-term money-market securities, commercial paper and repos, which experience little secondary trading.

The money market is really a market for money, rather than securities. Those who buy five-day commercial paper are really selling money, the securities merely document the money transfers. The buyers know in advance when they need the money and try to match terms to these needs. Liquidity comes from this foreknowledge instead of the ability to sell longer securities before they mature. The issuers, on the other hand, are not looking for credit so much as they are managing their cash flow with fewer liquid assets than they would need otherwise.

In contrast, six-month securities are bought either as short-term investments—for example, by people anticipating a fall in the long market—or for liquid reserves, but usually not to match a known cash need. In this case, the sellers are getting short term credit.

The upward slope at the short end of the yield curve reflects imbalances between supply and demand in these two sectors. There is probably an excess demand for very short-term securities, by people warehousing cash, and an excess supply of six-month bills, CDs, and Acceptances reflecting the short-term borrowings of government and banks. These longer issuers show little interest in lowering borrowing costs by selling into the lower-yielding sector. For banks, it would add to the refinancing risk, and for the government, it would complicate monetary policy by adding to the stock of money substitutes. In any case, they do not do it enough to flatten the yield curve. Nor do the cash warehousers extend for more yield, because they would either lose the risk-free liability match or lengthen their average liquid asset holding at the expense of higher-yielding opportunities. The difference in the function of the two markets makes the securities less interchangeable than at other parts of the curve, and it is a barrier to arbitrage in the way transit costs shield two distant markets from the full effect of competition.

The undersupply at the short end and oversupply at six months would be greater still, and the curve more positively sloped, were it not for the term repo. Arbitrageurs borrow at the repo rate for the shorter terms (like those of commercial paper) to carry the longer ones. In the process, they increase the supply of short-term and the demand for long-term (six months) securities, narrowing the natural gap just noted, but they do not eliminate it.

Exhibit 21 shows why this is so. The yield curve on repos is higher than the one on bills by an amount that measures the liquid premium. (This point holds better for CDs than for Treasury bills, which yield less than their repos for reasons other than liquidity as well.) In the chart, the arbitrageur buys a bill with N months to maturity and does a repo for T months. At this point, the repo cost

## Exhibit 21. The Relationship between the Repo and Bill Rates

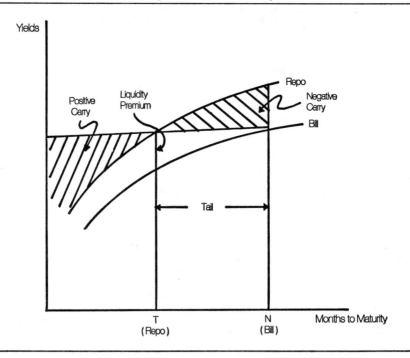

equals the bill yield and the carry is, therefore, zero. If he did a shorter repo, his carry would be positive, and if a longer one, negative. After T months, he must refinance or sell the bill, at potentially higher rates. The months remaining on the bill at this point are called the tail. The longer the tail, the greater the potential price change on the bill or, what comes to the same thing, the longer the period of refinancing risk.

Assuming for a moment that arbitrageurs are content with a zero carry (or any fixed carry), a steeper yield curve or a smaller liquidity premium allows a shorter tail and, therefore, less risk. If either of these got out of line, the curve too steep or the premium too small, the demand for bills and supply of repos would rise until the curve and premium were in balance. Similarly, an increase in the liquidity premium would lengthen the required tail, raise the risk, and, consequently, lower the demand for bills and the supply of repos. In this case, the curve would get steeper.

The point is that the short-term market is held in check by: (1) the perceived risk for a given tail; (2) the outlook for yield changes; and (3) the liquidity premium, which as suggested in the diagram, increases with term. Arbitrageurs would have to be quite bullish to buy enough bills to flatten the yield curve and accept the liquidity premium as a negative carry. Barring this, there is no market force that would entirely offset the imbalance between supply and demand described earlier.

# Chapter 3

# Parametric Analysis of Fixed Income Securities

**Stanley Diller**
**Bear, Stearns & Co. Inc.**

## Introduction

The work in this chapter extends on my earlier work on mortgage products. The novel part of that paper, as of the product, was its analysis of the option-like nature of mortgages brought about by the homeowner's ability to prepay for the purpose of refinancing at a lower rate. The present paper expands this topic beyond mortgages and sets forth a fairly general framework for analyzing all types of fixed income securities.

The framework makes use of the conventional "investment period" over which portfolio returns are projected under various yield scenarios. Securities are equivalent when they give the same returns (income and price change) under the same conditions. They may be called correlates when their prices move together, in which case, one may serve as a hedge or a surrogate for the other. The question is how do we know how closely their prices are correlated?

The answer has two parts. First, what triggers the price change, i.e., what are the independent variables? If the bonds have different maturities or if they represent different sectors, their yields may change unequally, although usually in the same direction. If options are involved, a change in perceived variance (see below) will change values even without yield changes. Second, the price impact of a given yield change depends on the mathematics governing the securities. Each security has a unique curve (or function) mapping every yield into a price. Two securities are perfectly correlated when they have the same such curves.

But it is awkward to match up the actual curves of different securities to determine how similar they are and, therefore, how good a surrogate one is for the other. Instead, people describe these curves with such parameters as duration and convexity. The first is the tangent to the curve, which gives a linear approximation of the price change, and the second measures the divergence between the curve and the tangent or, in other words, between the actual and the linear approximation of the price changes associated with a given yield change.

Both the curves and the parameters may be computed for any given security, whether an option, bond, pass-through, future, or for a portfolio comprising all of them, long and short. The price-yield curve, or what I prefer to call the performance profile for the whole portfolio, is merely the sum of the individual curves, and, similarly, for the parameters.

For most analytical purposes, these profiles (i.e., the curve giving the portfolio value at each yield) contain all we need to know about the securities. It does not matter whether the changes in a portfolio's value as yields change are due to the options, futures, bonds, it contains, and so on or whether the options have one strike price or another. The special features of each security are important only insofar as they influence the performance profile. Nor do we care whether the profile describes one security or many.

Many swaps, for example, pit composites, such as short and long or high and low coupon bonds on one side against a single bond with term or coupon equal to the pair's average on the other. Composites have become even more popular with the emergence of derivative securities such as options, futures, and interest rate swaps. There is no limit to the possible number of combinations involving these instruments and the various cash securities. Once formed, any combination gives rise to a performance profile that can be compared with any other. The sources of the profile cease to matter. Instead of apple and orange comparisons of disparate securities, we have a single framework in which everything looks alike. Instead of strike prices, delivery dates, and the like, we have duration, convexity, and a few other parameters that describe each performance profile.

Just as many securities can be synthesized into a single performance profile, so a single security can be analyzed into several profiles. Prepayable securities, for example, can be decomposed into call-free securities and options, short-term securities into long-term securities and futures, and so on. It is still true that the performance profile or its parametric representation is the bottom line. The decomposition merely provides a better understanding of the result. As long as a bond's components are additive, its performance profile may be considered as the sum of the component's profiles.

The advantage of this approach is that it provides a single framework for analyzing all kinds of securities and portfolio problems limited only by the need for a single driving variable, a given yield, or several that are tied together in a known way. Although far from exhaustive, the present paper sets forth in some details the framework just summarized.

The chapter begins with the price yield function for ordinary bonds. Then, it describes (without mathematics) the main ideas of option theory. These two securities, bonds and options, can be synthesized into callable securities, which are considered next; first, bonds and then pass-throughs. Then, a more general explanation of parametric analysis and its applications in hedging and arbitrage is provided, including a section on dumbbelling. This is followed by a summary of the general framework and then a brief discussion of asset-liability management.

Several people in the Financial Strategies Group contributed to the writing of this paper. Dennis Adler and Tim Beaulac wrote most of the mortgage software. Ravi Dattatreya, who developed our options product, extended the theory and software into many parts of the mortgage product, especially coupon spreads and hedging. May Jou wrote many of the parametric programs. And Hon-Fei Lai, who is responsible for all our optimization work, including dedicated portfolios, wrote many of the routines needed for asset liability management and parametric analysis. I helped design the overall framework, as well as approaches to various specific questions.

## Price-Yield Curve

The simplest performance profile is the price-yield curve of an ordinary bond, which gives the prices at different yields, as illustrated in Exhibit 1. The bond's duration, 9.46 at a 10% yield, is shown as the tangent to the curve at that point. It serves as a linear estimate of the percentage price change associated with a given

**Exhibit 1.   The Price-Yield Curve of a Current 30-Year Bond at 10 Percent**

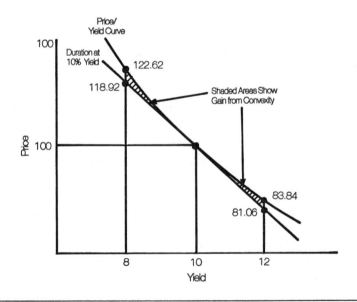

yield change. A 200-basis-point-yield change in either direction, by this estimate, implies an 18.92 percent price change in the opposite direction. But the actual price rises 22.62% when the yield falls 200 basis points and falls 16.16% (not 18.92%) when the yield rises 200 basis points. In either case, the *actual* price change is better for those who are long the bond than the one implied by duration. The difference is due to the convexity of the price-yield curve.

The following section on bond convexity relies on work done by Hon-Fei Lai.

The conventional use of duration to estimate the vertical (i.e., price) change along a curve associated with a given horizontal (i.e., yield) change is part of a more general method involving a Taylor series. This method estimates the vertical movement ($\Delta P$) in the following way:

$$\text{Price Change} = \Delta P = \frac{dP}{dY}\Delta Y + \frac{1}{2}\frac{d^2P}{dY^2}\Delta Y^2 + \dots$$

Define:

$$\text{Modified Duration} = D = -\frac{100}{P}\frac{dP}{dY}$$

and

$$\text{Convexity} = C = \frac{100}{P}\frac{d^2P}{dY^2}$$

Then:

$$\Delta P = \left[\left(\frac{-P}{100}\times D\right)\times \Delta Y\right] + \left[\frac{1}{2}\left(\frac{P}{100}\times C\right)\times \Delta Y^2\right] + E$$

Where $E$ is the residual or unexplained part of $\Delta P$.

The first term is the duration estimate of the price change, and the second term is the part we attribute to *convexity*. The latter represents a parabolic approximatic of the price-yield curve over the distance spanned by $\Delta P$.

But even the parabolic adjustment is incomplete. Further terms in the Taylor series, representing higher-degree polynomials, are needed to estimate the price change *parametrically*, as distinct from using the actual price-yield formula. These extra terms (not shown) are incorporated in the residual term $E$.

Exhibits 2 and 3 decompose the price changes on a full and zero coupon bond for various maturities and yield changes. The part *not* explained by duration grows with the bond's duration and with the size of the yield change. In the extreme case of a 400-basis-point decline on a 40-year zero, duration accounts for only 42% (152.38 / 365.25) of the total price change. It accounts for only 82% of the price change in the much less extreme case of a 200-basis-point change on a 30-year full coupon bond. Zeros are more convex than current coupon bonds only when their durations are greater. For the *same* duration, their convexity is *less*. For example, the durations of the 30-year current and the 10-year zero coupon bonds are almost the same, 9.46 and 9.52. But for a 400-basis-point yield change, duration accounts for 68% of the price change in the first case and 81% in the second. In fact, the duration of a 20-year zero, 19.05, accounts for 66% of the price change, not very different from the 68% for a current coupon with half the duration.

This point helps explain why intermediate zero coupon bonds trade above the yield curve while long zero coupons trade below, a subject considered below.

## Options

The main idea of options, at least what one needs to know about them for the present discussion, can be brought out with a few exhibits. The first (Exhibit 4) gives a probability distribution on expiration day of the prices of the security underlying the option, which I will characterize as a call-free bond. The *strike price* is the one at which you can buy the bond. The *expected price* is merely the current one, for there is no forecasting in option pricing.

**Exhibit 2. Decomposition of Percentage Price Changes into Parts Attributable to Duration, Convexity and Residual for Selected Yield Changes and Maturities (Assumes 10 Percent Yield and Starting Coupon)**

| Matu-rity | Dura-tion | Price Changes | Yield Changes (basis points) | | | | | | | | |
|---|---|---|---|---|---|---|---|---|---|---|---|
| | | | -400 | -300 | -200 | -100 | 0 | 100 | 200 | 300 | 400 |
| 5 | 3.96 | Total | 17.06 | 12.47 | 8.11 | 3.96 | 0.00 | -3.77 | -7.36 | -10.78 | -14.06 |
| | | Due to Duration | 15.44 | 11.58 | 7.72 | 3.86 | 0.00 | -3.86 | -7.72 | -11.58 | -15.44 |
| | | Due to Convexity | 1.50 | 0.84 | 0.37 | 0.09 | 0.00 | 0.09 | 0.37 | 0.84 | 1.50 |
| | | Residual | 0.12 | 0.05 | 0.01 | 0.00 | 0.00 | -0.00 | -0.01 | -0.04 | -0.10 |
| 10 | 6.23 | Total | 29.75 | 21.32 | 13.59 | 6.50 | 0.00 | -5.97 | -11.47 | -16.53 | -21.19 |
| | | Due to Duration | 24.92 | 18.69 | 12.46 | 6.23 | 0.00 | -6.23 | -12.46 | -18.69 | -24.92 |
| | | Due to Convexity | 4.23 | 2.38 | 1.06 | 0.26 | 0.00 | 0.26 | 1.06 | 2.38 | 4.23 |
| | | Residual | 0.60 | 0.25 | 0.07 | 0.01 | 0.00 | -0.01 | -0.06 | -0.21 | -0.49 |
| 15 | 7.00 | Total | 39.20 | 27.50 | 17.29 | 8.14 | 0.00 | -7.27 | -13.76 | -19.59 | -24.82 |
| | | Due to Duration | 30.74 | 23.06 | 15.37 | 7.69 | 0.00 | -7.69 | -15.37 | -23.06 | -30.74 |
| | | Due to Convexity | 7.01 | 3.94 | 1.75 | 0.44 | 0.00 | 0.44 | 1.75 | 3.94 | 7.01 |
| | | Residual | 1.45 | 0.59 | 0.17 | 0.02 | 0.00 | -0.02 | -0.14 | -0.47 | -1.08 |
| 20 | 8.58 | Total | 46.23 | 32.03 | 19.79 | 9.20 | 0.00 | -8.02 | -15.05 | -21.22 | -26.66 |
| | | Due to Duration | 34.32 | 25.74 | 17.16 | 8.58 | 0.00 | -8.58 | -17.16 | -25.74 | -34.32 |
| | | Due to Convexity | 9.40 | 5.29 | 2.35 | 0.59 | 0.00 | 0.59 | 2.35 | 5.29 | 9.40 |
| | | Residual | 2.51 | 1.01 | 0.28 | 0.03 | 0.00 | -0.03 | -0.24 | -0.77 | -1.74 |
| 25 | 9.46 | Total | 55.35 | 37.42 | 22.64 | 10.32 | 0.00 | -8.72 | -16.16 | -22.55 | -28.08 |
| | | Due to Duration | 37.86 | 28.39 | 18.93 | 9.46 | 0.00 | -9.46 | -18.93 | -28.39 | -37.86 |
| | | Due to Convexity | 12.70 | 7.14 | 3.17 | 0.79 | 0.00 | 0.79 | 3.17 | 7.14 | 12.70 |
| | | Residual | 4.80 | 1.86 | 0.52 | 0.06 | 0.00 | -0.05 | -0.41 | -1.30 | -2.91 |

**Exhibit 3.  Decomposition of Percentage Price Changes of Zero Coupon Bonds into Parts Attributable to Duration, Convexity and Residual for Selected Yield Changes and Maturities (The Starting Yield Is 10 Percent in All Cases)**

| | | | Yield Changes (basis points) | | | | | | | | |
|---|---|---|---|---|---|---|---|---|---|---|---|
| Matu-rity | Dura-tion | Price Changes | -400 | -300 | -200 | -100 | 0 | 100 | 200 | 300 | 400 |
| 5 | 4.76 | Total | 21.20 | 15.47 | 10.04 | 4.89 | 0.00 | -4.64 | -9.04 | -13.22 | -17.19 |
| | | Due to Duration | 19.05 | 14.28 | 9.52 | 4.76 | 0.00 | -4.76 | -9.52 | -14.28 | -19.05 |
| | | Due to Convexity | 1.99 | 1.12 | 0.50 | 0.12 | 0.00 | 0.12 | 0.50 | 1.12 | 1.99 |
| | | Residual | 0.16 | 0.07 | 0.02 | 0.00 | 0.00 | -0.00 | -0.02 | -0.06 | -0.14 |
| 10 | 9.52 | Total | 46.91 | 33.34 | 21.09 | 10.02 | 0.00 | -9.06 | -17.27 | -24.70 | -31.43 |
| | | Due to Duration | 38.09 | 28.57 | 19.05 | 9.52 | 0.00 | -9.52 | -19.05 | -28.57 | -38.09 |
| | | Due to Convexity | 7.62 | 4.28 | 1.90 | 0.48 | 0.00 | 0.48 | 1.90 | 4.29 | 7.62 |
| | | Residual | 1.19 | 0.49 | 0.14 | 0.02 | 0.00 | -0.02 | -0.13 | -0.41 | -0.96 |
| 15 | 19.05 | Total | 115.81 | 77.81 | 46.63 | 21.04 | 0.00 | -17.31 | -31.55 | -43.30 | -52.99 |
| | | Due to Duration | 76.19 | 57.14 | 38.09 | 19.05 | 0.00 | -19.05 | -38.09 | -57.15 | -76.19 |
| | | Due to Convexity | 29.75 | 16.73 | 7.44 | 1.86 | 0.00 | 1.96 | 7.44 | 16.73 | 29.75 |
| | | Residual | 9.89 | 3.93 | 1.10 | 0.13 | 0.00 | -0.12 | -0.90 | -2.89 | -6.55 |
| 20 | 28.75 | Total | 217.05 | 137.10 | 77.51 | 33.16 | 0.00 | -24.80 | -43.37 | -57.30 | -67.76 |
| | | Due to Duration | 114.29 | 85.71 | 57.14 | 28.57 | 0.00 | -28.57 | -57.14 | -85.71 | -114.29 |
| | | Due to Convexity | 66.38 | 37.35 | 16.60 | 4.15 | 0.00 | 4.15 | 16.80 | 37.35 | 66.39 |
| | | Residual | 36.37 | 14.04 | 3.82 | 0.44 | 0.00 | -0.36 | -2.83 | -8.94 | -19.87 |
| 25 | 38.00 | Total | 365.76 | 216.17 | 115.02 | 46.50 | 0.00 | -31.62 | -53.15 | -67.35 | -77.90 |
| | | Due to Duration | 152.38 | 114.29 | 76.19 | 38.10 | 0.00 | -38.10 | -76.19 | -114.29 | -152.38 |
| | | Due to Convexity | 117.55 | 66.12 | 29.30 | 7.35 | 0.00 | 7.36 | 29.30 | 66.12 | 117.55 |
| | | Residual | 96.83 | 35.76 | 9.44 | 1.06 | 0.00 | -0.87 | -6.35 | -19.00 | -43.07 |

**Exhibit 4.  Expiration Day Distribution of Prices of Underlying Bond**

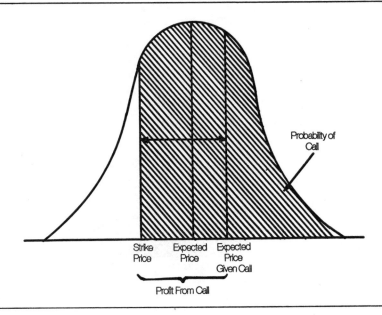

The *expected-price-given-call* is the expected price[1] on the assumption that the option will be *in-the-money*, represented, as is the probability of call, by the shaded area. It is the mean value of the shaded area. The "profit from call" is the difference between the "expected-value-given-call" and the exercise or "strike" price: you buy at the lower and sell at the higher price. The value of the option may be viewed as the present value of the product of the probability of call and the profit from call.

Exhibit 5 shows the impact of volatility on option values. The dashed line represents more volatile or dispersed prices. At expiration, the option holder is stopped out at the strike price. If the bond is above the strike price, the option is worth the difference between the bond and strike prices; the greater this difference, the more the option is worth. If the bond is below the strike price, the option is worthless but equally so regardless of how far the bond

---

1. "Expected price" is a mathematical term denoting the mean of a probability distribution, it should not be interpreted as a forecast.

**Exhibit 5.  The Impact of Volatility on Option Values**

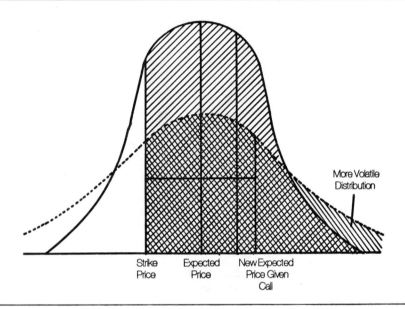

Strike | Expected | New Expected | More Volatile
Price | Price | Price Given | Distribution
| | Call |

is below the strike price. The flatter price distribution heightens both tails but with unequal effect. Raising the lower tail is harmless to the option holder since he is stopped out, but he fully enjoys the increased upper tail. As a result, the *new* expected-price-given-call and, therefore, the profit from call is greater than before. As a general matter, whoever is stopped out benefits from a more volatile environment, a fact that the insurance industry calls *moral hazard.*

Imagine redrawing the chart in Exhibit 4 for different values of the expected price. As it moved to the left, the whole curve would shift, while the strike remained fixed. The result is a lower probability of and profit from call. As it moved to the right, both would rise. But the product of the two, the present value of which is the current option value, does not change one for one with the expected bond price.

Instead, it traces a path like the one given in Exhibit 6. The bold line segments represent parity, or expiration, value. When the bond is below the strike, the option expires worthless; when above, its expiration value equals the difference between bond and strike. (The 45-degree diagonal equates the option price with this difference.)

The slope of the tangent to the option curve gives the *hedge ratio* at the contact point, which gives the option price change per unit bond price change. A typical value for an at-the-money option is one-half, which implies that a hedged writer (or seller) would carry half a bond for each option or, in other words, two options per bond. But having put on this hedge, the writer cannot walk away: as the bond moves, the hedge ratio moves as well, necessitating a so-called rebalancing. The hedge ratio varies from zero for deeply out-of-the-money to one for deeply in-the-money options. How fast it moves within this range, represented by the degree of curvature or *convexity* of the option curve, is the core of option analysis.

The shaded area in Exhibit 6 represents the *time value* of the option at various market prices. It is greater the more volatile that

**Exhibit 6.   The Relationship between Option Price and Bond Price**

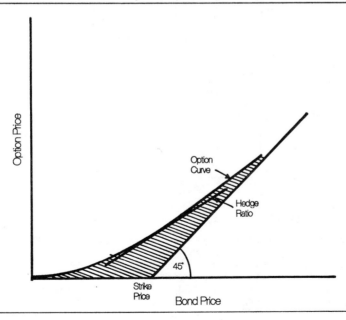

bond prices are and the longer the term to expiration. Analytically, these two influences are the same. The reason lies in the random walk assumption that the price changes in any period are independent of those in previous periods. As a result, the variance over two periods is twice the one-period variance.[2] There is a family of curves similar to the one shown in Exhibit 6, one for each variance or term.

Exhibit 7 magnifies the at-the-money part of the previously described curve. The option price rises a greater fraction (2/3) of the bond price rise than it falls (1/3) relative to a price fall. This difference is due to *convexity*. In contrast a bond future would rise and fall (roughly) in the same proportion as the bond's rise and fall as long as the starting durations were the same.

**Exhibit 7.   The Convexity of the Option Curve**

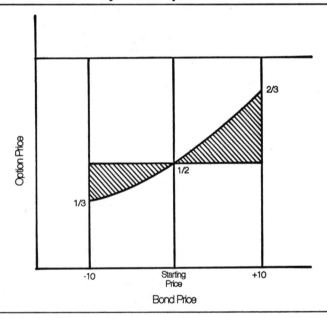

2. The option value depends directly not on variance, but on its square root, the standard deviation. But only the former is additive. The standard deviation over two periods is the square root of the sum of one-period variances and hence rises not with time but with the square root of time. Since at-the-money option values tend to grow proportionately with the standard deviation of the underlying security prices, they too grow with the *square root* of term to expiration. Doubling the term raises the value roughly by the square root of two, or 1.4.

The impact of this convexity is illustrated in Exhibit 8, which describes the effect of a bond price change on a hedged option writer. It assumes a starting hedge ratio of 1/2, which means that the hedged writer buys one bond and sells two options. It further assumes, as above, that the option rises 2/3 of the bond's rise and falls 1/3 of the bond's fall, for the 10-basis-point bond movements assumed. When the bond rises 10 points, either option rises 6 2/3 and the pair 13 1/3, which gives a net loss of 3 1/3. When the bond falls 10 basis points, either option falls 3 1/3 and the pair only 6 2/3, also for a net loss of 3 1/3. In other words, either way the writer loses 3 1/3 points.

If he were sure of a 10-basis-point move and got the present value of 3 1/3 dollars up front as a premium, he would break even. If he did get that, but the actual price movement were more than 10 basis points, he would lose; if less, he would win. The premium set in the market would depend on the consensus about the potential price movement, in either direction.

I believe this highly schematic example captures the main point of option modeling, which is to make possible a mapping between expected price movement and required premium. Formal models work with the standard deviation instead of the range of prices, and they work incrementally. The Black-Scholes model, for example, sets the premium such that its fall due to the passage of time (a gain to the short seller) just offsets the loss described above for small units of time and price change. Instead of assuming the option writer keeps taking it on the chin until expiration, the models evoke a process in which the writer is zigging and zagging or, in the current euphemism,[3] rebalancing. The method, often called

**Exhibit 8. The Option Writer's Loss**

| Bond Price | Option Price | Short Position | Profit/Loss |
|:---:|:---:|:---:|:---:|
| +10 | 6⅔ | −13⅓ | −3⅓ |
| −10 | −3⅓ | 6⅔ | −3⅓ |

---

3. The phrase (or term) is a *euphemism* because it occurs *after* the losses due to convexity. While it cuts the size of a given loss, it leads to a greater number of losses, including the double-losses due to whipsawing.

*delta-hedging*, involves realignments of the hedge ratio. Keep in mind these changes are made *after* the loss and involve turnover cost as well. In theory, the time gains (i.e., being short a falling value) just offset these losses, but the theory relies on a constant degree of price variability. In practice, the degree of fixed-income market variability has been quite unstable.

The changing estimate of volatility is the main risk in option trading. The contest among arbitrageurs is not built around who has got the best model but rather who has got the best estimate of variance or, better, who can price correctly the risk of not having a good estimate. The models merely map variance into the price, and the reverse, the latter being called *implicit variance*, namely the variance that equates the model's estimated option price with the market value. This number plays a role in option trading similar to the one played by the implied repo rate in futures trading.

Another hedging approach involves creating a synthetic option by trading on a decision rule. To synthesize a call at 80, for example, arrange to buy the bond whenever it rises to 80 and to sell it whenever it falls to a tick below 80. In that case, you own the bond at 80 and above and are out below 80, the equivalent of owning a call at 80. As with delta-hedging, this approach involves two costs: first, you buy at a higher price than you sell and, second, there are turnover costs. Both costs rise with market volatility since they depend on the number of turnovers. Clearly, the more liquid the market for the underlying security, the lower the cost of synthesizing the option. (I think the greater liquidity of futures over bonds is the main reason for the market preference for options on futures over options on bonds). The dependence of hedging cost on market volatility is the main vehicle for translating the market's perception of volatility into option prices.

### Volatility versus Time

The driving force in option evaluation is the trade off between volatility and time. Volatility determines how much the hedged writer will lose (or the hedged buyer gain) from a given option convexity. The more convex the option the more its value diverges from the linear projection of change assumed by the starting hedge ratio, as illustrated in Exhibit 9. The wider the price move, suggesting more volatility, the greater the divergence. To gain from this volatility the investor must be net long convexity. If instead, your long and short positions moved along the same curve, as in the typical bond-versus-futures (but not GNMA versus futures) hedge, you would have no reason to welcome volatility. This volatility is worth more, the greater the option's convexity. The more convexity, the more divergence between the option and bond price movements. (Do not confuse this point, that convexity is worth more when there is more volatility, with the false notion that volatility makes convexity larger. In fact, the reverse is true: convexity falls as either the term to expiration or the bond volatility gets larger. Convexity is a mathematical property of options, and indeed of bonds, as well, as shown above; volatility is a perception that determines how much this property is worth.)

You pay for this divergence through the option premium. The more you pay, the farther it can fall over time. It helps to imagine

**Exhibit 9.  Change in Option Value as Bond Price Changes**

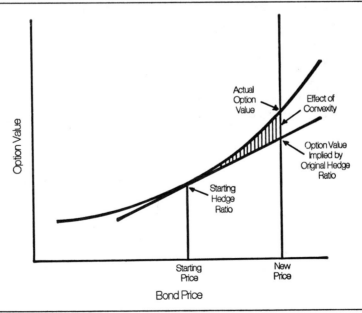

a horizontal force representing price volatility and a downward force representing the loss in time value. The market resolves these forces by setting the premium to a level such that the resulting fall due to time just offsets the divergence between the option and bond for a given range of bond prices. The short position gains from the fall due to time and loses from the divergence due to price movements, and the reverse is true of the long position.

Exhibit 10 illustrates these two effects for an option on a bond future. It describes the relative movement of an option and future after a month's time. The starting hedge ratio is 0.58. The futures prices are given in Column 1, starting with 75.00 at the middle of the page. The option was purchased at 2.52 (2 52/64) but has lost 20/64s from the passage of time (4th column). The long option position involving 1/0.58 options, is down $0.31 (Column 6). In other words, without price movement, the long position falls. As long as the price moves less than 2 1/2 points, remaining between 72 16/32 and 77 16/32, the position loses. But any movement beyond that results in a net gain.

There are many ways to trade off time and convexity by taking opposite positions in securities with different amounts of either attribute. By *time*, I mean the fall of the option price as expiration gets nearer, with bond prices constant. By *convexity*, I mean the divergence of the option price from the price projected with the starting hedge ratio as the bond price changes, for a given term to expiration. For a given underlying security, say a Treasury bond, and a given assumed volatility, the two parameters depend on the term to expiration and the market level in relation to the strike price.

For at-the-money options, convexity grows and value falls at growing rates as expiration gets nearer. That means that if you are long the near and short the far option, that is, long the *spread*, you are net long convexity and net short time value. In that case, you win if prices move a lot and lose if they do not. Exhibit 11 shows the opposite case, being long the *reverse spread*. The dashed line shows the net position, the shaded area being the profit. As long as yields fall between 10.6 percent and 11.9 percent at the one-

## Exhibit 10. Future Call Options Table

Date: 01/21/83

OPTION: June 74
Standard Deviation: 0.137
Futures Price (32nd): 75.00

Current Price (64th): 2.52
Hedge Ratio: 0.583
Short Term Rate: 8.25

Horizon Date: 02/21/83

| Future | | Option | | | |
|---|---|---|---|---|---|
| Price (32nd) | Move (32nd) | Price (64th) | Move (64th) | Hedge Ratio | Move at Current Hedge* |
| 67.00 | -8.00 | 0.09 | -2.43 | 0.073 | 2.00 |
| 67.16 | -7.16 | 0.12 | -2.40 | 0.090 | 1.75 |
| 68.00 | -7.00 | 0.14 | -2.38 | 0.107 | 1.50 |
| 68.16 | -6.16 | 0.19 | -2.33 | 0.131 | 1.27 |
| 69.00 | -5.00 | 0.23 | -2.29 | 0.156 | 1.05 |
| 69.16 | -5.16 | 0.28 | -2.24 | 0.181 | 0.83 |
| 70.00 | -5.00 | 0.35 | -2.17 | 0.213 | 0.65 |
| 72.16 | -4.16 | 0.42 | -2.10 | 0.245 | 0.47 |
| 71.00 | -4.00 | 0.50 | -2.02 | 0.278 | 0.30 |
| 71.16 | -3.16 | 0.60 | -1.56 | 0.316 | 0.17 |
| 72.00 | -3.00 | 1.06 | -1.45 | 0.354 | 0.04 |
| 72.16 | -2.16 | 1.17 | -1.35 | 0.392 | -0.08 |
| 73.00 | -2.00 | 1.31 | -1.21 | 0.433 | -0.15 |
| 73.16 | -1.16 | 1.45 | -1.06 | 0.473 | -0.22 |
| 74.00 | -1.00 | 1.60 | -0.56 | 0.513 | -0.30 |
| 74.16 | -0.16 | 2.14 | -0.38 | 0.553 | -0.30 |
| 75.00 | 0.00 | 2.32 | -0.20 | 0.593 | -0.31 |
| 75.16 | 0.16 | 2.50 | -0.02 | 0.632 | -0.32 |
| 76.00 | 1.00 | 3.07 | 0.19 | 0.668 | -0.28 |
| 76.16 | 1.16 | 3.29 | 0.41 | 0.703 | -0.23 |
| 77.00 | 2.00 | 3.51 | 0.63 | 0.737 | -0.18 |
| 77.16 | 2.16 | 4.11 | 1.23 | 0.768 | -0.10 |
| 78.00 | 3.00 | 4.36 | 1.48 | 0.796 | 0.00 |
| 78.16 | 3.16 | 4.61 | 2.09 | 0.824 | 0.10 |
| 79.00 | 4.00 | 5.23 | 2.35 | 0.850 | 0.22 |
| 79.16 | 4.16 | 5.51 | 2.63 | 0.870 | 0.36 |
| 80.00 | 5.00 | 6.15 | 3.27 | 0.891 | 0.50 |
| 80.16 | 5.16 | 6.43 | 3.55 | 0.912 | 0.65 |
| 81.00 | 6.00 | 7.08 | 4.20 | 0.926 | 0.82 |
| 81.16 | 6.16 | 7.38 | 4.50 | 0.941 | 0.99 |
| 82.00 | 7.00 | 8.04 | 5.16 | 0.958 | 1.16 |
| 82.16 | 7.16 | 8.34 | 5.46 | 0.967 | 1.35 |
| 83.00 | 8.00 | 9.01 | 6.13 | 0.977 | 1.54 |

*Current Hedge: Long 1 CALL + Short 0.583 futures.

## Exhibit 11. Position Diagram at Horizon

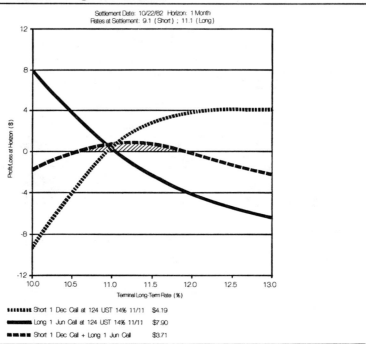

Settlement Date: 10/22/82  Horizon: 1 Month
Rates at Settlement: 9.1 (Short) ; 11.1 (Long)

ıııııı Short 1 Dec Call at 124 UST 14% 11/11   $4.19
▬▬ Long 1 Jun Call at 124 UST 14% 11/11   $7.90
■■■■ Short 1 Dec Call + Long 1 Jun Call   $3.71

month horizon, the net short position in a falling time value outweighs the net short position in convexity.

Deeply in- and out-of-the-money options have much less convexity *and* time value. In fact, some people use the deeply in-the-money options, with hedge ratios near one, as substitutes for futures. To some extent one can hedge low-convexity, long-term options with out-of-the-money, short-term options, which are more readily available.

### Callable Bonds

Option theory is the most direct way of analyzing the prepayment of bonds and pass-throughs. Yet arbitrary concepts like average life and assumed prepayments are more widely used, mainly because their broad acceptance makes them convenient. But they lead to relative prices that have little economic basis and confuse investors. The problem is that prepayment is contingent on future interest rates and can be estimated only probablistically. Assigning one prepayment rate for the life of the pass-through, especially one based on very recent experience, or assuming some *worst* case and calling the resulting estimate *conservative* instead of merely arbitrary, is inadequate. Instead, treating the prepayment as a call option written by the investor provides a more reasonable framework on which to build. Since they involve fewer complications, I start with callable bonds and then extend the analysis to pass-throughs.

A callable bond combines a long position in a call-free bond with a short position in an option. The option is not exercisable until the first call date, i.e., *European* and exercisable any time thereafter until the bond's maturity, i.e., *American*. Ravi Dattatreya's model is *binomial*, starting with a yield distribution that he translates into a price distribution with the yield-to-price formula. As the bond ages, the price volatility implied by a given yield volatility falls, approaching zero as the bond approaches maturity. He also has a (fairly arbitrary) yield dampener in recognition of people's perception that interest rates are unlikely to increase indefinitely. Most option models find the expiration-day volatility by multiplying the user-given one-day variance by the number of trading or calendar days to expiration. For callable bonds, this is a long time, and a linear projection of variance overstates the option's value. Therefore, some dampening is needed.

To use the model one must enter a call-free yield; that is, an estimate of what the yield would be if the bond were not callable. The estimate usually is based on a low coupon bond of the same type, perhaps adjusted for coupon influence other than call, or on some spread over treasuries. Alternatively, one can assume a call-free yield variance and let the model find the call-free yield consistent with the callable bond price and call-free yield variance.

## Duration of Callable Bonds

There are good reasons for knowing how to calculate the duration of callable bonds. Many techniques like hedging, immunization, and gap management depend on duration. People using these methods often avoid callable bonds and pass-throughs because they do not know how to calculate their durations. When it comes to hedging portfolios in which these types of securities appear, they are unable to do this. The options approach suggests a reasonable solution.

The duration of a callable bond is the weighted-average duration of its components, the weights being their dollar values with a negative sign for the short option position.

$$D_{CB} = \frac{P_{NCB} \times D_{NCB} - P_C \times D_C}{P_{CB}}$$

The *modified duration* of the hypothetical, noncallable ($D_{NCB}$) is calculated with the usual formula:

$$D_M = \frac{D}{1 + \dfrac{R}{X}}$$

where $D$ is ordinary duration and $X$ is the compounding frequency. Modified duration gives the *percentage* price change per basis-point-change in yield (multiplied by 100). It is the *price elasticity* with respect to yield. This number typically is used to compare the price volatilities of different bonds. In this context it bears little relationship to time. That is obviously the case with options, the durations of which can be many times greater than their terms to expiration. Moreover an option price is driven not by its own yield, but by that of the underlying security. If that's a bond future, the chain of events goes from the yield change on the underlying bond to the bond's price change to the future's price change to the option's price change. This sequence results because we think in terms of yield but are interested, ultimately, in price movement. In other words, the driving force is the plain vanilla interest rate, from which flows the various price movements. The (modified) duration of the option is given by the following formula:

$$D_C = \frac{H \times P_{NCB} \times D_{NCB}}{P_C}$$

that is, it is the product of the hedge ratio ($H$), the price ($P_{NCB}$) and the duration ($D_{NCB}$) of the non-callable bond, all divided by the option price ($P_C$). The formula is quite intuitive. The expression $P_{NCB} \times D_{NCB}$ gives the dollar movement in the bond per basis-point-yield change. Multiplying that by the hedge ratio gives the dollar movement of the option. And dividing that by the option price gives the percentage movement of the option.

Assume one wants to calculate the duration of a callable bond on the following facts:

| | Bonds | | Option | |
| | Callable | Noncallable | | |
|---|---|---|---|---|
| Coupon | 15 | 15 | Call Price | 115 |
| Maturity | 20 Yrs. | 20 Yrs. | First Call Date | 5 Yrs. |
| Price | 110.30 | 127.19 | Price | 16.89 |
| Yield | 13.50 | 11.50 | Hedge Ratio | 0.39 |

$$\text{Duration (noncallable)} = D_{NCB} = \qquad = 7.48$$

$$\text{Duration (option)} = D_C = \frac{0.39 \times 127.19 \times 7.48}{16.89} = 21.97$$

$$\text{Duration (callable)} = D_{CB} = \frac{127.19 \times 7.48 - 16.89 \times 21.97}{110.30} = 5.26$$

In this case, the yield on the noncallable bond is estimated and the price inferred. The difference between the two bond prices is the implied option price (127.19 − 110.30 = 16.89). An alternative method enters the standard deviation of the noncallable yields from which the model calculates the option value and through that the noncallable bond yield. The hedge ratio is calculated by the option model. First, it calculates the option curve, giving the option price for each bond price, and then derives the first derivative of the option price with respect to the bond price, which is the hedge ratio.

The calculated duration of the callable bond neither ignores the call nor assumes the bond will be called on the first call date. Instead, it is based on the *contingency* of call, the probable outcome of which is driven by the variance of the distribution of bond prices. Clearly, the calculated duration changes with call-free yields as the probability of call changes. Therefore, in hedging callable bonds, one must constantly recalculate duration and where necessary, change the hedge.

Often one needs to know a bond's maturity for the purpose of display or of calculating summary statistics like the average maturity of a portfolio. This is a problem when there is contingent prepayment. The option approach described here makes possible some reasonable estimates, keeping in mind that with indefinite prepayment the ideas of yield and maturity are indefinite. The proposed method calculates the duration of the callable bond in the way just described and finds the combination of maturity and yield that is consistent with this duration, given price. The result is the equivalent of an average life, calculated on contingent rather than on assumed prepayment, and the proposed yield merely is the yield to this average life.

## Performance of Callable Bonds

In deciding whether to buy callable bonds people often estimate their performance under various market scenarios relative to that of noncallable bonds. These estimates depend largely on conjectured behavior of callable bond yields under various noncallable yield scenarios. But the option model can do better. The callable bond *yield* change is not an autonomous event, about which one has an informed opinion, but rather the result of the call-free-yield change causing the call-free price, and through that the option value change, and through that the callable bond price and finally, yield change. In other words, the driving force is not the callable yield itself, but rather the impact of the call-free yield change on the option value.

Exhibit 12 shows how the callable yields change as the call-free yields change, allowing for the changing option value. When the call-free yield changes from 11.5 to 10, and its price from 126.80 to 142.17, the option value changes from 16.62 to 23.49. The callable bond price, merely the difference between the call-free bond and the option prices, goes from 110.18 to 118.68, a rise of 8.50, instead of the 15.37 point rise of the call-free bond, and the callable yield falls 108 instead of the 150 basis points of the call-free yield. But the callable yield change is an inference, not a driving force.

The rates of return on callable bonds depend only on the impact of the hypothetical *call-free* bond's yield change on its price and that of the call option, the algebraic sum of which gives the callable price change, from which the rate of return is calculated.

### Option Analysis of Pass-throughs

Basically, the owner of a pass-through or mortgage, as of a callable bond, can be said to be long a hypothetical noncallable security and short a call option. The value of his position is the value of the first less that of the second. The expected change in the pass-through's value as interest rates change is the expected change in the first less that in the second, both changes being quite amenable to rigorous analysis. The pass-through's duration is equal to that of the call-free component less that of the option, weighted by their respective values. In other words, the option approach provides an objective evaluation of mortgage securities and also makes it possible to apply the same type of analysis to mortgages as to ordinary bonds. For hedging and gap management, one needs an accurate measure of duration. For horizon analysis, one must know how interest rate movements affect prepayment and

## Exhibit 12. Callable Bond Analysis Report

| Call Free Bond | | Callable Bond | |
|---|---|---|---|
| Coupon: | 15.000 | Coupon: | 15.000 |
| Maturity: | 10/15/02 | Maturity: | 10/15/02 |
| | | Call Price: | 115.00 |
| | | Call Date: | 10/15/87 |
| Price: | 126.80 | Price: | 110.18 |
| | | Call Value: | 16.62 |
| | | Implied Std: | 0.225 |

| Yield | | Price | | Yield | | Price | | Call | Yield |
|---|---|---|---|---|---|---|---|---|---|
| Acutal | Move | Acutal | Move | Acutal | Move | Acutal | Move | Value | Spread |
| 10.00 | -1.50 | 142.17 | 15.37 | 15.37 | -1.08 | 118.68 | 8.50 | 23.49 | -2.42 |
| 10.10 | -1.40 | 141.05 | 14.26 | 14.26 | -1.01 | 118.10 | 7.91 | 22.96 | -2.39 |
| 10.20 | -1.30 | 139.95 | 13.15 | 13.15 | -0.94 | 117.52 | 7.34 | 22.43 | -2.36 |
| 10.30 | -1.20 | 138.86 | 12.06 | 12.06 | -0.87 | 116.94 | 6.76 | 21.92 | -2.33 |
| 10.40 | -1.10 | 137.79 | 10.99 | 10.99 | -0.80 | 116.37 | 6.19 | 21.42 | -2.30 |
| 10.50 | -1.00 | 136.73 | 9.93 | 9.93 | -0.73 | 115.80 | 5.62 | 20.92 | -2.27 |
| 10.60 | -0.90 | 135.68 | 8.88 | 8.88 | -0.66 | 115.24 | 5.05 | 20.44 | -2.24 |
| 10.70 | -0.80 | 134.64 | 7.84 | 7.84 | -0.59 | 114.67 | 4.49 | 19.97 | -2.21 |
| 10.80 | -0.70 | 133.62 | 6.82 | 6.82 | -0.52 | 114.11 | 3.93 | 19.50 | -2.18 |
| 10.90 | -0.60 | 132.61 | 5.81 | 5.81 | -0.45 | 113.56 | 3.37 | 19.05 | -2.15 |
| 11.00 | -0.50 | 131.61 | 4.81 | 4.81 | -0.37 | 112.99 | 2.81 | 18.62 | -2.13 |
| 11.10 | -0.40 | 130.62 | 3.83 | 3.83 | -0.30 | 112.43 | 2.24 | 18.20 | -2.10 |
| 11.20 | -0.30 | 129.65 | 2.85 | 2.85 | -0.22 | 111.86 | 1.67 | 17.79 | -2.08 |
| 11.30 | -0.20 | 128.69 | 1.89 | 1.89 | -0.15 | 111.30 | 1.11 | 17.39 | -2.05 |
| 11.40 | -0.10 | 127.74 | 0.94 | 0.94 | -0.07 | 110.74 | 0.56 | 17.00 | -2.03 |
| 11.50 | 0.00 | 126.80 | 0.00 | 13.50 | 0.00 | 110.18 | 0.00 | 16.62 | -2.00 |
| 11.60 | 0.10 | 125.87 | -0.93 | 13.58 | 0.08 | 109.63 | -0.55 | 16.24 | -1.98 |
| 11.70 | 0.20 | 124.95 | -1.84 | 13.65 | 0.15 | 109.08 | -1.10 | 15.87 | -1.95 |
| 11.80 | 0.30 | 124.05 | -2.75 | 13.73 | 0.23 | 108.54 | -1.64 | 15.51 | -1.93 |
| 11.90 | 0.40 | 123.15 | -3.64 | 13.30 | 0.30 | 108.00 | -2.18 | 15.15 | -1.90 |
| 12.00 | 0.50 | 122.27 | -4.53 | 13.88 | 0.38 | 107.46 | -2.72 | 14.81 | -1.88 |
| 12.10 | 0.60 | 121.40 | -5.40 | 13.95 | 0.45 | 106.92 | -3.26 | 14.47 | -1.85 |
| 12.20 | 0.70 | 120.53 | -6.27 | 14.03 | 0.53 | 106.38 | -3.60 | 14.15 | -1.83 |
| 12.30 | 0.80 | 119.68 | -7.12 | 14.11 | 0.61 | 105.85 | -4.34 | 13.83 | -1.81 |
| 12.40 | 0.90 | 118.84 | -7.96 | 14.19 | 0.69 | 105.31 | -4.87 | 13.52 | -1.79 |
| 12.50 | 1.00 | 118.00 | -8.80 | 14.26 | 0.76 | 104.78 | -5.40 | 13.22 | -1.76 |
| 12.60 | 1.10 | 117.18 | -9.62 | 14.34 | 0.84 | 104.26 | -5.92 | 12.92 | -1.74 |
| 12.70 | 1.20 | 116.36 | -10.43 | 14.42 | 0.92 | 103.74 | -6.44 | 12.62 | -1.72 |
| 12.80 | 1.30 | 115.56 | -11.24 | 14.50 | 1.00 | 103.22 | -6.96 | 12.34 | -1.70 |
| 12.90 | 1.40 | 114.77 | -12.03 | 14.58 | 1.08 | 102.71 | -7.47 | 12.06 | -1.68 |
| 13.00 | 1.50 | 113.98 | -12.82 | 14.65 | 1.15 | 102.20 | -7.98 | 11.78 | -1.65 |

through that yields. To evaluate pass-through coupon spreads and project their changes under different interest rate conditions, one must understand their dependency on changing interest rates. These and other advantages flow out of the option approach.

The mortgagor (i.e., borrower) has a par call against the lender at any time, and there is no call protection. As in the callable bond case, the lender or investor owns a call-free mortgage or pass-through and is short an option. Instead of conjecturing about what the paydown will be or merely projecting recent experience, the proposed model evaluates this option and then equates the pass-through value with the dollar-weighted difference between the hypothetical call-free pass-through and the option values.

There is, however, an important difference between callable bonds and pass-throughs with respect to the option approach. Most people assume that corporations call their bonds whenever they have an economic incentive and do not when they do not. That means if market rates beyond the protection period are low enough to cover refunding cost, allowing for timing discretion, the issuer calls his bond. It also means he does not call the bond when the market rates are too high.

Neither point holds true for mortgages. GNMA 17s could not have survived in a strict economic world. For whatever reason, homeowners do not consider their mortgages in strictly economic terms. For example, how many corporations call 8% bonds? Yet even deeply out-of-the-money pass-throughs pay down. In fact, since the lower coupon mortgages are older, and therefore their homeowners more likely to move, the non-economic paydown is greater than on higher coupons, although on average, not enough to offset the differences due to economic incentive.

The result is a continuum from low to high coupons of too much exercise down to too little relative to economic incentive. Among out-of-the-money pass-throughs, currently those under 14% or so, the lower coupons pay down less in absolute terms but more in relation to what is expected on purely economic grounds. Among the in-the-money coupons, the higher coupons pay down more but to a smaller degree than they should on economic grounds.

Much conjecture exists about the reasons for prepayment experience across coupons: from the loan-to-value ratios, time in home, origination date in relation to inflation, assumability, turnover cost on new mortgages, business cycle influences on unemployment, and family formation and breakup, and so on, all on top of current yields, the sole factor in the option approach.

The way Ravi Dattatraya and I have handled this problem so far is to calculate what we call a *drag ratio* for each coupon, defined as the ratio of the market value of the implied option relative to its mathematical value. This ratio has been fairly stable over time and fairly insensitive to interest rates. Exhibit 13 plots these drag ratios for a 12 percent GNMA for the past year.

The stability, or at least the predictability, of the drag ratio is crucial to the option approach. Otherwise, there is little to gain from relabeling our ignorance about prepayment to ignorance about drag ratio. Our tests to date suggest that we are not merely

**Exhibit 13. Historical Drag Ratio—GNMA 12%**
**Ref 8%; Std 0.2; Strike 103**

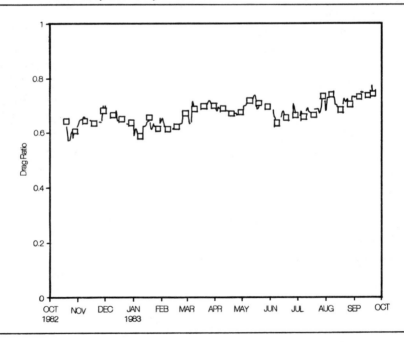

in a relabeling game but instead are adding value with this more elaborate framework. But at the same time I am aware that this subject is the weakest part of the model. Fitting historical drag ratios is not the same thing as understanding their movement and being able to project them under different market conditions.

The drag problem arises whenever an option is held by people whose exercise depends on more things than the spread between the market and strike prices. For example, fixed-rate committments from mortgage bankers that leave the mortgagor free to walk away if rates go lower are not exercised to full advantage by people who are primarily concerned with getting any mortgage or even the house itself. Some people accept the original rate even when they would be better off walking, while others fail to close even as rates go up, in some cases, no doubt, because they decide not to buy the house and cannot transfer the committment. Insurance companies run into similar things with the prepayment clauses on single-premium annuities, cash value loans, and various guaranteed-rate products. In some cases, the option holder is reluctant to jeopardize personal relationships with the implied-option writer, although this feeling diminishes as the option moves deeper into-the-money.

Still there is no reason for more than prudent scepticism about the option approach on grounds that it relies on some empirical regularity instead of pure deduction. Virtually all financial theories lean on assumptions that are at best derived empirically. Indeed, the option model itself relies on an estimate of variance that often turns out badly. The value of a theory depends not on *whether* it has an empirical underpinning but on how tractable this underpinning is. Perhaps the main virtue of any theory is that it defines a variable that can be tracked and projected more successfully than the variables that come to mind without the theory. From what I know now, I would rather worry about the drag ratio than the paydown rate itself since it takes care of at least part of the market influence on paydown.

Applying option theory to pass-throughs has the same advantages as those described above for callable bonds. It makes it easier to project rates of return over different scenarios by tracking separately the call-free and option components. It makes possible hedging a long pass-through position with a short bond future position against the call-free component and a long option position against the option component. By providing an easy way to calculate their durations, the options approach makes it easy to include pass-throughs in portfolios that are managed by controlling duration. Finally, it provides a way of projecting coupon spreads under different interest rate conditions, as well as basing coupon arbitrages on inconsistencies in option valuation.

Exhibit 14 shows how a GNMA 13 moves relative to a hypothetical call free GNMA, which behaves roughly like a Treasury bond. Both GNMAs are assumed to pay down 0.1 percent per month for demographic (or rate insensitive) reasons. The ratio of the market call value to the model call value, what we call the drag ratio, is 0.70. The standard deviation is 0.200, a little high by current standards. When the call-free price rises from 110.91 to 124.20, the call rises from 10.47 to 16.27. The callable GNMA price, the difference between the call-free and option prices, rises from 100.44 to 107.93, the latter being the difference between 124.20 and 16.27. In other words, for a 13.30 point price rise in the call-free GNMA, the callable GNMA rises 7.49 points.

This divergence underlies the problem mortgage bankers had last year when they tried to hedge their current mortgage production with bond futures. While the futures, which they were short, fully participated in the rally, the mortgages they were long did not. The reason is that the rising price of the (short) option component detracted from the rise in the call-free component. Note that for the same yield changes, the call free GNMA's price rises more than it falls; for 150 basis points, 13.30 versus 10.95 points. This is because its duration, which gives (in percentage terms) the price sensitivity to yield changes, itself changes with yield. This latter effect is called *convexity*.

People who describe themselves as being hedged almost always mean that they have equated the dollar-durations of their long and short positions. This is acceptable when these positions are similar, for then the durations themselves will change in the same way. But if they are not, particularly if one side includes an

## Exhibit 14. GNMA Option Analysis Report

|  | Call Free GNMA |  |  |  | Callable GNMA |  |  |  |  |
|---|---|---|---|---|---|---|---|---|---|
|  | Coupon: | 13.000 |  |  |  | Coupon: | 13.000 |  |  |
|  | Price: | 110.91 |  |  |  | Price: | 100.44 |  |  |
|  |  |  |  |  | Market Call Value: | 10.47 |  |  |  |
|  |  |  |  |  | Model Call Value: | 15.03 |  |  |  |
|  |  |  |  |  | Drag Ratio: | 0.70 |  |  |  |
|  |  |  |  |  | Std. Dev.: | 0.200 |  |  |  |
| Dem. CMP Rate: | 0.1 |  |  |  | Dem. CMP Rate: | 0.1 |  |  |  |
|  |  |  |  |  | Strike Price: | 103.00 |  |  |  |

| Yield | | Price | | Yield | | Price | | Call | Yield |
|---|---|---|---|---|---|---|---|---|---|
| Acutal | Move | Acutal | Move | Acutal | Move | Acutal | Move | Value | Spread |
| 9.93 | -1.50 | 124.20 | 13.30 | 11.81 | -1.05 | 107.93 | 7.49 | 16.27 | -1.88 |
| 10.03 | -1.40 | 123.23 | 12.32 | 11.87 | -0.98 | 107.44 | 7.00 | 15.79 | -1.84 |
| 10.13 | -1.30 | 122.27 | 11.37 | 11.93 | -0.92 | 106.96 | 6.52 | 15.31 | -1.81 |
| 10.23 | -1.20 | 121.33 | 10.42 | 12.00 | -0.86 | 106.49 | 6.05 | 14.84 | -1.77 |
| 10.33 | -1.10 | 120.39 | 9.49 | 12.05 | -0.79 | 106.02 | 5.58 | 14.37 | -1.73 |
| 10.43 | -1.00 | 119.47 | 8.57 | 12.12 | -0.73 | 105.56 | 5.12 | 13.92 | -1.70 |
| 10.53 | -0.90 | 118.56 | 7.66 | 12.19 | -0.67 | 105.10 | 4.66 | 13.47 | -1.66 |
| 10.63 | -0.80 | 117.67 | 6.76 | 12.25 | -0.60 | 104.64 | 4.21 | 13.02 | -1.62 |
| 10.73 | -0.70 | 116.78 | 5.88 | 12.31 | -0.54 | 104.18 | 3.75 | 12.60 | -1.59 |
| 10.83 | -0.60 | 115.91 | 5.00 | 12.39 | -0.46 | 103.63 | 3.20 | 12.28 | -1.56 |
| 10.93 | -0.50 | 115.05 | 4.14 | 12.47 | -0.39 | 103.09 | 2.65 | 11.96 | -1.54 |
| 11.03 | -0.40 | 114.20 | 3.29 | 12.54 | -0.31 | 102.55 | 2.11 | 11.65 | -1.52 |
| 11.13 | -0.30 | 113.36 | 2.45 | 12.62 | -0.23 | 102.01 | 1.57 | 11.35 | -1.50 |
| 11.23 | -0.20 | 112.53 | 1.63 | 12.70 | -0.15 | 101.48 | 1.04 | 11.05 | -1.47 |
| 11.33 | -0.10 | 111.71 | 0.81 | 12.78 | -0.08 | 100.96 | 0.52 | 10.76 | -1.45 |
| 11.43 | 0.00 | 110.91 | 0.00 | 12.85 | 0.00 | 100.44 | 0.00 | 10.47 | -1.43 |
| 11.53 | 0.10 | 110.11 | -0.80 | 12.93 | 0.08 | 99.92 | -0.52 | 10.19 | -1.40 |
| 11.63 | 0.20 | 109.32 | -1.58 | 13.01 | 0.15 | 99.42 | -1.02 | 9.91 | -1.38 |
| 11.73 | 0.30 | 108.55 | -2.36 | 13.06 | 0.23 | 98.92 | -1.52 | 9.63 | -1.36 |
| 11.83 | 0.40 | 107.78 | -3.13 | 13.16 | 0.31 | 98.42 | -2.02 | 9.36 | -1.33 |
| 11.93 | 0.50 | 107.02 | -3.88 | 13.24 | 0.38 | 97.93 | -2.50 | 9.09 | -1.31 |
| 12.03 | 0.60 | '06.28 | -4.63 | 13.31 | 0.46 | 97.45 | -2.99 | 8.83 | -1.29 |
| 12.13 | 0.70 | 105.54 | -5.37 | 13.39 | 0.53 | 96.97 | -3.47 | 8.57 | -1.26 |
| 12.23 | 0.80 | 104.81 | -6.10 | 13.46 | 0.61 | 96.49 | -3.94 | 8.31 | -1.24 |
| 12.33 | 0.90 | 104.09 | -6.82 | 13.54 | 0.69 | 96.03 | -4.41 | 8.06 | -1.21 |
| 12.43 | 1.00 | 103.38 | -7.53 | 13.61 | 0.76 | 95.56 | -4.88 | 7.82 | -1.19 |
| 12.53 | 1.10 | 102.68 | -8.23 | 13.69 | 0.84 | 95.10 | -5.34 | 7.58 | -1.16 |
| 12.63 | 1.20 | 101.98 | -8.92 | 13.78 | 0.92 | 94.59 | -5.85 | 7.40 | -1.15 |
| 12.73 | 1.30 | 101.30 | -9.61 | 13.86 | 1.01 | 94.08 | -6.36 | 7.22 | -1.13 |
| 12.83 | 1.40 | 100.62 | -10.29 | 13.94 | 1.09 | 93.58 | -6.86 | 7.04 | -1.12 |
| 12.93 | 1.50 | 99.95 | -10.95 | 14.03 | 1.18 | 93.08 | -7.35 | 6.87 | -1.10 |

Goldman, Sachs & Co.—Financial Strategies Group

option, the durations of the two positions will not stay equal as yields change. That is the problem with hedging mortgages or options with futures.

For that we must consider *convexity*. The above discussion makes clear the importance of convexity to the performance of options and of the securities that embody them, such as mortgages and callable bonds. With that in mind, it is much better to match not only the durations but the convexities of opposing positions in hedging, arbitrage, and asset-liability management. Better still, since convexity is a good thing, arrange for more of it in the long than the short position.

### Hedging Pass-throughs

The interplay of bond and option convexity is the core of hedging pass-throughs. In the typical hedge, like the one in Exhibit 15, bond futures are dollar-duration-matched with a pass-through as if it were a deliverable bond. Since the pass-through is less convex than the bond future, the hedge breaks down in either direction. When rates rise, the pass-through falls faster than the bond future because its duration actually rises, while that of the future declines (see below). The problem is much worse in the other direction when the option is in-the-money and holds back the rise in the pass-through.

I would like to pursue this matter with further examples because it epitomizes the main theme of this paper. Exhibit 16 divides a 13% GNMA into a hypothetical call-free and an option component and shows how the prices and durations of either component change as yields change. The call-free component is comparable with a bond or futures but, in this case, it is *not* dollar-duration-matched with the callable GNMA.

The convexity of the call-free component is revealed by its unequal price changes for equal yield changes, rising 31.15, while falling only 20.99 points for 300-basis-point-changes. The convexity of the option is much greater, with prices rising and falling 18.92 and 7.61. The callable composite—long the call-free and short the option—is actually concave, its price rising *less* than it falls, 12.23

# Exhibit 15. Gains or Losses from Hedging a GNMA under Different Yield Conditions

ProfitLoss

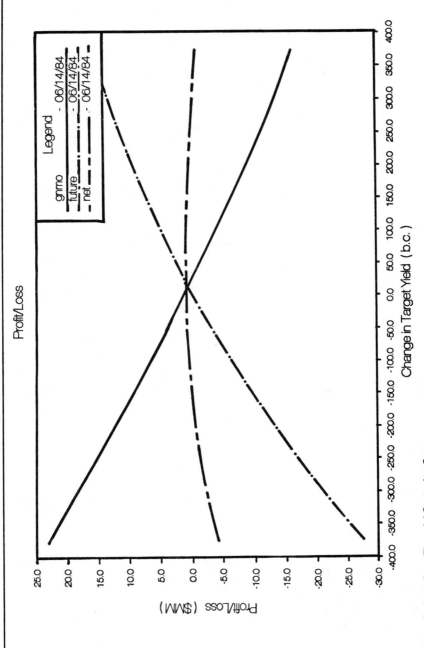

# Exhibit 16. GNMA Price and Duration Analysis, 09/20/83

|  | Demographic Rate (CMP): | 0.10; | Std. | 0.200; | Strike: | 103.0; | Short Rate: | 10.000 |
| Call Free GNMA: | Coupon: | 8.000; | Price: | 76.000; | Yield: | 11.609; | Duration: | 7.18 |
| Callable GNMA: | Coupon: | 13.000; | Price: | 100.889; | Age: | 25 Mos; | Duration: | 4.68 |
| | Option: | | Price: | 10.666; | Drag: | 0.750; | Duration: | 30.82 |

| Yields | | Price Changes | | | Durations | | | Dollar Durations | | |
|--------|---------|-----------|--------|----------|-----------|--------|----------|-----------|--------|----------|
| Yields | Changes | Call Free | Option | Callable | Call Free | Option | Callable | Call Free | Option | Callable |
| 8.51 | -3.00 | 31.15 | 18.92 | 12.23 | 8.60 | 26.88 | 3.82 | 1227.52 | 795.23 | 432.29 |
| 9.01 | -2.50 | 25.00 | 14.83 | 10.17 | 8.34 | 27.50 | 3.95 | 1139.59 | 701.31 | 438.27 |
| 9.51 | -2.00 | 19.29 | 11.14 | 8.15 | 8.10 | 28.14 | 4.09 | 1059.17 | 613.48 | 445.69 |
| 10.01 | -1.50 | 13.96 | 7.79 | 6.17 | 7.85 | 28.79 | 4.25 | 985.80 | 531.30 | 454.50 |
| 10.51 | -1.00 | 8.99 | 4.77 | 4.22 | 7.62 | 29.46 | 4.41 | 918.56 | 454.74 | 463.82 |
| 11.01 | -0.50 | 4.34 | 2.05 | 2.30 | 7.39 | 30.16 | 4.59 | 856.97 | 383.49 | 473.48 |
| 11.51 | 0.00 | 0.00 | 0.00 | 0.00 | 7.18 | 30.82 | 4.68 | 800.63 | 328.73 | 471.90 |
| 12.01 | 0.50 | -4.07 | -1.81 | -2.26 | 6.97 | 31.57 | 4.76 | 748.86 | 279.60 | 469.26 |
| 12.51 | 1.00 | -7.89 | -3.39 | -4.50 | 6.76 | 32.34 | 4.83 | 701.22 | 235.30 | 465.92 |
| 13.01 | 1.50 | -11.47 | -4.76 | -6.71 | 6.57 | 33.09 | 4.91 | 657.47 | 195.40 | 462.11 |
| 13.51 | 2.00 | -14.84 | -5.94 | -8.90 | 6.38 | 33.69 | 4.98 | 617.16 | 159.35 | 457.81 |
| 14.01 | 2.50 | -18.01 | -6.90 | -11.11 | 6.20 | 34.67 | 5.01 | 580.00 | 130.66 | 449.34 |
| 14.51 | 3.00 | -20.99 | -7.61 | -13.38 | 6.03 | 35.64 | 4.99 | 545.72 | 108.82 | 436.90 |

Goldman, Sachs & Co.—Financial Strategies Group

versus 13.38. The range of callable prices is merely the difference between the ranges of call-free and option prices. That is, 31.15 − 18.92 = 12.23; 20.99 − 7.61 = 13.38. This inversion or concavity is more likely to occur when the option is more in-the-money.

Exhibits 17 and 18 give the same data for 11% and 15% coupons. The 11% preserves its convexity, but just barely, while the 15% becomes quite concave, its price range for a 300-basis-point fall and rise being up 9.29 to down 11.66 points.

The duration tables in these exhibits also mirror this behavior. In all cases, the call-free durations fall and the option durations rise as yields rise. The callable durations rise for the concave coupons, 13s and 15s, and are fairly flat for the 11s as yields rise. This is merely another way of saying that the two higher coupons are the opposite of convex (or concave) and the other is linear. These adjectives describe the curve of future values of each security under different yield scenarios. Keep in mind that while the component prices themselves are additive, the durations, representing percentage price changes, first must be dollar-weighted.

Since the call-free component looks just like a bond or futures contract, we can learn from the above relationships how the hedge actually works. The GNMA 13 underperforms the call-free component in a rally and does better when prices fall. But the size of the shortfall is much greater than that of the relative gain (18.92 versus 7.61). That is on a one-for-one basis. In hedging, one would use the futures equivalent of the call-free component to hedge more than one GNMA, the exact number being N in the following equation:

$$N \times \text{Dollars} \times \text{Duration (callable)} = \text{Dollars} \times \text{Duration (call free)}$$
$$N = \frac{800.63}{471.90} = 1.70$$

That means the long side of a hedged position would rise 20.79 (i.e, 1.70 × 12.23) in contrast to 31.15 for the short position and fall 22.75 (i.e., 1.70 × 13.38) in contrast to 20.99 for the short position. It loses either way, which is what being short the convexity really means.

Yet, this hedge started with the same dollar-duration on both sides. Clearly, there is more to hedging than assuring this equality.

# Exhibit 17. GNMA Price and Duration Analysis, 09/20/83

| | | | |
|---|---|---|---|
| Demographic Rate (CMP): | 0.10; | Strike: 103.0; | Short Rate: 10.000 |
| Call Free GNMA: Coupon: | 8.000; | Std: 0.200; Yield: 11.614; | Duration: 6.97 |
| Callable GNMA: Coupon: | 11.000; | Price: 76.000; Age: 25 Mos; | Duration: 5.63 |
| Option: | | Price: 90.420; Drag: 0.700; | Duration: 30.20 |
| | | Price: 5.230; | |

| Yields | | Price Changes | | | | Durations | | |
|--------|---------|-----------|--------|----------|-----------|--------|----------|-----------|
| Yields | Changes | Call Free | Option | Callable | Call Free | Option | Callable | Call Free |
| 8.61 | -3.00 | 25.71 | 11.14 | 14.57 | 8.27 | 26.30 | 5.46 | 0.61 |
| 9.11 | -2.50 | 20.68 | 8.54 | 12.14 | 8.04 | 26.92 | 5.51 | 0.57 |
| 9.61 | -2.00 | 15.98 | 6.24 | 9.74 | 7.81 | 27.55 | 5.55 | 0.52 |
| 10.11 | -1.50 | 11.58 | 4.21 | 7.38 | 7.59 | 28.18 | 5.60 | 0.47 |
| 10.61 | -1.00 | 7.47 | 2.52 | 4.95 | 7.38 | 28.90 | 5.63 | 0.42 |
| 11.11 | -0.50 | 3.62 | 1.16 | 2.46 | 7.17 | 29.58 | 5.63 | 0.38 |
| 11.61 | 0.00 | 0.00 | 0.00 | 0.00 | 6.97 | 30.20 | 5.63 | 0.34 |
| 12.11 | 0.50 | -3.39 | -1.00 | -2.39 | 6.78 | 30.93 | 5.62 | 0.30 |
| 12.61 | 1.00 | -6.59 | -1.85 | -4.73 | 6.59 | 31.67 | 5.60 | 0.26 |
| 13.01 | 1.50 | -9.59 | -2.57 | -7.02 | 6.41 | 32.36 | 5.58 | 0.22 |
| 13.61 | 2.00 | -12.42 | -3.09 | -9.33 | 6.23 | 33.05 | 5.52 | 0.20 |
| 14.11 | 2.50 | -15.09 | -3.52 | -11.57 | 6.06 | 33.97 | 5.45 | 0.17 |
| 14.61 | 3.00 | -17.61 | -3.88 | -13.73 | 5.90 | 34.91 | 5.39 | 0.15 |

Goldman, Sachs & Co.—Financial Strategies Group

**Exhibit 18. GNMA Price and Duration Analysis, 09/20/83**

| | | | | | |
|---|---|---|---|---|---|
| Demographic Rate (CMP): | 0.10; | Std: | 0.200; | Strike: | 103.0; | Short Rate: | 10.000 |
| Call Free GNMA: | Coupon: 8.000; | Price: | 76.000; | Yield: | 11.509; | Duration: | 7.17 |
| Callable GNMA: | Coupon: 15.000; | Price: | 109.272; | Age: | 25 Mos; | Duration: | 3.23 |
| Option: | | Price: | 17.989; | Drag: | 0.750; | Duration: | 31.10 |

| Yields | | Price Changes | | | Durations | | | |
|---|---|---|---|---|---|---|---|---|
| Yields | Changes | Call Free | Option | Callable | Call Free | Option | Callable | Hedge Ratio |
| 8.51 | -3.00 | 35.49 | 26.21 | 9.29 | 8.59 | 23.63 | 2.99 | 1.00 |
| 9.01 | -2.50 | 28.49 | 20.96 | 7.54 | 8.34 | 24.41 | 2.98 | 0.98 |
| 9.51 | -2.00 | 21.98 | 16.08 | 5.91 | 8.09 | 25.34 | 2.99 | 0.95 |
| 10.01 | -1.50 | 15.91 | 11.52 | 4.39 | 7.85 | 26.48 | 3.01 | 0.93 |
| 10.51 | -1.00 | 10.25 | 7.28 | 2.97 | 7.61 | 27.90 | 3.04 | 0.90 |
| 11.01 | -0.50 | 4.95 | 3.31 | 1.65 | 7.39 | 29.73 | 3.10 | 0.86 |
| 11.51 | 0.00 | 0.00 | 0.00 | 0.00 | 7.17 | 31.10 | 3.23 | 0.82 |
| 12.01 | 0.50 | -4.64 | -2.71 | -1.93 | 6.96 | 31.87 | 3.41 | 0.76 |
| 12.51 | 1.00 | -8.99 | -5.16 | -3.83 | 6.76 | 32.64 | 3.61 | 0.70 |
| 13.01 | 1.50 | -13.07 | -7.35 | -5.73 | 6.56 | 33.41 | 3.80 | 0.63 |
| 13.51 | 2.00 | -16.91 | -9.30 | -7.62 | 6.38 | 34.01 | 4.02 | 0.56 |
| 14.01 | 2.50 | -20.53 | -11.07 | -9.45 | 6.20 | 34.99 | 4.20 | 0.49 |
| 14.51 | 3.00 | -23.93 | -12.27 | -11.66 | 6.02 | 35.99 | 4.27 | 0.44 |

Goldman, Sachs & Co.—Financial Strategies Group

It works fine as long as duration is a good predictor of price change or as long as it is off to the same degree on either side. For example, that is true in the typical cash-and-carry position in which one goes long a deliverable bond and short an equal dollar-duration number of bond futures. Duration fails here to the same degree on either side. But the presence of the option makes that *not* the case with GNMAs and bond futures.

Except for a few, but admittedly important, cases—in which there are no options, and the durations of each security, not just the average, on either side are close—one must go beyond duration-matching in designing hedges. One must equate not the tangents to the price yield (or future value) curves of the long and short positions, but the curves themselves. But, since it is hard to deal with the curves themselves, we use the Taylor series approximations. Matching the convexities of either side, for example, is a big step forward, but still not complete when options are present. We saw above how options with different terms and strike prices react differently to the passage of time and changes in perceived volatility. These reactions can be measured by other parameters like time value, which gives the fall in an option's value as it ages one day. But, like the price-yield curve, these relationships are not linear and, therefore, require more than one parameter to estimate the option's movement for more than very small changes in yield, time, and variance. In effect, we need Taylor series approximations of these relationships as well. Finally, any single parameter, for example, convexity may depend, as illustrated above, on other variables like term and variance. These dependencies may be embodied in still other parameters.

*Performance Profiles*

So far I have talked about single securities, whether bonds, pass-throughs, options, or futures. I have used the price-yield curve interchangeably, i.e., the locus of prices at different yields, and the future value or performance profile curve, which gives the locus of values at any time, now or later, of a given security at different prevailing yields. The price-yield curve is a special case of a performance profile for instantaneous yield changes on a single bond.

But the performance profile is a much broader concept giving the total value, including reinvestment, of one or more securities, held long or short, under various terminal interest rates at some horizon. Since any security or portfolio can be translated into a performance profile, it may be viewed as a common denominator for comparing all possibilities. All kinds of positions are judged with the same criteria: what do I get and when do I get it. An important by-product of this approach is that it focus on the similarities rather than the differences among securities and encourages comparative analysis.

The performance profiles can be drawn for individual bonds or whole portfolios. They can represent the market values of a cash stream, whether assets or liabilities, under various yield conditions. They are a useful framework for hedging traders' positions and for asset-liability management. In all these cases, and many more, the problem is to match performance profiles, as if one literally laid the curve of one position over that of another. Duration-matching and more elaborate forms of parametric analysis are merely means to this end.

One very important assumption in this approach is that some basic yield is the driving force behind any performance profile. Once we know the yield, the various models of bonds, options, futures, callable bonds, pass-throughs, CMOs and so on will produce a performance profile that puts everything on the same terms. Of course, there is no one driving force. Not all yields move the same, giving rise to the basis changes that some people call risks and others opportunities. Changing variance, drag ratios, and paydown rates are still other disturbances. In principle, one can simulate outcomes for varying quantities of these influences, but then there are a lot of numbers.

## Parametric Analysis

While they provide a good intuitive understanding of the analysis, and, when graphed, nice visual impact, the performance profiles are unwieldy. It is difficult to set up a hedge by matching the performance curves of the two sides. Matching the tangents to these curves, what we call duration, is a lot easier. If that does not suffice, we can match convexity and other parameters.

Doing that is what I call parametric analysis. This subject comes up in such varying contexts as hedging, swapping, yield-spread analysis, and asset-liability management; indeed, wherever we need to know how securities will behave under various market conditions. In this section, I merely touch on these applications, emphasizing their common roots in arbitrage.

In each case, we consider two positions equivalent, in some respect, if they move together—particularly as yields change but also over time and, to some extent, for different variances. To some approximation, they move together if their parameters are the same, and the closeness depends on which parameters are equal and how large the movements are in yield, time, and variance.

Exhibit 19 finds a parametric equivalence between a long GNMA, on one hand, and a long zero coupon, a short bond future, and a short CD (representing the cost of financing the GNMA and zero) on the other. The exhibit calculates the number of zeros, futures, and CDs needed to make the *net* dollar-weighted duration and convexity equal to zero. Exhibit 20 graphs the behavior of this position under different interest rates for a given horizon. (To avoid clutter, the CD, which would appear as a horizontal line, is omitted.) The zero puts back the convexity that is lost in going long a GNMA: as a result, instead of losing from a yield move in either direction, we get a flat performance profile.

But, cutting the net convexity to zero in this way is not free: the zero yields less than the GNMA. Moreover, since the zero adds not only convexity but duration as well, the latter must be neutralized by selling futures which, with a positive yield curve, involves a further yield give-up. In other words, its higher yield may be thought of as compensation for the GNMAs low or negative convexity. The amount of this compensation should equal the cost of neutralizing the damage that is being compensated. This cost, in turn, is what it takes to buy enough zeros to replace the lost con-

# Exhibit 19. Maximization of Total Yield
## (Weighted by Market Values)

| | | | | Bond or Underlying Bond | | | | | Options & Callable Features | | | | | Futures | | | | | | | Gain from | |
|---|---|---|---|---|---|---|---|---|---|---|---|---|---|---|---|---|---|---|---|---|---|---|
| Bond # | Par Holding | Sector | Name | Coupon | Mature | Yield | Price | Volat Factor | Price | Strike Price | Expire | Std Dev | Hedge Ratio | Price | Del'ry | Del'ry Factor | Market Holding | Eff Team | Modified Duration | Dollar Duration | Convex-ity | Eff Yield |
| 1 | 413 450 | Treasury | ust | 0 000 | 021513 | 12 70 | 2 90 | 1 00 | | | | | | | | | 11 987 | 28 76 | 27 038 | 324 121 | 44 604 | 12 70 |
| 2 | 100 000 | GNMA | gnma | 14 000 | 051512 | 12 98 | 102 13 | 1 00 | 9 78 | 103 00 | 0 39 | 0 20 | 0 40 | | CMP = | 0 10 | 102 631 | 12 19 | 5 286 | 542 526 | 16 447 | 13 46 |
| 3 | 114 619 | CD | cd | 9 900 | 051584 | 9 90 | 100 00 | 1 00 | | | | | | | | | -114 618 | 0 00 | 0 003 | -0 309 | 0 000 | 10 04 |
| 4 | 173 099 | Fubond | fut | 8 750 | 111508 | 12 87 | 69 49 | 1 00 | | | | | | 64 38 | 061584 | 1 073 | 0 000 | 24 50 | 7 739 | -866 338 | -61 050 | 4 80 |
| | | | | | | | | | | | | | Total or average | | | | 0 000- | 10 01 | 0 000 | 0 000 | 0 000 | -1 35 |

# Exhibit 20. Gains or Losses from Hedging a GNMA with a Zero and Futures

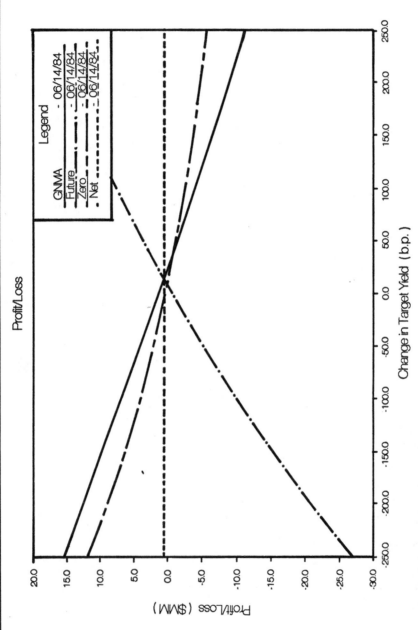

Profit/Loss

Legend

GNMA — 06/14/84
Future —·— 06/14/84
Zero —··— 06/14/84
Net ······· 06/14/84

Profit/Loss ($MM)

Change in Target Yield (b.p.)

Goldman Sachs & Co.—Financial Strategies Group

vexity. In other words, the proper price spread between a GNMA 12 and 14 is the one that leaves the higher coupon buyer with enough money to buy enough zeros or long-term options to make his combined position behave like a 12.

The same method can be used to evaluate many other spreads. For example, the price differential between a callable and a call-free bond with the same coupon and maturity should be equal to the cost of the compensating zero. Exhibit 21 graphs a synthetic call-free bond comprising a callable and zero coupon bond over different terminal yields. As long as these performance profiles are the same, the positions are equivalent and should cost the same. As a result, the value of the zero should control the call differential.

Using an option instead of a zero introduces variance as a more explicit factor in the price (or yield) differentials of callable securities. (It is there implicity owing to the potential arbitrage between zeros and options, on which I say more below.) As a result, it is reasonable to expect a positive correlation between these dif-

**Exhibit 21. A Non-Callable Bond versus a Callable Bond + a Zero**

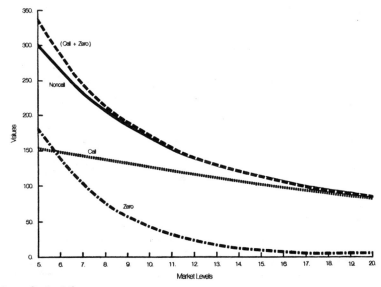

Goldman, Sachs & Co.

ferentials and the variance implied by traded option values. The growing availability of options and zeros assures that the market mechanisms are there to bring about what in the past was merely a theoretical goal.

While empirically testing these propositions is beyond the scope of the present paper, Ravi Dattatreya has produced the chart given in Exhibit 22 comparing the estimated and actual prices of a GNMA 12. These estimates come about in the following way. First, he finds the price of a hypothetical GNMA 12 assuming it had the same yield as a GNMA 8 and that they both had the same *demographic* paydown rate. He takes that price to be the one for a hypothetical call-free GNMA 12. Next, he finds the value of the call option using the *average* drag ratio[4] over the study period. Finally, Dattatreya subtracts this option value from the call-free GNMA 12 price.

**Exhibit 22. Actual and Predicted Prices of GNMA 12.00**
**Ref 8%; Std 0.2; Strike: 103**

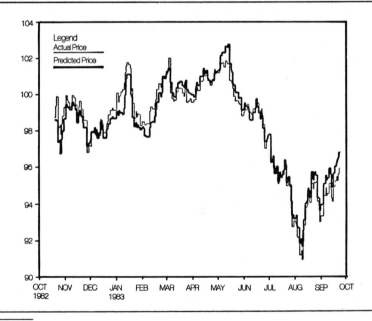

---

4. See earlier section "Option Analysis of Pass-throughs."

The fit is quite good, reflecting the stability of the drag ratio over the study period. Recall that this ratio divides the option value implied by the market spread between a given coupon and an (assumed noncallable) low coupon by the theoretical option value. The latter, in turn, depends on the price variance as implied, for example, by traded bond options. In practice, one would estimate the future ratio by using the implied variance from the nearest options market and projecting recent drag ratio experience assuming coeval implied variances instead of the constant variance assumed in the exhibit.

### The Parametric Analysis of Dumbbelling

An important characteristic of *bond* convexity is that it rises at a faster rate than duration, as illustrated in Exhibit 23 which happens to be drawn for zero coupon bonds.

**Exhibit 23. Convexity versus Duration and the Effect of Dumbbelling**

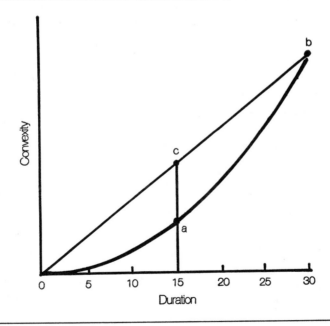

Imagine a dumbbell comprising overnight money and a 30-year zero weighted equally to give an average duration of 15 years. The convexity of this dumbbell is read from the line connecting the two ends which, in this case, is half way between zero and b, i.e., c. In contrast, the convexity of a single zero with the same duration is only a. Because of the shape of the convexity-versus-duration curve, the dumbbell always is more convex than a single bond with the same duration.

Exhibit 24 compares the performance of dumbbells and single bonds in light of changing interest rates. Part A compares a 7-year 11% bond with an equal-duration dumbbell comprising a 2- and 30-year bond. Part B compares a 15-year zero coupon bond with an equal-duration dumbbell comprising overnight money and a 30-year zero. All yields start at 11%. Each column gives the change in value on a $100 investment implied by a yield change from 11% to the terminal yields given in each row. For example, a 7-year bond with an 11% coupon rises $10.22 when its yield falls from 11% to 9%. The last column of either part shows the difference between the dollar changes of the dumbbell and bullet.

When the yield falls 300 basis points, the dumbbell in Part A with duration 4.79 rises $2.14 more than the 7-year bond with the same starting duration. For a 100-basis-point-fall, the difference is only $.20. While the differences are smaller for a yield rise, the value of the dumbbell consistently falls less than that of the bond. The dumbbell's advantage is much greater in Part B, where the durations and, therefore, convexities, are much larger. For a 300-basis-point-yield-fall, the difference between the dollar changes of the dumbbell and the 15-year zero is $14.41 per $100 invested. Even a 100-basis-point-fall leads to a $1.16 difference.

The convexity differences described are large because the dumbbells used are stretched. Narrower dumbbells fall somewhere between the stretched dumbbells and bullets. Hedgers must balance the greater convexity of a stretched dumbbell with greater yield curve risk resulting from unequal changes along the yield curve.

The greater convexity of dumbbells over equal-duration bullets makes them more valuable in the face of changing interest

**Exhibit 24. Relative Performance of Dumbbell and Single Bonds Given Changing Yields (Price Changes from 11% Starting Yield)**

| | | | A. 11 Percent Coupon | | |
|---|---|---|---|---|---|
| Terminal Yields (%) | 2 Yr. (21.75) | 30 Yr. (8.72) | 7 Yr. (4.79) | D'bell* (4.79) | D'bell -7 Yr. |
| 8 | 5.44 | 33.94 | 15.84 | 17.98 | 2.14 |
| 9 | 3.59 | 20.64 | 10.22 | 11.09 | 0.87 |
| 10 | 1.77 | 9.46 | 4.95 | 5.15 | 0.20 |
| 11 | 0.00 | 0.00 | 0.00 | 0.00 | 0.00 |
| 12 | -1.73 | -8.08 | -4.65 | -4.52 | 0.13 |
| 13 | -3.13 | -15.03 | -9.01 | -8.53 | 0.48 |
| 14 | -5.08 | -21.06 | -13.12 | -12.11 | 1.01 |

| | | | B. Zero Coupon | | |
|---|---|---|---|---|---|
| Terminal Yields (%) | O/N (0) | 30 Yr. (28.44) | 15 Yr. (14.22) | D'bell* (14.22) | D'bell -15 Yrs. |
| 8 | 0.00 | 136.13 | 53.66 | 68.07 | 14.41 |
| 9 | 0.00 | 77.08 | 33.07 | 38.54 | 5.47 |
| 10 | 0.00 | 32.98 | 15.33 | 16.49 | 1.16 |
| 11 | 0.00 | 0.00 | 0.00 | 0.00 | 0.00 |
| 12 | 0.00 | -24.70 | -13.23 | -12.35 | 0.88 |
| 13 | 0.00 | -43.22 | -24.65 | -21.61 | 3.04 |
| 14 | 0.00 | -57.13 | -34.53 | -28.57 | 5.96 |

*0.56 × (2 Yr.) + 0.44 × (30 Yr.)
**0.50 × (0) + 0.50 × (30 Yr.)

rates. With options one must pay for this advantage, and so it is with bonds. The form of the payment is the lower yield on dumb-bells, which is described in Exhibit 25. The positive slope of the yield curve makes the yield, c, on a single bond higher than the yield, d, on a dumbbell combining bond a and b to get the same average duration, D. The yield spread c-d may be viewed as the price of the convexity, analogous to the option premium. In choos-ing the dumbbell over an equal-duration single bond, one sacri-fices yield for the chance of doing better if yields change in either direction, as in the case of an option.

Exhibit 26 shows the difference in rates of return over one quarter between a dumbbell comprising 2- and 30-year bonds and a single 7-year bond with the same duration. The latter performs better as long as future yields stay within a rough window of a 75-basis-point fall and 120-basis-point rise. Outside the window, the dumbbell outperforms the single bond.

**Exhibit 25.  Yield Spreads between Dumbbells and Single Bonds with the Same Duration**

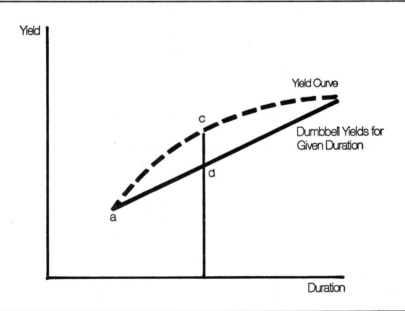

**Exhibit 26. Equal Dollar Duration Dumbbell and Bullet**

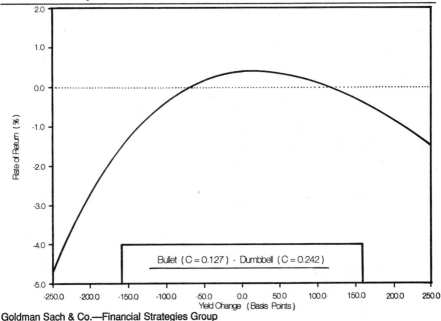

Goldman Sach & Co.—Financial Strategies Group

Viewed this way, the dumbbell-single bond spread, and through that the shape of the whole yield curve, is a measure of the value of convexity. Recalling the previous discussion of options, the value of convexity depends entirely on expected volatility. On that score, the yield curve should take on more curvature when volatility is expected to be greater.

As long as there is curvature the dumbbell will yield less than the bullet. But that is not the case when the curve is flat, as it has been at times in the recent past from intermediates to long bonds. It is interesting that at such times the 20-year yield often hangs above the curve, while it tends to be on the curve when there is curvature. The convexity analysis provides at least a plausible explanation of this phenomenon: when the curve is flat, the dumbbell around the 20-year would give more convexity without a yield penalty. The preference for this dumbbell forces the 20-year yield above the curve.

The pricing of *long* zeros provides an analogous point. Since they are more convex than the available coupon bonds, they are more valuable for a volatility play. Therefore, they should sell at lower yields than the longest coupon bonds available. Dumbbells with long zeros have lower yields but higher convexity than those with long coupon bonds, lower yields not only because the zeros have lower yields but also because their greater duration forces more weight onto the shorter end.

The demand for convexity, derived from expected volatility, influences ("determines" would be a little strong) how much long zeros trade through the yield curve. Investors' willingness to pay up for these zeros, for use as hedging or dumbbelling vehicles or as means of getting a lot of duration, encourages bond stripping. The limit on this activity stems from the problem of getting rid of the shorter coupons, which are by-products of the main event, at yields that do not give back the gains on the long end.

Since the supply of these coupons depends not on the perceived demand for them, but rather on the demand for the long coupons—much like the supply of tar depends on the demand for gasoline—their yields can be arbitrary. As a result, there can be some real arbitrage opportunities in this sector.

## Leverage versus Convexity

A bond with twice the duration of another has more than twice the convexity, as illustrated in Exhibit 27: two ten-year bonds do not make a 20. Therefore, equating dollar-durations for a hedge is not sufficient even when options are not involved. Getting a given dollar-duration by investing fewer dollars invested in a longer duration produces more convexity than with more dollars in a shorter duration.

Exhibit 28 compares the performance of a 21-year zero coupon bond with a combination of a current coupon bond and enough futures to give the same dollar-duration as that of the zero. After three months, the combination does better than the zero as long as the yield change remains within a rough window of 80 basis points below and 145 basis points above the starting yield.

## Exhibit 27. The Impact of Leverage on Convexity

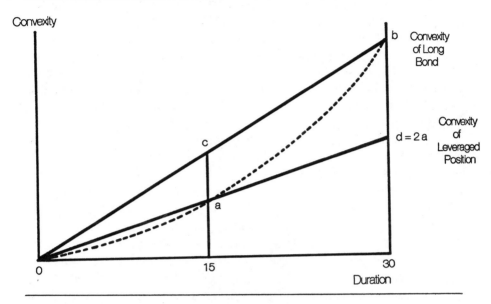

## Exhibit 28. Synthetic Zero versus Strip

### Synthetic Zero: 0.1 UST 8 1/4 of 05/15/05 + 0.2 Sept. future
### Strip: 1 UST 05/15/05

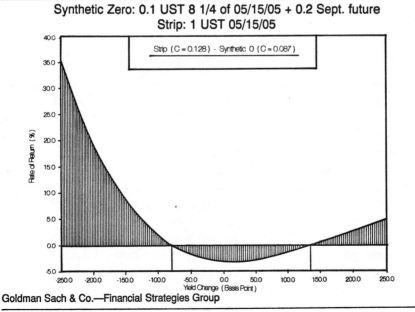

Goldman Sach & Co.—Financial Strategies Group

Again, we have the same trade-off between convexity and yield. When yields do not change, the bond-futures combination does far better than the zero. This is not only because the zero has a lower yield than the long coupon bond; rather, the positive yield curve implies that extending duration with futures increases portfolio yield for the same reason that cutting duration by shorting futures lowers yield. Buying futures is the same as carrying bonds on borrowed money and getting the spread between the long bond yield and the short-term borrowing rate.

This idea sheds added light on the cost of long zeros. When we say they trade "through the curve," we mean at a lower yield than the long current coupon bond. But this bond has a lot less duration than a long zero. A better reference would be a synthetic bond with the same convexity as the zero, for example, a leveraged holding of several bonds adding up to the same dollar-duration as that of the zero. With a positive yield curve, the yield on this synthetic, comprising the yield on the original investment and the positive carry on the leveraged position, would be much higher than the yield on the zero. This difference measures the cost of convexity for long zeros.

### Summary

This paper has outlined a framework for bringing together many seemingly different topics of fixed income analysis: hedging, immunization, pass-throughs, options, callable bonds, yield curves, asset-liability management, and horizon analysis, etc. Behind them all is the single concept that fixed income securities can be described by their future rates of return driven by yield changes, yield volatility, and time. The sensitivity of returns to the three independent variables is measured by *parameters* like duration, convexity, and time value, etc. By reducing all securities—whether bonds, pass-throughs, options, and futures, etc.—to their parametric values, we create a fungible mass in which everything looks like everything else, the values (e.g., duration), being additive where the qualitative attributes (e.g., strike price) are not.

Too much fixed income research focuses on the special features of securities (e.g., paydown rate) and strategies (e.g., immunization). That gives rise to a tunnel vision that segments the markets and encourages local expertise without a global framework. The special features of a given security matter, in the framework I am suggesting, only as they influence rates of return, especially the price movement resulting from changes in yield and perceived yield volatility. For example, most people limit their analysis of options to their gains or losses at expiration under various interest scenarios. But I am not necessarily interested in that particular day, especially since it may mean nothing to the rest of my portfolio. Instead, I want to know how the option behaves under these scenarios during its entire life. Better still, I want to know how its behavior will affect that of my whole portfolio, not just at expiration, but tomorrow and the day after. That way I have only one question—how does my whole portfolio behave under various market conditions, not just my options at expiration or my pass-throughs to their average life, but the whole portfolio in continuous time?

I define a performance profile as the rates of return for a given horizon on one or more securities under various terminal yield conditions. Imagine a matrix where the rows represent different horizons and the columns different yield changes. Each row would be a performance profile, over a different horizon. They are the core of the framework described in this paper. Parameters like duration and convexity are important only for their convenience in representing a performance profile for a very short horizon. They substitute a few numbers for a whole curve. They can be matched with their counterparts in other portfolios or liability streams more easily than can the respective profiles they represent. But we must keep in mind that they are merit performance profiles writ small.

Hedging means matching the performance profiles of the opposing sides of a position—not just the durations per se, but the total profiles, the durations being merely means to that end. The same goes for asset-liability management, where conventional duration-matching is not an end in itself but merely a means of matching performance profiles. Duration-matching works only insofar as the profiles diverge equally from their respective tangents in both the long and short positions. When the divergences are different, more parameters are needed to describe them. Except where options are present, introducing convexity should be enough. But when options play an important role, higher order terms may be needed to approximate the curvature of the price-yield function, that is, the composite curve relating the yield to the bond price and the bond price to the option price. Further, the parameters measuring the sensitivity of the option values to changes in perceived variance, as well as to the passage of time, come into play.

The other major topic covered in this paper is the pervasive role of volatility in fixed income markets. The main idea is that perceived volatility determines the value of convexity and through that the relative values of various securities. As long as the convexity of these securities—whether various GNMA coupons, callable bonds, dumbbells versus single bonds, zero coupon bonds, or options—can be isolated, we can put a value on different degrees of perceived volatility. The mechanism is always the same: the values of any two positions with the same starting duration but different convexities diverge as yields change, and by more the larger the change. This divergence always favors the long position with greater convexity. The greater the perceived volatility, the more the convexity is worth.

Usually one must pay for this advantage, directly in the case of options, but more often in the form of yield give-ups. There are arbitrage opportunities in the various prices of convexity in different markets—whether GNMA coupon spreads, various option spreads, zero coupon dumbbells, and so on. In principle, the cheapest form of convexity can be determined by synthesizing it with various equal-duration positions and picking the one with the lowest price. Because of their high convexity, options and long zeros are useful components of the synthetic.

Ideally, one would use long options whose convexities correspond to those found in callable securities. But they are not available in quantity (yet). Long zeros, which have roughly the same convexity as long options, are fairly good substitutes. Short options, on the other hand, provide the needed convexity only for a short time. Since their convexity is very sensitive both to yield movement and to the passage of time, using them to hedge longer option exposures involves much maintenance and is impractical.

Much of the popular thought about options concerns the expiration value of various combinations like straddles, strangles, spreads, butterflies, and so on. Basically, these are marketing words that add nothing to the clarity of the subject. They conceal the real motivation for using options which is to create desired performance profiles that reflect the impact of volatility.

# Chapter 4

# The Yield Surface

Stanley Diller
Bear, Stearns & Co. Inc.

## Introduction

Bond analysis has evolved through the last decade or so along two quite different and often conflicting paths. One approach is to evaluate bonds as income streams that are held to maturity. As with other income properties, value is measured as a multiple of the income of one year or its reciprocal yield. The other approach projects performance in the form of the expected rate of return over some arbitrary investment period, which allows for expected price change, as well as income.

The income approach to bond analysis originated with financial intermediaries, who made it their goal to maximize the spread between the streams of income and carrying cost, without being concerned with how the present values (or prices) of these streams diverge with changes in market yields. This approach works when the patterns of the two streams are the same, for then their respective present values react equally to yield changes. Both sides can be unwound anytime at a wash. But when the patterns are different, particularly with respect to maturity or prepayment contingency, the income spread over cost does not adequately describe the intermediary's economic condition.

105

If, due to early maturity or prepayment, one side must be rolled over at an adverse rate, the net income will fall. No accounting system can hide that once it happens. It can, however, and usually does, ignore its precursor in the form of the shortfall in the market value of assets relative to liabilities (or net worth) resulting from the same yield changes that are not yet reflected in new cash flows. Since net worth is the present value of net income, its changes due to changing yields merely anticipate the net income changes that occur only at the time of the actual rollovers.

Why not recognize the problem early by marking to market the portfolios? One perfunctory reason often given is that the assets and liabilities are often non-marketable and, therefore, have no price. Apart from the fact that there is a market for virtually all financial instruments, if often in the form of the whole institution holding them, the reason for the market valuation is not to sell anything but to get an early reading on a company's financial condition when it is still possible at least to avoid making the problem worse. Afterward, when the income is down, there is not much left to do.

The real reason for not revaluing assets and liabilities is the hope that yields will bounce back before net income is damaged beyond repair. For example, if, because of a fall in yield, callable assets underperform call-free liabilities (in the market value sense before the bonds are actually called) the valuation assumes that yields will stay down and bring about the actual prepayments that necessitate rollovers at adverse rates. If the yields rebound before these events materialize however, the matter can be resolved without loss. The presumption underlying the accounting system is that in time what goes up must come down. Instead of frightening the public with suggestions that the institutions in which it has deposited its savings might have problems, when, in time, conditions will improve, it is better (the argument goes) to paper over the problem and patiently wait for rates to come back. In the meantime, the institutions can benefit from the higher income that goes with mismatching maturity and call exposure and as a result (hopefully) offer the public lower cost financial services. If rates don't bounce back soon enough, there is always some agency to step in and temporize with open-mouth operations until the rates return.

While there is some merit in this argument, it puts no limits on how much mismatching an institution can prudently bear. Too often, the present system leads to a current income at any cost mentality, which instantly rewards high risk-taking to an extent that is often hidden in accounting legerdemain. The next step is for the accounting system to replace the financial condition as the thing that must be managed.

The bear market of a decade ago exposed the futility of concealing net worth losses that later showed up as unconcealable net income losses. Ironically, the false sense of security that the accounting shield engenders encouraged a greater so-called duration gap than people otherwise would have risked. Under regulatory pressure, the intermediaries reduced their gap, by bringing the durations of their assets and liabilities closer, but at the cost of reducing the yield curve component of their spread.

To regain their former spread, they took on the more insidious but no less risky convexity mismatches, the early form of which involved buying fairly high coupon mortgages and selling same-duration bullets, often in the form of interest-rate swaps. Later, they were interested in the more exotic interest-only mortgage strips and equivalent CMO tranches. The relatively high conventional yields on these positions cannot be construed as income for the purpose of locking in spreads but are merely advanced payments anticipating their underperformance. In principle, a reserve should be set up against these expected losses in either net worth or future net income. This is because of the callable assets' underperforming the call free liabilities, which would have the effect of penalizing their nominal yields and making callable bonds seem less desirable.

The idea is not to avoid call exposure but rather to make sure that one is properly paid for bearing it. What is determined as appropriate is not a matter of personal opinion but rather of what call-exposure is worth in the market. The market does not actually price call-exposure per se, for there is an infinite variety of call and partial prepayment features around. Indeed, the variety has grown out of control with the Byzantine cash flow structures of the more recent CMOs, which are incomprehensible from the point of view of ordinary call exposure. Instead, they, as well as their more conventional predecessors, must be evaluated through their effect on the bond's price behavior under changing market conditions, which anticipates the actual prepayments.

The best way to get at this prospective price behavior is to break it down into the duration and convexity of the function relating the callable bond price to the call-free yield that is assumed to drive it. These parameters are evaluated and traded as though they were bonds in themselves instead of merely the attributes of actual bonds. They are symbols that have been reified into material objects that trade in a commodity market. This is how futures and options may be interpreted, the former representing duration and the latter, convexity.

In principle, they are the only source of value of on-the-run Treasury bonds, whose yields are fully explained by their durations and convexities. This is not true of other bonds, whose yields are influenced by additional attributes that are often collected under the rubric, "basis." The distinction between the generic components and the basis is central to fixed income analysis and to this paper.

One reason for separating them is to get closer to the point where a higher yield implies a better value. This is not true of generic yield—with a positively sloped yield curve, a longer bond has a higher yield without necessarily having greater value. This is the reason that, in comparing bonds with unequal durations, people compare their spreads over the yield curve, instead of their absolute yields, i.e., to remove the generic duration effect.

Convexity is also a generic attribute. Since it is desirable, more so the greater is volatility, and people give up yield to get it. Conversely, people can get higher yield by foregoing (or selling) it. That too is a generic effect. More yield for selling convexity is no indication of better value. Because the appreciation for this effect is more recent than that for duration, people are less aware of its generic quality. Too often, they misconstrue the higher yield they get for selling convexity as better value and, conversely, the yield give-up required to get more convexity as worse value. This confusion between generic and basis components of yield is a central problem in fixed income analysis.

In order to separate the generic and basis components of value, some kind of filter is needed. Since treasuries, by definition, are entirely generic, they are used to fit the yield curve, which describes the generic duration effect. The yield spreads of non-Treasury bonds off this curve is their basis. But a more general formulation is needed to estimate the generic duration and convexity effects, especially since their correlation makes it harder to isolate their separate effects.

This more general yield curve or surface (for it has three dimensions) relates yield not just to duration, as in the ordinary curve, but to convexity as well. It is calculated on the theory that the expected instantaneous rate of return (ER) is the same on all Treasury positions lying on the surface. They are not only the same but equal specifically to the overnight rate. Each such position has a yield, duration, and convexity that, in the context of the model, give rise to the same ER and, therefore, add up to the overnight rate. In this regard, the surface is analogous to an "equal product curve," which gives the various combinations of a group of inputs that produce the same output. The surface, in the form of an algebraic equation, gives the combinations of yield, duration, and convexity that give the same ER.

The effect of this equation is to constrain the allowable combinations of the three attributes. In particular, for a given duration, yield and convexity are inversely related. Since a bullet has less convexity than a same-duration dumbbell, for example, it must have a higher yield in order for both to lie on the surface. It not only must be higher, but by a specific amount—the surface actually denominates the yield value of both duration and convexity.

Although the surface, like the yield curve, is based on treasuries, for they alone (and their derivatives, like future, options, and swaps) have only generic value, an ER, like conventional yield, can be calculated for non-treasuries as well. Since (by definition) the generic duration and convexity components of these specific ERs are equal to their surface counterparts, the ERs can differ from the short term rate only by the amount of the yield differential at the same duration and convexity which, therefore, measures the basis values of these bonds. Since they adjust both for duration and convexity, these spreads can replace the more cumbersome performance simulations that people use to compare dissimilar bonds.

One curious feature of the model is the linear relationship it posits between yield and duration, with convexity constant, and between yield and convexity, with duration constant. That may seem to be in conflict with the curvilinear shape of the observed yield curve. But this curve embodies the combined effect on yield of duration and convexity in the proportions in which they appear in individual bonds. Its curvature is attributable, in large part, to that of the curvilinear relationship between convexity and duration. When duration rises, convexity rises much more, and their net impact on yield is a blend of their separate impacts. When these parameters are analytically decoupled, the curvature disappears.

One apparent advantage of conventional yield over the surface approach is its apparent verisimilitude. Yield seems to represent, in an objective way, the actual investment process. A little realism would indeed be welcome in an investment world that increasingly has become a state of mind. Unfortunately, the realism of yield is largely chimerical, the triumph of familiarity over objectivity.

There is nothing realistic about discounting future money back to the present. It seems so only because it looks like the reverse of compounding present into future money, as one does with a savings account or insurance policy. But the symmetry holds only with one present and one future payment, as in a Treasury strip. In all other cases, the assumptions needed to establish it range from the unlikely to the absurd: from the assumption that the coupons on a bullet can be reinvested at a constant rate, to the assumption that the inverse relationship between prepayment and reinvestment rates can be subsumed in a yield-to-call or a PSA yield.

It is time for people to recognize that the compound interest formula is merely a metaphor for what can be a fairly arbitrary method of valuing bonds. Imputing to it a spurious realism evokes the false impression of a simple dollars and cents world that can be mastered with rules of thumb and instinctive judgment. In fact, fixed income analysis has become increasingly abstract and incompatible with the simplified, compound interest world into which people try to force it. What makes an analysis credible is not its apparent verisimilitude but rather its ability to inspire constructive behavior.

Several members of the Bear Stearns Strategies Group helped me in the course of writing this paper. Neil Baker and Bill Marden helped with historical data and yield curve fitting. YK Chan, whose specific contributions are noted in the text, proposed casting the yield curve problem in terms of the differential equation that is the core of the model. Avram Altaras combined this equation with a model I developed several years ago, the main idea of which is that yield depends not on duration per se but on estimated price volatility, which is the product of duration and estimated yield volatility, or what I call adjusted duration. For some reason, these adjustments lead to much better fitted yield curves, whether the two dimensional ones described in the earlier paper or the three dimensional ones in the present one. The earlier model includes a method of measuring the market's estimate of relative yield changes, which Avram Altara's adapted to the present model. He did all the other programming needed for the paper as well and helped me to think through the overall model. Whatever the ultimate impact of this work proves to be, his contribution, particularly insofar as he brought to bear his own initiative and ingenuity, deserves the highest merit.

## Yield Curve Equilibrium

According to the prevailing theory, observed and expected Treasury yields form an interlocking system that gives each investment period a unique expected return. For any such period, this expected return can be obtained by rolling over shorter bonds during the period; selling a longer one at the end of the period; or holding a bond that just spans the period. In the latter case, the rate is known with certainty. (Assume that we are dealing with strips.) In the other cases, it is expected to occur on the strength of the observed rates and the rates at which the rollovers or sales are expected to occur. In theory, the observed rates come about in a way that, in combination with the rate expectations, they give an expected total return equal to the rate that can be locked in with a single bond. Each observed rate on the curve determines the expected total return from rolling over shorter or selling longer bonds over an investment horizon equal to its term to maturity.

The future rates that together with the observed rates equate expected holding period returns can be inferred from the observed rates. These inferred, or, as they are called, forward rates are hypothetical, for there is no actual market in them. They are introduced as the conditions for bringing about the equality of expected returns.

The assumed connection between observed and expected yields or other prices does not represent a special yield curve theory, but rather is indicative of a general effort to bridge related markets. For example, futures models posit a cash-and-carry mechanism by which the deliverable bond is carried on repo at some gain or loss that is just offset by the change in the futures relative to the cash price. Option models posit some yield volatility that determines the theoretical value of the option relative to the underlying bond. An expected volatility is translated into an option price through its supposed impact on the cost of hedging an options position. Conversely, a volatility can be inferred from the relative prices of an option and its underlying bond just as a forward can be inferred from successive observed yields, and, in theory, it represents a forecast of future volatility the way a forward represents a forecast of a future yield. Still another example is the yield differential on bonds denominated in different currencies. In principle, this differential reflects the exchange rate expectations of people who start in one currency, invest in another, and convert the foreign denominated payments back into the original currency. This so-called round trip is the supposed mechanism for translating expected changes in an exchange rate into a current yield differential.

In each case, current price differentials anticipate changes in yield, volatility, exchange rates, as well as (in connection with mortgage pass-throughs) prepayment rates, and other variables that influence value, always within a framework that stipulates equal performance for comparable market exposures. The reason for acknowledging the anticipatory role of price and yield differentials is not to gain their help in predicting interest rates and bond performance, which the evidence suggests they do quite poorly, but to gain a better understanding of current price structure. Although the procedures put forward to show how current price differentials anticipate future events seem quite plausible, their verisimilitude is beside the point. The important thing is not why people think as they do or even whether they think as they appear to with respect to changing interest rates or volatility, but that imagining it so provides a basis for understanding the current price structure.

I noted earlier that for a given horizon, a forward rate comes into play whether one rolls over a shorter bond or sells a longer bond. Both hypothetical trades occur at presumed rates that originate in the future and are, therefore, forward rates. Either approach to the equalization of expected rates of return amounts to the same thing. They are not alternative theories but, rather, alternative ways of describing the same theory, the core of which is not rolling over shorter bonds at forward rates, but rather equalizing expected returns.

It is better to view all the implied forecasts that equate values across markets, whether forward rates predicting future interest rates, implied volatilities predicting future volatility, implied exchange rates (in inter-currency yield differentials) predicting future exchange rates, relative yield changes predicting future yield curve shapes, not as explicit forecasts, but rather as tautologies expressing the conditions for a unified bond market.

The current preference for casting yield curve theory in terms of rolling over shorter bonds instead of selling longer ones reflects the convention prevailing at the time the theory was developed. Then, as now, economists (who developed the theory) thought more in terms of abstract interest rates than of yields on live bonds. Therefore, it was more natural for them to consider strings of hypothetical forward rates, representing bonds spanning the same period, than to consider the price changes needed to equalize holding period rates of return.

For mathematical convenience, the present study uses an instantaneous holding period, which means that the expected return is equal to the overnight rate. In this limiting case, the only alternative to locking in the rate is to carry a longer bond. With a positive yield curve, the bond will accrue more interest than the short (i.e., overnight) rate. To limit its expected return to the overnight rate, its price must be expected to fall and, therefore, its yield to rise. More generally, for any yield curve, there must be an expected percentage price change ($\Delta P$) associated with what I call a Breakeven Yield Change (BYC) that compensates for the yield differential. The price and yield changes are linked by duration (D) in the following equation:

$$\Delta P_i = D_i \times BYC_i,$$

with the subscript (i) denoting the bond with the $i^{th}$ duration. The price change is equal to the difference between the bond yield ($Y_i$) and the short rate ($Y_o$):

$$Y_i - Y_o = D_i \times BYC_i$$

rearranging terms gives:

$$Y_o - Y_i = D_i \times BYC_i$$

which says that the expected instantaneous rate of return, that is, income plus expected price change, on any bond is equal to the short rate.

A paper I wrote several years ago[1] argued that the breakeven yield change on any bond with duration (i), i.e. $BYC_i$, is equal to some multiplier ($W_i$) times the one on the shortest bond ($BYC_1$):

$$BYC_i = W_i \times BYC_1$$

Substituting this expression into the previous equation gives:

$$Y_o = Y_i - D_i \times W_i BYC_1 \qquad (1)$$

Where:

$Y_o$ = the short-term rate,
$Y_i$ = the yield on the $i^{th}$ duration bond
$D_i$ = its duration
$W_i$ = the yield change multiplier on the $i^{th}$ duration bond
$BYC_1$= the breakeven yield change on the shortest bond

According to the model described, $W_i$ falls at a diminishing rate as duration gets larger, which means that longer yields are expected to change less than shorter yields. More than that, the use of $W_i$ implies that all longer yield changes ($BYC_i$), and their associated price changes, are determined by the shortest, or reference, yield change ($BYC_1$). However, (switching for the moment to more general notation), since a longer bond's duration ($D_i$) measures its price sensitivity to its own ($Y_i$) rather than its reference yield ($Y_R$) change, a chain derivative is needed to couple it with a term measuring the sensitivity ($W_i$) of its own to its reference yield changes:

$$\frac{1}{P_i}\frac{dP_i}{dY_R} = \frac{1}{P_i}\frac{dP_i}{dY_i} \times \frac{dY_i}{dY_R}$$

or

---

1. "The Yield Curve: A New Approach," Bear, Stearns & Co. Inc. 1980, New York. There is also a somewhat different version published in the Financial Analyst Journal, March/April 1981, New York pp. 23-41.

$$D^*_i = D_i \times W_i$$

(I call this new parameter ($D^*$) adjusted duration.)

The present model, like the earlier one, holds together only with adjusted, not ordinary, duration. The same is true of convexity; it must be "adjusted" by multiplying ordinary convexity by $W_i^2$. These adjusted parameters make it possible to relate all price changes to the same yield change and thereby make duration a generic measure of price volatility.

Their efficacy should be judged not by the plausibility of the relative-yield-change model used to get them (described in the earlier paper) but by their ability to explain actual data. In this regard, I will show later that: (1) they make it possible to fit well-formed Treasury strip curves, as they did the coupon curves in the earlier paper; (2) the strip curve, in turn, gives rise to a yield surface off which the corporate and mortgage spreads are quite stable through time; and, (3) the adjusted parameters explain what for many people has been a paradox, namely, why, when there is an inverted yield curve, a dumbbell, which is more convex and, therefore, should yield less, seems to yield more than a same-duration bullet.

At the time that my earlier paper was written, the assumption of lower yield volatility on longer bonds was supported by the data to such a degree that the magnitudes of $W_i$, estimated in the course of fitting the prevailing yield curves, were devilishly close to those observed in historical correlations. Since that time, however, the evidence is a lot less supportive, with parallel-shifting yield curves instead of the twisting ones implied by the falling $W_i$ being all too evident. It may still be true that longer yields are expected to be less volatile, even if they do not behave that way. And it may be that in retrospect the past five or six years will seem aberrant over a longer history. In any case, it should be clear that the falling $W_i$ fills a theoretical need in the context of the present model and is not offered here as a factor in hedging. On the other hand, it is worth noting that the estimates of $W_i$ obtained in the course of fitting the strip curves are much closer to 1.0 now than they were at the time of the earlier paper, which suggests that people are expecting more parallel-shifting yield curves.

The distinction between own and reference yields is also very important for callable bonds. In that case, the reference yield belongs to a hypothetical call-free bond, the yield on which is in turn driven by a shorter reference yield in the way just described. This call free yield drives a call-free price that in turn drives an option price. The callable price is the difference between these prices, and its changes are the differences between their changes. The callable bond's duration ties its price change not to its "own" but to its reference yield changes. A similar arrangement works for all derivative securities, changes in the values of which depend on those of the bonds from which they are derived, which in turn depend on the yield changes of still other bonds. As long as the parameters linking these changes are known, there is no limit to how many of them can be chained. But to make different bonds truly comparable, the final link in the chain must be the same yield change for all of them. Otherwise, "same duration" would not mean "same price volatility."

Another feature of the present approach is its disassociation of duration from calendar time. Most people distinguish long from short bonds, not because they pay out over a longer period, but because their prices are more volatile. Duration is a measure of that volatility. The duration of a short-term option, for example, its percentage price change relative to its underlying bond's yield change, can exceed 200, and it can be negative for an interest only-mortgage strip with positive cash flow.

## Abstracting Bond Attributes

What is important about the typically upward direction of most yield curves is not why they rise, but that they do mostly rise, whether because people expect rates to rise, think long bonds are riskier or, simply, because they want them less than shorter bonds. Whatever the reason, a rising curve implies that people are paid to extend. But the amount they are paid diminishes and ultimately turns negative as they extend along the curve. One reason for this pattern is that "adjusted duration," i.e., (D*), rises more slowly than duration itself; therefore, the actual increase in price volatility is less than it seems. The other reason is that rising duration implies even faster rising convexity, which has a downward influence on yield.

The relative magnitudes of the upward duration and downward convexity influences on yield vary along the curve. At low duration levels, the net influence of extension on yield is strongly upward; further on, with convexity larger, it levels off; and still further on, with convexity rising sharply, extension actually lowers yield. Since the yield value of convexity rises with perceived market volatility, it overtakes the duration effect sooner when volatility is higher.

This way of thinking about the yield curve helps to explain the moderately inverted curve currently prevailing. Some people have (I think incorrectly) interpreted the lower long term yield to mean a rise in the value of convexity instead of what I think is merely a weaker duration effect giving way sooner to convexity.

The familiar curve relating yield to duration is a two-dimensional slice into the three-dimensional world of yield, duration, and convexity, or what I am calling the yield surface. By ignoring convexity, the conventional yield curve does not remove its yield effect but instead merely conceals it within what looks like a changing duration effect. As duration increases, it affects yield directly, through the extension effect, and indirectly through its effect on convexity. Although the direct effect alone can be either upward or downward, depending on whether the yield curve is positively or negatively sloped at the lower end, the indirect effect is always downward—people are always willing to pay for convexity. The total duration effect on yield (as reflected in the conventional yield curve) is really a blend of these two effects, proportioned by the amounts of either parameter found in the observed bonds.

According to the model I am using, the separate yield effects of a unit change in either parameter (with the other held constant) are the same at all parameter levels. But that appears to conflict with the curvilinear shape of the conventional yield curve. The difference can be explained in the following way. As I maintain, while the yield per unit of convexity is constant (on a given day), more and more convexity units come into play per duration unit as duration grows, with each convexity unit having the same yield impact. That is why each new duration unit appears to have a different yield impact. In other words, the non-linear relationship between convexity and duration, by which convexity rises roughly with the square of duration, is projected onto the conventional yield curve.

As a result of this relationship, when conventional bonds are interpreted as portfolios of strips, it becomes clear that the convexity of any position rises with the dispersion of its cash flows, which can be measured as the variance of each payment's duration around the mean duration. This is why, for the same duration, current-coupon bonds and dumbbells are more convex and, therefore, give less yield than zero coupon bonds and bullets. Since the yield value of convexity depends on market volatility, the yield spreads between dumbbells and bullets, as well as between current- and zero coupon bonds, rise with market volatility.

Relating yield spreads to differences in duration and convexity has been one of the key developments in fixed income analysis over the past several years. The emergence of financial futures and of interest swaps gave people a more abstract sense of duration, just as the emergence of options and restructured mortgages made them think of convexity more as a thing in itself than a property of a specific bond. This appreciation for and explicit pricing of disembodied yield, duration, and convexity is the most important development in fixed income analysis that has yet occurred. Although the need for this type of analysis was always present, for example, in dealing with callable bonds, it took the emergence of derivative securities to make people acknowledge it. I suspect this is because such conventions as yield-to-call, yield-to-average life, and worst-case yield, however misleading they may be, give at least the semblance of a cash flow reality. With futures, options, and CMOs, these conventions become meaningless and must give way to a more abstract representation of value. For this reason, fixed-income culture is evolving along a similar path as most other sciences into a less tangible world of metaphor and computational rules in place of an experience based reality.

Putting actual values on the attributes themselves, instead of on the bonds to which they belong, creates common denominators for comparing different types of bonds. Yield, duration, and convexity, respectively, are the same and should be worth the same no matter which bonds they belong to. Modern arbitrage has largely come down to buying them where they are cheap and selling them where they are dear, while accepting the basis difference between the bonds on either side. For example, one can buy the relatively cheap convexity embodied in a super-PO and sell the fully priced convexity embodied in conventional options. The basis in this case largely reflects the greater uncertainty about the convexity estimates for super-POs due to their dependence on uncertain prepayment estimates, which gives rise to a compensatory yield that looks like cheapness. To the extent that the estimation errors wash out over time, the super-POs should appeal more to the long-term outlook of financial accounting systems than to a dealer's mark-to-market system. That suggests the possibility of a symbiotic relationship between dealers who sell super POs to, for example, banks which take back plain vanilla options. In effect, the banks wind up with cheaper dirty (due to estimation error) convexity, while the dealers get more expensive clean convexity.

Although one may think in terms of buying or selling a given attribute, such as convexity, in reality each attribute comes packaged with several others in the proportions defined by each bond. Convexity cannot be bought in a given instrument without also buying its duration. But since the packages, i.e., the mixes of yield, duration, and convexity, are all different, it is possible to combine several packages (or bonds) to achieve a desired net mix in the form of a synthetic bond. Such bonds play a crucial role in creating the yield surface.

## Time Value

People are divided now between concern for a bond's price behavior under different market conditions and for its cash flow yield.

The real difference between the two approaches is that the former takes for granted, while the latter largely ignores, market volatility. In the conventional yield paradigm, for example, the investor puts out cash with the certainty of getting it back later "plus interest." He might accept very little interest, at the limit nothing, but he would not accept less than nothing, when he could merely hold on to his money and get nothing.

That paradigm holds only for the unrealistic assumption that yields are either constant or changing in a known way, notwithstanding that the main subject of default free bond analysis is the performance impact of uncertain yield change. If yield could be assumed to be constant, turnover costs aside, there would be no reason to accept anything below the highest yield, even for a short holding. Yet, people routinely accept the equivalent of negative yields when they go short futures or long options because they expect yields to change. They accept the possibility of a negative yield in the event their expectations fail to materialize.

The income loss on futures comes about from their price rise over time, which, in turn, coincides with the net income flow or carry of a leveraged position in the underlying bond. With a positive yield curve, a covered futures seller earns more interest on the bond than he pays out on the repo. This net income is just offset by the so-called price backwardation, i.e., the position of the futures' price below the cash bond price by an amount equal to the net income to delivery. As delivery gets closer, both the income and backwardation get smaller, until both disappear on the final day. In closing out his short futures position, assuming no yield change, the covered seller pays more for his futures contract than that for which he sold it, with the difference being just equal to the net income. But an uncovered seller, i.e., one who intentionally lowers his duration, would not recover in the form of carry what he lost in the price increase and would experience, therefore, an uncompensated income loss. This loss is equivalent to the yield give-up he would incur by swapping a longer into a shorter bond. On the other hand, if the yield on the deliverable instrument is lower than the repo rate, as in the case of gold or ordinary bonds in an inverted yield curve environment, the futures contract starts above the cash price, which is called a contango, and falls to it, giving the uncovered seller a gain. Either way, two seemingly different trades, i.e., selling futures and switching from a longer to a shorter bond, have the same effects on both duration and yield because they embody the same yield curve.

But the futures' "yield" cannot be calculated as a conventional internal rate of return because futures have no cash flow. Instead, it reflects a price change over time assuming constant yield. This is the more general way of calculating yield, i.e., as a change in market value, including accrued interest. It can be expressed either in arithmetic terms, as a profit or loss, or percentage terms, as a rate of return. This is what I am calling "time value." It can be calculated for all yield-driven securities like futures, options, callable bonds and mortgages, short or multiple bond positions, as well as ordinary bonds. The "constant market conditions" means that, while the whole yield curve is constant, bonds age along it.

The main component of time value for coupon-bearing bonds is accrued interest, while for zero coupon bonds, options, and futures, it is their scheduled price changes in either direction.

## Expected Return

However, "constant market conditions" is an incomplete basis for valuation—it excludes too many motives people have for choosing particular bonds: without the expectation of rising yields, they have no reason to accept a lower yield on shorter bonds; and without recognizing the potential for yield volatility, no reason to pay up for convexity. In other words, the constancy assumption underlying conventional yield cannot account even for routine investment decisions. For this, a new value measure that takes care of both the income effects of stable and the performance effects of changing yields is needed.

One candidate is the Expected Return developed by YK Chan. Using a Taylor expansion of a bond's instantaneous Expected Return (ER) due to income, drift, and volatility, he developed the following equation:[2]

$$ER = R_0 - D \times my + \tfrac{1}{2} C\sigma^2 y^2 \tag{3}$$

The three terms correspond with time value ($R_0$), the price consequence of yield drift ($-D \times my$) and of random yield volatility ($\tfrac{1}{2} C \times \sigma^2 y^2$), both yield changes being expressed in percentage terms. Underlying this model is the assumption that yields change by the same percentage all along the curve.

This model, in effect, reinterprets "constant market conditions" to mean not constant yields but constant expectations of yield change, both directional and random. Recall that an existing yield structure embodies these expectations.

---

2. The following derivation was supplied by YK:

Let:

V=the value, i.e., price plus accrued interest of a given bond

y=yield

m=means of log normal distribution of potential yields (expressed as percentage)

$\sigma^2$=variance of this distribution (expressed as percentage)

$R_0$=instantaneous rate of return assuming no change in yield

D=duration

C=convexity

The Lognormal model for y implies for a short interval dt:

$E(dy) = mydt$

$E(dy^2) = \sigma^2 y^2 dt$

Taylor Expansion of dV:

$$dV = \frac{\partial V}{\partial y}dy + \frac{1}{2}\frac{\partial^2 V}{\partial y^2}dy^2 + \frac{\partial V}{\partial t}dt$$

Divide by V dt:

$$\frac{1}{V}\frac{dV}{dt} = \frac{1}{V}\frac{\partial V}{\partial y}\frac{dy}{dt} + \frac{1}{2}\frac{1}{V}\frac{\partial^2 V}{\partial y^2}\left(\frac{dy}{dt}\right)^2 + \frac{1}{V}\frac{\partial V}{\partial t}$$

$$= -D\frac{dy}{dt} + \frac{1}{2}C\left(\frac{dy}{dt}\right)^2 + \frac{1}{V}\frac{dV}{dt}$$

Take expectations:

$$E\left(\frac{1}{v}\frac{dV}{dt}\right) = -Dmy + \frac{1}{2}C\sigma^2 y^2 + R_0$$

## Combined Model

Avram Altaras and I combined the earlier model (Equation 1) with YK's (Equation 3) into a new model (Equation 4), which equates YK's expected return (ER) with the short-term rate $(Y_o)$ and makes all yield changes functions $(W_i)$ of the shortest yield change $(BYC_1)$

$$Y_0 = R_i - D_i \times W_i \times BYC_1 + \tfrac{1}{2}C_1 \times W_i^2 \times \sigma_1^2 \tag{4}$$

or letting

$$D_i^* = W_i \times D_i \tag{5}$$
$$C_i^* \times W_i^2 \times C_i \tag{5a}$$

gives

$$Y_0 = R_i - D_i^* \times BYC_1 + \tfrac{1}{2}C_i^* \times \sigma_1^2 \tag{6}$$

Like the earlier model, the new one equates the expected instantaneous rates of return on all treasuries with the short-term rate. But instead of depending only on a bond's expected price change to offset its yield difference versus the short-term rate, as the earlier model did, the new one looks to a bond's convexity as well and, thereby, links the yield curve with market volatility. This additional variable is the third dimension implied in the term "yield surface."

Given that people spend a lot of time figuring out which treasuries to own, it may appear a little odd to claim they all have the same instantaneous expected return, as though they were all worth the same. But having the same expected return does not make them equally desirable to all people. Leaving aside the middle term (involving duration) of Equation (6), the other two, representing income and convexity, pair off in infinite ways to give the same expected return. People with a strong preference for current income over performance potential, or who disagree with the level of volatility that equates expected returns, are not indifferent about which bonds they get merely because they have the same expected return. The model gives them no reason for disparagement.

Instead, by forcing the yield, duration, and convexity terms to add up to the same short-term rate, it specifies the proportions of each component needed to do so. For example, given the duration, there are specific proportions of yield and convexity that satisfy the market and, distinct from opinions, determined tradeoff between yield and convexity. People who give up convexity for yield too often give up too much merely because they are willing, rather than because the market makes them do so. My quarrel with them is not that they sell convexity but that they sell it too cheaply. The proper price is determined in the market for generic convexity, not by the conventions governing a specific source of it, or by the buyer's threshold of pain. One's willingness to accept less yield should be gotten for giving up convexity is no reason for doing so any more than is paying a doctor what one would be willing to pay him to relieve a pain instead of what one is asked to pay him.

Although everyone faces the same market trade-offs among yield, duration, and convexity, they choose different proportions because they have different needs and risk preferences. Many of them determine the durations and convexities of their low-risk portfolios according to the corresponding attributes of their liabilities, adopted indexes, or self imposed performance standards. They diverge from these standards and incur the risk of underperforming them to the extent their market opinions make it seem worthwhile, their performance evaluations tolerate near-term underperformance, or they are willing to bear the risk. The different outcomes of these considerations lead to investors' holding different amounts of yield, duration, and convexity while facing the same market prices and the same "expected return."

How can they all have the same expected return with wildly different portfolios? Because expected return is an ex ante notion that is based on assumptions about volatility and relative yield change, while performance is an ex poste notion that depends on what these variables turn out to be. Equilibrium does not mean that everything turns out the same. It merely means that current prices are consistent with prevailing opinions about future yields, volatility, etc. But even fairly priced positions perform quite differently, depending on how the projected variables actually turn out.

## Strip Curve

Since they cover a wider range of duration and convexity than ordinary bonds, Treasury strips are good for estimating the yield values of these parameters. Fitting Equation 6 to them makes it possible to denominate the independent impacts on yield of either parameter and through them determine the surface itself.

Several fitted strip curves are illustrated in Exhibit 1. To fit a curve, four parameters must be estimated: $Y_0$, the short term interest rate; $W_i$, the relative yield change factor on the $i^{th}$ duration bond; $BYC_1$, the breakeven yield change on the shortest bond; and $\sigma_1^2$, the volatility of the shortest bond yield. (The shortest bond is just a little longer than the period of the short-term rate.) In fitting the curve, all four parameters can be estimated by iteration, or, if one chooses, some may be forced to assume particular values. For example, for our own work, Avram Artelas forced the long bond yield volatility (i.e., $W_{10}^2 \times \sigma_1^2$) to equal the value implied in the option market. The price data for these fits are taken directly from our quote sheets.

Forcing the volatility this way anchors the strip curve to the options market, the place where most people acknowledge perceived volatility to be explicitly revealed. It is also a way of dealing with the difficult problem of separating the influences of W and $\sigma$, which are jointly responsible for capturing the odd shape of the strip curve. Since on a given day they could have mutually canceling errors, the magnitude of either one alone is somewhat arbitrary. (A similar interaction between call-free spreads, volatility, and prepayment is the main reason I have never been interested in tracking the "implied volatility" of mortgage prices).

The awkwardness of having two interacting parameters is unavoidable, for both are needed to fit the strip curve. To see why, recall that the convexity of strips is closely related to the square of

# Exhibit 1. Examples of Strip Curves Fitted with Yield Surface Model

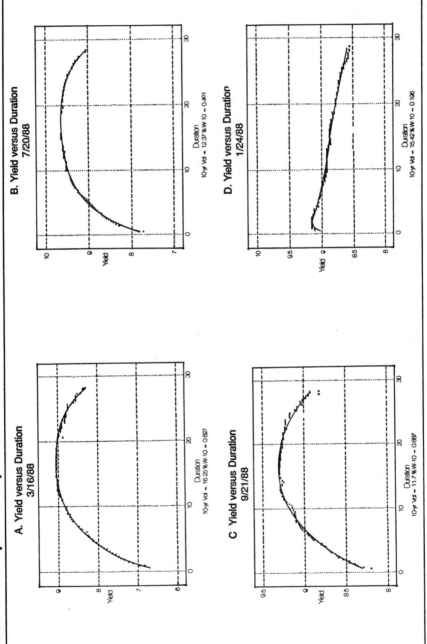

### A. Yield versus Duration
3/16/88

10-yr Vol = 16.25%/W-10 − 0.627

### B. Yield versus Duration
7/20/88

10-yr Vol = 12.37%/W-10 − 0.491

### C. Yield versus Duration
9/21/88

10-yr Vol = 11.7%/W-10 − 0.687

### D. Yield versus Duration
1/24/88

10-yr Vol = 15.42%/W-10 − 0.198

their duration. Therefore, if duration and convexity were enough by themselves, a 2-power polynomial of yield on duration and duration squared would fit the strip curve. In fact, it takes a 7-power polynomial to fit the curve as well as the present model does with half as many parameters. And these fits are quite good, notwithstanding the smoothness and continuity imposed on them by Equation 6.

Before considering the yield surface in more detail, I will review some well-known ideas about duration and convexity, which I originally described in 1984 in "The Parametric Analysis of Fixed Income Securities." Then, I will expand on that paper's discussion of synthetic securities, which take on new meaning in the context of the yield surface. I discovered that any three bonds on the strip curve (or elsewhere on the surface) can generate the same surface as the one that comes from inserting different values of (adjusted) duration and convexity into Equation 6. That is an important result because it implies that one can actually buy any duration-convexity pairs on the surface, not just those occurring in individual bonds.

## Duration and Convexity[3]

Duration and convexity describe how a bond's price changes in percentage terms as its own yield changes. In Exhibit 2, the yield fall, $Y_b - Y_a$, is associated with the price rise, $P_b - P_a$.

It has become conventional to divide the total price change into a linear component, $P_c - P_a$ and a remainder $P_b - P_c$; it is often convenient to use the linear component, called duration, as a surrogate for the total price change when the yield change is small. Duration is the slope of the tangent to the price-yield curve at the starting yield $Y_a$. Being linear, its contribution to the price change is a constant multiple of the yield change. For example, a 5 duration implies a 5% price change for a 100 basis-point yield change, a 10% price change for a 200 basis-point yield change, etc.

---

3. This section is a brief review of well known ideas that can be passed over by people already familiar with the subject.

**Exhibit 2.   The Duration and Convexity of a Call-Free Bond**

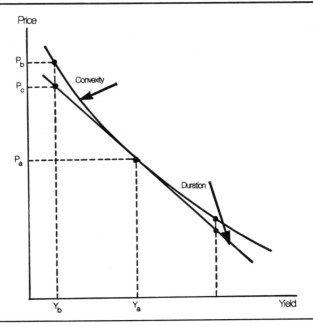

But the actual price change is not a constant multiple of the yield change. For symmetrical yield changes, prices rise more than they fall, and the difference grows with the range of yield changes. This is due to the bond's convexity. With an equal chance of a yield rising or falling, i.e., a zero expected yield change, the bond's expected price change is positive, since the magnitude of its rise exceeds that of its fall. The expected price change grows with both convexity and the range of potential yield movement (or volatility).[4]

How much people pay for this expected price gain, whether directly, in the form of option premiums, or indirectly, by giving up yield, has come to be known as the trade-off between yield and convexity. For a given duration, the yield that should be given up

---

4. For most purposes, the two way breakdown of price change suffices, with "convexity" being used to describe the whole nonlinear part. Strictly speaking, however, convexity refers to the second term of the Taylor expansion of the total price differential and is defined as the second derivative of price with respect to yield, all divided by the price. All the calculations in this paper use this more rigorous definition.

for another unit of convexity depends on the expected yield volatility. Conversely, the market's expected yield volatility can be inferred from the yield that has been given up for a given convexity.

Most people recognize this trade-off in the mortgage and corporate markets, where convexity is mainly known for its absence or worse, its negative value, and expect to be compensated with extra yield. With treasuries, however, they consider convexity more of a curiosity; its differences from one bond to another seem too small to matter. In that regard, they are mistaken. I have already argued that convexity is the major factor in the difference between the strip and current coupon yield curve and between dumbbell and bullet yields. Indeed, with same-duration treasury combinations, what I am calling synthetics, the income-convexity trade-off is the only thing left to analyze, and can involve magnitudes that rival those of embedded options.

## Synthetic Bonds

Synthetic bonds (as I am defining them) are combinations of long and short positions (i.e., positive and negative holdings) with a targeted net duration. Although they can include any number of bonds, they usually involve long and short positions in three bonds of which two popular types are dumbbells (i.e., longer and shorter bonds straddling an intermediate or bullet) and (what I call) Leveraged Extensions, LEs, (carrying several pars of a shorter bond on repo to get the same total duration as that of a longer bond). Dumbbells are more convex and lower yielding, while the LEs are less convex and higher yielding than their corresponding bullets.

Exhibits 3 and 4 illustrate these differences for dumbbells and LEs, respectively. The yield and convexity values of the targeted bonds are given along the curves and of the synthetics along the lines. The whole analysis depends on the shape of the yield curve in Panel A and the convexity-duration curve in Panel B. The yield-convexity trade-off for either synthetic type is reflected in the dif-

**Exhibit 3.   Yield and Convexity Differences Between a Dumbbell
and a Target Bullet**

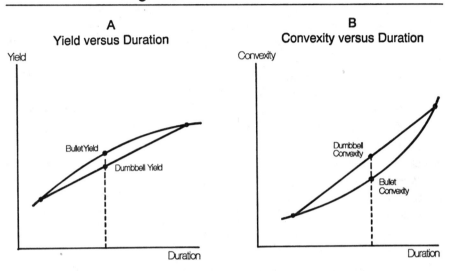

**A**
Yield versus Duration

**B**
Convexity versus Duration

**Exhibit 4.   Yield and Convexity Differences Between a Leveraged
Extension and a Target Bullet**

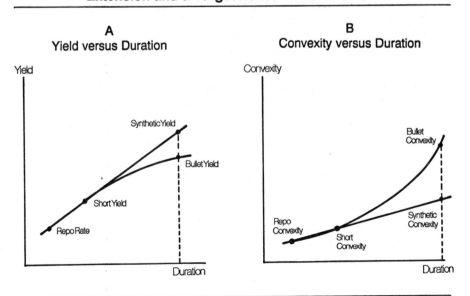

**A**
Yield versus Duration

**B**
Convexity versus Duration

ferences between the curves and lines, representing yield and convexity, in the two panels.

With either type of synthetic, yield grows linearly with duration; it grows along the line connecting its components. Suppose, for example, you synthesize a 10 year bond with four 2 year bonds (assuming they add up to the same duration as a 10 year). To equate the market values of both 10-year positions, suppose that one 2 year bond is bought for cash and the others on repo.

The synthetic's yield is the market-weighted yield of its components, with minus signs for the short positions. Roughly speaking, that translates into an effective yield equal to the sum of the yield on the cash purchase and the net carry (interest received less interest paid) on those bought on repo, expressed as a percentage of the cash investment. Therefore, if one invested 100 dollars in a 2-year bond at 8% and bought three more on repo, each with a 100 basis points of carry (implying a 7% repo rate), the effective yield on the synthetic would be (roughly) 11%, compared with a yield on the 10-year of, say, 9%.

The synthetic's higher yield comes from its extending along the line in Exhibit 4A, where the yield pickup per unit duration is greater than it is along the curve. Increasing duration in this fashion makes yield rise linearly, in contrast to the diminishing rate along the curve itself. Buying the synthetic and selling the same duration on the curve, therefore, gives a zero duration position with positive income.

But this income is not free; it comes with negative convexity. The reason is given in Exhibit 4B, which shows how an LE's convexity grows linearly with duration, while the corresponding bullet's convexity grows much faster along the curve. On the other hand, Exhibit 3B shows that dumbbells have more convexity than same-duration bullets; the line representing their average convexity lies above the curve representing bullet convexities.

The yield and convexity curves go a long way toward explaining the yield surface. For they show how long and short positions in various bullets and synthetics can create any combination of yield, duration, and convexity. For example, the one just noted, going long the LE and short the bullet, produces positive income, negative convexity, and zero duration. Extending the LE, while retaining the bullet position, gives a positive duration and negative convexity, as some mortgages have, while reversing the position gives a negative duration (and income) and a positive convexity, like that of a put option. In principle, this method can reproduce the duration and convexity combinations usually associated with embedded options.

The yield and convexity curves go hand in hand in creating these combinations, but there is an important difference between them: while the convexity-duration curve is purely mathematical, the yield curve is determined in the market. If the income convexity trade off implied by the two curves gets out of line with investors' volatility perceptions (and, therefore, with the value they ascribe to convexity), it is the yield curve, not the convexity-duration curve, that must adapt.

Therefore, one would expect to find that the yield curve takes on more curvature, as reflected by the dumbbell-bullet yield spreads, when perceived volatility, as reflected, say, in the options market, increases. In that case, one would expect the strip curve to diverge more from the current Treasury curve, as well as the conventionally calculated callable bond yield spreads to rise.

These expectations are based on the idea that higher perceived volatility makes convexity worth more, and that, in turn, should lower the relative yields of securities as it increases.

The actual correlations between the degree of curvature (as measured by the dumbbell-bullet yield spread) and options-implied volatility are suggestive but not compelling. Exhibit 5 plots the option market's implied volatility and Exhibit 6, the dumbbell bullet spread, in this case the 7-year versus a duration-weighted 2- and 30-year dumbbell, over the period September 2, 1987 to October 12, 1988. The correlation coefficient is 0.56. But this number is sensitive to which period is used, for most periods ranging between 1/3 and 2/3. Keep in mind that according to the model that I am using, volatility only partly explains the shape of the yield curve. The rest is due to the relative yield change estimates.

**Exhibit 5.    Implied Yield Volatility of Options on Bond Futures between September 2, 1987 and October 12, 1988. (Averagae of 3 Nearest-to-Money Puts and Calls)**

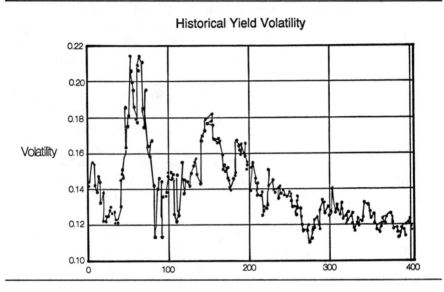

Historical Yield Volatility

**Exhibit 6.    Yield Spread between Dumbbell (2-yr, 30-yr) and Bullet (10-yr) between September 2, 1987 and October 12, 1988**

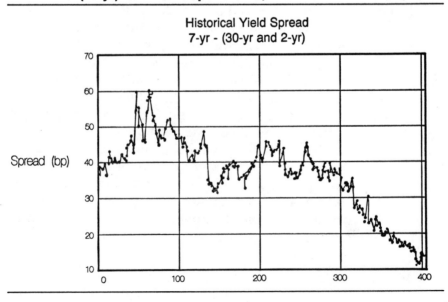

Historical Yield Spread
7-yr - (30-yr and 2-yr)

## Income-Convexity Trade-Off

Dumbbells and Leveraged Extensions are examples of equal-duration synthetics that are often compared with their matching bullets in respect to income and performance under assumed market conditions. Taking opposite positions in the synthetic and bullet typifies what has become the core of modern strategy, namely the trade-off between income and convexity. A given outcome is often characterized by a U- or inverted U-curve like the one used to describe a dumbbell-bullet arbitrage in Exhibit 7.

Since the bullet has a higher yield and lower convexity than the dumbbell, it performs better as long as yield changes are within the range bounded by the curve's intersections with the zero-line. The curve's height at no-yield-change reflects the bullet's greater time value, the effect of which diminishes as the yield changes bring its lower convexity more into play.

**Exhibit 7.   Rates of Return Differences between Equal-Duration Dumbbell and Bullet over Future Yield Scenarios**

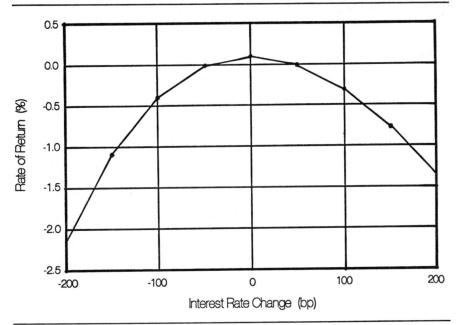

The net positions people choose are best thought of as means of shaping the U-curve according to their preferences and needs. The S&Ls, for example, traditionally buy the higher-yielding, negatively convex mortgage instruments, against which they sell a lower-yielding, positively convex bond or interest swap. Since their accounting systems favor the settlement yield over future price behavior because they do not mark-to-market, many thrifts prefer high and, therefore, narrow curves, the height reflecting the high no-change rate of return (roughly comparable to yield) and the narrowness, the poor performance under changing yields. Since this shape does not occur to the desired degree in natural securities, dealers carve them out of the cash flows of mortgage-backed securities in the form of CMOs and mortgage strips.

Some mutual funds also are big convexity sellers, being forced by competitive pressures to take in high current income, which, when netted against premium losses from prepayment, they can report to current and prospective shareholders as yield and pay out as dividends, at the expense of underperforming in volatile environments. Since the public appears to view many of the mortgage-backed funds as money market substitutes, they pay more attention to their high current yield than to their often lower performance over time. That is perhaps the most compelling example of the inadequacy of cash flow yield as a performance measure.

Preferring income over convexity is not inherently wrong as long as the right amount of income is received for the amount of convexity that is sold. But how does one know what that is? Although the U-curves show the no change rates of return relative to the breakeven yield ranges for any equal duration comparison, they do not denominate a continuous trade-off between yield and convexity, i.e., so many basis points per unit of convexity. The surface, on the other hand, does it for both duration and convexity.

In addition to accommodating different performance measurement needs, cash flow repackagers are bridging still another, less conspicuous gap, namely, the one between the perception and the mathematical evaluation of risk. People tend to undervalue remote contingencies, as when they fail to use seat belts or read the fine print of their contracts. As a result, they impute more stability to the CMO tranches that get first claim on prepayments that fall within some seemingly safe speed range. When these conditions are met, which is most of the time, these tranches offer much more generous spreads over the curve than the corporate bullets with which they are often compared. But when the conditions are not met, some of these tranches deteriorate quickly as, for example, when unusually high prepayments are used to pay off the super-POs and thereby reduce the cushion against subsequent unusually low speeds. The super POs, in turn, are correspondingly undervalued by the underestimation of their benefits in a high speed environment.

People mistakenly try to analyze these complex bonds within a conventional cash flow framework. But their cash flows have no rhyme or reason apart from their impact on the bond's performance, which itself can be estimated only with additional programs. As a result, the knowledge we can gain about these bonds is indirect and analytical rather than hands-on and intuitive. This development is one more step in the evolution of fixed income markets from the tangible world of loans and pay backs to the abstract world of performance profiles and attributes. Denying this process by forcing these bonds into conventional molds is futile.

## Yield Surface

The yield surface is a three-dimensional yield curve that makes yield a function of both duration and convexity. Each point on the surface represents a triplet of adjusted duration ($D_i^*$), adjusted convexity ($C_j^*$), and time value, or yield ($R_{ij}$), the i and j being any numbers. The "adjustments" are for relative yield changes as described in Equations 5A and 5B. The surface is generated by inserting any values of $D_i^*$ and $C_j^*$ in Equation 6, the parameters of which are estimated in the course of fitting the strip curve, and calculating the associated $R_{ij}$. Each pair of $D_i^*$ and $C_j^*$ gives a unique value of $R_{ij}$, which is the time value associated with the $i^{th}$ adjusted duration and the $ji^{th}$ adjusted convexity.

Although there are infinitely more points on the surface than there are actual bonds, they should not be regarded as hypothetical, for each one can be synthesized with long and short positions in any three bonds (a, b, and c) lying on the strip curve (or elsewhere on the surface). In other words, each $R_{ij}$ calculated with Equation 7 for a given pair of $D_i^*$ and $C_i^*$ can be recreated by solving three equations for the position weights, $X_a$, $X_b$, and $X_c$, of the three arbitrarily chosen bonds.

For example, to synthesize the triplet $D_i^*$, $C_j^*$, and $R_{ij}$ with bonds a, b, and c, solve the following equations for the position weights:

$$X_a D_a^* + X_b D_b^* + X_c D_c^* = D_i^*$$

$$X_a C_a^* + X_b C_b^* + X_c C_c^* = C_j^*$$

$$X_a + X_b + X_c = 1$$

Then, having determined the values of $X_a$, $X_b$, and $X_c$, solve the following equation for $R_{ij}$.

$$X_a R_a + X_b R_b + X_c R_c = R_{ij}$$

It will be the same as the one calculated with Equation 6, as long as the three bond yields lie on the surface. Therefore, every point on the surface can be accounted for either with the equation or with a synthetic calculated in the manner just described.

One big advantage of the surface over a two-dimensional yield curve is that it works for synthetics as well as individual bonds. Same duration dumbbells, for example, lie on the same surface, but not on the same yield curve, as their matching bullets. The reason is that, for a given duration, the surface implies a different yield for each convexity, while the yield curve implies only one yield, no matter what the convexity is. That is why the surface can accommodate synthetics, as well as callable bonds, which have different convexities for the same duration, while the yield curve is limited to bullets.

Separating the yield impacts of duration and convexity has become much more important with the emergence of mortgage products, especially CMOs, with their often exotic parametric combinations. With current treasuries, on the other hand, each duration has its particular convexity, which makes it seem as if yield is related to duration alone. But with mortgages (or callable bonds), as well as with synthetics, the convexity at a given duration level can be anything and create the appearance of an unstable relationship between yield and duration instead of a stable one alongside a different one between yield and convexity.

This point was clarified for me when a customer declined an offering of a super PO at even yield with an ordinary PO that was shorter and much less convex. The customer insisted on getting a higher yield on the longer PO to cover the carrying cost of his hedging it to the shorter PO's duration. Although he knew he had to give up yield for convexity on an equal-duration trade, he thought that a positively-sloped yield curve entitled him to more yield for more duration, irrespective of the greater convexity that goes with it, and relied on the hedging cost to determine how much. But if he had hedged the longer bond to the shorter bond's duration, he would have retained the longer bond's convexity, less the much smaller amount of convexity embodied in the hedging instrument he was selling. Therefore, he would have wound up with the shorter PO's duration but with much more convexity, for which he should have been willing to give up yield. Even yield would have been a gift. It is no longer available.

But the question remains, how much yield should he have been willing to give up? That depends on the yield value of the added convexity less the yield value of the added duration and less the yield value of the convexity lost in the course of lowering duration. A number like that does not roll off the fingers. But the surface provides it easily because it makes the yield impacts of duration and convexity independent of each other. The proper yield differential between the super and ordinary PO is simply the difference between the yields at their respective duration-convexity intersections on the surface.

They can be read from a table like the one in Exhibit 8A. Across any row are the time values for a given adjusted duration and any adjusted convexity. Down any column are the time values for a given adjusted convexity and any adjusted duration. In either case, the time value change per unit parameter change is the same at all parameter levels, which means that the relationship between time value and either parameter is linear when the other parameter is held constant (or when it also is allowed to change linearly). The range of positive and negative time values is unlimited.

The table in 8B is merely a denser version of the one in 8A, focusing on the parameter ranges found in ordinary bonds. To locate the point corresponding to an actual bond, you calculate first its adjusted duration and convexity and then find them in the table. (Since the time value changes are linear along both rows and columns, interpolation is simple.) The difference between two time values in the table representing the adjusted durations and convexities of any two bonds measures the part of their gross spread that is ascribable to their parametric differences. Any remaining yield difference represents a pure sectorial spread.

The calculations needed to locate individual bonds on the surface are illustrated in Exhibit 9. The duration, convexity, and time value are calculated separately for each bond with the means at disposal. With callable securities some sort of option model is needed to calculate them. The $W_i$ are always calculated for call-free bonds. The means for doing that are provided in the course of fitting the strip curve which, among other things, results in a function that relates to each duration (i) a value, $W_i$. (My earlier article described such a function.) With callable bonds, the $W_i$ refers to the underlying call-free bond, the yield on which is assumed to drive the call-free price which, in turn, drives the option price, with the two of them, finally, determining the callable bond price. The $W_i$ affects the latter price only through the call-free yield. It has no direct effect on the option.

## Exhibit 8A. Treasury Time-Value Surface, 9/21/88

| | Adjusted Convexity | | | | | | | | | | |
|---|---|---|---|---|---|---|---|---|---|---|---|
| | -2.000 | -1.200 | -0.400 | 0.400 | 1.200 | 2.000 | 2.800 | 3.600 | 4.400 | 5.200 | 6.000 |
| -15.000 | 7.977 | 7.081 | 6.184 | 5.287 | 4.391 | 3.494 | 2.597 | 1.700 | 0.804 | -0.093 | -0.990 |
| -13.875 | 8.151 | 7.255 | 6.358 | 5.461 | 4.564 | 3.668 | 2.771 | 1.874 | 0.978 | 0.081 | -0.816 |
| -12.750 | 8.325 | 7.428 | 6.532 | 5.635 | 4.738 | 3.842 | 2.945 | 2.048 | 1.151 | 0.255 | -0.642 |
| -11.625 | 8.499 | 7.602 | 6.705 | 5.809 | 4.912 | 4.015 | 3.119 | 2.222 | 1.325 | 0.429 | -0.468 |
| -10.500 | 8.673 | 7.776 | 6.879 | 5.983 | 5.086 | 4.189 | 3.292 | 2.396 | 1.499 | 0.602 | -0.294 |
| -9.375 | 8.847 | 7.950 | 7.053 | 6.156 | 5.260 | 4.363 | 3.466 | 2.570 | 1.673 | 0.776 | -0.121 |
| -8.250 | 9.020 | 8.124 | 7.227 | 6.330 | 5.434 | 4.537 | 3.640 | 2.743 | 1.847 | 0.950 | 0.053 |
| -7.125 | 9.194 | 8.298 | 7.401 | 6.504 | 5.607 | 4.711 | 3.814 | 2.917 | 2.021 | 1.124 | 0.227 |
| -6.000 | 9.368 | 8.471 | 7.575 | 6.678 | 5.781 | 4.885 | 3.988 | 3.091 | 2.194 | 1.298 | 0.401 |
| -4.875 | 9.542 | 8.645 | 7.748 | 6.852 | 5.955 | 5.058 | 4.162 | 3.265 | 2.368 | 1.471 | 0.575 |
| -3.750 | 9.716 | 8.819 | 7.922 | 7.026 | 6.129 | 5.232 | 4.335 | 3.439 | 2.542 | 1.645 | 0.749 |
| -2.625 | 9.890 | 8.993 | 8.096 | 7.199 | 6.303 | 5.406 | 4.509 | 3.613 | 2.716 | 1.819 | 0.922 |
| -1.500 | 10.063 | 9.167 | 8.270 | 7.373 | 6.477 | 5.580 | 4.683 | 3.786 | 2.890 | 1.993 | 1.096 |
| -0.375 | 10.237 | 9.340 | 8.444 | 7.547 | 6.650 | 5.754 | 4.857 | 3.960 | 3.064 | 2.167 | 1.270 |
| 0.750 | 10.411 | 9.514 | 8.618 | 7.721 | 6.824 | 5.927 | 5.031 | 4.134 | 3.237 | 2.341 | 1.444 |
| 1.875 | 10.585 | 9.688 | 8.791 | 7.895 | 6.998 | 6.101 | 5.205 | 4.308 | 3.411 | 2.514 | 1.618 |
| 3.000 | 10.759 | 9.862 | 8.965 | 8.069 | 7.172 | 6.275 | 5.378 | 4.482 | 3.585 | 2.688 | 1.792 |
| 4.125 | 10.933 | 10.036 | 9.139 | 8.242 | 7.346 | 6.449 | 5.552 | 4.656 | 3.759 | 2.862 | 1.965 |
| 5.250 | 11.106 | 10.210 | 9.313 | 8.416 | 7.520 | 6.623 | 5.726 | 4.829 | 3.933 | 3.036 | 2.139 |
| 6.375 | 11.280 | 10.383 | 9.487 | 8.590 | 7.693 | 6.797 | 5.900 | 5.003 | 4.106 | 3.210 | 2.313 |
| 7.500 | 11.454 | 10.557 | 9.661 | 8.764 | 7.867 | 6.970 | 6.074 | 5.177 | 4.280 | 3.384 | 2.487 |
| 8.625 | 11.628 | 10.731 | 9.834 | 8.938 | 8.041 | 7.144 | 6.248 | 5.351 | 4.454 | 3.557 | 2.661 |
| 9.750 | 11.802 | 10.905 | 10.008 | 9.112 | 8.215 | 7.318 | 6.421 | 5.525 | 4.628 | 3.731 | 2.835 |
| 10.875 | 11.975 | 11.079 | 10.182 | 9.285 | 8.389 | 7.492 | 6.595 | 5.699 | 4.802 | 3.905 | 3.008 |
| 12.000 | 12.149 | 11.253 | 10.356 | 9.459 | 8.562 | 7.666 | 6.769 | 5.872 | 4.976 | 4.079 | 3.182 |
| 13.125 | 12.323 | 11.426 | 10.530 | 9.633 | 8.736 | 7.840 | 6.943 | 6.046 | 5.149 | 4.253 | 3.356 |
| 14.250 | 12.497 | 11.600 | 10.704 | 9.807 | 8.910 | 8.013 | 7.117 | 6.220 | 5.323 | 4.427 | 3.530 |
| 15.375 | 12.671 | 11.774 | 10.877 | 9.981 | 9.084 | 8.187 | 7.291 | 6.394 | 5.497 | 4.600 | 3.704 |
| 16.500 | 12.845 | 11.948 | 11.051 | 10.155 | 9.258 | 8.361 | 7.464 | 6.568 | 5.671 | 4.774 | 3.878 |
| 17.625 | 13.018 | 12.122 | 11.225 | 10.328 | 9.432 | 8.535 | 7.638 | 6.741 | 5.845 | 4.948 | 4.051 |
| 18.750 | 13.192 | 12.296 | 11.399 | 10.502 | 9.605 | 8.709 | 7.812 | 6.915 | 6.019 | 5.122 | 4.225 |
| 19.875 | 13.366 | 12.469 | 11.573 | 10.676 | 9.779 | 8.883 | 7.986 | 7.089 | 6.192 | 5.296 | 4.399 |
| 21.000 | 13.540 | 12.643 | 11.747 | 10.850 | 9.953 | 9.056 | 8.160 | 7.263 | 6.366 | 5.470 | 4.573 |
| 22.125 | 13.714 | 12.817 | 11.920 | 11.024 | 10.127 | 9.230 | 8.334 | 7.437 | 6.540 | 5.643 | 4.747 |
| 23.250 | 13.888 | 12.991 | 12.094 | 11.197 | 10.301 | 9.404 | 8.507 | 7.611 | 6.714 | 5.817 | 4.920 |
| 24.375 | 14.061 | 13.165 | 12.268 | 11.371 | 10.475 | 9.578 | 8.681 | 7.784 | 6.888 | 5.991 | 5.094 |
| 25.500 | 14.235 | 13.339 | 12.442 | 11.545 | 10.648 | 9.752 | 8.855 | 7.958 | 7.062 | 6.165 | 5.268 |
| 26.625 | 14.409 | 13.512 | 12.616 | 11.719 | 10.822 | 9.926 | 9.029 | 8.132 | 7.235 | 6.339 | 5.442 |
| 27.750 | 14.583 | 13.686 | 12.790 | 11.893 | 10.996 | 10.099 | 9.203 | 8.306 | 7.409 | 6.513 | 5.616 |
| 28.875 | 14.757 | 13.860 | 12.963 | 12.067 | 11.170 | 10.273 | 9.376 | 8.480 | 7.583 | 6.686 | 5.790 |
| 30.000 | 14.931 | 14.034 | 13.137 | 12.240 | 11.344 | 10.447 | 9.550 | 8.654 | 7.757 | 6.860 | 5.963 |

## Exhibit 8B. Treasury Time-Value Surface, 9/21/88

| | | | | | Adjusted Convexity | | | | | | |
|---|---|---|---|---|---|---|---|---|---|---|---|
| | | 0.000 | 0.220 | 0.440 | 0.660 | 0.880 | 1.100 | 1.320 | 1.540 | 1.760 | 1.980 | 2.200 |
| | 0.000 | 8.053 | 7.807 | 7.560 | 7.314 | 7.067 | 6.820 | 6.574 | 6.327 | 6.081 | 5.834 | 5.587 |
| | 0.500 | 8.131 | 7.884 | 7.637 | 7.391 | 7.144 | 6.898 | 6.651 | 6.404 | 6.158 | 5.911 | 5.665 |
| | 1.000 | 8.208 | 7.961 | 7.715 | 7.468 | 7.221 | 6.975 | 6.728 | 6.482 | 6.235 | 5.989 | 5.742 |
| | 1.500 | 8.285 | 8.039 | 7.792 | 7.545 | 7.299 | 7.052 | 6.806 | 6.559 | 6.312 | 6.066 | 5.819 |
| | 2.000 | 8.362 | 8.116 | 7.869 | 7.623 | 7.376 | 7.129 | 6.883 | 6.636 | 6.390 | 6.143 | 5.896 |
| | 2.500 | 8.440 | 8.193 | 7.946 | 7.700 | 7.453 | 7.207 | 6.960 | 6.713 | 6.467 | 6.220 | 5.974 |
| | 3.000 | 8.517 | 8.270 | 8.024 | 7.777 | 7.531 | 7.284 | 7.037 | 6.791 | 6.544 | 6.298 | 6.051 |
| | 3.500 | 8.594 | 8.348 | 8.101 | 7.854 | 7.608 | 7.361 | 7.115 | 6.868 | 6.621 | 6.375 | 6.128 |
| | 4.000 | 8.671 | 8.425 | 8.178 | 7.932 | 7.685 | 7.438 | 7.192 | 6.945 | 6.699 | 6.452 | 6.205 |
| | 4.500 | 8.749 | 8.502 | 8.255 | 8.009 | 7.762 | 7.516 | 7.269 | 7.023 | 6.776 | 6.529 | 6.283 |
| | 5.000 | 8.826 | 8.579 | 8.333 | 8.086 | 7.840 | 7.593 | 7.346 | 7.100 | 6.853 | 6.607 | 6.360 |
| | 5.500 | 8.903 | 8.657 | 8.410 | 8.163 | 7.917 | 7.670 | 7.424 | 7.177 | 6.930 | 6.684 | 6.437 |
| | 6.000 | 8.980 | 8.734 | 8.487 | 8.241 | 7.994 | 7.747 | 7.501 | 7.254 | 7.008 | 6.761 | 6.514 |
| | 6.500 | 9.058 | 8.811 | 8.565 | 8.318 | 8.071 | 7.825 | 7.578 | 7.332 | 7.085 | 6.838 | 6.592 |
| | 7.000 | 9.135 | 8.888 | 8.642 | 8.395 | 8.149 | 7.902 | 7.655 | 7.409 | 7.162 | 6.916 | 6.669 |
| | 7.500 | 9.212 | 8.966 | 8.719 | 8.472 | 8.226 | 7.979 | 7.733 | 7.486 | 7.239 | 6.993 | 6.746 |
| | 8.000 | 9.289 | 9.043 | 8.796 | 8.550 | 8.303 | 8.057 | 7.810 | 7.563 | 7.317 | 7.070 | 6.824 |
| Adjusted Duration | 8.500 | 9.367 | 9.120 | 8.874 | 8.627 | 8.380 | 8.134 | 7.887 | 7.641 | 7.394 | 7.147 | 6.901 |
| | 9.000 | 9.444 | 9.197 | 8.951 | 8.704 | 8.458 | 8.211 | 7.964 | 7.718 | 7.471 | 7.225 | 6.978 |
| | 9.500 | 9.521 | 9.275 | 9.028 | 8.781 | 8.535 | 8.288 | 8.042 | 7.795 | 7.548 | 7.302 | 7.055 |
| | 10.000 | 9.599 | 9.352 | 9.105 | 8.859 | 8.612 | 8.366 | 8.119 | 7.872 | 7.626 | 7.379 | 7.133 |
| | 10.500 | 9.676 | 9.429 | 9.183 | 8.936 | 8.689 | 8.443 | 8.196 | 7.950 | 7.703 | 7.456 | 7.210 |
| | 11.000 | 9.753 | 9.506 | 9.260 | 9.013 | 8.767 | 8.520 | 8.273 | 8.027 | 7.780 | 7.534 | 7.287 |
| | 11.500 | 9.830 | 9.584 | 9.337 | 9.090 | 8.844 | 8.597 | 8.351 | 8.104 | 7.858 | 7.611 | 7.364 |
| | 12.000 | 9.908 | 9.661 | 9.414 | 9.168 | 8.921 | 8.675 | 8.428 | 8.181 | 7.935 | 7.688 | 7.442 |
| | 12.500 | 9.985 | 9.738 | 9.492 | 9.245 | 8.998 | 8.752 | 8.505 | 8.259 | 8.012 | 7.765 | 7.519 |
| | 13.000 | 10.062 | 9.815 | 9.569 | 9.322 | 9.076 | 8.829 | 8.582 | 8.336 | 8.089 | 7.843 | 7.596 |
| | 13.500 | 10.139 | 9.893 | 9.646 | 9.400 | 9.153 | 8.906 | 8.660 | 8.413 | 8.167 | 7.920 | 7.673 |
| | 14.000 | 10.217 | 9.970 | 9.723 | 9.477 | 9.230 | 8.984 | 8.737 | 8.490 | 8.244 | 7.997 | 7.751 |
| | 14.500 | 10.294 | 10.047 | 9.801 | 9.554 | 9.307 | 9.061 | 8.814 | 8.568 | 8.321 | 8.074 | 7.828 |
| | 15.000 | 10.371 | 10.124 | 9.878 | 9.631 | 9.385 | 9.138 | 8.892 | 8.645 | 8.398 | 8.152 | 7.905 |
| | 15.500 | 10.448 | 10.202 | 9.955 | 9.709 | 9.462 | 9.215 | 8.969 | 8.722 | 8.476 | 8.229 | 7.982 |
| | 16.000 | 10.526 | 10.279 | 10.032 | 9.786 | 9.539 | 9.293 | 9.046 | 8.799 | 8.553 | 8.306 | 8.060 |
| | 16.500 | 10.603 | 10.356 | 10.110 | 9.863 | 9.616 | 9.370 | 9.123 | 8.877 | 8.630 | 8.383 | 8.137 |
| | 17.000 | 10.680 | 10.434 | 10.187 | 9.940 | 9.694 | 9.447 | 9.201 | 8.954 | 8.707 | 8.461 | 8.214 |
| | 17.500 | 10.757 | 10.511 | 10.264 | 10.018 | 9.771 | 9.524 | 9.278 | 9.031 | 8.785 | 8.538 | 8.291 |
| | 18.000 | 10.835 | 10.588 | 10.341 | 10.095 | 9.848 | 9.602 | 9.355 | 9.108 | 8.862 | 8.615 | 8.369 |
| | 18.500 | 10.912 | 10.665 | 10.419 | 10.172 | 9.926 | 9.679 | 9.432 | 9.186 | 8.939 | 8.693 | 8.446 |
| | 19.000 | 10.989 | 10.743 | 10.496 | 10.249 | 10.003 | 9.756 | 9.510 | 9.263 | 9.016 | 8.770 | 8.523 |
| | 19.500 | 11.066 | 10.820 | 10.573 | 10.327 | 10.080 | 9.833 | 9.587 | 9.340 | 9.094 | 8.847 | 8.600 |
| | 20.000 | 11.144 | 10.897 | 10.650 | 10.404 | 10.157 | 9.911 | 9.664 | 9.417 | 9.171 | 8.924 | 8.678 |

The time value for any bond is its instantaneous rate of return assuming no yield change but allowing for aging along the yield curve. It can be calculated for any security with a positive price. (With fully leveraged positions, which have no market value, the time value can be calculated in arithmetic instead of percentage terms, as simply the instantaneous change in value.) The time value on the surface itself can be calculated by using Equation 6 after inserting the other values, all of which are known. The translation of time value into yield must be based on a particular parameter set and yield curve and requires merely solving for the yield that, in light of the other information, would give the time value.

Since there is no single yield curve relating yield to duration, but rather a different one for each collection of duration-convexity pairs, the "yield curve" I referred to a moment ago is really the yield surface. That means a bond's time value is actually the change in its value (including accrued interest) resulting from a change in its adjusted duration and convexity over an instant, assuming no autonomous yield change.

## Call-Adjusted Spreads

The widely recognized dependency of yield on both duration and convexity has brought forth a variety of so-called option-adjusted spreads on callable bonds and mortgages (hereafter, callable

**Exhibit 9.  Surface Values Coinciding with the Parameters of Selected Bonds, 9/21/88**

|                      | $D$    | $C$   | $W$   | $D^*$  | $C^*$ | $R$   |
|----------------------|--------|-------|-------|--------|-------|-------|
| 5-Year Strip         | 4.789  | 0.126 | 0.943 | 4.519  | 0.112 | 8.626 |
| 5-Year Strip         | 9.562  | 0.480 | 0.891 | 8.527  | 0.382 | 8.943 |
| 5-Year Strip         | 19.113 | 1.872 | 0.799 | 15.269 | 1.195 | 9.073 |
| 5-Year Strip         | 28.239 | 4.055 | 0.722 | 20.396 | 2.115 | 8.834 |
| 10-Year Current Bond | 6.488  | 0.281 | 0.925 | 6.000  | 0.241 | 8.710 |
| 30-Year Current Bond | 10.211 | 0.898 | 0.885 | 9.036  | 0.703 | 8.661 |

bonds). The surface provides a convenient reference for such calculations; spreading two bond yields off the surface at their own values of adjusted duration and convexity effectively "adjusts" the gross yield spread between the bonds for the impact of their parametric differences.

The need for an "adjustment" (as in call-adjusted spread, not to be confused with the relative yield change adjustment) is based on the convenience of separating gross yields into a generic part and a basis. The generic part is what the market pays people for taking on a given duration and convexity, irrespective of the bonds used to get them. That means one gets a given yield for having a certain duration and a certain convexity, however one got them. The surface describes these yields for all possible adjusted duration-convexity pairs. The spread off the surface effectively eliminates the generic part of a gross yield. The remainder is associated with such things as credit quality, liquidity, prepayment risk, event risk, as well as unexplained effects that people collect under the term "basis."

This separation is the heart of hedging, which usually connotes a position with gross attributes on one side and generic attributes on the other, with either side including its appropriate time value or yield.[5] The difference between the sides, i.e., the basis, comprises the non-generic attributes and their associated yield. In fact, hedging is often thought of as basis management. The reason for holding this kind of position is either to lock in an extra yield on the basis or to gain from an expected basis yield change, having eliminated the generic yield changes from both sides. One can, of course, take a stand on one or more of the generic attributes as well, the most popular one now being the income convexity tradeoff I mentioned earlier. In this case, instead of equating the convexities of both sides the way one usually equates the durations, one consciously gives one side more convexity at the expense of income or more income at the expense of convexity. Strictly speak-

---

5. When the "arbitrage" position represents the assets and liabilities of a financial institution, the name of the subject becomes asset-liability management, which is merely arbitrage writ large, with the basis representing the institution's vantage point. When the latter does not contain enough spread, or juice, the institution must fall back on accepting some combination of generic risks. Optimizing this combination is for many of them the heart of their asset-liability management.

ing, that should not be called arbitrage any more than intended duration gaps are because both are generic; however, current convention regards the income-convexity trade-off, not the duration imbalance, as arbitrage.

Distinguishing the basis from the generic components of these positions is essential to their success. People too often attribute the higher yields on corporates and mortgages to the basis instead of the generic effect of accepting lower convexity. If they properly hedged this "basis" by holding the same duration and convexity, not just duration, on both sides, they would give back the higher income they got for accepting less convexity. That is, in fact, how one can distinguish basis from generic income: is it still there after a proper hedge?

A bond's spread off the surface is the difference between its time value and that on the surface at the same adjusted duration and convexity. It represents what is left of the total time value after the generic component is removed.

In this respect, it differs from most other call-adjusted spreads, which are calculated in one of two ways: one method estimates the price of the embedded option and then converts it into a yield equivalent, usually by adding the option price to the callable bond price and then recalculating the yield. Since this hypothetical call-free bond's duration is greater than the callable bond's, this method understates the yield equivalent of the option's estimated dollar-impact on performance. The other method lowers the conventional yield by some estimate of the underperformance of the callable relative to a same-duration call-free bond over a range of symmetrical yield changes driven by an assumed volatility. In both cases, the call-adjusted spread is the difference between the adjusted yield and the yield on the curve at the same duration.

In either approach, a change in the value of convexity, due, for example, to a change in perceived volatility, affects the bond's call-adjusted yield but not that of the Treasury curve that serves as the reference. Since convexity, like duration, contributes to the generic component of yield, a change in its value should be recognized not only in the bond but in the reference yield as well—both yields determine the spread. Otherwise, the conventional call-adjusted spread and, more important, its changes over time will reflect not just the changes in the basis yield but in the generic value of convexity as well. This is not so with the surface which keeps up with the value of convexity.

That can be seen in Exhibit 10 which gives weekly observations of the time values of various GNMAs and their surface counterparts over the past year. The curves pick up the spread widening that occurred in October 1987 and the subsequent tightening down to the present. Panel F shows the widely recognized tightening of GNMA 13 spreads, which it attributes more to the upward movement of the surface at the GNMA 13's coeval adjusted duration and convexity than to the GNMA's time values falling. As a result, people who were long these bonds would not have enjoyed the gain from this tightening unless they were also short the surface.

The remarkable correlations between the GNMA time values and their surface counterparts inspire a healthy skepticism about the independence of the two calculations, although none that I am able to validate. The upper curves in Exhibit 10 plot simply the no-change rates of return (RORs) of each GNMA, invoking the option model only to value the GNMA at the horizon in calculating the RORs. The lower curves are the time values on the surface calculated at the same adjusted durations and convexities as the GNMAs. The option model is invoked only to calculate the GNMA's duration and convexity, the $W_i$ (for the adjustment) being taken from the underlying reference bond. The surface itself is calculated in the way I described earlier. It is hard to see how these calculations would cause a spurious correlation between the two sets of curves.

These correlations are lower for the higher coupons, whether because they are more subject to the technical market conditions arising from their use as CMO collateral or because they put more strain on YK's option model.

The inverse relationship between coupon and spread is shown more clearly in Exhibit 11. Since the higher coupons have lower convexities, they are expected to and, indeed, have higher spreads over the yield curve (not shown—i.e., for a given duration) and

## Exhibit 10.

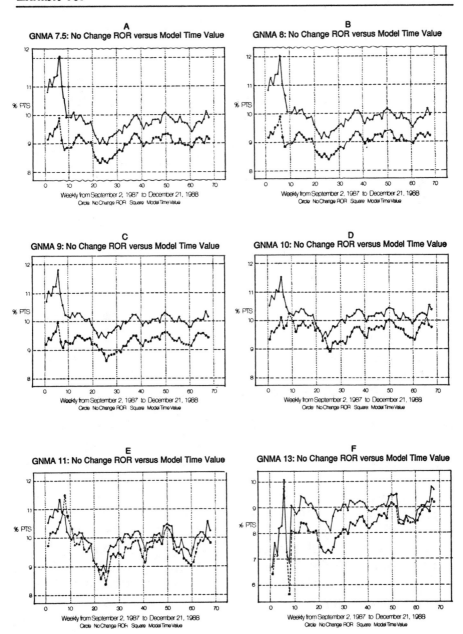

**Exhibit 11. Spreads Off the Yield Surface**

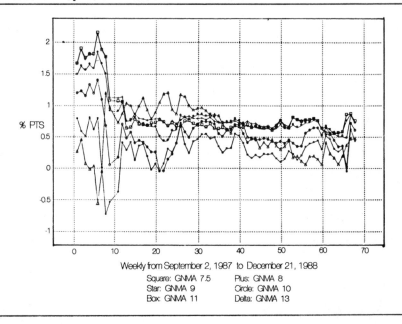

Weekly from September 2, 1987 to December 21, 1988

| | |
|---|---|
| Square: GNMA 7.5 | Plus: GNMA 8 |
| Star: GNMA 9 | Circle: GNMA 10 |
| Box: GNMA 11 | Delta: GNMA 13 |

often higher absolute yields. But when adjusted for duration and convexity, i.e., spread off the surface, their yields are lower. This probably reflects the excess demand of current income buyers, like most S&Ls and some mutual funds, in the face of a relatively inelastic supply of the 11s and higher coupons and the withdrawal of the 10s from the floating supply for use as CMO collateral. As long as these GNMAs yield more on an absolute or duration-only-adjusted basis, these buyers are willing to accept lower yields on a duration-and-convexity adjusted basis, as reflected by their lower spreads off the surface. The lower coupons, on the other hand, have been good buys, offering about twice the spreads of agencies (not shown) on a fully adjusted basis. But, here again, as in the case of super POs that I described earlier, part of their apparent cheapness is compensation for the uncertainty about the prepayment estimates and the magnitudes of the parameters that are based on them. To the extent any estimation errors are random over time, they should wash out, as long as people give them the time to do so. But if the errors are biased, they then constitute a new risk.

## Empirical Yield Curves

I explained earlier how yield curves, though seemingly relating yield to duration alone, embody the effect of convexity as well. That is why the ordinary and strip yield curves shown in Exhibit 12 are different even where their durations overlap. But, notwithstanding people's appreciation for the effect of convexity on yield and their knowledge of the convexity difference between strips and coupon bonds, the prevailing explanation of the difference between the curves does not involve convexity. Instead, through the

**Exhibit 12. Strip and Parbond Curves versus Adjusted Duration**

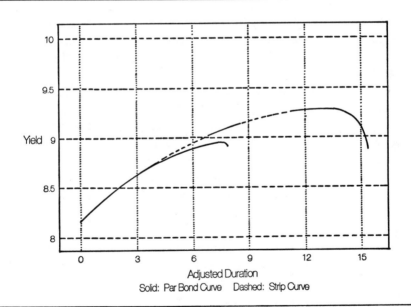

Adjusted Duration
Solid: Par Bond Curve    Dashed: Strip Curve

so-called spot-curve,[6] it relates the difference to a shortcoming in the way conventional yields are calculated: since these yields are associated with bonds rather than times, the 2-year coupon on 5- and 10-year bonds are discounted at different rates. In contrast, the spot method discounts all coupons paid at the same time at the same rate, irrespective of the yields on the bonds to which they are attached.

In rough terms, the spot curve method works as follows: it discounts the 6-month coupon on the 1-year bond at the 6-month spot rate and subtracts the present value from the one-year bond price. That leaves an adjusted price at the beginning and a bullet (coupon and principal) at the end, from which it calculates the 1-year spot rate. The 6-month and 1-year spot rates are used to discount the first two coupons of the 18-month bond, with the resulting present values being subtracted from its price, leaving an adjusted price at the beginning and a bullet at the end, from which it calculates an 18-month spot rate. In this fashion, it calculates the whole spot curve.

This method succeeds in capturing the faster rise and subsequent decline of the strip relative to the ordinary yield curve, but with a waviness that is out of keeping with a theoretical curve. The main reason for this property is that the coupons on two consecutive bonds, six months apart, share all but the last discount rate, which must absorb the whole difference between their conventional yields. As a result, when the latter are rising along the curve, the spot rates rise faster; and when falling, the spot rates fall faster as well. But, since the original yields do not lie along a smooth curve, the method of concentrating the whole conventional yield difference on the final discount rate which is, in fact, the spot rate, makes the latter more volatile than the strip yields they are supposed to describe.

Moreover, the rough similarity between the strip and spot curves appears to be merely an accidental effect of the spot curve's exaggerating the curvature of the ordinary yield curve. The yield curve shape that it is exaggerating has little to do with the differ-

---

6. The spot rate is a curious misnomer: the rate from which it is being differentiated, namely the conventional yield to maturity, is also a spot rate; it also originates in the present in contrast to a forward rate which originates in the future.

ence between spot and ordinary yields, but depends instead on the duration and convexity influences I've been describing, which the spot curve merely inherits.

Instead of inferring the strip from the coupon curve with the spot rate method, Equation 6, as I showed earlier, fits a curve directly to the strip yields. Avram Altavas used that curve, in turn, to reconstitute the yields on ordinary bonds in a reverse spot curve approach. Working with one bond at a time, he discounted each of its coupons and principal by the same-duration yields on the strip curve, with the 2-year coupon discounted at the 2-year yield, the 3-year coupon at the 3-year yield, and so on. The sum of the resulting present values is the reconstituted price which, in theory, is what an ordinary bond can be stripped and sold for on the strip market. The difference between that and the actual price is the stripper's profit or loss.

The reconstituted replaces the actual price in calculating the reconstituted yield. What makes this yield interesting is that it gives a much smoother yield curve than do the actual Treasury yields, as illustrated in Exhibit 13. Panel A plots the actual and Panel B the reconstituted yields versus duration. As is usually the case with actual-yield curves, the intermediate yields sag below the implied curve. That is not the case with the reconstituted yields, which form a nice, clean line.

The string of these reconstituted yields is equivalent to a current-bond yield curve extracted from the surface. Exhibit 14 gives a smooth curve taken from the surface in the following way: a hypothetical bond is created at each duration such that its coupon and yield are equal, which determines its convexity as well. A string of these yields comprises a current-bond yield curve, which is superimposed on the reconstituted yields, making it appear as if it were fitted to them.

Frankly, I do not know why the reconstituted yields and the current-bond curve extracted from the surface are so smooth, while the actual yields sag in the intermediate sector. But the smoothness comes at the cost of substituting theoretical for actual prices. That is a real loss—a bond's price, as distinct from its yield, duration, and convexity, is one of the few facts one encounters in

**Exhibit 13.**

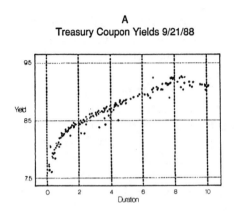

**A**
Treasury Coupon Yields 9/21/88

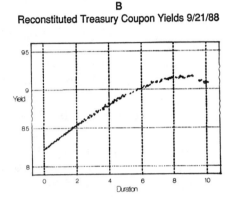

**B**
Reconstituted Treasury Coupon Yields 9/21/88

**Exhibit 14. Parbond Curves and Reconstituted Yields versus Duration, 9/21/88**

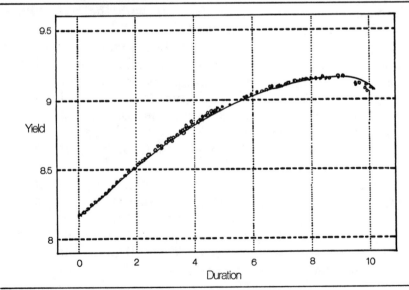

this work, and one does not like to ignore a fact. The problem is that ordinary and strip yields are not entirely consistent, although the inconsistency is usually too small to make remedial arbitrage worthwhile. Why it exists at all deserves an explanation.

Ultimately, what I am calling reconstituted yields should replace conventional yields and end the problem that the spot curve is intended to resolve. The strip curve is better suited than the conventional curve to be the arbiter of value because it is cleaner, being the only case where yield really is defined and having only one yield per duration. One reflection of its superiority is that it can be directly fitted far more accurately than the conventional curve notwithstanding the supposedly lower liquidity and, hence, presumably greater pricing errors of strips.

## Inverted Yield Curves

The main problem people have had with the duration-convexity model of the yield curve has been its inability to explain the shape of inverted yield curves. According to the model, a dumbbell should yield more than a same-duration bullet because it is more convex. But that is not the case when (as they usually are) inverted curves are concave from above. Then the dumbbell line lies above the curve, as shown in Exhibit 15A, which plots a replica of a typical inverted yield curve prevailing in 1980.[7] A dumbbell line connecting any two points on the curve, measuring the average yield at any duration, lies above the curve, which means each dumbbell has a higher yield than its same-duration bullet. This higher yield, combined with the dumbbell's higher convexity, is in conflict with the inverse relationship between them implied by the present model.

But an upwardly concave yield curve is not possible with the model described in Equation 6: with its middle (or duration) term held constant, all pairs of the yield and convexity terms must add up to the single short-term rate. As a result, if yield is higher, con-

---

7. Since there were no strips in 1980, Avram Altavas inferred one from a conventional curve of November 6, 1980, using the reverse of the reconstituted yield procedure. He fitted the inferred strip yields in the same way as he fitted the more recent actual strip yields.

vexity must be lower, or the converse. Therefore, a dumbbell cannot have both a higher yield and more convexity than a same-duration bullet.

The resolution of the apparent conflict between the model and observed yield curves lies in adjusting duration and convexity by the relative yield change factor, W. Equation 6 implies no particular relationship between yield and convexity for a given duration but rather between yield (or, more accurately, time value) and adjusted convexity for a given adjusted duration. Therefore, the model must be tested with a yield curve plotted against adjusted, not plain, duration.

An example of such a curve is given in Exhibit 15B. Substituting adjusted for plain duration has the effect of compressing the horizontal axis, much as logarithms do. As a result, the curve flips over and becomes concave from below, like a positively-sloped yield curve, and the dumbbell line winds up below the curve.

This resolution of what has been a major theoretical problem is no mere academic quibble. Instead, like the well-behaved strip curves the model produces, it confirms the importance the model attaches to the relative yield change adjustment of duration and convexity. If this adjustment was not appropriate and, therefore, the resolution of the problem an empty formalism, the strip curve estimated in the course of calculating the adjustments would fit the strip yields poorly. In other words, the observable quality of the fitted curve is a measure of the substantive value of the adjustment.

Behind this adjustment is the idea that people are ultimately concerned with a bond's price changes, not yield changes, and look to the latter only to estimate the former. Some index of estimated relative price change appears to be an important determinant of relative yield levels. By itself (i.e., unadjusted) duration does not serve this role.

The relative yield change adjustment, whatever allegory is used to motivate it, is basically a means of making duration a better index of how the market ranks the potential price changes of different bonds. Better indexes, as well as more useful random variables than the short-term yield, will emerge in the future, and

**Exhibit 15A. Strip Yield versus Duration, Treasury Strip Curve
Inferred from Current Bond Yields, 11/6/80**

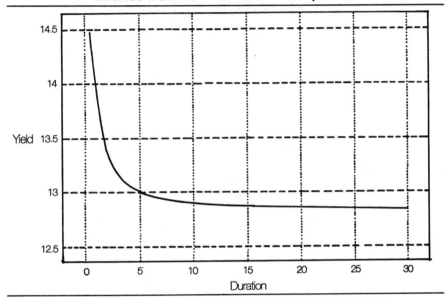

**Exhibit 15B. Strip Yield versus Adjusted Duration, 11/6/80**

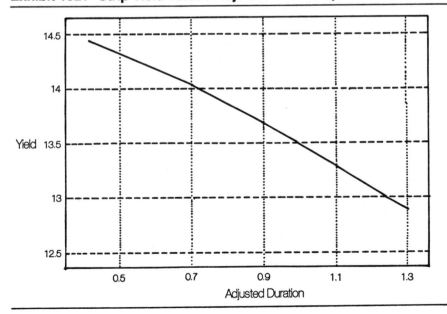

the models that depend on them will win out. But not because they are based on more plausible assumptions or their underlying metaphors have more verisimilitude, but because they more accurately describe the market data.

# Chapter 5

# Valuing Debt Securities Under Uncertainty: The Option-Adjusted Spread Model

**David Sykes**
**Bear, Stearns & Co. Inc.**

## Introduction[1]

The last decade has seen extraordinary changes in the fixed income markets. Along with the massive growth of the secondary mortgage market, there has been a tremendous increase in the diversity and level of sophistication of the products available in virtually every sector. Indeed, the term "fixed income market" has become a misnomer especially considering the proliferation of securities that have interest-rate-contingent cash flows, as do callable bonds, floating rate securities, and virtually all mortgage products. Thus, with the uncertainty of future interest rates, and the often complex relationship of bond cash flows and interest rates, it has become increasingly difficult for market participants to assess the risks and benefits of these securities.

1. The author would like to thank Blaine Roberts, David Chow, Richard Ellson, David Foulds, and Peter Cherasia for helpful discussions; Robert Ge for invaluable programming assistance in developing the Bear Stearns OAS model; Victoria Lee for her graphs and general assistance; and Marie Falvey for final preparation of the manuscript.

Out of the variety of models that have been proposed for evaluating variable cash flow securities, the "Option-Adjusted Spread" (OAS) model stands out clearly as the best available methodology. This chapter describes the theoretical and practical foundations of this emerging new convention. The methodology consists of three basic components:

1. a large sample of potential interest rate paths are generated using a probabilistic model that is consistent with the current term structure;

2. for each rate path, cash flows are generated;

3. a value of the security is found for each future path by discounting the cash flows at the projected risk-free rates plus a spread; this generates a distribution of values for the security; for a given price, the OAS is the spread such that the average of the distribution of values equals that price.

This framework has several notable features:

- OAS is a general stochastic model, equally applicable to all bond investment decisions in a world of uncertainty.

- Discount rates are derived from the entire term structure and, thus, OAS provides a much more accurate valuation of time to receipt than if a single discount rate is used.

- OAS is a spread over future risk-free rates that takes into account interest rate and any cash flow uncertainty.

- If markets were ideally efficient and complete, and the OAS model's projections perfectly accurate, then any positive OAS would represent a riskless arbitrage.

- Positive OASs are justified to the extent that less than ideal markets result in illiquidity or hedging costs that exceed risk free rates. Compensation may also be required for any credit risk or uncertainty regarding the model's projections.

- As an expected or average value, the OAS valuation is neutral with respect to the dispersion of a security's values across scenarios.

Regarding the last point, OAS assumes that with an accurate assessment of a security's performance under alternative scenarios, pure variability can be hedged away. To the extent that markets are incomplete and thus perfect hedges are not generally feasible, however, variability does represent a risk for which investors must be compensated.

In this chapter we will explore the strengths and limitations of the OAS model in detail. What is clear is that, with the ever increasing levels of sophistication in today's markets, the OAS model is far superior to the traditional yield-to-maturity (YTM) valuation methods. The YTM convention evolved when most bonds were true, fixed cash flow instruments. To "buy and hold" investors of fixed cash flow bonds, YTM valuation is reasonable in as much as the yield spread earned on a duration-matched position is fixed at the time of purchase and is, generally, not subject to change because the projected cash flows do not change. Under these conditions, the uncertainty of future changes in interest rates is of no direct consequence.

This rationale is not sufficient when cash flows are interest rate dependent, however, because YTM valuation is cash flow dependent. That is, as realized cash flows differ from those used in the YTM calculations, realized returns will differ from the YTM. Moreover, using static YTM methods to calculate hedging parameters such as modified duration and convexity may result in a severe misrepresentation of a variable cash flow bond's performance profile. These have been hard lessons for many investors who have persistently applied fixed cash flow YTM valuation and accounting methodologies to variable cash flow securities. Sound economics require that investments in interest-rate-contingent cash flows be valued and managed using techniques that explicitly account for the uncertainty of future interest rates and the variability of cash flows

In the next sections of the chapter, we discuss the theoretical foundation of the OAS framework, the steps necessary to implement the theory and finally the applications of OAS analysis to a variety of mortgage products, including generic fixed coupons, strips, and CMO bonds.

## The Theoretical Framework

*Valuing Time to Receipt: The Term Structure*

Debt securities can differ in a variety of ways: liquidity, credit risk, call features, etc. One characteristic common to all debt instruments, however, is the obligation to deliver a stream of future cash flows. Therefore, the term structure of interest rates is the logical starting point in developing a valuation framework. The term structure refers to the discount rates that the market assigns to cash flows that differ only in terms of their maturity. As a matter of convenience, it is also referred to as the spot rate yield curve for "pure" discount bonds; that is, zero coupon bonds that are highly liquid, and default-free. Given the term structure, any liquid, default-free bond can be valued by interpreting the bond as a portfolio of pure discount bonds and discounting each cash flow by the spot rate corresponding to its time to receipt. As a means of evaluating the "lowest common denominator" among bond characteristics (namely, the time value of money), the term structure provides the foundation for valuing debt securities. The value of any other characteristics of a bond must be regarded as incremental to the value associated with the time to receipt of the cash flows.

*Valuation in a Dynamic, Certain World: The Expectations Hypothesis*

Although the term structure provides a sound basis for evaluating a bond at a given point in time, it does not account for the dynamic aspects of investing in debt securities. As interest rates change over time, the value of a bond investment also changes.

This creates periodic opportunity costs (values) that must be included in any true economic valuation framework. That is, returns should measure not only the cash inflow but also the inter period changes in the value of the investment, since the latter represents an equally valid change in the value of the investor's assets. Thus, to account for the dynamics of bond investing, we need a basis for projecting future values of interest rates.

**Arbitrage-Free Interest Rate Projections.** Dynamics can be incorporated into the static term structure framework by invoking the expectations hypothesis. This hypothesis provides an explanation for the term structure in terms of investor expectations for the one-period rate. It is based on the notion that spot rates will be driven toward equilibrium values that eliminate arbitrage opportunities across maturities. This theory can be explained in terms of a simple example.

Assume that there are only two periods. If the current one-period spot rate is 6.00% and the market expects the one-period rate one period from now to be 8.08%, then the equilibrium value for the current two-period spot rate is 7.035%. This is derived by noting that if an investor plans to invest for two periods by rolling over a sequence of one-period securities, then the investor expects the investment to increase by a factor of $(1.06) \times (1.0808) = 1.1465$, implying a periodic return of 7.035%. Therefore, to prevent arbitrage possibilities the two-year spot rate today must also be 7.035%. This example is summarized in Exhibit 1.

**Exhibit 1.  A Two-Period Term Structure Derived from Investor Expectations**

Expected future value for the one-period rate: 8.08%

| Maturity | Term Structure |
|----------|----------------|
| 1 period | 6% |
| 2 periods | 7.035% |

Conversely, and more central to our purpose, if the current term structure is in equilibrium, then the market's expectation for the one-period rate one period from now, r1, can be extracted by solving:

$$(1.06) \times (1 + r1) = (1.07035)^2$$

Given the 3-year spot rate, we can similarly generate the market expectations for the one-period rate two periods from now, and so forth. Future short-term interest rates derived in this fashion are called *implied forward rates*.

The expectations hypothesis provides a means of projecting a future interest rate path that is arbitrage-free relative to the current term structure. For example, according to the term structure in Exhibit 1, a pure discount bond with a maturity of two periods has a value of:

$$\$87.29 = \$100/(1.07035)^2$$

On the other hand, based on the 8.08% expectation embodied in this term structure, the value of a sequence of one-period pure discount bonds also has a value of:

$$\$87.29 = \$100/(1.06) \times (1.0808)$$

where the $87.29 invested in the first one-period bond matures to $92.53 at the end of period one, and is then reinvested in a second one-period bond which, at the new 8.08% short rate, matures to a value of $100. Thus, the two maturity strategies are equivalent and there is no arbitrage.

Note that whether the investor purchases a two-period security or two sequential one-period securities, the holding period return is 7.035%. By extension, a return of 7.035% would also be earned if a security with a maturity greater than two periods is purchased and resold at the end of period two; the resale value at the end of period two is given by discounting the remaining cash flows across the implied forward path back to period two. Thus, the expectations hypothesis also generates holding period returns that are economically sound as well as arbitrage-free relative to the term structure.

**Dynamic Valuation Under Certainty.** Ignoring the problem of uncertainty, we now have a dynamic framework for assessing the relative value of alternative bond investments. The methodology can be explained in the context of an example.

Consider a two-period bond with cash flows of $40 and $60 at the end of periods one and two, respectively. Using the term structure in Exhibit 1, the "fair" or arbitrage-free value of a sequence of one-period, pure discount bonds that match the bond's cash flows is, as shown in Exhibit 2, $90.11. Thus, if the security is default-free and liquid, it should be priced at $90.11. However, assume the bond is not default-free and is priced at $88.98. We would like to assess the incremental return or spread over risk-free rates that is implied by this lower price. In our dynamic framework, this can be measured by finding the spread over the implied forward path that discounts the securities cash flows to the market price of $88.98. Through a process of iteration, this spread is found to be 85 basis points. The calculation is shown in Exhibit 2.

**Exhibit 2.   Dynamic Valuation of a Two-Period Bond**

| Period | Cash Flows |
|--------|------------|
| 1 | $40 |
| 2 | $60 |

Valued at pure discount rates:

$$\$90.11 = \$40/1.06 + \$60/(1.06) \times (1.0808)$$

Spread implied by market price:

$$\$88.98 = \frac{\$40}{[1 + (6 + .85)/100]}$$

$$+ \frac{\$60}{[1 + (6 + .85)/100] \times [1 + (8.08 + .85)/100]}$$

Thus, the $88.98 price of the bond implies an 85 basis point spread over the projected path of risk-free rates. Alternatively, given the link between the future rate projections and the current term structure, this 85 basis point can be interpreted as the spread earned relative to a portfolio of pure discount bonds that replicates the bond's cash flows.

The dynamic framework provides a sound basis for evaluating relative richness or cheapness. To illustrate, assume that other bonds with default risk comparable to the example in Exhibit 2 are found to earn a spread of 100 basis points over the implied forward path. Then theoretically, the fair price of the Exhibit 2 bond is determined by discounting the cash flows at 100 basis points:

$$\$88.79 = \frac{\$40}{[1 + (6 + 1.0)/100]} + \frac{\$60}{[1 + (6 + 1.0)/100] \times [1 + (8.08 + 1.0)/100]}$$

Thus, comparing the fair price of $88.79 with the hypothetical market price of $88.98, the bond in Exhibit 2 is found to be relatively rich.

**OAS versus Yield Spreads.** This method of calculating spreads is the basic methodology used to calculate an "option-adjusted spread" (OAS). In fact, as discussed below, the spread calculated here can be regarded as the special case of an OAS when there is no interest rate uncertainty. It is arguably superior to the more conventional method of comparing the yield to maturity (YTM) on a bond to the YTM of a risk-free bond (such as a Treasury) that has a comparable maturity. The dynamic OAS methodology fully incorporates the market's assessment of the time value of money: cash flows are discounted along a rate path that reflects the full range of the term structure. Comparing YTMs is, at best, a comparison of average discount rates and, as such, can result in misleading conclusions.

To illustrate, note that the bond in Exhibit 2 has a weighted average life (WAL) of 1.6 periods, and a YTM of 7.614% at the $88.98 price. Interpolating the term structure in Exhibit 1, the 1.6 period pure discount rate is 6.621%. Thus, in contrast to an 85 basis points OAS, the bond has a WAL spread to the term struc-

ture of 99.3 basis points. Now consider a bond perfectly comparable to the bond in Exhibit 2, except that it is a "bullet" with one
cash flow of $100 paid at the end of 1.6 periods. Since the bullet
also has a WAL of 1.6 periods, it would also be priced at 99.3 basis
points over the curve, resulting in a price of $88.92. Thus, under
the yield spreads methodology these two investments are equivalent: both have WAL of 1.6 periods and YTMs of 7.614%. However, at $88.92, the bullet can be shown to have an OAS of 115
basis points versus the 85 basis points of the Exhibit 2 bond.[2] Thus,
the YTM "averaging" of the term structure results in a significant
undervaluation of the bullet in the current environment. In general, the potential for error is greater, the more discount rates differ across maturities, as when the yield curve is either very steep
or very inverted.

The potential for misguided conclusions with yield spreads is
even greater in real life when, for example, a mortgage security
with a WAL of ten years (and cash flows spread out over nearly
30 years) and a ten-year agency bullet are both evaluated relative
to the ten-year Treasury yield, despite the drastic differences in
their cash flows. Moreover, deterministic yield spread comparisons
are even more questionable when the cash flows and, therefore,
the WAL is uncertain, as is the case for virtually all mortgage
products.

### Valuation Under Uncertainty: Summarizing the Possibilities

The future path of the risk-free rate is, of course, uncertain. The
future consists of an infinite number of possibilities, some of
which are more likely than others. So rather than assessing the
value of an investment on the basis of any single scenario, such as
the implied forward path, it seems more reasonable to assess value
in a manner that summarizes the universe of all possible out-

---

2. $88.92 = $100 / (1.07614)^{1.6}$

$$= \frac{\$100}{\{[1 + (6 + 1.15)/100] \times [1 + (7.248 + 1.15)/100]^{.6}\}}$$

where 7.614 is the interpolated spot rate plus the WAL spread of 99.3, and 7.248 is the implied
forward rate interpolated to 1.6 years.

comes. This is especially true when a bond's cash flows are contingent upon the future course of interest rates. To devise a method of summarizing the future, however, we must first define the character of the future possibilities in analytical terms.

We would like the valuation framework under uncertainty to retain the appealing arbitrage-free property developed in the previous section. To the extent that rates deviate from the forward path, however, unexpected arbitrage opportunities will exist. For example, assume that the one-period rate actually goes to 9.00%, in contrast with 8.08% expectation in Exhibit 1. Then, when the $87.29 cost of a two-period bond paying $100 is invested in a one-period bond, it will mature, as before, to $92.53. However, at a new one-period rate of 9.00%, the $92.53 reinvested in a second one-period bond will mature to a value of $101, implying arbitrage opportunities at the original price of $87.29. Ex post, the arbitrage-free price for a two-period investment under this scenario would have been:

$$\$86.55 = \$100/(1.06)(1.09)$$

Thus, different interest rate paths correspond to different fair values. The multitude of possible paths generates an array, or distribution, of "potential" fair values. Which of these values ultimately turn out to be the arbitrage-free price is as uncertain as the course of interest rates itself. Nevertheless, the basic arbitrage idea underlying implied forward rates provides a meaningful basis for an assumption about the "center" of the universe of possible interest rate paths.

**Centering the Universe.** Assume that the observed term structure is consistent with the assumption that the market prices pure discount bonds to equal their expected or average value across all possible evolutions of the short-term rate. That is, the market values pure discount bonds at a price that corresponds to earning a zero (option-adjusted) spread to future risk-free rates. Under this assumption, the central or expected rate path about which all other possible paths are dispersed will depend on the level of interest rate volatility, since in this context, volatility refers to the average annual percent deviation of interest rates from their expected value. Thus, zero volatility corresponds to the case of interest rate certainty since all possible paths will correspond to the expected path and, consequently, the distribution of alternative values for a pure discount bond will correspond to a single price. If this single (expected) price is the market price, then to retain the arbitrage-free property described in the previous section, the expected path must be the implied forward path. Thus, we generalize the earlier arbitrage-free model to uncertainty by modeling certainty as the limiting case of zero volatility.

At positive levels of interest rate volatility, the alternative future paths will become dispersed around the expected path. Thus, the expected path that is consistent with the assumption that pure discount bonds are priced to an OAS of zero clearly depends on the manner in which rates are dispersed; that is, on the mathematical process by which interest rates evolve over time. Thus, to embody this assumption in an OAS model, the rate process must be specified and solved for the appropriate expected path, given the term structure and volatility level.

To illustrate, assume the term structure of Exhibit 1. In addition, assume that there are two equally likely future states of the world, and that the short-term rate evolves at a constant percentage drift, d, plus or minus the volatility rate, v. Thus, if state one occurs, the short-term rate one period hence is 6xexp(v+d); if state two occurs, the short rate will be 6xexp(-v+d). Exhibit 3 presents future rate scenarios at 0% and 20% volatilities in accordance with the assumption that the current term structure price for each pure discount bond is equal to the expected price generated by the model at a zero OAS.

To verify this, consider the pure discount bond paying $100 in period two. It is priced at $87.29 by the current term structure. When there are multiple rate paths, the value of the bond is determined by discounting the cash flows along each path and taking the average. Using the implied forward rate calculated earlier for the case of 0% volatility, the price is $87.29 under either scenario; therefore, the average price is clearly $87.29. Under 20% volatility, however the expected future rate implied by the observed price of

**Exhibit 3.**

Term Structure

| Maturity | Rate |
| --- | --- |
| 1 period | 6.000% |
| 2 periods | 7.035% |

0% Volatility

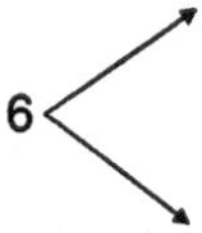

| | |
| --- | --- |
| 8.08 | State 1 |
| 8.08 | State 2 |

Expected Future Rate: 8.08%
Implied Drift Rate: 29.77%

20% Volatility

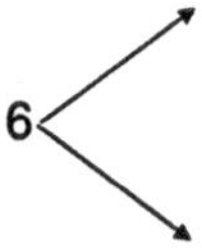

| | |
| --- | --- |
| 9.703 | State 1 |
| 6.504 | State 2 |

Expected Future Rate: 8.10%
Implied Drift Rate: 28.07%

$87.29 is 2 basis points higher at 8.10%. This is determined by solving for the drift term, d, that results in scenario prices that generate an average equal to the target price of $87.29.

**Relative Valuation Under Uncertainty: Fixed Cash Flows.** Consider the bond example in Exhibit 2 which pays $40 and $60 in periods one and two, respectively. Under certainty, this bond had an OAS of 85 basis points at its observed market price of $88.98. Under uncertainty, the process of determining the incremental spread implied by the price of $88.98 is basically the same. In this framework, however, the cash flows are discounted across each path plus a proposed spread to determine a price for each scenario. The average of the resulting prices is then calculated and compared to the given market price. If the average price is higher, a lower spread is tried; if the average price is too low, a higher spread is tried, and so forth until the average price matches the market price.

For the case of 0% volatility, the spread implied by the price of $88.98 is, again, 85 basis points. If we add 85 basis points to the scenarios under 20% volatility, however, the average price is slightly too high at $88.99, implying an OAS greater than 85 basis points. Through iteration, we find the spread that generates an expected price of $88.98 is 85.4 basis points. That is, the bond has an OAS of 85.4 basis points. See Exhibit 4. As explained in the following section, the additional 0.4 basis points reflects the OAS model's valuation of the bonds convexity at 20% volatility.

**Evaluating Convexity with the OAS Framework.** Unlike the naive certainty model, the OAS valuation methodology accounts for the value of a bond's convexity, a characteristic that has no value, or

**Exhibit 4.  OAS Computation at 20% Volatility**

State 1

$$\$88.22 = \frac{\$40}{[1 + (6 + .854)/100]} + \frac{\$60}{[1 + (6 + .854)/100] \times [1 + (9.703 + .854)/100]}$$

State 2

$$\$89.74 = \frac{\$40}{[1 + (6 + .854)/100]} + \frac{\$60}{[1 + (6 + .854)/100] \times [1 + (6.504 + .854)/100]}$$

Expected Price 88.98 = (88.22 = + 89.74) / 2

relevance, in a world of certainty. This feature of OAS analysis is relevant even for fixed cash flow bonds that exhibit a significant degree of positive convexity—for example, long-term bonds trading at a deep discount.

The valuation of convexity can be illustrated graphically by translating the OAS framework into the static terms of a price-yield diagram. In Exhibit 5 the alternative paths of the risk-free rate plus spread are expressed in terms of their YTM equivalents. As such, there is a probability distribution over yields centered on the yield that corresponds to the expected path. The prices associated with each yield (rate path) also have a probability distribution induced by the distribution over yields. The case of certainty is illustrated in Exhibit 5A, where yields equal the "expected" yield with a probability of one and, consequently, the price distribution has converged to the single price associated with the expected yield.

Exhibit 5B presents an illustration of the effect of interest rate uncertainty when there is zero convexity: the price-yield curve is linear. In this case, uncertainty is of no consequence in valuing the security. Because the transformation from yield to price is linear, the expected price corresponds to the price that the price-yield curve associates with the expected yield. Moreover, it is also true that the expected value is independent of the slope of the price-yield curve. Although the dispersion or standard deviation is greater as the curve steepens, the expected value is the same. Thus, OAS valuation is neutral with respect to valuation dispersion. Intuitively, it makes sense that interest rate risk is of no consequence in a linear world since it can always be eliminated by a perfectly accurate hedge. More generally, it also makes sense in any world in which markets are complete in the sense that any security's profile can always be perfectly synthesized by an appropriate combination of instruments.

Buying convexity is often described as taking a bet on interest rate volatility. When a position has net positive convexity, any movement in rates will generate a positive change in the net position. Thus, convexity has greater value, the greater the level of volatility. The OAS framework captures this relationship between

**Exhibit 5.**

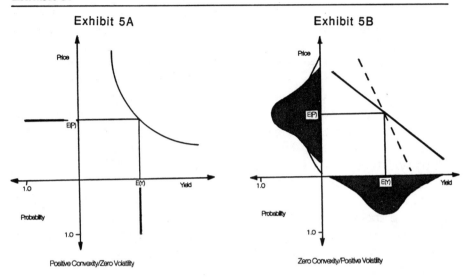

### Exhibit 5A

Price

E(P)

1.0    E(Y)    Yield

Probability

1.0

Positive Convexity/Zero Volatility

### Exhibit 5B

Price

E(P)

1.0    E(Y)    Yield

Probability

1.0

Zero Convexity/Positive Volatility

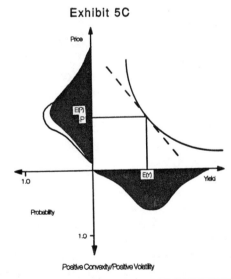

### Exhibit 5C

Price

E(P)
P

1.0    E(Y)    Yield

Probability

1.0

Positive Convexity/Positive Volatility

convexity and volatility. As illustrated in Exhibit 5C, the tendency for price increases to exceed price decreases is reflected in the curvature of the price-yield curve, which takes on a "convex" shape.

In the stochastic OAS framework, the dominance of upside potential over downside causes the induced distribution of prices to be skewed toward values above the expected price associated with zero convexity. That is, positive convexity causes an increase in the expected value of the security and, thus, by considering the difference between the two expected prices (under zero versus positive convexity) the OAS framework generates an expected value of positive convexity. Of course, negative convexity is similarly valued as the expected price is skewed below the zero convexity price. The greater the level of volatility, the more price expectations will be skewed and, thus, the greater the OAS assessment of the value (or cost) of convexity.

This convexity valuation can be translated into basis points by rescaling the yield axis so that the distribution is recentered over the given price. With positive convexity, this rescaling will require a positive "spread" so as to lower the expected value. This spread represents the increase in expected return due to positive convexity. If convexity is negative, a negative spread would be required to raise the expected price, representing the decrease in expected return due to negative convexity. In the OAS framework, this spread (OAS) is actually added to the various future short-rate paths, however, the basic interpretation is the same. Thus OAS analysis has relevance even for straight, fixed cash flow securities. In addition to incorporating the entire term structure into valuing the timing of cash flows, the OAS model also assesses the value of bond characteristics that only have relevance when uncertainty is included in the analysis.

**Relative Valuation Under Uncertainty: Variable Cash Flows.** To illustrate valuation when cash flows are contingent on interest rates, we convert the bond from Exhibit 2 into a 10% coupon bond with an initial principal face amount of $86. To be consistent with the cash flows of $40 and $60, we must assume that the general provisions of the bond contract call for a principal paydown of $31.40 in period one, with the remaining balance of $54.60 paid at the end of period two. Assume that the bond contains a call provision whereby the issuer has the option to pay the bond off completely at the end of period one. Assume further that the issuer will find it optimal to exercise this option only if the short-term rate at the beginning of period two is less than 8%. Exhibit 6 presents the cash flows that will result if the option is exercised optimally.

Assume, as before, that the bond is trading at a price consistent with a present value calculation of $88.98 for the base case cash flows of $40 and $60. Then, with a principal face of $86, the bond's trading price is 103.47 (= $88.98/86). What is the OAS implied by this price now that the bond is callable? At a 0% volatility, the call is always out-of-the-money, so the bond is equivalent to the original noncallable version of the bond except that it has a

**Exhibit 6.**

---

*Callable Bond*

| | |
|---|---|
| Coupon | 10% |
| Face | $86 |

*Paydown Provisions*

Period 1: $31.40
Period 2: $54.60

*Call Provisions*

Bond is redeemable at par after one period at the option of the issuer.

*Cash Flows*
*20% Volatility*

| 1 | 2 | |
|---|---|---|
| $40 -> | $60 | State 1 |
| $94.6 -> | $0 | State 2 |

---

stated face amount. Consequently, the OAS is 85 basis points as previously calculated.

Investors will be affected adversely if the call option is exercised because the 10% coupon is at a premium relative to the discount rates and, thus, early return of principal reduces this coupon income. This is reflected in the value of the OAS at 20%. The spread over the rate paths needed to produce an average price of 103.47 is only 28 basis points. Thus, the option "costs" the investor 57 (= 85 – 28) basis points in spread.

In Exhibit 7, the effect of the call option is illustrated in terms of the static price-yield diagrams introduced in Exhibit 5. Without the call option, the price-performance curve of the bond would correspond to the fully convex curve. Because of the call option, however, when yields decline and the option is exercised, the upside potential of the bond is limited. This skews the distribution of scenario prices downward and, as a result, the expected price falls below the observed price corresponding to the expected yield. The difference in value reflects the convexity cost attributable to the call. Alternatively, the convexity cost can be assessed in terms of the reduction in OAS required to shift the skewed distribution up-

**Exhibit 7.   Convexity Cost of a Corporate Call**

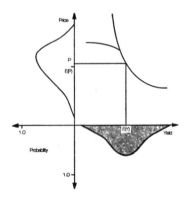

ward so that it generates an expected price equal to the observed price.

## Implementing The Theoretical Framework

### A Term Structure Proxy: The Treasury Yield Curve

There is, of course, no real market for pure discount bonds and, thus, the "true" term structure is not directly observable. Nevertheless, the term structure is readily exemplified in the market by the current coupon Treasury yield curve with due attention to certain differences. First, the Treasury securities are coupon bonds, not discount (zero coupon) bonds, and this will be reflected in relative yield levels. Moreover, factors other than maturity differences are also variable along the Treasury yield curve. For example, differences in liquidity, preferences for specific maturity ranges, and varying demand and supply conditions are among the factors that can influence the shape of the curve at any point in time. While the net effect of these influences is difficult to assess and will vary over time, the systematic influence of the coupon payments associated with Treasury curve securities can be extricated by using a simple arbitrage argument. (Interested readers are referred to Appendix A.) Thus, if the net effect of influences other than coupon can be regarded as negligible, a proxy for the term structure curve can be derived from the current coupon Treasury curve.

**The OAS over Treasury Rates.** Given the term structure proxy, we can derive an implied forward short-rate Treasury path. This path provides the basis for centering the range of future interest rate paths. That is, the expected path of future rates is defined so that the model generates on-the-run Treasury prices that match their current market prices. Thus, the model assumes that Treasuries are fairly priced and, as such, provide a reasonable benchmark against which other securities can be evaluated. As such, the OAS on a security represents an expected incremental return over Treasury rates. Alternatively, given the manner in which future short-term rates are derived from the current Treasury curve, the OAS can also be interpreted as the spread earned relative to a portfolio of Treasuries that replicates the cash flows of the security being evaluated.

## Sampling the Future: Monte Carlo Simulation

As previously discussed, there are, an infinite number of possible paths that short term rates could follow. Therefore, in practice it is necessary to generate a random sample of paths to represent the entire universe of possibilities. This is accomplished using a random sampling process known as Monte Carlo Simulation, whereby computer-generated random numbers are used to construct interest rate paths. The process is designed so that percent changes in interest rates have two components: a deterministic "drift" term and a random term. The volatility assumption controls the degree of randomness in the latter term by determining the standard deviation of the probability distribution of percent changes in interest rates. We follow the convention of assuming that these interest rate changes are normally distributed.

Given the interest rate process, a Treasury yield curve, and an assumed level of volatility, drift terms are derived so that the model generates expected Treasury prices equal to their observed market prices. That is, we solve for an expected path that forces on-the-run Treasuries to have an OAS of zero. Thus, the Monte Carlo Simulation process is designed so that the sample rate paths generated are representative of an entire universe of possibilities that is consistent and arbitrage-free relative to the current coupon Treasury curve.

To evaluate a security, we need the cash flows corresponding to each interest rate path. For straight securities, such as noncallable agencies, corporates, etc., the cash flows are the same for each path. Securities that have interest-rate-contingent cash flows (e.g., mortgage securities and callable bonds), require a method of generating cash flows (e.g., an econometric prepayment model). To calculate an OAS, the cash flows corresponding to each rate path are discounted along that path plus a spread. The OAS is the spread that results in an average present value that matches the security's market price. Conversely, given a "fair" spread over Treasuries, the fair or theoretical price for the security is given by the average price that results from discounting the cash flows across their corresponding rate paths plus the "fair" spread.

## Application To Fixed Coupon Mortgage Securities

Although the OAS valuation framework is clearly applicable to any bond investment, its development was largely motivated by the rapid growth of the secondary mortgage market in recent years. Whereas less accurate valuation methods, such as yield spreads, have been adequate for straight bonds, the complex effect of prepayments on the investment profile of mortgage products generated a definite need for a more sophisticated valuation framework. This section describes the application of the OAS model to mortgage products.

### *Projecting Mortgage Cash Flows*

The prepayment option contained in most mortgage contracts creates uncertainty as to the timing and amount of the cash flows from mortgage securities. Therefore, assessing the value of these securities requires some means of projecting prepayment rates. Bear Stearns maintains an econometric model that relates prepayments to the current level of mortgage rates, the mortgage age, season of the year, and various economic variables related to housing inflation and the level of economic activity. This model provides the method for generating mortgage cash flows in Bear Stearns' OAS model.

The dominant factor driving prepayment activity on fixed-coupon mortgages is the refinancing incentive dictated by the mortgagor's coupon relative to prevailing mortgage rates. As short-term rates decrease (increase), mortgage rates generally decrease (increase) which, to varying degrees, heightens (diminishes) the financial incentive to prepay. Thus, to generate cash flows that correspond to a given path of the short-term, risk-free rates, we must generate a corresponding path of long-term mortgage rates. This can be accomplished in a variety of ways. One method involves using a statistically estimated equation that relates mortgage rates to a moving average of the short-term Treasury rate. One can also generate long-term rates by defining a second random process that has a specified degree of correlation to short-term rates. A third method involves the assumption that future expectations are preserved over time, only the levels are adjusted to reflect the most recent observation of the short-term rate. Thus, at any point along a given path, one can derive a long-term rate from these expectations. Other methods have been described. Each method has strengths and weakness, but under reasonable assumptions, most of the alternative methods generate similar results.

Once the set of mortgage rate paths is generated from the short-term paths, these rates are fed into the Bear Stearns prepayment model. The prepayment model then generates a corresponding path of monthly prepayment rates for each interest rate scenario. These prepayment rates will reflect the agency, net and gross coupon, and aging effects over the life of the MBS. Finally, the prepayment rates are used to calculate monthly cash flows for each future rate scenario. Thus, the effect of cash flow variability on investment performance is fully incorporated into the valuation analysis.

### Agency Pass-Throughs

The fixed-coupon MBS issued by GNMA, FNMA, and FHLMC are perhaps the most straightforward of the ever increasing variety of products available in the secondary mortgage market. By virtue of their agency status, these securities have minimal, if any, credit risk. They are subject to interest rate risk, however, since the value of their coupon payments is inversely related to interest rate levels. But of even greater significance, is the "call" risk associated with the prepayment option. The effect of call risk on the value of an MBS is similar to the effect discussed above of calls on straight bonds: the call option reduces convexity as increases in value are limited by the possibility of call. However, call risk can be even more significant for MBS because prepayment activity can also magnify price decreases, thus reducing convexity on the downside as well.

**Prepayment Variability and the MBS Coupon.** The extent of the effect of the prepayment option on MBS value depends on the sensitivity of prepayments to interest rate changes. In options terminology, prepayment sensitivity depends primarily on the extent to which the option is "in-the-money," defined in terms of the level of the underlying mortgage coupon relative to prevailing mortgage rates. MBS with a coupon at, or slightly premium, to current mortgage rates will generally exhibit the greatest prepayment sensitivity, and thus the greatest prepayment risk. This is because a decrease in rates can generate a substantial increase in prepayment activity as mortgagors move to refinance at lower available mortgage rates. Conversely, if rates increase, prepayments rates can slow significantly as many mortgagors who might otherwise refinance, postpone in hopes that rates will return to lower levels. Thus, MBS with coupons near prevailing rates generally exhibit a high degree of prepayment variation as rates either increase or decrease.

The prepayment option on deep discount MBS is far out-of-the-money. As rates rise, an already existing disincentive to refinance is only made stronger, so generally prepayments on discounts will respond by slowing down, but to a lesser extent than for current coupon MBS. As rates decline, on the other hand, the existing disincentive to refinance is diminished. Depending on how out-of-the-money the option is, prepayments may accelerate considerably as mortgagors who have postponed refinancing now find it economically feasible to do so.

That mortgagors with high premium coupons have not already exercised their in-the-money option to prepay, indicates a relative insensitivity to refinancing incentives. Accordingly, as rates fall, prepayments rates on premium MBS do not usually accelerate to any degree. Conversely, as rates rise, prepayments may be relatively more susceptible to decreases as mortgagors who would otherwise refinance, lose their incentive to do so. Thus, while current coupon mortgages exhibit a high degree of prepayment response to both rate increases and rate decreases, high premium and deep discounts exhibit asymmetrical responses. Prepayments on premiums are generally more susceptible to slowing down, while prepayments on discounts generally have more potential to accelerate.

**The Convexity Implications of Prepayment Variability.** OAS analysis evaluates the implications of prepayment variability by first determining the spread over risk-free rates that would be earned if prepayments were fixed at the current projected rate. We call this the fixed cash flow (FCF) spread. The FCF spread is then compared to the OAS found when cash flows are allowed to vary according to the prepayments projected for each possible future path. The difference between the two is referred to as the convexity cost, since it reflects the impact of prepayments on the convexity value of the MBS.[3]

Exhibit 8 presents graphical illustrations of the effect of prepayments in terms of price-yield curves. The data from which the graphs are derived were generated from an application of the Bear Stearns OAS model to an analysis of GNMA pass-throughs. The results of the analysis are summarized in Exhibit 9. Exhibit 8A illustrates the convexity cost of prepayment variability for GNMA 11s. The dashed line is fitted to price-yield points that were generated in calculating the OAS while holding cash flows fixed at the currently projected rate of 174% PSA. If these cash flows were guaranteed at a price of 102:9, then, as shown in Exhibit 9, an investor would earn a YTM of 10.65 and an expected return over future risk free rates (i.e., an OAS) of 138 basis points.

The cash flows that the buyer of a GNMA 11 ultimately receives are not certain; rather, they are contingent on future interest rates that are uncertain. This uncertainty has a complex effect on

---

3. The positive convexity of the FCF version of the MBS indicated in Exhibit 8 will increase in value with the level of volatility, as discussed earlier. However, except at very high levels of volatility, the portion of the FCF spread attributable to positive convexity is generally relatively small compared to the impact of prepayments. Therefore, convexity cost is usually evaluated relative to the FCF spread at zero volatility: that is, by comparing the OAS to the spread that would be earned if there was neither interest rate nor cash flow uncertainty.

**Exhibit 8.**

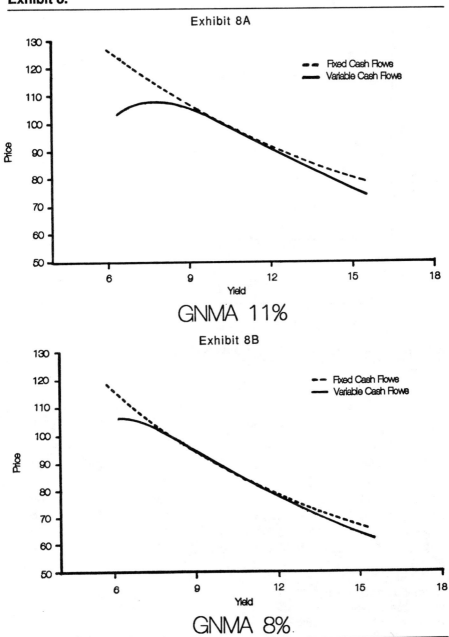

Exhibit 8A

GNMA 11%

Exhibit 8B

GNMA 8%.

**Exhibit 8.   (continued)**

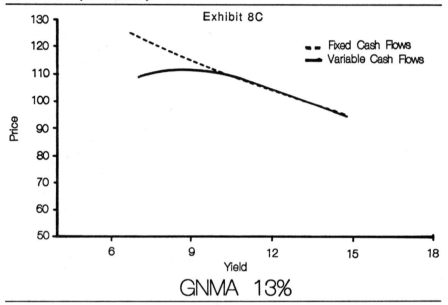

Exhibit 8C

Legend:
- - Fixed Cash Flows
— Variable Cash Flows

Price (y-axis), Yield (x-axis)

GNMA 13%

**Exhibit 9.   Option-Adjusted Spread Analysis on GNMAs**

| Coupon | WAM | Price | PSA | Yield | Fixed Cash Flow Spread | Convexity Cost | Option Adjusted Spread |
|--------|-----|-------|-----|-------|------|------|------|
| 8.00 | 335 | 87: 1 | 69% | 10.27 | 103 | 23 | 80 |
| 9.00 | 337 | 92:14 | 91% | 10.48 | 123 | 33 | 90 |
| 10.00 | 348 | 97:20 | 123% | 10.60 | 134 | 49 | 86 |
| 11.00 | 348 | 102: 9 | 174% | 10.65 | 138 | 63 | 75 |
| 12.00 | 302 | 105:16 | 229% | 10.66 | 138 | 58 | 80 |
| 13.00 | 264 | 108:16 | 262% | 10.63 | 134 | 50 | 84 |

Current mortgage rate: 11%
Interest rate volatility: 12%
Prices as of March 5, 1989

the expected value of the MBS. In down rate scenarios, the value of the security increases in response to lower discount rates. However, prepayments also accelerate as mortgage rates decline, and the more rapid return of principal compresses value in two ways. First, early return of principal reduces coupon income that, in a low rate environment, is at a substantial premium to the risk-free discount rates. Second, value is also compressed by the early return of any premium paid for the MBS. This upside compression on price increases is illustrated by the variable cash flow (VCF) price-performance curve in Exhibit 8A. This curve is fitted to price-yield points generated by the OAS model when cash flows were allowed to vary with each interest rate path. The reduction in upside convexity on the GNMA 11s is clearly illustrated as the VCF price-yield curve falls below the FCF curve when yields decline.

Convexity is also reduced on the downside. When interest rates increase, slower prepayments offset the price decrease to the extent that any premium paid is received later. However, this offset is typically dominated by an amplification of price decrease caused by higher outstanding principal balances in a higher discount rate environment. More intuitively, the value of the investment is reduced in these scenarios by a slower return of principal at a time when reinvestment rates are attractive relative to the MBS coupon. This reduction of convexity on the downside is shown in Exhibit 8A by the divergence of the VCF price-yield curve below the FCF curve.

If the investor were actually buying 174% PSA GNMA 11 cash flows, then he would be buying the FCF curve in Exhibit 8A and earning a projected OAS of 138 basis points over risk-free rates. However, the investor is, in fact, buying the VCF curve which, at a price of 102:9, earns a projected OAS of 75 basis points. Thus, the difference of 63 basis points reported in Exhibit 9 is the "convexity cost" of prepayment variability. In this manner, convexity cost can be interpreted as the difference in the value of the two price performance curves.

The analysis of prepayment variability is similar for discount and premium MBS, with the primary difference being the extent of prepayment sensitivity to changing interest rates. Because discounts and premiums are usually less prepayment-sensitive, the convexity cost is typically less severe for these MBS. This is illustrated by the OAS results presented in Exhibit 9 and the graphs in Exhibits 8B and 8C that are based on the underlying price yield points. The convexity cost of GNMA 8s, for example, is 23 basis points as compared to the 63 basis points of convexity cost on the GNMA 11s. Similarly, the GNMA 13s exhibit a lesser convexity cost at 50 basis points. Note that market pricing reflects an awareness of the relative degree of call risk in that the GNMA 9s and 8s are priced at decreasing FCF spreads, which after adjusting for the convexity cost, results in OAS' of about the same magnitude across all coupons. However, on the basis of an OAS of 90 basis points, the GNMA 9s are the most attractive of the GNMA coupons; and the current coupon GNMA 11s are relatively rich at an OAS of 75 basis points.

On the surface, it might seem that a discount MBS would increase in value as prepayments accelerate, since faster prepayments mean discounted principal is returned earlier. However, faster prepayments also mean a reduction in coupon income that may now be at a sizable premium to the declining short-term discount (reinvestment) rates. This loss of future income can compress price increases so much so that the net effect of prepayment acceleration is a reduction in upside convexity. Downside convexity is clearly reduced since slower prepayments mean discounted principal is returned later. Furthermore, price decreases will also be accelerated to the extent that short-term discount rates are now higher than the mortgage coupon; principal would be more profitably reinvested at the higher risk-free rates. Thus, although prepayment variability generally has less of an impact on discount MBS than it does on current coupon MBS, it is, nevertheless, significant and disadvantageous in both rising and declining rate environments. (See Exhibit 8B.)

Premium MBS benefit when prepayments slow since premium principal is returned more slowly. However, this advantage to slower prepayments is often overshadowed by the disadvantage of having higher outstanding balances in a high discount rate environment; that is, it would be more advantageous to have princi- pal returned earlier so as to take advantage of the higher prevail- ing reinvestment rates. Depending on the relative magnitude of these offsetting effects, the overall effect on downside convexity is usually relatively small, as is illustrated in Exhibit 8C. As interest rates decrease, on the other hand, the premium holder is hurt dou- bly by prepayment acceleration: premium principal is returned earlier and, moreover, it is returned earlier when reinvestment rates are low and, consequently, the premium coupon paid on the outstanding balances is especially valuable. Thus, the reduction in upside convexity from prepayment variability can be severe for high premiums. (See Exhibit 8C.)

**The Sensitivity of OAS to Volatility.** To the extent that prepay- ment variability is a function of interest rate variability, higher lev- els of interest rate volatility will generate more extreme levels of prepayment variation. Thus, convexity costs will be greater and OASs smaller at higher levels of volatility. In terms of options the- ory, the prepayment options that the MBS investor is short have more value at higher volatility and, therefore, the value of the MBS is less. Exhibit 10 presents the OASs of selected GNMA cou- pons at interest rate volatilities ranging from 0% to 20%. Note that increasing volatility has a lesser impact on the discount coupons since they are subject to relatively less prepayment volatility.

**Exhibit 10. Option-Adjusted Spreads Volatility Sensitivity**

| | | Volatility | | | |
|---|---|---|---|---|---|
| | | 0% | 5% | 10% | 15% | 20% |
| Coupon | FCF Spread | OAS | OAS | OAS | OAS |
| 8.00 | 103 | 97 | 86 | 70 | 50 |
| 10.00 | 134 | 123 | 99 | 64 | 25 |
| 11.00 | 139 | 122 | 92 | 50 | 3 |
| 13.00 | 132 | 123 | 97 | 60 | 16 |

The results in Exhibit 10 indicate that interest rate volatility is an important parameter in OAS analysis. Not only are the OAS levels sensitive to volatility for all coupons, but also relative richness and cheapness can be affected by the volatility level. For example, at 5% volatility, the GNMA 8s are about 25 basis points rich to the other coupons. However, at 20% volatility this is reversed, with the 8s being at least 25 basis points cheaper than the next cheapest coupon. Thus, it can be important to assess correctly the level of volatility in carrying out an OAS evaluation. Of course, there is no precise "correct" volatility assumption; rather, OAS trading strategies are best evaluated by looking at a range of volatilities around a base volatility rate that is derived from recent interest rate movements or implied by observed option price movements.

### Derivative Products

Mortgage products derived by slicing, stripping, and otherwise restructuring the cash flows of fixed coupon MBS are playing an increasing role in the secondary mortgage market. As of November 15, 1988, there were over $240 billion in outstanding derivative products as compared to a generic MBS market of just over $700 billion. Many of these derivative products alter conventional MBS characteristics, such as long duration or high prepayment risk, and thus provide access to the mortgage market for many investors who would otherwise be shut out by regulatory or other constraints. Other products appeal to specific investor needs such as the hedging properties of interest-only (IO) and principal-only (PO) strips.

Although the structure from which a derivative product originates alters the character of prepayment risk relative to the collateral, it is rarely if ever completely eliminated. Therefore, the OAS framework is an important tool for assessing the investment character of these securities. This is especially the case for bonds from some of the more exotic structures, where the nature of the prepayment risk may be difficult to assess. Using the OAS framework to evaluate the convexity implications of prepayment variability for derivative products is relatively straightforward. Cash flows for the underlying fixed-coupon MBS collateral are projected for each scenario in the usual fashion for fixed-coupon pass-throughs. Then, the entire bond structure of the security being analyzed is amortized for each scenario. This produces the cash flows of the derivative product for each scenario. Given the cash flows, the OAS is calculated in the usual fashion: find the spread to the short-term rate path that generates a distribution of prices that has an expected value equal to the market price. Conversely, given a "fair" spread to treasuries, a theoretical price can be calculated by adding this spread to the rate paths and calculating the average price.

**Interest-Only (IO) and Principal-Only (PO) Strips.** IO/PO strips are created by selling the interest and principal portions of the cash flows from a pool of mortgages or mortgage securities as separate securities. The holder of the IO is entitled to all interest payments from the mortgages and none of the principal; the PO buyer has rights to all principal payments and none of the interest. By stripping in this fashion, the bullish qualities of prepayments are decomposed and isolated into the PO, and the bearish character into the IO. The result is securities that make ideal instruments for investors wishing to hedge interest rate risk, or to take a position on prepayments.

The high concentration of bearish and bullish properties in IO and PO securities makes OAS analysis especially critical to an informed evaluation. Exhibit 12 presents the results of an analysis of an IO/PO strip derived from FNMA 8.50 MBS collateral. Because the collateral is at a discount relative to current mortgage rates, there is more potential for prepayments to increase rather than slow down from its current projected rate of 130% PSA.

Consider the implications of prepayment variability for the PO. The PO is a pure discount instrument in the sense that no coupon interest is earned on the outstanding balance. As such, the sooner principal is returned to the PO holder, the higher the return on the investment; and, conversely, slower prepayments reduce return. Thus, a PO holder can only benefit when prepayments accelerate and, conversely, the holder unequivocally loses when prepayments decelerate. To the extent that there is an asymmetry toward greater potential for prepayment increases, the result of prepayment variability is a net increase in convexity, and thus a net increase in value. Exhibit 12 presents the OAS evaluation of this net increase in upside convexity for the FNMA 8.50% backed PO. Under certainty, at 0% volatility, the PO has a projected YTM of 9.63, which corresponds to a spread over treasuries of about 35 basis points. If cash flows were fixed at the projected PSA level, then the price-performance profile of the PO would correspond to the FCF price-yield curve in Exhibit 14A. As prepayment variability is introduced with an increase in volatility to 12%, the net positive effect on performance is seen by the 37 basis points increase in OAS from 35 basis points to 72 basis points. This enhancement of the price-performance profile from prepayment variability is illustrated in Exhibit 11A by the shape of the VCF price-yield curve relative to the FCF curve. Although prepayment variability increases the rate at which the PO price decreases, it increases the rate of price increase to an even greater extent, with the net effect being worth an additional 37 basis points in OAS.

The IO piece lives off the principal balance: there will be IO cash flows only as long as there is an outstanding principal balance. Moreover, the greater the outstanding balance, the greater the IO cash flows. Thus, with respect to prepayment variability, the IO holders are situated directly opposite to the PO holders: IO holders can only lose as prepayments accelerate and, conversely, only benefit as prepayments slow down. The net effect of prepayment variability in the case of the FNMA 8.50% IOs is an extreme degree of negative convexity. Moreover, as illustrated in Exhibit 11B, the price-yield relation becomes inverse over a substantial range, making the IO a natural hedge against interest rate risk. The inverse relation occurs because as interest rates decline, the positive impact of lower discount rates on value is more than offset by the adverse effect of accelerating prepayments.

According to the results reported in Exhibit 12, the negative convexity resulting from prepayment variability costs the IO investor 117 basis points as the OAS goes from 244 at 0% volatility to 127 at 12% volatility. The high degree of sensitivity of the OAS

**Exhibit 11.**

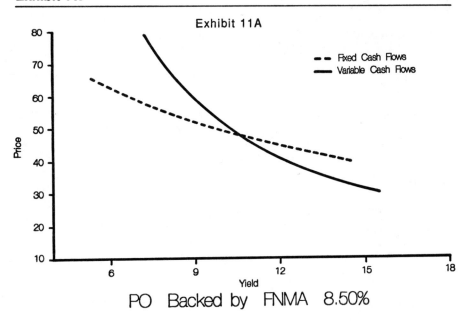

Exhibit 11A

PO  Backed  by  FNMA  8.50%

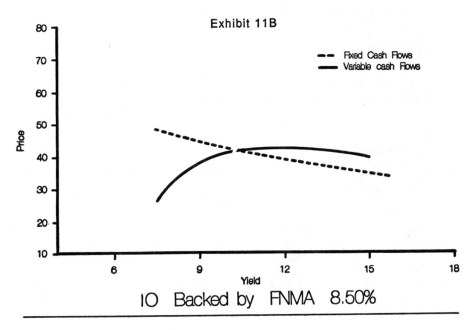

Exhibit 11B

IO  Backed  by  FNMA  8.50%

**Exhibit 12. Option-Adjusted Spread Analysis on IO/PO MBS Strip**

| Collateral: | FNMA MBS | Projected PSA: | 130% |
| | WAC 8.50% | Average Life: | 9.23 |
| | WAM 335 months | | |

| | | | | Volatility | | |
| | | | 0% | 12% | 15% | 18% |
| | Price | Yield | Fixed Cash Flow Spread | OAS | OAS | OAS |
| Collateral | 90:16 | 10.48 | 121 | 94 | 82 | 68 |
| PO | 50: 4 | 9.63 | 35 | 72 | 92 | 118 |
| IO | 40:12 | 11.71 | 244 | 127 | 67 | -1 |

to the level of volatility reflects the manner in which the opposing effects of prepayment variability have been concentrated into the IO and PO securities. In aggregate, the prepayment risk is consistent with that of the underlying collateral; that is, the price-weighted average of the IO and PO OAS is approximately equal to the OAS of the collateral. Thus, by extracting and isolating the effects of prepayment variability in this way, two highly sensitive securities are created with an aggregate prepayment risk equivalent to that of the collateral. Because of the high degree of prepayment sensitivity, OAS analysis is especially critical to a proper evaluation of IO and PO strips.

**CMO Bonds.** A Collateralized Mortgage Obligation (CMO) slices mortgage cash flows into a number of bond classes of varying face amounts.[4] CMO bonds can take on a wide variety of performance

---

4. For details see the following Bear Stearns Mortgage Research papers see: David Sykes "CMO Concepts" (1987r); David Sykes, Brett Graham "Investment Opportunities in Residuals" (1988r); Blaine Roberts, Nancy Wilt, and Sarah Wolf "Advances and Innovations in the CMO Market" (1988r).

characteristics, thus providing investors with a broad menu of alternative mortgage products from which to choose. CMO structures may include bonds with coupons that float at some spread over an index (typically a LIBOR rate or COFI), bonds with paydown schedules that are more or less fixed (PACs and TACs), accrual (Z) bonds, and so on. Because the vast diversity of CMO products available precludes a comprehensive discussion, our application of OAS analysis to CMO bonds will be limited to the bonds derived from the structure presented in Exhibit 13.

The "Y" bonds in the CMO structure denote PAC (Planned Amortization Class) bonds. These are fixed coupon bonds that will maintain a specified amortization schedule as long as prepayments fall within a specified range. For the structure in Exhibit 13, this range is from 85% to 300% PSA. The numbers 1, 2, and 3 denote the sequential order of paydown; that is, Y1 receives all principal payments until its balance is paid down, then Y2 receives all principal payments until it is paid down, and so on. After the Y classes have paid down, the accrual class Z bonds begin to pay down in the sequence indicated.

### Exhibit 13. Option-Adjusted Spread Analysis on CMO Bonds

Collateral: FNMA MBS      Projected PSA:   160%
           WAC 10%           Average Life:    7.93
           WAM 347 months

|  |  |  |  |  |  |  | 12% Volatility | |
| % of Issue | Bond Type | Coupon | Price | Yield | Avg. Life | Fixed Cash Flow Spread | Convexity Cost | OAS |
|---|---|---|---|---|---|---|---|---|
| 9.50% | Y1 | 7.1 | 90:31 | 9.970 | 3.9 | 58 | 6 | 52 |
| 17.32% | Y2 | 8.5 | 92:28 | 10.030 | 5.7 | 89 | 11 | 78 |
| 12.98% | Y3 | 9.7 | 98:11 | 10.090 | 7.9 | 80 | 15 | 65 |
| 5.98% | Z1 | 10.0 | 99:14 | 10.200 | 11.1 | 97 | 17 | 80 |
| 1.68% | Z2 | 10.0 | 98:25 | 10.310 | 17.8 | 109 | 25 | 84 |
| 45.55% | G | 10.0 | 99: 1 | 10.270 | 3.3 | 131 | 69 | 61 |
| 7.00% | Z3 | 10.0 | 90:22 | 10.860 | 18.1 | 164 | 88 | 77 |

Class Z bonds do not receive interest until they begin to pay down. Prior to paydown, their principal balance accrues at the stated coupon rate. Moreover, in this structure the first two Z bonds (Z1 and Z2) are also PACs with a planned paydown schedule that is, like the Y bonds, guaranteed for prepayment rates between 85% and 300% PSA. Thus, this structure creates 5 classes of bonds that receive a considerable amount of protection from prepayment variability. Given their sequential order of paydown, the investor can choose from average lives as short as 3.9 years to as long as 17.8 years.

Slicing the cash flows into the above structure does not reduce the prepayment risk associated with the FNMA 10 collateral; it only rechannels it. Thus, the minimal prepayment risk enjoyed by the PAC classes is afforded by enhanced prepayment risk (relative to the collateral) borne by the regular fixed-coupon class G, and the accrual class Z3. In the structure, the G class is paid down first to the extent that the PAC schedules are met. Thus, if prepayments do occur at 160% PSA, the G bond will pay down with an average life of 3.3 years. To the extent that prepayments deviate from this speed, however, and it is necessary to rechannel cash flows to meet PAC schedules, the average life on the G bond may be altered dramatically.

Similarly, if a 160% PSA speed is realized, the Z3 bonds will accrue at its coupon rate of 10% until all other bonds are paid down. At that time, paydown will commence on this bond, resulting in an average life of 18.1 years. As with the G bond, however, this average life may vary substantially with the requirements of the PAC schedules under changing prepayments speeds. Thus, the structure offers investors comfortable with prepayment risk two alternatives: a bond with a very short projected average life of 3.3 years (the G bond), and a bond with a much longer projected average life of 18.1 years (the Z3 bond).

The reallocation of the prepayment risk of the underlying collateral to the various bond classes is assessed readily by the OAS analysis. The convexity costs of the PACs are all relatively low, ranging from 6 basis points on the Y1 bond to 25 basis points on the Z2 bond. The increase in convexity cost across the PAC bond classes primarily reflects their sequential order of paydown. As a bond is outstanding for a longer period of time, it suffers greater exposure to the possibility that prepayments will breach the PAC range. In the meantime, the prepayment variation that does breach the PAC range is initially absorbed by the G class followed by the Z3 class. This is reflected by the high convexity costs of 69 and 88 basis points, respectively.

Exhibit 14 illustrates the lost convexity from prepayment variation for the Y2 PAC bond and the G bond. Note that the VCF curve diverges from the FCF curve only at very high and very low yield levels. This corresponds to rate levels where prepayments fall out of the PAC range. The extent to which the G bond is exposed to prepayment risk is reflected in the high degree of negative convexity in the VCF price-yield curve.

**Exhibit 14.**

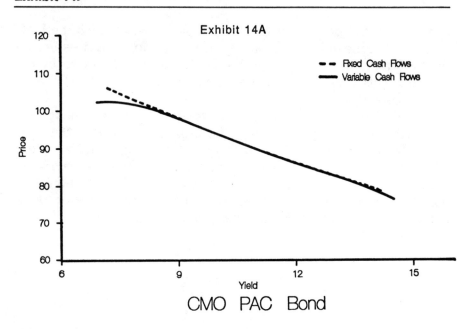

CMO  PAC  Bond

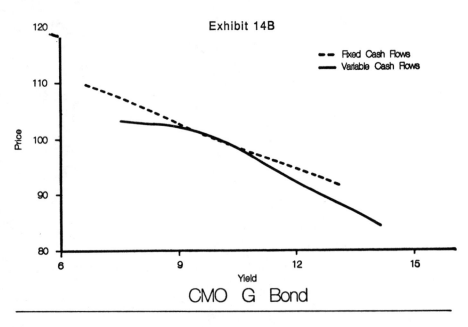

CMO  G  Bond

## APPENDIX A

The arbitrage argument for eliminating coupon effects can be illustrated by considering a simple two-period world with a one-period T bill trading at a YTM of 6%, and a two-period 7% coupon Treasury trading at a yield to maturity of 7%. Since the T Bill has no coupon, is highly liquid and default-free, we will assume that the pure discount rate applicable to cash flows one period out is 6%. What discount rate should be applied to a single cash flow received two periods from now? If the cash flows of the current coupon security can be matched by a portfolio of pure discount bonds, then to prevent arbitrage opportunities, this portfolio must trade to the same price as the coupon bond. Thus, the two-period spot rate, r2, can be extracted by solving the arbitrage-free pricing equation shown in Table A1.

### Table A1.

To prevent arbitrage between the zero coupon market and the current coupon Treasury market, a two-period spot rate is implied by the pricing equation:

Price 2-Period Treasury = Value of Portfolio of "Zeros" with Equivalent Cash Flows

$$\$100 = \frac{\$7}{(1.06)} + \frac{\$107}{(1+r2)^2}$$

| Maturity | Treasury Curve | Implied Spot Rate Curve |
|---|---|---|
| 1 period | 6% | 6% |
| 2 periods | 7% | 7.035% |

| Time Period | Implied Forward Rate |
|---|---|
| 1 | 6.00% |
| 2 | 8.08% |

# Chapter 6

# Risk-Adjusted Measurement (RAM): A Replacement for OAS Models

David J. Gordon*
Paine Webber

Michael Zaretsky
Kidder, Peabody & Co.

## I. Introduction

The proper valuation and hedging of complex fixed-income securities[1] is of paramount importance to anyone who invests in or trades these securities. Currently, many portfolio managers are relying on Option-Adjusted Spread (OAS) models to guide their investing and hedging decisions. Investors use OAS models to maximize the expected value of their portfolio returns by simply choosing to invest in securities that have the highest OAS spreads. The assumption is that the comparison of OAS spreads constitutes

---

1. We will assume that the purpose of the RAM model is to create a methodology for finding the relative values and hedging requirements of U.S. dollar-denominated fixed-income securities whose values can be expressed as some function of the process of short-term, default-free, U.S. dollar interest rates.

---

This paper was written when David J. Gordon was working at Kidder, Peabody & Co.

a definitive methodology for the resolution of the question of relative valuation.

Unfortunately, OAS models have two fundamental flaws embedded in their statistics and their assumptions. Furthermore, these models are unpalatable because they allow one to explain the shape of the U.S. Treasury yield curve only by using drift, the change over time of the centers of the probabilistic riskless interest rate distributions.

To satisfy the need for a consistent and flexible security pricing methodology, we have developed a general and powerful type of model called Risk-Adjusted Measurement or, simply, RAM. RAM technology allows us to value fixed income securities in an arbitrage free or consistent manner while permitting us to reserve the flexibility to explain the shape of the U.S. Treasury yield curve using drift and a risk premium. A risk premium is the difference in the expected returns of two securities whose returns have different degrees of riskiness.

The freedom to choose and weight the forces that may shape the yield curve is important for two reasons: this freedom enables us to value and to hedge securities under a wide range of assumptions and, therefore, this freedom enables us to quantify the sensitivity of our valuations and hedge ratios to changes in these assumptions.

This chapter is organized as follows. Section II describes the flaws embedded in the OAS models. This section contains a theoretical example in which the most undervalued of a pair of securities is not the security which has the highest OAS spread. This example is followed by an examination of why the OAS models fail and a description of the theoretical problems which lead to the OAS models' error in relative valuation. This section concludes with a discussion of another of the OAS models' flaws, the general lack of flexibility in the choice of the various forces that may shape the yield curve.

Section III describes how the use of the RAM model would produce a consistent analysis of the relative valuation problem that the OAS models failed to correctly solve. This description is followed by an overview of the theoretical content and usefulness of the RAM model. The following section introduces our complete battery of hedging statistics and examines our two basic relative valuation statistics, LOCAL VALUE and GLOBAL VALUE.

A complete proof of the RAM model's theoretical consistency is given in Section V. This section begins with a basic arbitrage argument and proceeds to cover the elegantly simple formulation of the RAM equations.

Finally, we examine the implications of the RAM model and suggest additional exciting areas that may be explored in the future with the use of the RAM model.

## II.  Limitations of OAS Models

As we have mentioned, OAS models fail to provide investors with consistent valuations and sufficient flexibility. We will start with the critical flaw, inconsistency. Typically, publishers of OAS statistics claim that securities that have the highest OAS spreads are those that can be proven by arbitrage arguments to be the most undervalued.

We will refute this assertion with both an example and a theoretical argument. To demonstrate the imperfection of the OAS spread analysis, we have constructed a hypothetical situation, involving two securities, in which the security with the highest OAS spread is actually the most overvalued security. This example takes place in a simplified world where there are no taxes or transactions costs, and borrowing and lending rates are equal to the riskless interest rate, the rate of return on an investment which matures in one period of time and does not have any variability in its payoffs. In addition, to minimize the complexity of this example, we will compute OAS spreads using annual returns instead of bond equivalent returns. This alteration does not affect the validity of our conclusions in the slightest degree.

In order to proceed, we must specify the interest rate process, the set of probability-weighted interest rate scenarios. We will use a simplified binomial interest rate process which is a discrete approximation of a continuous interest rate process. Let both securities have one period, which is one-year long, until maturity, the time when the final cash flows from the securities will be received. Furthermore, let the one-period riskless interest rate, for borrowing or lending, be 10%.

Let us define a state to be the unique combination of the riskless interest rate and the time period, and let us assume that there are two possible future states—X, the "down" state, and Y, the "up" state—that can occur one period from the present time. We will assume that each of these states has a 50% probability of occurring. Finally, let us set the returns of each of the two securities in each possible state. In state X, security A will return 5.71%, and security B will return -6.67%. In state Y, security A will return 16.29%, and security B will return 30.67%.

At this stage, we are ready to calculate the OAS spreads of the two securities. The expected return of security A is 11%, and the expected return of security B is 12%. Since the riskless interest rate is 10% and the time period is one-year long, we can conclude that the OAS of security A is 100 basis points and the OAS of security B is 200 basis points.

We can prove that security B is overvalued with respect to security A by demonstrating that we can replicate the state-dependent payoffs of one dollar's worth of security B by constructing a portfolio whose initial cost is less than one dollar. A portfolio that borrows 2.5432 dollars and invests 3.5293 dollars in security A will replicate the payoffs of one dollar's worth of security B. However, this portfolio only costs .9861 dollars. Thus, we can see that security B is overvalued by 1.39% with respect to security A. Furthermore, by buying the aforementioned replicating portfolio and selling short one dollar's worth of security B, we can produce a profitable riskless arbitrage. This arbitrage would allow us to realize a profit of 1.39% immediately on the amount of security B that is sold short.

In essence, we have demonstrated how the OAS models fail to provide consistent measures of relative valuation. Proponents of the OAS models have stated that the "cheapest" or most undervalued securities are those with the highest OAS spreads. Here, we have proven that these proponents are mistaken and that OAS spreads cannot be used to determine the relative values of securities. In our example, we have shown that the most overvalued security was actually the security with the highest OAS spread, and that we could actually make an immediate riskless profit by selling short the security with the highest OAS spread, borrowing money, and buying a weighted amount of the security with a lower OAS spread.

After examining how the OAS models can fail in practice, we will explain, in theory, why the OAS models can fail to provide consistent relative valuations. The failure of the OAS analysis is a direct result of the use of OAS spread-dependent riskless interest rate processes. We will now describe the OAS models' usage of these processes and how this usage will produce incorrect relative valuation statistics. OAS models value securities using a two-step algorithm. In the first step, the OAS models solve for the set of state-dependent riskless interest rates that can be used to produce theoretical values for "on-the-run" Treasury securities that match the market values of those securities.

The OAS models begin by creating a set of state-dependent bond equivalent riskless interest rates. This set comprises a discrete approximation of the continuous riskless interest rate process. In general, the bond-equivalent interest rates of any one period are forced to approximate a lognormal distribution with a constant level of "volatility," the standard deviation of the logarithms of the bond-equivalent riskless interest rates.

Then, the OAS models use this set of state-dependent riskless interest rates in conjunction with the following recursive methodology to find the theoretical value of a security. In any state, the theoretical value of a security is the average of the conditional probability weighted end-of-period values of that security divided by one plus the one-period version of the bond-equivalent riskless interest rate of that state. By starting with the states that are in the maturity period of the security and working back in time, the current theoretical values of the security can be calculated.

If using one set of state-dependent riskless interest rates produces theoretical values of the "on-the-run" Treasury securities that differ from the market values of these securities, then the set of state dependent riskless interest rates is altered. This alteration affects the drifts of the set; a drift is the relationship between the median of the distribution of the logarithms of the bond-equivalent riskless interest rates at time t and the median of the distribution at time t+1.

We will call the final set of state-dependent riskless interest rates that can be used to equate theoretical and market values for Treasury securities, the "Treasury set." Once the Treasury set has been determined, the relative valuation statistic, the "OAS spread," of a security is produced by finding the increment that must be added to all elements of the bond-equivalent riskless interest rates of the Treasury set to equate the theoretical and market values of that security.

The failure of these OAS models arises from the implicit assumption that the effective state-dependent riskless interest rate, the rate at which an investor can borrow and lend, is the sum of the bond-equivalent riskless interest rate of the Treasury set and the OAS spread. To shed light on this problem, we must define an OAS framework as the methodology that is used to value securities at a single OAS spread. Even though any single OAS framework values securities in an arbitrage-free fashion, OAS models' relative valuations are often meaningless since the frameworks that are employed to value different securities may contain different sets of effective state-dependent riskless interest rates. In fact, when comparing securities that have different OAS spreads, OAS models are actually using different sets of effective state-dependent riskless interest rates to value these securities.

In practice, since the existence of an undervalued or overvalued risky security does not necessarily imply anything about the set of state-dependent riskless interest rates, it is logical to assume that the set of state-dependent riskless interest rates is invariant with respect to the relative value of any risky securities. An exception to this rule would exist for the riskless interest rate, which is the one-period borrowing and lending rate, of any single state only if we could find, in that state, a truly riskless portfolio of undervalued or overvalued risky securities that could be bought and sold short to simulate borrowing and lending.

Nonetheless, in general, to consistently value securities, we need to use a single set of state-dependent riskless interest rates to produce statistics that would allow us to directly compare the values of two securities. As we have seen, the use of OAS spreads which are computed using multiple sets of state-dependent riskless interest rates can lead to incorrect investment decisions because of the glaring discrepancies between the various sets that the OAS models use to produce their valuation statistics.

As mentioned earlier, even if the OAS models' methodology were consistent, the OAS models would still be unpalatable because of the lack of flexibility of their assumptions. OAS models are predicated on a stringent set of assumptions governing the required return of fixed income securities. OAS models incorporate the "expectations hypothesis" which postulates that, in any single state, the expected returns of all securities are identical regardless of what the variability of the returns of these securities may be. This expectations hypothesis is implemented by simply setting the drifts of the set of state-dependent riskless interest rates to explain the U.S. Treasury yield curve.

OAS models ignore the variability or riskiness of returns when they are determining the rate they will use to discount cash flows. In other words, they assume that a very interest rate-sensitive instrument, such as the 30-year Treasury bond, must have the same expected return as a very interest-rate insensitive instrument, such as a Treasury bill.

Since OAS models cannot analyze the effects of using different expected rates of return for different securities in an arbitrage-free or consistent pricing environment, these OAS models fail to provide investors with any information relating to the sensitivity of their valuations and hedge ratios to a change in the assumptions governing the relationship between the expected returns of different securities. This is unfortunate for investors who do not believe that the expectations hypothesis holds for all securities and would like to value and hedge securities based on alternative expected rate of return assumptions. It is also unfortunate for investors who have not decided to accept any particular theory governing the relationship between the expected rates of return of different secu-

rities and would like to compare and contrast the numerical results that may be obtained under a variety of such assumptions.

## III.  The RAM Approach

The RAM model does correct the aforementioned flaws of the
OAS models. In this section, we will show that the RAM model
produces consistent results based on arbitrage pricing and discuss
how the RAM model can be used to examine the effects of utilizing different combinations of interest rate process drift and risk
premiums on valuation and hedging statistics. However, this section will only summarize the theoretical composition of the RAM
model. A complete theoretical discussion can be found in the last
section.

In contrast to the OAS models, whose valuation methods
were shown to be inconsistent in both theory and practice, the
RAM model does produce consistent relative valuation measures
for the pair of theoretical securities in the example of the previous
section and, in general, the RAM model does value securities in a
consistent manner.

As described previously, the OAS models use a variable set of
state-dependent riskless interest rates to value a security. However, the existence of an undervalued or overvalued security does
not necessarily imply that there should be a change in the set of
state-dependent riskless interest rates. To incorporate this idea, the
RAM model values securities by holding the set of state-dependent
riskless interest rates constant and by allowing the risk premium
to vary. The RAM model allows the risk premium to vary in order
to describe the set of possible movements of a security's value
over time, a set which we will call the security's value process,
while maintaining a match between the model's theoretical value
for a security and the market's current value for that security.

In order to understand how the RAM model produces the correct conclusion in the relative pricing example of the previous section, a quick summary of our RAM methodology is in order. The
RAM model's value for a security is equal to the current value of a
portfolio that consists of a varying and dynamically revised posi-

tion in a single benchmark risky security combined with borrowing or lending at the riskless interest rate and that is constructed such that this portfolio's payoffs exactly duplicate the payoffs of the security that we wish to value. In effect, in each state, our methodology makes the required risk premium of a security a function of the elasticity of that security's returns with respect to our benchmark security's returns.

If we postulate a simple relationship between our theoretical benchmark security's one-period risk premium and the risk of that security's one-period returns, then we do not need to explicitly specify the process of the benchmark security's value in order to value other securities. Assuming that we have already determined the riskless interest rate process, the only remaining parameter necessary for security pricing is our Risk Adjustment Factor (RAF). As we will demonstrate later, if we define the state dependent RAM RISK of a security to be the standard deviation of that security's one-period returns multiplied by the negative of the correlation between the level of the riskless interest rate and the security's returns, then we can set a security's state-dependent risk premium to be the product of its RAM RISK and the RAF. Therefore, the use of our RAF in tandem with our riskless interest rate process precisely defines an arbitrage-free set of values for all securities.

For the purposes of computing valuation and hedging statistics, we will assume a security will follow the value process that results from the use of the RAF of that security which is the RAF that will have our model produce that security's market value. The only exception to this rule concerns our GLOBAL VALUE statistic, and we will delay a complete discussion of the analysis of our RAM statistics. (See Section V.)

Nonetheless, for the purpose of showing the RAM model's ability to correctly compare the securities with one period to maturity in our theoretical example, it is sufficient to note that the most undervalued of our pair of theoretical securities is the one with the highest risk adjustment factor, RAF. We have chosen to derive this simplified valuation rule because our other valuation statistics incorporate the value of an additional security, the benchmark secu-

rity, and because we wish to show the correctness of our methodology without adding this additional information to our analysis.

We have derived this simplified rule for this specific case
using the following logic. Since we have two securities that have
one period to maturity, the most undervalued security of the pair
will be the one that can be used to produce the most profitable
one-period arbitrage against some benchmark security portfolio.
Our LOCAL VALUE statistic, which we will examine in Section
IV, measures the exact value of such a one-period arbitrage.

In addition, it can be shown that the difference between the
LOCAL VALUEs of two securities is proportional to the RAFs of
the two securities in question if the securities have returns that are
positively correlated. This last fact is proven in Appendix B.

Finally, we need to determine the sign of the proportionality
variable. An examination of the last equation in Appendix B reveals that the sign of the difference between the securities' LOCAL
VALUEs is merely the sign of the difference between the
securities' RAFs if the securities have higher payoffs in the "up"
state than in the "down" state. Since both securities A and B have
higher payoffs in the "up" state than in the "down" state, we can
conclude that, in our example involving securities A and B, the
most undervalued security is the one with the highest RAF.

Having established our simplified relative valuation rule, we
can proceed to show that the RAM model functions properly in
our theoretical example. Let us recall the details of our securities'
state-dependent returns and the riskless interest rate from the previous section. In state X, security A will return 5.71%, and security
B will return -6.67%. In state Y, security A will return 16.29%, and
security B will return 30.67%. Also, the riskless interest rate is 10%
per period.

Calling upon Equation 11 in Section V we find that the RAF
of security A is .18904 and that the RAF of security B is merely
.10712. Thus, by the rule we previously discussed, the RAM model
correctly finds security A to be an arbitrageably better investment
than security B.

In fact, the RAM model shows that we can create a riskless
arbitrage profit by selling short W dollars of security B, buying the

RAM hedge of 3.5293•W dollars of security A, and borrowing 2.5293•W dollars at the riskless rate. This portfolio, which has a net cost of zero dollars, produces an end of period profit of .01529•W dollars, regardless of what interest rate state is reached at the end of the period.

In general, the RAM model does more than merely produce correct results under a single set of assumptions; its wealth of flexibility allows it to be used to find the robustness of its own results with respect to its risk premium and drift assumptions. One of the strengths of the RAM model lies in its ability to use both a risk premium and interest rate process drift to explain the shape of the Treasury yield curve in an arbitrage-free framework. While OAS models always assume that the risk premiums of all securities are uniformly zero, our RAM model allows us to set a variable risk premium subject to the constraint that the risk premium of a security must be proportional to the theoretical risk of the returns of that security.

This property allows us, if we wish, to set the expected return of the 30-year Treasury bond to a significantly higher level than that of the three-month Treasury bill without allowing any arbitrage opportunities between these two securities to exist. On the other hand, the versatility of the RAM model also would allow us to utilize the expectations hypothesis in our pricing methodology by setting the risk premium equal to zero.

This versatility also allows an investor to accomplish two interrelated goals. An investor can use the RAM model to value and find the hedge of a security under any combination of a risk premium and interest rate process drift. Then, an investor can use the RAM model to gather enough data to enable him to examine the sensitivity and stability of a security's valuation and hedging statistics under a variety of conditions.

In summary, as we have shown or described, the RAM model correctly chooses the more undervalued of our two theoretical securities and allows the investor to perform various sensitivity analyses that the OAS models cannot do. Combining flexibility with consistency, our RAM model succeeds where the OAS models have failed.

## IV. Interpreting RAM Statistics

After setting the appropriate assumptions concerning the riskless interest rate process and the RAF, the RAM model will produce information that will help an investor choose securities and manage the risk of these securities.

Our battery of hedging statistics covers every major, distinct source of risk, with the exception of credit risk, for fixed-income securities. The first two, RAM DURATION and RAM CONVEXITY, are the RAM model analogs for the familiar method of quantifying interest rate risk. These statistics measure the first and second derivative of a security's value, with respect to a change in the RAM model's initial riskless interest rate, divided by the security's value. Since these two statistics assume a specific type of yield curve shift for a shift in the riskless rate, we have defined another statistic, RAM YIELD CURVE, to examine the change in a security's value for a steepening or inverting of the yield curve.

Our last two statistics concern areas of importance that are not directly related to interest rate risk. These statistics concern our volatility and prepayment assumptions. RAM VOL measures the change in the value of a security for a change in the RAM model's assumed level of volatility for the bond-equivalent riskless interest rate. Similarly, RAM PREPAY measures the change in the value of a security for a change in that security's prepayment function.

While the interpretation of our hedging statistics is quite simple, the interpretation of our relative valuation statistics can be a little more difficult. As a consequence of the possibly complex nature of a security's value process, the set of probability-weighted security value scenarios, measuring the "undervaluation" or "overvaluation" of any security requires a degree of judgment. The absence of a perfect relative valuation statistic is not a problem that is unique to the RAM model. Cox and Rubinstein encountered a very similar problem when they searched for a relative valuation statistic for stock options.[2] In fact, our relative valuation statistics were inspired by their "Equalizing Ratio" statistic.

---

2. John C. Cox and Mark Rubinstein, *Options Markets*, Englewood Cliffs, NJ: Prentice-Hall Inc. 1985: pp. 310-313.

There are two reasons for the need for judgment in the valuation of securities. First, a proper and useful valuation statistic must take into account the hedging requirements of a security. Since securities can vary over different states, both in the sign and the magnitude of their hedging requirements, a perfect definition of relative valuation is both elusive and problematical.

Furthermore, even if a security were to have a constant hedging requirement over all states that occur prior to the security's maturity, we would still be left with the general dilemma of deciding how quickly the market value of an improperly valued security should converge to its theoretical value. More precisely, when we are defining a relative valuation statistic for the RAM model, we have considerable latitude in deciding how quickly the RAF of a security, the RAF implied by the security's market value, will converge to some theoretical RAF such as the RAF of the benchmark security.

In the absence of an ideal solution to the pair of aforementioned problems, we have sought to define reasonable and useful statistics to guide investors in their task of portfolio selection. We have chosen to create two statistics, LOCAL VALUE and GLOBAL VALUE, that use radically different methods of determining the RAF that a security will have in the future, and to incorporate into both of these statistics the one period hedging requirement of the security being valued.

Specifically, both statistics, when applied to security x, give the value of a one-period arbitrage in which a weighted amount of security x is purchased, an investment in riskless securities is made, and an appropriate benchmark portfolio is sold short. The LOCAL VALUE statistic is the value that the arbitrage would have if security x maintains, over the period of the arbitrage, the RAF that its market value implies at the present time. In contrast, the GLOBAL VALUE statistic is the value that the arbitrage would have if our security were to be valued at the benchmark security's RAF at the end of the period of the arbitrage.

As we have said, each of these measures seeks to weigh the value of an arbitrage that includes a short position in an appropriate benchmark security portfolio. In reality, we need exactly two different "appropriate" portfolios with two different signs of RAM RISK. This need arises because our valuation statistics only have meaning if we consistently measure the value of a long position in the security being examined and because this security may have a RISK of either possible sign. Therefore, we have defined two benchmark security portfolios that each require the same initial investment, one dollar, but have RAM RISK values of equal magnitudes and opposite signs.

The choice of the appropriate benchmark portfolio depends on the relationship between the sign of the RISKs of security x and the benchmark. A security with the same RISK sign as the benchmark security in the current state is measured against a portfolio that consists of a one-dollar long position in our benchmark security. A security with a different RISK sign than that of the benchmark security in the current state is measured against a portfolio that consists of a one-dollar short sale of our benchmark security and a one-dollar riskless loan. In effect, the payoffs of this last portfolio are the negatives of the payoffs of a one-dollar investment in the benchmark security plus the payoffs of a two-dollar riskless loan because the proceeds from making a short sale can be invested in riskless securities.

At this point, we have all of the information that we need to precisely define our valuation statistics. Symbolically: Let:

$m$ = the benchmark security

$p(x,s)$ = the value of security or portfolio x in state s.

$bp(x,r,s)$ = the appropriate benchmark portfolio that corresponds to the sign of security x's RISK which is evaluated in state s using the end-of-period RAF r.

$RAF\_of(x)$ = the RAF of security x, i.e., the RAF that the model would have to use to equate its theoretical value for security x with the market value of security x.

$syn\_bp(x,r,s)$ = the synthetic benchmark portfolio that consists of a long position in security x and a position in riskless securities and is balanced, assuming that security x will have an end of period RAF of r, such that the portfolio constitutes a perfect hedge in state s for $bp(x,r,s)$.

Then we can write:

$$LOCAL\ VALUE(x,m,s) =$$
$$p(bp(x,RAF\_of(x),s),s)-p(syn\_bp(x,RAF\_of(x),s),s) \qquad (1)$$

$$GLOBAL\ VALUE(x,m,s) =$$
$$p(bp(x,RAF\_of(m),s),s)-p(syn\_bp(x,RAF\_of(m),s),s) \qquad (2)$$

In general, we believe that the GLOBAL VALUE statistic gives an investor a long-term view of the value of holding a security while the LOCAL VALUE statistic gives an investor a very short-term view of the value of holding that same security. We also believe that the GLOBAL VALUE is the more important of our two statistics and that investment decisions should be primarily based upon its value.

However, when one is waiting for a security's implied or market RAF to converge to the benchmark security's RAF, it is important to be aware of the LOCAL VALUE of one's security since this will show what the cost or profitability of hedging this security will be if the security does not change its RAF in the near future. This situation is similar to the familiar case in which an investor wishes to know not only how undervalued a security is but also how much it will cost him to roll or finance this security once he purchases it.

Ultimately, we must leave investors with a caveat. The investor should keep in mind that, in any state, there may be combinations of a position in negative RAM RISK securities and a position in positive RAM RISK securities that can produce a synergistic risk and return profile that cannot be precisely measured by our statistics since such combinations can produce synthetic riskless securities whose expected rates of return may differ from those of the actual riskless securities. Aside from creating profitable arbitrage opportunities between the synthetic and actual riskless securities, synthetic riskless securities could change the effective riskless interest rate in a state and, thereby, change the required relationship between the returns of different securities with different risk levels in that state. In reality, however, the reliability of the relationships of the returns among the securities that theoretically would compose the new synthetic riskless securities probably is not great enough to warrant an investigation of the consequences of such second-order effects.

In summary, our statistics value a security by comparing the combination of a weighted position in that security and a position in riskless securities to a benchmark security portfolio that has the same RAM RISK sign. These statistics should give an investor the tools he needs to choose exceptional securities for his portfolio.

## V. Detailed Description of the Ram Model

The RAM model makes a few basic assumptions about the market-place. In the simplified world of this model, all securities can be bought or sold short, there are no taxes or transaction costs and, in any state, the one-period borrowing and lending rates are equal to that state's one-period riskless interest rate.

Conceptually, the RAM model values a security by finding the risk-adjusted, current theoretical value of all of the cash flows of that security. The RAM model uses a two-step algorithm to value securities. First, the model generates a set of state-dependent bond-equivalent riskless interest rates which discretely approximates a continuous interest rate process. Second, using this set of interest rates, arbitrage equations are used to value any security whose cash flows can be stated as a function of the riskless interest rate process.

Every set of state-dependent bond-equivalent riskless interest rates has the following properties. In each period, the distribution of the bond-equivalent riskless interest rates approximates a log-normal distribution with a volatility level that is constant for all time periods. This volatility level is simply the standard deviation of the natural logarithms of the bond-equivalent riskless interest rates. The median of the interest rate distribution in the first period is simply the current bond-equivalent riskless interest rate. At time t, the median of the bond-equivalent riskless interest rate distribution is determined by the center of the distribution at time t-1 and by the drift that corresponds to time t-1. The drift of t-1 is the change, from period t-1 to period t, in the median of the distribution of the natural logarithms of the bond-equivalent riskless interest rates.

Finally, this set of state dependent riskless interest rates is constructed such that it constitutes a binomial process. As before, we define a state to be a unique combination of the time period and the level of the riskless interest rate. By the definition of a binomial process,[3] each state must have exactly two immediate successor states, an "up" state and a "down" state, that occur one period in time after their predecessor state. The successor states of state s are the states that can theoretically occur at the end of the current time period if we are currently in state s. Of the two successor states of any state, the "up" state has the lower riskless interest rate and higher fixed-payment bond values.

Using this binomial interest rate process, we can define security valuation equations by considering the important restriction that is placed on any model which we wish to call "arbitrage-free" and by using two standard securities. The arbitrage restriction states that any portfolio that has riskless payoffs and that requires no initial investment must have payoffs that are equal to zero. The first standard security is a riskless security whose value consequently increases at the state-dependent riskless interest rate. The other standard security is a risky security which we will call the benchmark security.

From this point, unless otherwise stated, one should assume that the security values that are used in the arbitrage equations are theoretical values which are not necessarily equivalent to market values. In other words, these equations specify the values that securities would have if there were no arbitrage opportunities available in the securities market at any point in the interest rate process. In reality, arbitrage opportunities may exist, and securities may have market values that deviate considerably from our theoretical values.

In order to derive our security valuation equations, we must define:

3. Richard J. Rendleman, Jr., and Brit J. Bartter. "The Pricing of Options on Debt Securities," *Journal of Financial and Quantitative Analysis*, XV, No. 1, March 1980: pp. 11-24.

r      =    the riskless interest risk.

s      =    the state defined by the unique combination of a specific time period, t, and a specific level of the riskless interest rate, r.

t      =    the time period.

m     =    our benchmark risky security.

rf(s) =    one plus the one period return of the riskless security in state s.

r(i,s) =    one plus the one period return of security i in state s.

E[g(s)] = the expected value of the function g(s).

|x| =      the absolute value of x.

rp(x,s) = the risk premium for security x in state s = (E[r(x,s)]-rf(s))

p(x,s) =   the value of security x in state s.

p_u(x,s) =    the value of security x in state s's "up" successor state.

p_d(x,s) =    the value of security x in state s's "down" successor state.

u(x,s)    =    one plus the one period return of security x in state s's "up" successor state.

d(x,s)    =    one plus the one period return of security x in state s's "down" successor state.

sign(x)   =    {x/|x| for x<>0, 1 for x=0}

sd_p(x,s)=    the standard deviation of the value of security x in the successor states of state s.

sign_sd_p(x,s)    =    sd_p(x,s)*sign(p_u(x,s)-p_d(x,s))

sd_r(x,s) =    the standard deviation of the one-period returns of security x in the successor states of state s.

prob_u(s) =    the conditional probability of reaching the decreasing interest rate successor state of state s given the existence of state s.

prob_d(s) =    the conditional probability of reaching the increasing interest rate successor state of state s given the existence of state s.

δ(x,s)    =    the number of units of the benchmark security that will perform as a perfect hedge for a single unit of security x in state s.

Using the aforementioned arbitrage restriction, we now can find the relationship between the values of any security, x, our benchmark security, m, and the riskless security. This relationship will be explored for the case of a riskless arbitrage that involves security x, the benchmark security, and the riskless security.

This arbitrage will be started in state s and examined in the two successor states of state s. In accordance with the definition of and the restriction placed on a riskless arbitrage, we have specified that the arbitrage should require no investment in state s and that the arbitrage should have zero dollar payoffs in the successor states of state s.

The no-net investment condition is satisfied since, in our arbitrage, we can invest $p(x,s)$ dollars in security x, sell short $p(m,s) \bullet \delta(x,s)$ dollars' worth of the benchmark security, and sell short $p(x,s)-p(m,s) \bullet \delta(x,s)$ dollars' worth of the riskless security. A short position in the riskless security is equivalent to borrowing at the riskless rate, and a long position in the riskless security is equivalent to lending at the riskless rate.

Now, we will write the equations for the payoffs of our arbitrage in the successor states of state s.[4]

In the "up" state:

$$0 = u(x,s) \bullet p(x,s) - u(m,s) \bullet p(m,s) \bullet \delta(x,s) - (p(x,s) - p(m,s) \bullet \delta(x,s)) \bullet rf(s)$$

$$\text{or, equivalently} \tag{3}$$

$$u(x,s) \bullet p(x,s) = u(m,s) \bullet p(m,s) \bullet \delta(x,s) + (p(x,s) - p(m,s) \bullet \delta(x,s)) \bullet rf(s)$$

In the "down" state:

$$0 = d(x,s) \bullet p(x,s) - d(m,s) \bullet p(m,s) \bullet \delta(x,s) - (p(x,s) - p(m,s) \bullet \delta(x,s)) \bullet rf(s)$$

$$\text{or, equivalently,} \tag{4}$$

$$d(x,s) \bullet p(x,s) = d(m,s) \bullet p(m,s) \bullet \delta(x,s) + (p(x,s) - p(m,s) \bullet \delta(x,s)) \bullet rf(s)$$

---

4. The terminology and the basic arbitrage equations for this discussion has been drawn from Cox, John and Rubinstein, Mark. *Options Markets*, Englewood Cliffs, NJ: Prentice-Hall Inc., 1985.

These equations imply that the value of the hedge ratio, delta(x,s), must be:

$$\delta(x,s) = (p\_u(x,s)-p\_d(x,s))/(p\_u(m,s)-p\_d(m,s))$$

Noting that prob_u(s)+prob_d(s)=1, we can sum Equation 3 multiplied by prob_u(s) and Equation 4 multiplied by prob_d(s) and get:

$$
\begin{aligned}
&(prob\_u(s)\bullet u(x,s) + prob\_d(s)\bullet d(x,s))\bullet p(x,s)) \\
&= (prob\_u(s)\bullet u(m,s) + prob\_d(s)\bullet d(m,s))\bullet p(m,s)\bullet \delta(x,s) \quad (5) \\
&\quad + (p(x,s)-p(m,s)\bullet \delta(x,s))\bullet rf(s)
\end{aligned}
$$

By the definition of an expected return in our binomial model, the probability weighted average of the returns of a security in the two successor states of state s is the expected return of the security in state s.

$$prob\_u(s)\bullet u(x,s) + prob\_d(s)\bullet d(x,s) = E[r(x,s)] \qquad (6)$$

$$prob\_u(s)\bullet u(m,s) + prob\_d(s)\bullet d(m,s) = E[r(m,s)] \qquad (7)$$

Therefore, we can rewrite Equation 5.

$$
\begin{aligned}
E[r(x,s)]\bullet p(x,s) &= E[r(m,s)]\bullet p(m,s)\bullet \delta(x,s) \\
&+ (p(x,s) - p(m,s) \bullet \delta(x,s))\bullet rf(s)
\end{aligned}
\qquad \text{(rev.5)}
$$

By defining the functions $\omega(x,s)$ and rp(x,s), we can write:

$$E[r(x,s)] = \omega(x,s)\bullet E[r(m,s)] + (1 - \omega(x,s))\bullet rf(s) \qquad (8)$$

or

$$E[r(x,s)] = \omega(x,s)\bullet rp(m,s) + rf(s)$$

where
$$\omega(x,s) = \delta(x,s)\bullet p(m,s)/p(x,s) \text{ and}$$
$$rp(m,s) = (E[r(m,s)] - rf(s))$$

This final set of equations defines the required return of any security in terms of the risk premium, $rp(m,s)$, and the dollar hedge ratio or elasticity, $\omega(x,s)$, of the benchmark security with respect to security x. Since this hedge ratio is the result of the arbitrage conditions imposed in Equations 3 and 4, we know that a portfolio consisting of $\omega(x,s)$ dollars of the benchmark security and $(1 - \omega(x,s))$ dollars of the riskless security will exactly replicate the one-period returns of a one-dollar investment in security x in state s.

A thorough perusal of Equation 8 reveals that we have significant latitude in the setting of the return of the benchmark security or, equivalently, the risk premium of the benchmark security in every state s. Given this considerable degree of discretion, we wish to allow the risk premium of a security in state s to be a simple function of the risk of that security's returns in that state. Fortunately, it turns out that the condition that creates the direct relationship between the state-dependent risk premium of a security and some local measure of the risk of that security's return is, in itself, intuitively appealing. For each state, if we set the state-dependent risk premium of the benchmark security to be proportional to the state-dependent standard deviation of the benchmark security's one-period returns, then we can prove that the state-dependent risk premium of any security will be proportional to the state-dependent standard deviation of the one-period returns of that security.

This is the point in our analysis where the probabilities of the interest rate states are used since the standard deviations of the one-period returns of the benchmark security are a function of the conditional probabilities of the successor states of any given state. Given the cash flows of the benchmark security, our new rule for setting the benchmark security's state-dependent risk premium, and the riskless interest rate process, we can derive the value process of the benchmark security. Once we have the value of the benchmark security in each state, we can value any other security by an arbitrage argument without referring to the actual probabilities of each state again.

It is extremely important to note that all of these arbitrage relationships which we will discuss are based on the use of a single theoretical risk premium. In practice, there will be two basic types of risk premiums, the theoretical one and the one that can be used to force the RAM model to produce the market or actual value of a security. Unless otherwise stated, the reader should assume that the risk premium that we are using corresponds to a theoretical risk premium which can be used to produce theoretical security values which may or may not conform to market security values.

Let us define:

RAF $\quad$ = $\quad$ the risk adjustment factor, a measure of risk aversion that is constant across all states.

$$\text{RISK}(x,s) = \text{sd\_r}(x,s) \bullet \text{sign}(u(x,s) - d(x,s))$$
$$= \text{sign\_sd\_p}(x,s)/p(x,s)$$

If we construct the riskless interest rate lattice such that the conditional probability of each successor state, given the existence of the predecessor state, is 50%, then we can write:

$$\text{sign\_sd\_p}(x,s) = (\text{p\_u}(x,s) - \text{p\_d}(x,s)) / 2$$
$$E[r(x,s)] = (u(x,s) + d(x,s)) / 2$$
$$\text{RISK}(x,s) = (\text{p\_u}(x,s) - \text{p\_d}(x,s)) / (2 \bullet p(x,s))$$

With this relationship, we can find a new way to express the $\omega$ function.

$$\omega(x,s) = \delta(x,s) \bullet p(m,s)/p(x,s)$$
$$= (\text{p\_u}(x,s) - \text{p\_d}(x,s))/(\text{p\_u}(m,s) - \text{p\_d}(m,s)) \bullet p(m,s)/p(x,s)$$
$$= (\text{sign\_sd\_p}(x,s)/\text{sign\_sd\_p}(m,s)) \bullet (p(m,s)/p(x,s))$$

Using Equation 8:

$$E[r(x,s)] = \omega(x,s) \bullet rp(m,s) + rf(s)$$
$$= (\text{sign\_sd\_p}(x,s)/\text{sign\_sd\_p}(m,s)) \bullet (p(m,s)/p(x,s))$$
$$\bullet rp(m,s) + rf(s)$$
$$= (\text{RISK}(x,s)/\text{RISK}(m,s)) \bullet rp(m,s) + rf(s)$$

Here, we will incorporate the assumption that the risk premium of the benchmark security is proportional to the standard deviation of its returns by setting rp(m,s)=RAF•RISK(m,s). Using this new definition for rp(m,s), we can produce:

$$E[r(x,s)] = RAF \bullet RISK(x,s) + rf(s) \tag{9}$$

Finally, since

$$rp(x,s) = E[r(x,s)] - rf(s),$$

we know that:

$$rp(x,s) = RAF \bullet RISK(x,s)$$

Thus, we have proven that the risk premium of a security in a particular state is proportional to the standard deviation of that security's one-period returns over the following period of time.

In general, to value securities, we can utilize the new definitions that we have for E[r(x,s)] and RISK(x,s) that rely on the simplifying construction that forces the conditional probability of each successor state to be 50% and rearrange Equation 9 to produce:

$$p(x,s) = (p\_u(x,s) + p\_d(x,s) - RAF \\ \bullet(p\_u(x,s) - p\_d(x,s))) / (2 \bullet rf(s)) \tag{10}$$

Finally, we can also solve for the RAF:

$$RAF = (2 \bullet rf(s) \bullet p(x,s) - p\_u(x,s) - p\_d(x,s))/(p\_d(x,s) - p\_u(x,s)) \tag{11}$$

Because of the nature of our binomial arbitrage, we must place a simple set of conditions on the values that our RAF can assume in order to ensure that, in every state, no riskless, profitable arbitrage is available between the riskless security and any other security. These conditions and a proof of their necessity and sufficiency can be found in Appendix A.

## VI.   Conclusions

As we have seen, the RAM model will provide correct and useful relative value indicators. This is in contrast to the OAS models which produce statistics that we have proven to be unreliable and often incorrect. Furthermore, in addition to resolving the problems that are associated with the general methodology of the class of OAS models, the RAM model allows users to explore the sensitivities of any security's statistics to changes in the combination of interest process drift and a risk premium. At the same time, the RAM model is capable of limiting the choice of combinations to those which are completely consistent with any given U.S. Treasury yield curve.

The creation of the RAM model has opened many avenues of exploration to us. For instance, in future papers, we will examine and highlight the effects of varying the drift and the risk premium on the calculated valuation and hedging requirements of a variety of types of securities. This will allow us to determine the sensitivity of the statistics of classes of securities to such variations. Knowledge of such sensitivities is extremely important for all investors who need to understand the reliability of the relative valuation and hedging statistics that are generated under a single set of assumptions.

## APPENDIX A:
## LIMITATIONS ON THE RISK ADJUSTMENT FACTOR (RAF)

This appendix derives the restrictions on our RAF variable and draws heavily upon the definitions and equations of two previous sections, IV and V.

Because of the nature of our binomial arbitrage argument, we must place limits on our RAF. By the definition of a binomial process, any state has exactly two immediate successor states. Accordingly, in any state, a security has only two possible one-period returns. If these returns do not bracket the return of the riskless security, then a riskless, profitable arbitrage can be constructed. Therefore, we must subject the returns of all securities to the some constraints.

We will consider the case where $d(x,s) < u(x,s)$. Note that a completely analogous proof that reaches the same exact conclusions can be made for the case where $u(x,s) < d(x,s)$.

For the case where $u(x,s) < d(x,s)$, we need to prove:

$$d(x,s) < rf(s) < u(x,s)$$

for all securities, x, in all states, s.

Taking the left side of the inequality:

$$d(x,s) < rf(s)$$

By definition, $d(x,s) = p\_d(x,s)/p(x,s)$. Thus we have:

$$p\_d(x,s)/p(x,s) < rf(s)$$

Equation 10 states that:

$$p(x,s) = (p\_u(x,s) + p\_d(x,s) - RAF \bullet (p\_u(x,s) - p\_d(x,s))) / (2 \bullet rf(s))$$

Therefore, if we substitute for $p(x,s)$ in our last inequality, then we will get:

$$(2 \bullet p\_d(x,s) \bullet rf(s)) / (p\_u(x,s) + p\_d(x,s) - RAF \bullet (p\_u(x,s) - p\_d(x,s))) < rf(s)$$

At this point, we would like to multiply this last equation by the left hand side denominator and divide it by rf(s). In order to determine the resultant type of inequality, we need to know the signs of these two multiplicative terms. Rf(s) will always be positive since the one-period riskless interest rate will never be less than zero. Since rf(s) is always positive and since there is limited liability which implies that security values are always nonnegative, Equation 10 tells us that the left hand side denominator is always positive. Performing the aforementioned multiplications, we arrive at:

$$(2 \bullet p\_d(x,s)) < (p\_u(x,s) + p\_d(x,s) - RAF \bullet (p\_u(x,s) - p\_d(x,s)))$$

Rearranging:

$$p\_d(x,s) - p\_u(x,s) < -RAF \bullet (p\_u(x,s) - p\_d(x,s)))$$

For the riskless security, $p\_d(x,s) - p\_u(x,s) = 0$, and this proof is trivial. For all other securities, given our assumption that $d(x,s) < u(x,s)$, we can conclude that:

$$p\_u(x,s) - p\_d(x,s) > 0$$

Therefore, we can divide the previous equation by $p\_u(x,s) - p\_d(x,s)$ and get:

$$-1 < -RAF$$
$$1 > RAF$$

Similarly, we can take the right hand side of the equation and analyze it in the following way.

$$rf(s) < u(x,s)$$
$$rf(s) < p\_u(x,s) / p(x,s)$$
$$rf(s) < (2 \bullet p\_u(x,s) \bullet rf(s)) / (p\_u(x,s) + p\_d(x,s) - RAF \bullet (p\_u(x,s) - p\_d(x,s)))$$
$$(p\_u(x,s) + p\_d(x,s) - RAF \bullet (p\_u(x,s) - p\_d(x,s))) < (2 \bullet p\_u(x,s))$$

$$-RAF \bullet (p\_u(x,s) - p\_d(x,s))) < p\_u(x,s) - p\_d(x,s)$$
$$-RAF < 1$$
$$RAF > -1$$

Combining our two results, we get the inequality which guarantees that no riskless, profitable arbitrage opportunities will arise between any security that is valued at a certain RAF and the riskless security.

$$1 > RAF > -1$$

## APPENDIX B:
## THE RELATIONSHIP BETWEEN LOCAL VALUES AND RAFS

This appendix establishes the relationship between the LOCAL VALUEs and the RAFs of securities and draws heavily upon the definitions and equations of two previous sections, IV and V.

As noted elsewhere in this paper, if the signs of the RISKs of two securities are the same, and if we assume that the RAF of these securities will remain constant over time, then we can simply use the RAFs of these two securities to determine which is a better investment in terms of the possible one-period arbitrage against the appropriate benchmark security portfolio. In fact, if we take equation 8 and substitute the definition of the state-dependent value of a security that we have in Equation 10, we get:

$$LOCAL\ VALUE(x,m,s) =$$
$$((p\_u(bp(x,RAF\_of\_(x),s),s) + p\_d(bp(x,RAF\_of\_(x),s),s)$$
$$-RAF\_of(m) \bullet (p\_u(bp(x,RAF\_of\_(x),s),s) - p\_d(bp(x,RAF\_of\_(x),s),s))) / (2 \bullet rf(s)))$$
$$- ((p\_u(syn\_bp(x,RAF\_of(x),s),s) + p\_d(syn\_bp(x,RAF\_of(x),s),s)$$
$$-RAF\_of(x) \bullet (p\_u(syn\_bp(x,RAF\_of(x),s),s) - p\_d(syn\_bp(x,RAF\_of(x),s),s))) /$$
$$(2 \bullet rf(s)))$$

By the definition of arbitrage, the net payoffs in both the up and down interest rate scenarios must be zero. In other words, the p_u and the p_d of the appropriate benchmark portfolio must be the same as the p_u and the p_d of the synthetic benchmark portfolio. Thus, we can rewrite this equation and produce:

LOCAL VALUE(x,m,s) = (RAF_of(x) - RAF_of(m))•(p_u(bp(x,RAF_of_(x),s),s)
- p_d(bp(x,RAF_of_(x),s),s)) / (2•rf(s))

Since the p_u(bp(x,RAF_of_(x),s),s), the p_d(bp(x,RAF_of_(x), s),s), and the rf(s) that the LOCAL VALUE statistic will incorporate do not vary between securities that have the same RISK signs, the difference between the LOCAL VALUEs of two securities that have RISKs of the same sign will be proportional to the difference between the RAFs of the two securities.

# Chapter 7

# Structure and Value in Regular Bonds*

Dennis Adler
Dillon, Read & Co. Inc.

## Introduction

Most bond investors do not like risk; they seek cash flows which are certain. Their requirements relate to the timing and size of each future payment and the certainty that the issuer will ultimately pay. The market's perception of the degree of uncertainty is reflected in the price paid for bonds of varying structure. While knowledge of the issuer's ability and desire to change the course of payments plays a role in the value of those bonds, some predictions of future events are only statistical. If we believe statistics are predictive, then we can relate value to the uncertainty in future cash flow in fixed income securities.

The advent of mortgage securities and CMOs has focused investors' attention on understanding prepayment risk since this is the principal component of uncertainty in the mortgage market. Research has resulted in the development of prepayment models

*This chapter would not have been possible without the creativity of Sam Adams. His work alone in the development of the option model and term structure model used here was absolutely essential to demonstrate the relationships which exist between bond structure and value.

225

to simulate this consumer option, integrated with more fundamental option theory relating interest rates to call option value. CMOs, in particular, segregate prepayment risk among their tranches. But the interaction between estimates of collateral prepayment rates and how that risk is divided among the tranches exacerbates the investor's ability to relate value to structure.

While portfolio managers and quantitative research teams are busy debating the relative merits of one structure over another, many are missing an opportunity to add value by applying similar analytical rigor to their corporate and municipal (regular) bond portfolios. It is often easy to find considerable differential between bonds of the same issuer, or similar credit, if evaluated on an option adjusted spread (OAS) basis. Often these differences are simply ignored. Routinely, investors enamored with option-adjusted analysis in mortgages do not apply the same focus to options embedded in bonds with call schedules, put options, and sinking fund open market features.

The classic buyer who demands only a pickup in yield-to-maturity determines value based on name, credit rating, and maturity. The compensation he may ascribe to the difference between dollar price and call price, or to the coupon alone, implies what value he gives to structure. Many consider book value or other tax or accounting-driven issues in swapping bonds. Those buyers who are evaluated on performance must consider structure. *Yield alone is a limited measure of performance.* It tells the buyer nothing about potential performance when rates move markedly away from their purchase yield. Calls or sinking funds limit upside in a rally. Puts may give added value because they perform like longer bonds as rates fall. Option adjusted yields are more predictive of performance because they consider the effects of movements away from purchase yields. The option components of bonds are only one component of risk.

We will not delve into how to evaluate credit, event risk, and liquidity risk as they are not within the realm of straightforward quantitative analysis. We will attempt to show how to evaluate other risks so that swap decisions become subjective only with respect to qualitative differences between cash flows. Examples of bond swaps are used extensively throughout the paper in order to illustrate how each of these risks are broken apart.

## THE STRUCTURE OF THE STRAIGHT BOND

The evaluation of structure and value begins with an understanding of the structure of straight (bullet) bonds, fundamentally a result of their cash flow and yield curve shape.

In its most primitive form, a bond is a series of cash flows with options attached to them. Bonds having no option features are typical of U.S. government, agency, and Yankee markets, but are more the exception among municipal and corporate bonds.

Straight or bullet bonds differ from each other in the shape (timing and dollars) of the promised cash stream and the certainty of payment (credit). What is needed is a mechanism to properly compare the risk of owning one straight bond to another.

### Improvements on Yield-to-Maturity

The structural features distinguishing bullet bonds from each other are revealed in their cash flows. Consider equal maturity bonds. The spectrum from zero coupon to high coupon changes the amount of cash received up front rather than at maturity. How we value these cash flows depends on the yield or discount rate applied. Yield-to-maturity calculations do not take into account the shape of the cash flow. They imply that all cash should be discounted at one rate, the yield-to-maturity rate. Term structure theory tells us that earlier cash should be valued at different discount rates than later ones. A more "wholesome" way to distinguish the value of two cash flows of equal credit risk is to discount each flow at its theoretical zero coupon yield applicable to a bond of a given credit.

Application of yield-to-maturity, as a measure of performance, ignores yield curve shape. Therefore, cash flow shape is likewise not taken in account when using yield-to-maturity. For instance, two bonds of the same maturity, but different in coupon, are not the same in the sense of term structure. High coupon bonds are "shorter." A 10-year 10% bond at par should be compared to 6.5-year zero coupon bond, both of which have the same duration (6.5).

In a flat yield curve environment, yield-to-maturity is fairly accurate in explaining differences in value. Taking a sharply upward sloping curve, however, earlier cash is worth more than later cash. A higher-coupon (lower duration) bond of the same maturity should, therefore, yield less.

We can define risk spread as the basis-point-value ascribed to a bond relative to the riskless term structure. The riskless term structure is identical to the *implied spot curve* derived from on-the-run treasuries (for taxable bonds).

In the example in Exhibit 1, there is a 35-basis-point difference between the *implied spot spread* of equal maturity, equal yielding 10-year bonds differing in coupon between 0% and 16%. The 16% bond is shorter on a duration basis, and should be compared to a lower maturity point on the implied spot curve. Its risk spread, therefore, is wider than all the other bonds. For all the bonds to

**Exhibit 1.  The Effect of Yield Curve Shape on Relative Value of Equal Maturity Equal Yield Bonds of Differing Coupon**

|  | Term (yrs.) | | | | | | | |
|---|---|---|---|---|---|---|---|---|
|  | 1 | 2 | 3 | 4 | 5 | 7 | 10 | 30 |
| Yield Curve | 6.0 | 6.30 | 6.70 | 7.25 | 7.70 | 8.10 | 8.30 | 8.50 |
| Implied Spot Curve | 6.0 | 6.31 | 6.74 | 7.35 | 7.86 | 8.33 | 8.54 | 8.78 |

| Coupon | Duration* | Risk Spread (bp) |
|---|---|---|
| 0 | 10 | −24 |
| 6% | 7.4 | −5 |
| 8.5% | 6.9 | 0 |
| 16% | 6.1 | 11 |

*All at yield: 8.3%, with a ten-year maturity.

have identical spot spreads, the 16% bond should yield 8.19%, while the 0% bond should yield 8.54%. Purely on an arbitrage basis, risk-free equal maturity bonds of lower coupon should yield more in a positively sloped yield curve. Conversely, inverted yield curves should cause higher coupon bonds to yield more.

## How to Calculate Risk Spread

We begin by separating a bond into individual cash flows, discounting each cash flow at the *riskless rate* and adding all of them together giving a *riskless price*. Most bonds are not riskless and are worth less than the riskless price, resulting in a risk premium. The difference between the riskless price and the actual price is the risk value in dollars:

$$\text{Risk value (RV)} = \text{Riskless price} - \text{Actual price (AP)} \qquad (1)$$

There are various ways to translate this RV to a risk value in basis points (RVBP). One simple way is to use duration. Since modified duration (MD) is defined as:

$$\text{MD} = \% \text{ change in price } / \text{ 100 basis points change in yield} \qquad (2)$$

Then:

$$\text{RVBP} = (\text{RV}/\text{AP}) \times 10{,}000 \ / \ \text{MD} \qquad (3)$$

For example, if a bond trades at 90 and has a modified duration (MD) of 5, with RV as calculated in Equation 1 being equal to 1, we calculate the risk value in basis points as:

$$\text{RVBP} = (1/90) \times 10{,}000 \ / \ 5 = 22.2 \text{ basis points}$$

Thus, if the difference between the actual price and the present value of the cash flows discounted at the riskless zero coupon curve were 1 point, the bond would be 22 basis points cheaper than the Treasury market. This 22 bp of premium could account for any of the risk factors (such as liquidity, sector, credit, etc.), other than duration and call risk.

## How to Analyze a Straight Bond Swap of Equal Duration

By equating the duration of each side of a swap, an investor maintains similar interest rate risk in parallel movements of the yield curve. Comparing two bonds in a bond swap, duration and spread to the riskless equivalent should be measured—not yield-to-maturity and term. In general, once duration is deemed equal, the investor must evaluate whether the differences in credit, liquidity, and sector risk compensate for the spread difference.

### Convexity

Convexity is the tendency for a bond's duration to change with a change in interest rates. Bonds (or cash flows) with positive convexity are those that increase duration as yields drop. They get longer in a rally and the investor benefits from retaining his high coupon longer. Similarly, as rates rise, investors favor shorter securities so they can get their money back sooner and benefit from higher reinvestment rates. Positive convexity is an advantage only in higher market volatilities.

All straight bonds have positive convexity, though some have more than others. *The higher the coupon or the more the cash flow is distributed around a bond's duration, the greater the convexity. Zero coupon bonds have a lower convexity than coupon bonds of the same duration.* But long zero coupon bonds have the most convexity in the bullet market, primarily because their duration exceeds that of normal coupon bonds of the same maturity.

### The Barbell/Bullet Comparison (An illustration of convexity and yield curve risks)

In swaps involving more than two securities non-parallel shifts in the curve become of paramount importance in risk management.

Equal duration, as well as equal or improved convexity do not guarantee better performance in all yield curve shifts. The classic example is the barbell/bullet trade. This analysis amplifies the importance of parallel versus non-parallel curve movement.

As an example of a barbell/bullet trade consider Swap Example 1 where we sell the 2-year and 7-year Treasury and buy an equal market value of the 5-years. For $100 million of 5-years, $29.1 million of 2-years, plus $71.4 million of 7-years are exchanged for a pickup of 2.4 basis points. In a positively sloped yield curve, selling a barbell and buying a bullet usually results in a higher yield. Why shouldn't this always be done? Because two risks remain: volatility and yield curve risk.

### Parallel Curve Shift

In a parallel yield curve shift, a barbell will outperform a bullet of equal duration. The cause of the outperformance of the barbell is evident in the duration differences as rates move. The barbell duration will change less than the bullet. This is another example of convexity. *Barbells have more convexity than bullets.* The lower the convexity (all other risks being equal), the poorer the performance in large parallel interest rate moves.

The effect of convexity is only experienced in large rate moves. With a 100-basis-points parallel shift in the curve, the barbell outperforms by .017%. Thus, convexity is synonomous with volatility risk.

### Non-Parallel Curve Shift

In Swap Example 1, if the market had moved over the course of a month in a non-parallel fashion by either flattening of steepening, the profit and loss would be affected greatly. As shown in Exhibit 2, a 20-basis-point tilt of the curve changes the profitability of the trade enormously—.25% in one month rate of return. The convexity effect of a 100-basis-point-parallel yield shock was only -.017%. *Yield curve risk predominates in equal duration barbell type swaps.*

## Swap Example 1. Buy Bullet/Sell Barbell

Equal Duration
(Settlement = 9/29/89)

| | Face Amount | Issuer | Coupon | Maturity | Price | Yield | Duration | Convexity |
|---|---|---|---|---|---|---|---|---|
| Sell: | -29.1 MM | U.S. Treas. | 8.250 | 8/31/91 | 100.1 | 8.20 | 1.8 | 1.9 |
| | -71.4 MM | U.S. Treas. | 7.875 | 7/15/96 | 97.3 | 8.40 | 5.3 | 16.3 |
| Buy: | 100 MM | U.S. Treas. | 8.250 | 11/15/94 | 99.5 | 8.35 | 4.2 | 10.3 |
| Difference | | | 0.265 | | 1.3 | .024* | 0 | -1.7** |

*Dollar-duration weighted
**A price change of -.017% per 100 basis points yield shock

**Exhibit 2.  One-Month Investment Horizon on Swap Example 1**

| | *Non-Parallel* Curve Shift | | |
| --- | --- | --- | --- |
| | *Flattening* | *No Change* | *Steepening* |
| 2-year | +10 bp | 0 | −10 bp |
| 5-year | 0 | 0 | 0 |
| 7-year | −10 bp | 0 | +10 bp |
| P&L* | −252,000 | +1,000 | +253,000 |

*Amount ($) earned per $100 million transacted.

Matching duration does not equate all risks; in fact, it actually amplifies yield curve risk. This effect is especially important to indexers or immunized portfolio managers who only match the duration of their index or liability but neglect the distribution of maturities along the curve.

Barbell/bullet transactions are mostly yield curve plays. Consider the following simple way to remember the effect, shown in Exhibit 3.

**Exhibit 3.  Barbell/Bullet as the Curve Flattens**

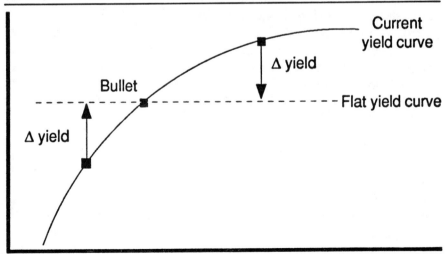

Assume a barbell is constructed to pivot on the bullet bond. If the curve moves from upwardly sloping to totally flat, because of its longer duration, the long bond will gain in value more than the short bond will lose. Recall duration is percent change in price per 100-basis-point-change in yield. If the change in yield is the same for both ends of the barbell, the change in price of the long bond exceeds the short bond's loss in price. The bullet has not changed value at all, acting as the pivot to the curve seesaw. In contrast, a steepening would favor the bullet.

*Always buy the curve when flattening is anticipated. Sell it and buy the middle if steepening is expected.*

Thus, swaps in which risk spread increases, while duration is maintained and convexity increases, should always be done unless a loss in risk spread appears justified by an anticipated steepening of the curve.

Of the various risks outlined for straight bond swaps, yield curve risk remains the most difficult to predict or to measure. This point should be emphasized: the relative importance of the different risk categories depends on the markets to be considered in a swap. Risks overlooked in one market may be exaggerated in another. In pure government trades, duration and yield curve risk are most important. In same sector corporate or municipal swaps, credit, liquidity, duration, and volatility are all important. The more similar with respect to each risk the bonds on either side are, the easier it is to determine the merits of a transaction. To limit portfolio enhancing transactions to the simplest of swaps, however, negates the advantage and opportunities to uncover excess value. Overly restrictive rules for bond swapping diminish performance. The fine-tuning of risk measurement is the challenge portfolio managers should seek to attain.

## BONDS WITH EMBEDDED OPTIONS

### Introduction

The following sections go beyond the comparison of non-call structures and seek to measure the effect of embedded options. It is in these structures where particularly large irregularities exist in market pricing and where opportunities for enhanced performance are the greatest.

Many corporate or municipal bonds have embedded options.[1] Three types of embedded options exist:

1. An issuer's call option exercisable at any time following a call protection period,

2. An open market option of the issuer to buy-in sinking funds and to accelerate the sinking fund,

3. A holder's right to put, exercisable at one time prior to maturity.

Type 1 is an American option while Types 2 and 3 are European. American options initiate on one date and remain active continuously thereafter. Many issuer calls originate at an elevated call price and step down in price at annual or semi-annual intervals. The same continuous American option remains but with a diminishing exercise price compensating for the lengthening time to call.

European options (Types 2 and 3) are exercisable on a one-time only basis. The sinking fund option is renewable but does not involve the redemption of the full number of bonds outstanding. The issuer's right to accelerate the sinking fund, normally called the "double-up" or "triple-up" option, simply allows a greater percentage of the total amount outstanding to be redeemed. The sinking fund option, because it is a compound option, is the most complex.

The put option allows the holder to put the security back to the issuer, usually at par, only one time. This European option, therefore, is more restrictive and of somewhat less value than the equivalent American call option.

What is the aim of evaluating these embedded options? It simply allows an investor to compare the risk of securities with

---

1. Consumer or mortgage type options which result from an individual loan's right to prepay will not be considered here.

differing structures within a consistent framework. To do this, we need an option model. Yield calculations just will not do, because they ignore the expected behavior of a bond when rates move away from the current market. An equally important consideration is that without an option model we cannot assess the effect of *changing values of the embedded options* as the protection period shortens, and as the bond is priced off a shorter position on the yield curve.

Many bonds contain more than one option. For example, typical long corporate bonds are callable at a premium and contain open market sinking fund options. Some put bonds are exercisable more than once. Other complex securities contain both put and call options.

Most of these individual embedded options affect each other; that is, they are not linear or independent of one another. The evaluation of each separately does not necessarily determine the overall value in a complex security. Many simple models try to measure the value of the options separated from the overall bond, either in yield premiums or discounts, or in price. For example:

Yield of callable bond = Yield of call free bond + Yield value of call      (4)

While this approach is easy to understand, the value of complex embedded options cannot be analytically separated from the security to which it is attached. Our option model is intended to allow for maximum flexibility in comparing embedded options in individual securities. For this reason, we consider all structural characteristics of the bond when running the model as well as the current market value (the current price and the current risk-free term structure of interest rates). Exhibit 4 shows model inputs and outputs.

Much of the discussion in this paper will focus on the sensitivity of bond value to each of the elements of structure. The effect of market environment will be treated separately.

**Exhibit 4.    Required Inputs and Outputs of an Option Model for Non-Mortgage Bonds**

MODEL INPUTS

Elements of Bond Structure:

1. Coupon
2. Maturity
3. Type of option (European or American)
4. Type of option (put or call)
5. First exercise date
6. First exercise price
7. Time between option exercise dates
8. Price decrement between option exercise dates
9. Amount of bonds potentially redeemed on each date
10. Number of option exercise dates
11. The uneconomic protection (in points)

Characteristics of the market environment:

12. The current market price, yield, or spread to benchmark security
13. The series of term and yield of a "risk-free" set of bonds. Usually, this is the series of on-the-run U.S. treasuries.
14. An assumed volatility of interest rates.

MODEL OUTPUTS

1. Option-adjusted spread
2. Option-adjusted duration

# The Option Model

## *Overview*

Our model is what is commonly referred to as a simulation model. The model begins with a series of future interest rate paths. A given bond, its elements of structure fully specified, is subjected to each path. One path is thought of as a predictable series of future interest rates. At any point, the bond will either be completely called, partially called or completely put, depending on the structure. In this way, a given structure interacts with a given future rate scenario. We then blend the results of many paths (usually over 100), using discounted cash flows to determine an average bond value. This approach is identical to that used for straight bonds in which we calculated a *riskless price* (Equation 1). This price is compared to the actual bond price to obtain a risk value. We then convert the risk value to basis points (RVBP).

### Option-Adjusted Spreads

The risk value in basis points for a bond containing options is the "option-adjusted spread." If the bond we analyze has no embedded options, then:

$$\text{Option-adjusted spread} = \text{spot spread}$$

Recall that the spot spread contains all risk premium that makes a noncallable bond trade above the treasury curve. These include all the qualitative risks: credit, sector, and liquidity. Thus, *the option-adjusted spread is the basis-point-premium of a bond which is comparable to an option-free bond of the same issuer.*

### Option-Adjusted Duration

Conventional duration represents the fulcrum point, or average, of the discounted cash flows to maturity. The option adjustment reflects the expected cash flows, assuming the probability of exercise of any embedded options. To truly evaluate a credit spread, not only must we option adjust the conventional maturity spread (e.g., 80 basis points off the 10-year bond), but we must also compare it to the appropriate point along the risk free curve. That point is given by the option-adjusted duration. The duration of a bond with embedded options is always less than the duration to maturity, since all options reflect the chance of early redemption.

As shown in Exhibit 5 for a callable bond, the option-adjusted duration (OAD) lies between the duration-to-call (DTC) and the duration-to-maturity (DTM). Put bonds (not shown) option-adjusted durations would also be between duration-to-put and duration-to-maturity. Many investors think of put bonds only when they trade to put. On an option-adjusted basis, these bonds are always longer than calculated from duration-to-put.

Exhibit 5 also illustrates that for callable bonds, option-adjusted spread is always less than or equal to the conventional spread; the difference is referred to throughout this paper as the embedded option value or cost. The higher the option value, the wider the conventional spread of callable bonds and the narrower the conventional spread of put bonds.

To refine an early statement, the option adjusted spread is the basis-point-(risk) premium of a bond which is comparable to that of an option-free bond of the same issuer and whose option-adjusted duration is identical to the conventional duration of the option-free bond.

**Exhibit 5.   The "True" Yield and Duration of a Callable Bond**

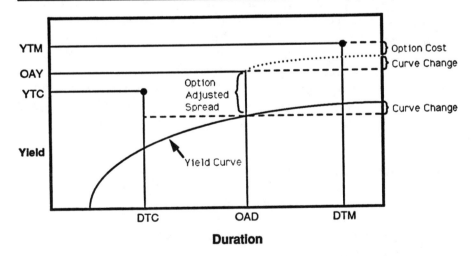

Yield-to-Maturity – Curve Change – Option Cost = Option-Adjusted Yield

Duration-to-Maturity ≥ Option-Adjusted Duration ≥ Duration-to-Call

An investor can truly determine relative value comparing the OAS of a bond with embedded options to a theoretical option-free bond of the same OAD. The conventional duration of an option-free bond is mathematically certain at any given yield. Option containing bonds change duration more radically as rates change because redemption becomes more or less likely. As we saw earlier for bullet bonds, this large potential change in duration is referred to as convexity. Unlike bullet bonds, however, convexity differences among equal duration option containing bonds can be very large.

Equally important to using option-adjusted duration to determine where a bond resides on the yield curve, OAD serves as a measure of interest rate risk. A bond containing calls or puts will not respond to interest rate movements exactly as its duration-to-maturity (call or put) would predict. Its response to interest rates is greater than its duration-to-put or call and slower than its duration-to-maturity. This has important implications for hedging and immunization. Bond traders should hedge bonds containing options by shorting bonds or futures of equal option-adjusted duration (adjusting for market-weighting). Similarly, portfolio managers who seek to match liabilities of known duration with callable assets must continually adjust to stay matched, using option-adjusted duration, not duration to maturity. Moreover, since these durations change with interest rates (as bonds become more or less likely to be called), immunized portfolios require continual rebalancing. For this reason alone, most managers of immunized portfolios stay away from securities containing options.

## The Callable Bond

### Structural Features of the Call

The call features of a typical callable bond are characterized by five simple parameters:

1. First (or current) call date, or call protection period (or refund date if refund protection is considered viable)

2. First call price

3. Par call date

4. Decrement in call price at each change date

5. Period between decrements (in months)

Examples are shown in Exhibits 6A and 6B.

With so many features that vary, issuers can change nuances in call protection very easily. Often, the market perceives these subtleties differently from the issuer. It is here where structuring

### Exhibit 6A. Typical Corporate Call Structures

|          |        |          |          | (1)   | (2)    | (3)      | (4)   | (5) |
|----------|--------|----------|----------|-------|--------|----------|-------|-----|
| GMAC     | 7 7/8% | 3/1/97   | 3/1/94   | 100   | 3/1/94 | 0        | 0     |     |
| GMAC     | 8%     | 1/15/02  | 1/15/87  | 104   | 1/15/97 | .4      | 12    |     |
| GTE      | 10.3%  | 11/15/17 | 11/15/97 | 105.15 | 11/15/07 | .515  | 12    |     |
| SO BELL  | 8.5%   | 8/1/29   | 8/1/94   | 103.83 | 8/1/19 | .153     | 12    |     |
| SO CENT  | 9 5/8% | 3/1/19   | 3/1/84   | 107.93 | 3/1/14 | .264     | 12    |     |
| DUKE     | 8 1/2% | 2/1/17   | 3/1/92(R)* | 105 | 3/1/12 | .298     | 12    |     |
| ARKLA    | 9 7/8% | 2/15/18  | 2/15/88(C)** | 109.88 | 2/15/08 | .49  | 12    |     |

*Bond is cash-callable  2/1/87 at 107.45    R = refundable
**Bond is refundable  2/15/98 at 104.94     C = callable

### Exhibit 6B. Typical Municipal Bonds Call Structures

|               |       |        | (1)    | (2) | (3)    | (4) | (5) |
|---------------|-------|--------|--------|-----|--------|-----|-----|
| N.J. TURNPIKE | 7.20% | 1/1/93 | 1/1/93 | 103 | 1/1/99 | .25 | 6   |
| IPA           | 7%    | 7/1/98 | 102    | 102 | 7/1/00 | .5  | 6   |
| TBTA          | 6.5%  | 1/1/16 | 1/1/96 | 100 | 1/1/96 | —   | —   |

Note: See explanations (1) through (5) in text above for column heading explanations.

new issues becomes a trade-off between the investor's and issuer's perception of the value of call options.

## Price Protection

On top of its structure, a bond's current market price affects option value very strongly. Option values are maximum at a bond's call price; thus, spreads should be widest at or near 100. (The absolute number of points of call protection is not a sufficient measure of protection because 2 points on a long bond is worth less in yield than 2 points on a shorter bond.) A more important measure of call protection should be the ratio of price protection to duration. Thus, a 7-year bond (duration=5.3) trading at 94.7 has similar call protection to a 4-year bond (duration=3.5) trading at 96.5.

Many investors only equate price discounts to call protection, but cushion (or high premium) bonds may also have significant call protection. For example, a 10-year bond callable in 5 years at par which is priced at 105 has roughly the same protection at a price of 93.

A rough measure of "price" call protection may be called the price protection ratio (PPR), which is measured in basis points:

$$PPR = \frac{|(CP - MP)| \times 100}{MD} \qquad (5)$$

where:
CP  =  First call price
MP  =  Market price
MD  =  Modified duration     (to call if MP > CP)
                             (to maturity if MP < CP)

For example, a bond callable at 102 trading at 92 with a duration to maturity of 5 has price protection of 200 basis points. For bonds callable at par:

$$PPR = |Yield - Coupon| \qquad (6)$$

## Time Protection

The second important structural effect is dependent on the ratio of call protection period to maturity. The importance of time protection is best understood when you consider the present value of known cash flows to the present value of the cash flows that are in doubt. A crude measure of this is the leverage ratio (LR):

$$LR = \frac{(DTM - DTC)}{DTM} \qquad (7)$$

where:
DTM = Duration-to-maturity
DTC = Duration-to-call  (if noncallable DTC = DTM; if putable replace DTC with DTP)

Generally, the larger the uncertain part of the bond's cash flow, the greater the call risk. The leverage ratio becomes a less meaningful number as it approaches 1.

## Yield Curve Effect

Less important in call structuring is the rapidity with which call price moves toward 100. The larger the price change per year, the less the call protection. Once bonds trade above 100, the exact schedule of call prices has more effect. Most investors are familiar with "yield-to-worst" calculations which vary call date/price combinations and seek the lowest yield. Ambiguities about which call is "worst" are particularly critical to bond evaluation in a sloping yield curve. A few 1/4 basis points in price not only changes the yield but also significantly changes the "spread" to the appropriate point in the term structure. For example, if yield-to-par call and yield-to-premium call were equal at 7%, but the yield curve at the premium call date was at 6.50% versus 6.90% at the par call, the investor gains some advantage in performance by referencing to a lower point on the curve.

In a flatter or inverted yield curve environment, the investor gains no advantage in considering his callable security spread to a lower point on the curve. *Option values decrease as the curve steepens.*

Another way to think about the term structure effect is to consider the call from the issuer's point of view. When the market rallies and the issuer's bonds become more economic to call, the issuer might consider refinancing to the original maturity of the bonds he calls. It will cost less to do so if the curve is flat. Thus, his incentive to refinance increases in a flat curve, to the disadvantage of the bond holder.

**Thus, call protection is influenced by three major variables:**

**1. Price discount or premium relative to call price**

**2. Time-to-call relative to time to maturity**

**3. The yield curve shape**

The interaction of these variables influences what an investor should pay for call protection. Sensitivity analysis of typical call structures should demonstrate the relative importance of these variables.

### Intermediate Corporate Bond Structures

Typical intermediate corporate bonds have a structure of either 10-year NC7, 7-year NC5, or 5-year NC4. Fannie Mae has recently introduced two less protected structures: 10-year NC5 and 5-year NC3. Most issues shorter than 5 years are noncallable, as are most medium term notes. Few have call premiums.

Of these three typical structures, the 10-year NC7 and the 7-year NC5 have similar option values of about 20 basis points at 12.5% volatility (see Exhibit 7). The 5-year structure has more call protection and implies a correction of 13 basis points from a 5 year bullet. The Fannie Mae structures offer significantly less call protection than typical corporate intermediate structures. Obviously,

**Exhibit 7.  Call Value\* in Typical Intermediate Callable Bonds
(In Basis Points)**

| Structure | Volatility | | | | | Lever-age Ratio\*\* |
|---|---|---|---|---|---|---|
| | *7.5%* | *10%* | *12.5%* | *15%* | *17.5%* | |
| 10-yr NC7 | 13 | 18 | 22 | 27 | 31 | .21 |
| 10-yr NC5 | 25 | 34 | 43 | 51 | 60 | .39 |
| 7-yr NC5 | 12 | 16 | 20 | 25 | 29 | .22 |
| 5-yr NC4 | 8 | 11 | 13 | 16 | 18 | .16 |
| 5-yr NC3 | 18 | 24 | 29 | 35 | 42 | .35 |

\* Assumes par bonds in 8% *flat* yield curve.
\*\*Leverage ratio is a measure of the importance of call structure.

the higher the implied volatility of the market, the greater the pay-up in yield for the call protection.

Call risk intensifies as the protection period diminishes. As shown in Exhibit 8 for 7-year NC5 bonds, the value of the embedded option is expected to increase markedly with decreasing call protection. Our model would imply that spreads on par bonds should increase rapidly with time. Initially, each year of added call protection is worth approximately 5 basis points at 12.5% volatility. By the time the bond becomes a 3-year bond with only one year left of protection, the option has more than doubled in value and the value will increase rapidly as the time to call diminishes. This is shown more clearly in Exhibit 9.

Exhibits 8 and 9 show how as call protection decreases, spreads should widen for bonds trading at par. When bonds become currently callable, the value of the option ceases to increase when priced at par. In currently callable bonds, slight changes in price have large effects on option value.

**Exhibit 8.  Value of Option as Bond Ages (In Basis Points)
7-year NC5 Bond at Par**

| Time-to-Maturity | Volatility | | | | | Leverage Ratio** |
|---|---|---|---|---|---|---|
| | *7.5%* | *10%* | *12.5%* | *15%* | *17.5%* | |
| 7 | 12 | 16 | 20 | 25 | 29 | .23 |
| 6 | 14 | 19 | 24 | 29 | 34 | .28 |
| 5 | 17 | 23 | 29 | 35 | 41 | .35 |
| 4 | 22 | 29 | 36 | 44 | 51 | .45 |
| 3 | 29 | 40 | 50 | 60 | 70 | .64 |
| 2* | | | | | | |
| 1 (currently callable) | 28 | 39 | 50 | 61 | 72 | 1.0 |

*Model is at Convergence Point—model results unreliable.
**Leverage ratio is a measure of the importance of call structure.

**Exhibit 9.  Option Value as a Bond Ages
7-year NC5 Bond at 100**

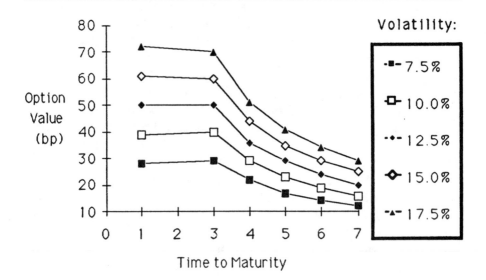

## Using the Leverage Ratio

The leverage ratio as defined in Equation 7 is a crude, but useful, estimator of relative option value in bonds with par calls (or puts) if they are trading at par. For examples, see Exhibits 7 and 8. A 7-year bond callable in five years has an LR=.23; and a 5-year bond callable in three years has an LR=.35. We would expect the option in the 5-year NC3 to be worth approximately 52% (.35/.23) more than in the 7-year NC5. At 12.5% volatility, the actual ratio of option values is 29 versus 20 basis points, or 45% higher.

## Prices Away From Par

A fairly effective rule of thumb for estimating the importance of price on option value is: The option diminishes to approximately one third of its value at par when yield moves to 100 basis points above the coupon. Or, when PPR=100bp, the option value falls to one third the value when PPR=0.

Given the definition of duration, 100 basis points in yield equals a price discount equal to its (modified) duration. For example, a 7-year NC5 trades at par 20 basis points cheaper than the NC equivalent 7 year bullet. The bullet yields 8.80%; the callable bond 9%. The bond's duration equals 5. Therefore, at a price of 95 (yielding roughly 10% on the callable issue) the option should be worth about 7 basis points. The comparable bullet should yield 9.93%.

## Cushion Bonds

The familiar notion of a "cushion" bond is one whose price performance tails off as it approaches and exceeds the call price. The tailing off, however, is only a function of the duration-to-maturity versus the duration-to-call. For a 10-year NC7 structure, the leverage ratio is .21 and the price of performance only diminishes by 79%. As a deep discount, the bond moves 6.5 basis points for every 1% in yield, at a high premium it moves 5.1 pts for every

1%. Not much cushioning. Older long bonds which have run out of call protection or long bonds with short calls, such as telephones (40-year NC5) have the greatest cushioning and, therefore, are the least desirable.

Many portfolio managers are more fearful of losing call protection on long bonds than on intermediates. Many are willing to pay up more for the protection in long bonds. A 5-year bond with one year of call protection has about the same duration uncertainty as a long bond (30-year) with three years of call protection. Both have a leverage ratio of about .75. Intermediates, especially aged intermediates, have enormous call risk, similar to that of long bonds with little remaining call protection. In fact, most longer bonds have higher call premiums which give added protection.

Whether your assets are matching duration of long liabilities such as life insurance or pension contracts, or short liabilities such as GICs, callable bonds can cause poor profitability and very large mismatches in maintaining a spread between assets and liabilities.

Throughout this discussion we should not lose sight of the objectives. If the market compensates an investor with sufficient excess yield for the call risk he bears, there is no reason not to buy a callable security. Investors should be especially willing to bear the risk if lower volatility is expected; in particular, if anticipated volatility is lower than that used in evaluating embedded option value.

### Long Bonds with Calls

In contrast to intermediates, most longer securities have call premiums and these premiums diminish to 100 over time. The importance and sensitivity of these characteristics of the call schedule will be reviewed.

Exhibit 10 illustrates the impact of structure on call values to various corporate long bonds. In contrast to Exhibit 7 which shows values for intermediates, long bond calls are worth at least twice the value. For example, the option embedded in a 10-year NC7 is worth 22 basis points, whereas a 30-year NR 10 (with a 104.5 call premium and 20-year par call) has an option valued at 55 basis

**Exhibit 10. Value of Call Option in Typical Long Bond Structures\***
**(In Basis Points)**

| Typical Sector | Structure | Call Premium | Par Call (yrs.) | Volatility | | | | |
|---|---|---|---|---|---|---|---|---|
| | | | | 7.5 | 10 | 12.5 | 15 | 17.5 |
| Industrial and Finance | 30-yr. NR10 | 104.5 | 20 | 22 | 32 | 42 | 53 | 64 |
| | 30-yr. NR10, Cash callable | 104.5, 109 | 20 | 27 | 44 | 64 | 84 | 105 |
| Utility | 30-yr. NR5 | 106.5 | 20 | 27 | 43 | 60 | 77 | 95 |
| Telephone | 40-yr. NR5 | 106.5 | 35 | 27 | 44 | 62 | 80 | 98 |
| | | 106.5 | 30 | 28 | 44 | 62 | 80 | 99 |
| | | 104.5 | 35 | 34 | 52 | 71 | 89 | 108 |
| | | 104.5 | 30 | 35 | 53 | 71 | 90 | 108 |
| TVA | 30-yr. NC5 | 104.4 | 25 | 40 | 58 | 76 | 95 | 114 |
| | 40-yr. NC10 | 106.2 | 35 | 26 | 38 | 49 | 61 | 73 |

\*9% coupons, 8% flat yield curve at par.

points. Both values represent 12.5% volatility. Unlike intermediates, the 55 basis points in long bonds do not represent the maximum option value. Even higher values occur as the dollar price approaches the call premium.

Exhibit 10 only shows option values for bonds trading at 100. We are using a flat yield curve which overstates call values relative to an upward sloping curve. Despite these various assumptions, some important conclusions can be drawn from this data (12.5% volatility is a standard for comparison): lower volatilities show less differences in option value; higher show larger effects. The conclusions about the relative structures are similar.

Utility and telephone bonds have the worst call protection. Either a 30-year or 40-year new issue trading at par have embedded options worth over 60 basis points at 12.5% volatility. The difference between a 30-year and 40-year with 5 years of refunding protection is only a few basis points. Most investors consider refund protection to be certain in utilities because they are regulated. Many utilities also have weak sinkers and Maintenance and Replacement (M&R) calls. The M&R call usually allows the issuer to redeem 1% of all outstanding debt in a given year at par. This is especially detrimental to the highest outstanding coupons which may be called in part or whole at a price well below their refund premium. This call is especially difficult, if not impossible, to value with an option model. It should be sufficient to know, however, that the call risk of high coupon utilities with M&R provisions is worse than calculated for the call schedule alone.

Call premiums are important. As shown in Exhibit 10, two points of additional premium on a 40-year telephone bond (from 104.5 to 106.5) is worth 10 additional basis points in option value. The time-to-par call is virtually insignificant in a typical new long utility bond.

There is considerable debate as to whether to consider the refund protection real or to consider the cash call (at issue) having importance to the call risk of the industrial bonds. Evidence from the bond rally in the early 1980s indicates that many industrial companies, if they have the cash, will not honor the refunding protection and will exercise the cash call if it is in their interest. In addition, most industrials also have sinking funds beginning in year 10. Some bank bonds also have sinking funds but insurance company paper does not. This feature will be in the sinking fund section to follow. It is important to realize, however, that the sinker is like a series of partial par calls and operates in addition to the call in limiting the upside movement in price when the bond trades above 100.

Industrial and finance long bonds with 10 years of true call protection reduce the value of the embedded option by about 30% relative to cash callable long industrials (42 versus 64 basis points at 12.5% volatility). The uncertainty concerning true refund protection in industrials has considerable impact. Without refunding protection, long industrials have the same weak call protection of long utilities.

The TVA bonds appear to have structures somewhat similar to utilities and telephones. The 40-year issue with 10 years of call protection has better call protection than the typical telephone bond by as much as 13 basis points (at 12.5% volatility). By contrast, the 30-year issue with a lower call price should trade 16 basis points richer than a typical 30 year utility, owing to its lower call premium.

### Effect of Premium Call

The premium call offers additional protection to most long bonds over other structures having only par calls. The premium does not offer enough additional protection to make new issue (par) long bond calls worth less than calls in intermediates. Long bond structures have much longer duration, and greater leverage, than intermediate structures. This is why, despite call premiums, there is greater call risk in most long bonds.

Call premiums do change the shape of the region over which spreads are expected to widen; however, Exhibit 11 contrasts the shape of spread premium expected for callable long bonds, with and without a call premium. Notice bonds with par calls peak in value at 100 and taper off rapidly.

In essence, the existence of a call premium which declines to par extends the region of prices over which yields remain wide to compensate investors for callability. The spread of bonds with a single call price should widen over a more restricted range of prices.

### Using a Call Model to Evaluate Swaps

Following the strategy outlined previously, any swap transaction can be separated into its component risks. Among noncallable bonds, call or convexity risk is small relative to credit, sector, and

## Exhibit 11. Option Cost and Price as Interest Rates Change

**Long Bond with 10-Year Premium Call**
Flat yield curve at 8%
Volatility=12.5%
(Settlement=8/25/89)

**Long Bond with 10-Year Par Call**
Flat yield curve at 8%
Volatility=12.5%
(Settlement=8/25/89)

30-year Bond -10-year Refund Protection
Call premium 104.5, par call year 20   | Structure |
Constant Option-Adjusted Spread =
95bp

30-year Bond -10-year call at 100

Constant Option-Adjusted Spread =
95bp

Exhibit 11A

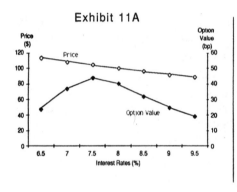

Exhibit 11B

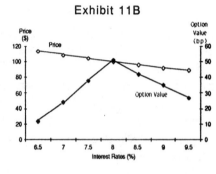

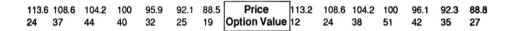

| 113.6 | 108.6 | 104.2 | 100 | 95.9 | 92.1 | 88.5 | **Price** | 113.2 | 108.6 | 104.2 | 100 | 96.1 | 92.3 | 88.8 |
| 24 | 37 | 44 | 40 | 32 | 25 | 19 | **Option Value** | 12 | 24 | 38 | 51 | 42 | 35 | 27 |

liquidity risks. In corporates, call risk can become the main source of risk, especially in similar credit or similar sector swaps.

Call models allow the investor to gain precision in evaluating the basis points value of call features. In evaluating swaps, the investor should analyze the change in option-adjusted duration and option-adjusted spread. He can look at the pickup or giveup in spread and determine if it is justified, given the other risks. While most investors insist on maintaining yield to maturity (YTM) in equal credit or sector swaps, option-adjusted yield (or spread) pickups can often be substantial, despite giveups in YTM. Theoretically and practically, from a performance basis, yield-to-maturity should be ignored in evaluating swaps containing options; the option components outweigh most other components of risk. Therefore, option-adjusted yield offers a better predictor of performance than yield-to-maturity.

In Swap Example 2, we see an equal option-adjusted duration swap of bonds of all the same issuer (GMAC). This swap is a synthetic combination of a noncallable bond plus and a call protected callable bond in exchange for one very callable issue. Given the same issuer is involved all sectors and credit risks are equal, both sides of the swap have the same option-adjusted duration (5.2 years). The swap generates a 10-basis-point pickup in Option-Adjusted Spread, despite a giveup of 14 basis points on a yield-to-maturity (duration-weighted) basis. The only risk not equalized is yield curve risk. This transaction will perform poorly only if the yield curve steepens substantially or if volatility is substantially lower than 12.5%.

In Swap Example 3, we sell a callable treasury and buy a straight bond of equal option-adjusted duration. This swap picks up 1-basis-point yield to maturity, but 32 basis points option-adjusted yield. It is a wonder that anyone owns callable treasuries at these levels.

Swap Example 4 shows a municipal swap. By exchanging New Jersey Turnpike 7.2s of '18 for Triboro Bridge and Tunnel Authority 6 1/2 of '16, we can see how mispriced the municipal market can be with respect to call risk. This transaction picks up 30 basis points on an option-adjusted yield basis. The NJs are callable in four years at 103, nine years at 100 and its price is 97 1/8. The TBTAs are callable later (in six and one half years) at 100, and the price is lower: 89 3/4. TBTAs clearly have more call protection and the model shows it.

Notice that Option Adjusted Spread only shows a pickup of 13 basis points while Option Adjusted Yield is +30 basis points. The difference reflects, in part, the lengthening of duration, on an option-adjusted basis, of 1.4 years (referred to as "curve change"

## Swap Example 2. Sell Callable/Buy Combination of Callable and NC

Same Issuer
Equal Option-Adjusted Duration
Volatility = 12.5%
(Settlement = 6/15/89)

| | Face | Security | Coupon | Maturity | Call $ | Call Date | Price | YTM | Dur | Option-Adjusted Yield | Option-Adjusted Spd. | Option-Adjusted Dur. |
|---|---|---|---|---|---|---|---|---|---|---|---|---|
| Sell: | 10.0 | GMAC | 8.75 | 6/15/01 | 103 | 6/15/89 | 96.07 | 9.27 | 7.3 | 8.88 | 57 | 5.2 |
| Buy: | 6.4 | GMAC | 8.00 | 01/15/02 | 103.2 | 1/15/89 | 91.34 | 9.17 | 7.7 | 8.96 | 67 | 6.5 |
| | 3.9 | GMAC | 9.80 | 05/01/93 | NC | | 102.61 | 8.98 | 3.3 | 8.98 | 66 | 3.3 |
| Differences (Dollar-duration weighted) | | | | | | | | -.14 | -1.3 | .08 | 10 | 0 |

**Swap Example 3. Callable versus Noncallable Treasury Swap**

Equal Option-Adjusted Duration
Volatility = 10%
(Settlement = 5/28/89)

| | Issuer | Coupon | Maturity | Call | Price | YTM | Option-Adjusted | |
| | | | | | | | Yield | Duration |
|---|---|---|---|---|---|---|---|---|
| Sell: | U.S. Treas. | 8.50 | 5/15/97 | Callable 94 at 100 | 100 | 8.50 | 8.19 | 5.5 |
| Buy: | U.S. Treas. | 7 3/8 | 5/15/96 | | 94.1 | 8.51 | 8.51 | 5.5 |
| Differences | | | | | | +1 bp | +32 bp | 0 |

# Swap Example 4.  Municipal Bond Swap

(Settlement = 10/09/89)

|  | Issuer | Coupon | Maturity | Call $ | Ratings | Price | YTM | Dur | Option-Adjusted | | |
|---|---|---|---|---|---|---|---|---|---|---|---|
|  |  |  |  |  |  |  |  |  | Yield | Spd. | Dur. |
| Sell: | NJ Tpke | 7.20 | 01/01/18-93 | 103 | A/A | 97.125 | 7.44 | 12 | 6.85 | -2 | 8.7 |
| Buy: | TBTA | 6.50 | 01/01/16-96 | 100.00 | Aa/A | 89.75 | 7.39 | 12 | 7.15 | 11 | 10.1 |
| Differences |  |  |  |  |  |  | -.05 | 0 | +.30 | +13 | 1.4 |

in Exhibit 5) Apparently, the risk-free curve used to determine the term structure sloped upward from duration = 8.7 to 10.1. It becomes apparent that for non-equal Option-Adjusted Duration swaps, the value of the curve shape must be considered. For this reason, *option-adjusted spread is preferred to option-adjusted yield as a measure of risk*. Option-Adjusted Spread is also a better measure of risk because it is calculated across the entire term structure, rather than at a specific point on the curve.

## The Sinking Fund Option

Many long corporate and municipal bonds contain sinking funds. This structural feature mandates the issuer to buy back a fixed minimum percentage of the original issue on a fixed schedule. For example, a 30-year bond may have a 5% annual sinker starting in year ten. Ten years later, half the issue is retired (5% × 10 years = 50%). The sinking fund average life is 20 years, the time an average dollar of principal is outstanding. Often, the issuer also may accelerate the sinking fund. The company may have the option to double. For our example, it could retire 10% each year starting in year 10, producing a double-up average life of 15 years. Investors recognize that sinking funds "shorten" their investment, particularly when a double-up or triple-up feature exists. This shortening can limit performance in a rally.

Sinking fund acceleration is another type of call option held by the issuer against the holder. An option still exists even without double-up or triple-up features. This right eliminates the holder's guarantee that the issuer will always pay par; at most, par is paid. This right is commonly known as the "open market option." It allows an issuer to buy securities in secondary markets to satisfy the sinking fund requirements. The option is a call; therefore, it will lower the value of the security relative to similar securities without any sinking funds. In fact, the sinking fund option represents a series of partial European calls, usually exercisable at par.

Most, if not all, bonds containing sinking funds also have regular call features. In contrast to the typical embedded American call option, the sinking fund option is not an option to retire the entire issue all at once. For this reason, average "term to exercise" (like its average life) is longer than an American call option exercisable at the beginning of the sinking fund. It is more akin to an American call exercisable near its average life. This lengthening of term to exercise reduces the strength of the sinking fund option relative to an American call; however, most sinking fund options have lower price protection. When an issuer retires a sinking fund payment, he pays at most 100. Call options on long bonds usually are at a premium, offering the holder greater protection. These two offsetting effects, greater time protection but poorer price protection, make the sinking fund option of comparable importance to the call option.

### Open Market Option

Why is the right to purchase in the open market a valuable option for the issuer? To understand this, begin by separating the action of the issuer when the bond trades above par versus below par. As with any call, when the bond is at a premium to the call price, it is in the issuer's interest to retire as many bonds as he can at 100 because (after considering taxes and reissuance costs) he can issue new bonds cheaper. The holder of the bonds who is sunk out (either pro rata or by lot) will lose value on his portion of the outstanding bonds. He is paid 100 when the open market pays in excess of 100. If retirement is pro rata, the holders loss is much similar to the holder of a premium GNMA whose prepayment rate accelerates. In the case of redemption by lot, the owner's loss is the risk of a lottery: he may be lucky and lose no bonds at all or he may lose a greater percentage than the average. Either by lot or pro rata, the holder can use statistics to determine his fate. This is traditionally done by calculating prices as a yield to average life or discounted cash flow, whichever is worse.

Exhibit 12 shows how yield is affected by the average term to sinking date for a bond priced at 97. At lower prices, the timing effect would appear to exaggerate yield. This difference in yield below par, however, is negated by the open market right. Here, although the issuer is mandated to retire some fixed percentage of

**Exhibit 12. Sinking Fund Analysis**

AMOCO 8 3/8%      6/15/05

| | |
|---|---|
| Callable | 103.25 6/15/89;  Par call 6/15/00 |
| Mandatory Sinker | 3.67%/year for 19 years starting in 1986 |
| Optional Sinker | 7.33%/year (double) |

| | |
|---|---|
| Settlement | 12/4/89 |
| Price | 97.00 |

| | *Term* | *Yield* |
|---|---|---|
| Maturity: | 15 1/2 years | 8.73 |
| Longest Average Life: | 10 years | 8.82 |
| Shortest Average Life: | 5 1/2 years | 9.04 |

the issue, if he has an open market option, he can pay less than 100. In fact, he can buy ahead his future sinking fund requirement at a discount to his original issue cost. Thus, the average holder, whose bonds are not bought by the issuer, gets a longer security which is something he does not want. He wants his money back at 100 as soon as possible.

## Cornering

Our analysis of the call risk of sinkers has so far only considered a holder of an arbitrarily small percentage of the issue: the innocent bystander not the typical sinking fund player or "cornerer." The main concern involves the limited upside of a sinking fund bond in a rally. All investors in sinkers lose performance in a rally. In a bear market, however, cornerers have an additional advantage. Those investors who accumulate sinking fund bonds, in effect, limit the issuer's option for open market purchase. The larger the accumulation, the greater the certainty of average life, and the more likely the issuer will be forced to pay par for discount sinking fund bonds. In a total corner, the issue's open market option ceases to exist.

The call option of sinking funds, as with regular calls, might imply to the average investor that sinkers with little true protection should have higher yields. For example, investors should pay up for distant sinkers relative to near active sinkers. In fact, the opposite is often true. As discount sinkers come closer to becoming active, their spreads to treasuries narrow considerably. This effect has nothing to do with option value.

Active corporate sinkers have natural buyers—the issuer and the collectors. This excess demand tightens spreads. Thus, *issuer buy-backs and collection of sinking funds is a supply and demand issue— not an option effect.* As sinkers age, if they remain at a discount to par, they become more valuable to the issuer or collector. An appealing strategy would be to purchase sinkers a few years before they become active and ride the narrowing, selling out just before they become active.

It is the callability of these bonds that can cause this strategy to backfire. If the bond should begin to trade near 100, not only will the demand-induced narrowing fade, but also the bond will widen in spread owing to the calls, just like any callable bond widens in a rally as the call price is approached. This widening was quite pronounced in the recent 150-basis-point rally of late spring-early summer 1989, and is shown in the average sector spread of active sinkers versus non-active and non-sinking fund industrial bonds in Exhibit 13. This behavior emphasizes the devastating performance of sinking fund bonds in a rally.

## Simultaneous Evaluation of Partial and Total Calls

Most sinking fund bonds also have normal (American) call options. In the typical new issue, the premium or cash call is, in effect, earlier than the sinking fund. A typical long sinker is cash callable at issue but the sinker begins in 10 years. The Amoco 8 3/8 of '05, shown in Exhibit 12, had a structure similar to this when it was issued.

Exhibit 14 illustrates the relative importance of the cash call to the sinker call as a sinker ages. Initially, the sinker has almost no value since the bond is immediately callable, even at a 8 3/8 point

## Exhibit 13. Average Option-Adjusted Spreads During a Rally

AA-rated Industrial Bonds
Active Sinkers versus Non-Active or Non-Sinking Fund Issues

| Date | Long Bond Yield | Average OAS (bp) | |
|------|-----------------|------------------|--|
| | | Non-Active Non-Sinkers | Active Sinkers |
| 3/13/89 | 9.34 | 57 | 19 |
| 11/24/89 | 7.87 | <u>76</u> | <u>51</u> |
| Difference: | 147 bp | 19 | 32 |

Source: Dillon, Read & Co. Inc. Fixed Income Research.

## Exhibit 14. Option Value of Each Call Component (In Basis Points)

Generic 30-Year Sinking Fund Bond, Coupon 8 3/8%

| | |
|---|---|
| Callable | 107.4 at issue; par call after 25 years |
| Mandatory Sinker | 3.67% per year for 19 years beginning in year 11 |
| Optional Sinker | 7.33% per year (double) |

| | Option Value (12% volatility) | |
|---|---|---|
| | New (107.4 call price) | 10 yrs. old (104.4 call price) |
| Cash Call | 63 bp | 64 bp |
| Sink Call | 13 bp | 21 bp |
| Cash + Sink Call Combined | 63 bp | 66 bp |

Price: 99
Flat yield curve: 8%

premium. The par sinking fund "call" begins 10 years out. Even after the bond's sinking activates, the total call (now at a 104.4 premium) dominates. The sinker calls should only contribute an extra 2bp to the yield.

Option models illustrate that both options, the partial and the total calls, compare in value when sinkers are active. Most sinkers have total calls which predate them. In those cases, sinking fund options can generally be ignored. Rarely does a series of partial calls have significant excess value relative to a total call, unless the partial calls begin prior to the total call. An example of this is shown in Swap Example 5.

The Citicorp 10 1/2% issue has a triple-up sinker option. Although there is call protection of almost seven years, in a worst case scenario roughly 60% of the issue could be called at par before the premium call even kicks in. The call on the remaining 40% will depend on where rates are in 1996; however, the present value of the full call at a premium versus the value of a series of sinks at par extending beyond 1996 would be negligible (see Exhibits 15A and 15B).

In the case of the 10 7/8% bond, the value of the sinker is equivalent to that of the 10 1/2s. The bond is more callable however, which costs the investor 10 basis points at a 12% volatility. The 20-basis-point yield-to-maturity pickup offsets this cost enough so that it still looks good on an option-adjusted spread basis at +6 basis points.

The reason that the sinking fund "call" has such a small effect on the overall option-adjusted spread of a typical bond is unintuitive. One would think that the addition of sinking fund options would always lower value to the owner, especially with par call prices. However, the shortening effect of the sinking fund dominates. A bond with a sinking fund implies the possibility of a shorter duration. Recall the "leverage effect" from our earlier analysis of simple calls. A 10-year NC3 bond with a 5 year average life has less option value than a non-sinker 10-year NC3. *Sinking funds lower the leverage of the total call.* Instead of a call on a typical 30-year bond, the sinker has the effect of making the call on a bond whose maturity is more like its average life. In sum, the sinking

# Swap Example 5. Comparison of Two Callable Sinking Fund Bonds

| | | | | | |
|---|---|---|---|---|---|
| Sell: | Citicorp | 10 7/8% | '10 | Callable 6/15/90 at 106.5 | Sinker 6/15/91 | Price = 101.43 |
| Buy: | Citicorp | 10 1/2% | '16 | Callable 2/1/96 at 104.5 | Sinker 2/1/92 | Price = 100 |

*Differences*

| | |
|---|---|
| Upgrade | A2/AA- to A1/AA |
| Yield to Maturity | +20 basis points |
| Option-Adjusted Spread | +6 basis points |
| Option-Adjusted Duration | -1.5 yrs. |

**Exhibit 15.**

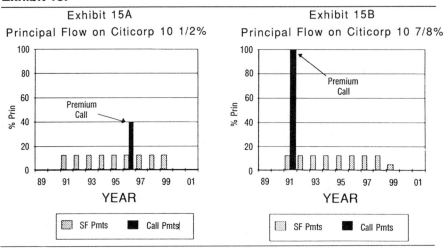

fund provision typically weakens the total call's impact, but adds more callability to the overall structure, principally through adding more calls at par.

The market's perception of the poor performance of sinking fund bonds as they approach a price of 100 has little to do with the existence of the partial par sinker. It is dominated by the total callability of the bond. As sinkers trade to a discount, they tighten, owing to collecting activity, or the investor's perception of potential cornering and open market purchase by the issuer.

## Put Bonds

In contrast to call options, where the issuer retains the right to call a bond back from the holder, put bonds offer the owner a rarely found level of control over the duration of his holding. The collector of put bonds tends to be a special sort of investor, one who is actually willing to pay up today for excess rights in the future. Until recently, few investors were willing to give up yield to maturity (or put in this case), yet many would forsake yield for noncallable paper, believing the call option which the issuer held was too valuable.

Embedded put options have a great performance characteristic. They lengthen in a rally just when an investor wants to retain his high coupon as long as possible. They shorten as rates rise, just when it is preferable to get principal back and reinvest at higher yields.

Typical put options are European and exercisable at par. They expire and become worthless on a specific date. Unlike the sinking fund option which is also European, the put is not usually renewable at a later date. There are a few put bonds with multiple exercise dates and these have additional value.

Many investors and traders who understand intuitively the relative value of call options in bonds fail to apply the same thinking to embedded puts. For example, we are familiar with the notion of call protection that is enhanced by time to expiration (time protection) and the difference between the current price and call price (price protection). In general, the shorter the time to call and the less the price protection, the more onerous is the call and the more yield the investor demands to take the call risk. In put bonds, generally, the closer the put is to exercise and the closer the bond trades to 100 (the put price), the more valuable the option tends to become, and the more the investor should be willing to pay up. *Put bonds should tighten to the curve as they approach 100,* just as callable bonds widen near their call price. (See Exhibit 16.)

One measure of the value of options is the degree of uncertainty they produce for the investor. In the case of puts, the greatest uncertainty exists when the bond trades near its put price. This is where the investor has his greatest advantage or leverage. To state it another way, an investor assigns little value to a put when it is quite certain that the bond should be put, or when it should be held to maturity. He might as well own a noncallable bond. This out-of-the-money condition only pays off if the bond begins to trade near the put price. Some investors will buy out-of-the-money puts if they do not have to pay up, because some upside advantage is retained at no additional cost.

Many investors are reluctant to buy put bonds at what looks like a low yield, especially if, as they move in either direction, the spread should widen (see Exhibit 16). This reflects a common mis-

**Exhibit 16. Expected Spread of a Put Bond as Dollar Price Changes**

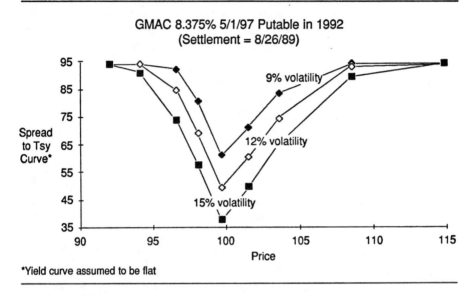

GMAC 8.375% 5/1/97 Putable in 1992
(Settlement = 8/26/89)

*Yield curve assumed to be flat

perception about the relationship between spread and price performance. Price performance can improve even if spreads widen.

Swap Example 6 illustrates how yield spreads can belie price performance for put bonds. Buying GMAC 8 3/8 '97 putable in 92 at +50 basis points over an equal option-adjusted duration treasury implies an option-adjusted pickup of 94 basis points.

The swap reflects a takeout of 2.49 points. To reverse, when the Treasury bond is 100 basis points higher in yield, the investor pays 2.12 points (a profit of .37); or given a 100-basis-point-rally, he pays 2.27 points to reverse (a gain of .22). In either case, the yield spread has widened, contrary to typical expectations.

### Puts and Calls Contrasted

The fact that the puts are European has two important implications when thinking about how to value them. If there is only one put option embedded, then the option is detachable. If there are multiple put options, then detachability depends on whether ear-

## Swap Example 6. Put Bond versus Noncall Bond

Volatility = 12%
(Settlement = 8/26/89)

|        |       |         | NC |
|--------|-------|---------|-------------------------|
| Sell:  | UST   | 8 5/8   | 11/5/93 |
| Buy:   | GMAC  | 8 3/8   | 5/1/97   Putable in 5/1/92 at 100 |

|             | Price   | Yield     | Spread (bp) | Option-Adjusted Spread | Duration | Option-Adjusted Duration |
|-------------|---------|-----------|-------------|------------------------|----------|--------------------------|
| UST         | 102.18  | 8.00      | 0           | 0                      | 3.5      | 3.5                      |
| GMAC        | 99.69   | 8.50(P)   | 50          | 94                     | 2.4      | 3.5                      |
| Differences |         | +50 bp    | +50 bp      | +94 bp                 | -.9      | 0                        |

### Effect of 100 bp rate shock*

**Price Performance**

|            | -100 bp | 0 bp   | +100 bp |
|------------|---------|--------|---------|
| GMAC       | 103.55  | 99.69  | 96.57   |
| U.S. Treas.| 105.83  | 102.18 | 98.68   |
|            | -2.27   | -2.49  | -2.12   |

**Yield Performance**

|            | -100 bp   | 0 bp     | +100 bp   |
|------------|-----------|----------|-----------|
| GMAC       | 7.75(M)   | 8.50(P)  | 9.85(P)   |
| U.S. Treas.| 7.00      | 8.00     | 9.00      |
|            | +75       | +50      | +85       |

**Option-Adjusted Durations**

|            | -100 bp | 0 bp | +100 bp |
|------------|---------|------|---------|
| GMAC       | 4.2     | 3.5  | 2.9     |
| U.S. Treas.| 3.5     | 3.5  | 3.5     |
|            | +.7     | 0    | -.6     |

*Maintaining Option-Adjusted spread of 94 bp on GMAC bond.

lier puts have been exercised. The options cannot be detached without changing the value of subsequent exercise dates. The final put option in a multiput bond is still detachable. In this way, put options resemble OTC call options on straight bonds. Therefore, they can be more easily evaluated and offset.

American options always increase in value as the time to expiration shortens—the familiar bane of poor call protection. European options have a more complex behavior. When puts expire they are worthless, so as expiration approaches, option values fall. The implication is shown in Exhibit 17. As the time to put on a 30-year bond decreases, the price is expected to increase at a constant (option-adjusted) spread, reflecting that the put bond has become more valuable. Likewise, a callable bond should become cheaper as its call protection decreases. The peak in the value of the put bond reflects its European rather than American exercise.

Similarly, Exhibit 18 shows how this type of option is most important for short terms to exercise. In general, as with calls, the "leverage" between time to put and time to maturity has a significant effect on the value of the embedded option; however, Euro-

**Exhibit 17. Time Value of Calls and Puts**

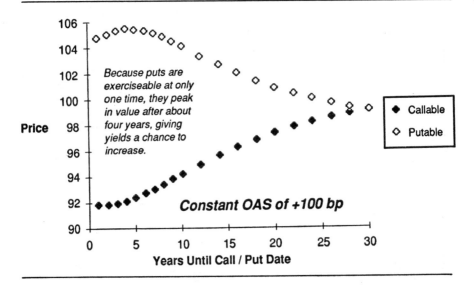

## Exhibit 18. Value of Different Types of Embedded Options (In Basis Points)

12% volatility
Flat yield curve at 8%
Bonds priced at par

| Term to Exercise | Option Type | Abs. Value European | Abs. Value American | Ratio Eur/Am | Leverage Ratio* |
|---|---|---|---|---|---|
| **10-Year Maturity** | | | | | |
| 1 | Call | 83 | **103** | 81% | .85 |
| 3 | Call | 57 | **66** | 86% | .60 |
| 5 | Call | 39 | **41** | 95% | .39 |
| 1 | Put | **74** | 91 | 81% | .85 |
| 3 | Put | **53** | 60 | 88% | .60 |
| 5 | Put | **37** | 38 | 97% | .39 |
| **5-year Maturity** | | | | | |
| 1 | Call | 61 | **71** | 86% | .76 |
| 3 | Call | 27 | **28** | 96% | .34 |
| 1 | Put | **58** | 66 | 88% | .76 |
| 3 | Put | **26** | 27 | 96% | .34 |

The **European option is more restrictive** (i.e., puts) because it is only exercisable at one time. Its absolute value and contribution to the value of a bond will tend to be less than an American option of the same maturity and term to exercise.

As expected, both types of **options gain value as the term to exercise shortens.** A 10-year bond callable in 5 years has less embedded option value than a 10-year bond callable in 3 years (41 bp versus 66 bp).

As the term to exercise lengthens, the **distinction between European and American options** diminishes. It is **most different for long maturities and short terms to exercise.**

(Option values in bold type indicate embedded options in typical corporate bonds.)

Leverage ratio is a measure of the importance of calls or puts to structure. It is a reasonably good estimator of option value in bonds callable at par, trading at par.

*(DTM-DTP)/DTM or (DTM – DTC) / DTM
DTM = Duration to maturity
DTP = Duration to put
DTC = Duration to call

pean options have less leverage effect. A 10-year bond with five years to call would have an option worth 41 basis points when trading at par (at 12% volatility). The analogous put would be worth slightly less, 37 basis points. However, in a shorter option with three years of call protection, the call goes to 66 basis points, a 60% increase. The 10-year bond with 3-year put is worth 53 basis points, a 43% increase in value.

The leverage effect can be thought of in present value terms. The difference in present value of owning a 5-year bond versus a 10-year bond is less than the difference between owning a 3-year bond versus 10-year bond. This is especially true at high interest rates, where discount rates favor shorter cash flows.

As time passes, the leverage effect gives way to the time value and the put disappears; however, the leverage effect tends to be most important. This leads us to a valuable conclusion about put bonds that is often ignored in the market. *Put bonds trading near par with short time periods to put are very valuable to the owner.* Thus, in theory, the market for short puts should tighten to the curve considerably. Since most investors shy away from paying up for anything, the extra payup expected for short put bonds is usually not found. (Have you ever seen a put bond priced through the curve?) This is precisely why investors should seek them out because they would be buying a bond rich in convexity for little additional payup.

### Multiple Put Bonds

To state the obvious, bonds with more than one put are more valuable than those with single puts. Exhibit 19 lists those multi-put bonds issued to date. The market is often mystified as to how to price the additional puts. Again, the analysis of these options is not straightforward and often not amenable to rules of thumb. While option models do not necessarily tell us absolute value, they are very powerful in determining the sensitivity of these various factors in a complicated structure such as a multi-put bond.

Consider Chrysler Financial 8.5% of '18. This bond has three put options and one call option on the same date as the final put.

**Exhibit 19. Corporate Bonds with Multiple Puts (as of 6/15/90)**

| Issuer | Coupon | Maturity | Put Dates | Issue Size |
|---|---|---|---|---|
| Associates | 12.4% | 10/1/95 | 90,92 | 100MM |
| Chrysler Finance | 8.5% | 2/1/18 | 92,96,00* | 200MM |
| IADB | 8.4% | 9/1/09 | 99,04 | 300MM |
| ITT Finance | 8.875% | 6/15/03 | 92,97 | 125MM |
| ITT Finance | 8.825% | 6/01/10 | 95,00,05 | 100MM |
| Commercial Credit | 8.70% | 6/15/10 | 93,96,99,02,05 | 100MM |
| GMAC | 8.875% | 6/01/10 | 95,00,05 | 500MM |
| Westinghouse Credit | 8.875% | 6/14/14 | 94,99,04 | 150MM |

*Callable in 2000 also

The simultaneous put and call in the year 2000, both at par, have the effect of a final maturity on that date. That is, either it will be in the interest of the issuer to retire the bonds at par or in the investor's favor to do so. Thus, this bond effectively has two put options. The incremental effect of the second one is easily determined by running the model with and without it (See Exhibit 20).

**Exhibit 20. Effect of Adding Puts**

Chrysler Financial 8 1/2 of 2/1/18      putable 2/1/92, 2/1/96, 2/1/00
Settlement = 10/6/89                     callable 2/1/00 at 100

| | Option Value (bp)* Volatility | | |
|---|---|---|---|
| | 9% | 12% | 15% |
| All Options | 51 | 67 | 83 |
| Without '96 Put | 46 | 61 | 75 |
| Difference | 5 | 6 | 8 |

*Bond priced at 100

The result found at a price of 100 shows at 9% volatility = 5 bp, 12% volatility = 6 bp and 15% volatility = 8 bp. As the bond price moves away from par, the option value drops.

Multiple put options should trade tighter than bonds of a similar maturity, dollar price, and distance to first put. Each additional put adds value to the bond, though more distant ones add incrementally less.

A series of put options cannot exceed, however, in overall value what an embedded call of similar strike and time to expiration is worth. We are assuming the call is an American option while the put is European. In the extreme, an infinite series of European options must equal one American option. This is why, all other things being equal, typical call options on bonds with 100 as a redemption price are more valuable options for the issuer than put options are for the investor.

Many put bonds are mispriced when they trade above par. The market often prices on a yield-to-put basis even when an issue trades above the put price. This is a convention. It is still used even though yield to maturity is the "yield-to-worst." The market continues to have a relatively poor understanding of how to price the put option. Put bonds, despite their obscurity, present opportunities to investors. Many put bonds may look unusually cheap or rich on an option adjusted basis as a result of naive pricing.

## Comment on the Use of Option Models

Many of the conclusions in this paper about the importance of various structural features of bonds are drawn from running our option model. The model's assumptions are based on current term structure theory and mimic the way most of the options are, in fact, exercised in real markets. If anything, we may overstate the call risk in favor of the investors. We make no provision for "uneconomic" exercise by the issuer. Furthermore, we make no distinction between how readily one issuer, or type of issuer, takes advantage of call options. For example, the model assumes utility companies call their bonds as readily as finance companies. In fact, there is evidence that finance companies exercise call options more frequently and at market levels much closer to the original cost of funds of the issue being refunded.

Generally, the question of relative callability of issuers is a qualitative one, not unlike credit analysis. We try here to present a framework which eliminates this "confusion," by looking at mathematically tractable questions only. This does not imply that other considerations are to be ignored.

The development of option models for embedded options is still an art and not a science, although many would argue otherwise. How future rate paths are generated varies from one model to the next, the amount of mean reversion, and the interpretation of volatility remains quite qualitative. Questioning whether volatility is long-term or short-term, and whether it varies over time, may produce different results. Furthermore, the handling of distributions of interest rates, and the effect of term structure are model dependent.

## Implied Volatility in Embedded Options

Volatility is an especially difficult issue. What volatility is reasonable to use? This question is clearly a market bet. Just as investors for years have made bets on the overall direction of the market, so should they make bets on the future volatility of the market. Callable bonds have excess value at low volatilities. If you believe volatility will go down, then you should use a low volatility when running comparisons between different structures. Many investors must take call risk by owning mortgage-backed securities and, thus, are already betting on volatility. They can weight their portfolio with corporate bonds to either offset (noncallables and puts) or enhance this call risk (with callable and sinkable bonds).

The appropriate benchmarks that should be used to determine historical volatility is also a somewhat ambiguous issue. Many investors look to the implied volatility of the options on bond futures. This only measures the market's view on short-term volatility, however. A longer-term volatility is implied by the long options embedded in bond structures. A better approach is by comparison:

1. Calculate the implied volatility of a given swap. This is the volatility at which the swap is done, where the spread change is equal to what the investor thinks the qualitative spread is worth. For example, if the swap is a +20 basis points option-adjusted (at 12% volatility), the investor believes a noncallable equivalent transaction should be +5 basis points. If run at 8% volatility, the swap is +5 basis points, and the implied volatility of the swap is 8%.

2. Compare this volatility to that implied by the new issue market. For example, what is the implied volatility of a 5-year NC trading 20 basis points richer than a 7-year NC5.

If you think the new issue market is reasonable, then a swap with a lower implied volatility should be executed. If you think that 20 basis points is too much for the new issue spread, calculate the implied volatility of what you think is reasonable. This should then be compared to that implied by the swap.

## Conclusion

An investor can learn much from running sensitivity analyses on differing bond structures. Poor conclusions can only reflect poor assumptions and, without computers to help interpret these complex interactions, we fail to make progress for investors to price the market more efficiently. Already in the last year, corporate investors have embraced put bonds. I believe much of this interest comes from a greater understanding and use of option models.

The municipal market is only beginning to analyze structure more closely. This should continue to progress as more paper moves into the hands of money managers who are paid on the basis of performance rather than on purchase yield. The municipal market has other qualitative problems which confound the use of options models. These include the impact of prerefunding on call evaluation and the lack of a clear term structure on which to base a "risk-free" set of rates. Nevertheless, even primitive models will help uncover many mispriced and poorly understood structural features.

The most important reason to use these models, however, remains as a method to create comparisons—not to determine absolute value but relative value. This is why the bond swap or relative ranking scheme is the fundamental way to look at quantitative analysis. Whether the option-adjusted spread is 50 basis points or 40 basis points for a given structure and credit should not matter. What should matter is whether this is more or less than another bond of similar credit, liquidity, or sector, but different structure.

# Chapter 8

# Simulation Methods for the Evaluation of Option Models

Richard M. Bookstaber
Morgan Stanley

## Introduction

The purpose of this chapter is to present a methodology for evaluating option models. The methodology begins with the observation that the objective of an option model is to replicate an option's payoff for a predetermined cost. It then employs simulation methods to gauge how well the model fulfills that objective.

The development of this evaluation methodology is motivated in part by the proliferation of option models over the past several years, models that claim superior performance based on more realistic characterizations of security returns, arbitrage-free yield curves, and a more complete treatment of the idiosyncratic cash flows and path-dependent nature of particular financial instruments.

Model evaluation has motivation beyond the options themselves. Option pricing theory has been applied to a wide variety of financial assets. Option-based models have become the standard for pricing callable bonds, mortgage-backed securities, and increas-

This chapter was adapted from Richard M. Bookstaber, *Option Pricing and Investment Strategies*, 3rd Edition. (Chicago, IL: Probus Publishing Co, 1991).

ingly complex swap-related strategies. For the investment firms that rely on option models for investment decisions, the swap and option-trading desks that use option models for managing their books, or the mortgage operations that rely on option-based models for pricing and hedging information, it is important to question the effectiveness of these models.

The usual starting point in evaluating a model is to summarize its assumptions and logical structure. We can ask whether an option model has realistic assumptions, and whether its design is consistent with the arbitrage and replication underpinnings of the theory. Since the basis of option pricing methodology is the creation of a dynamic hedge against the underlying asset, we might ask whether the underlying asset is indeed hedgeable.[1] Since the assumptions behind interest rates and term structure are so central to fixed income securities, we might ask whether the model incorporates sensible interest rate behavior.[2]

Unfortunately, with the increasing complexity of option models, it is difficult to pass even this starting point with any assurance. Furthermore, many models are shielded from careful scrutiny because of their proprietary nature, making more than a cursory evaluation impossible.

Another method of evaluating an option model is to see whether the prices it generates conform to market prices. This has been the principal evaluation method used in academic studies, with conformity of the model and market prices taken as evidence

---

1. If the underlying asset is not liquid, as would be the case, for example, with some corporate bonds (especially in the high yield sector), or if the hedging strategy requires a long-term hedge to be successful, as would be the case for many of the options embedded in fixed income instruments, we might reasonably wonder what claim the option pricing approach can actually have on the marketplace.

We can always go through the exercise of constructing an option model and pricing the contingent claim. But if the marketplace does not fulfill the basic assumptions required for the application of this model, we will be engaging in an academic exercise of the form: "If this asset were liquid, and if the hedge were followed over the life of the option, then this hedging strategy would imply a price of such-and-such would be necessary to eliminate arbitrage." If the hedge cannot be followed in practice, then there need be no link between this and what is observed in the market.

2. For example, some models allow negative interest rates. While it is easy in the computational process to restrict rates from going negative, we would then wish to ascertain what imposing such a restriction might mean for other characteristics of the model, such as the distribution of interest rates or the path of implied forward rates. Other models might employ methods of generating yield curves that bear little resemblance to the yield curves that are observed in practice, either in terms of shape or in terms of the probability of a particular type of yield curve materializing.

that the model is correct. While this method has been widely used in tests of option models in the academic literature, there are two problems with using this approach in many of the fixed income markets.

First, for many instruments, such as swaptions and new financial products, little market history exists, and the price history that does exist for many of the over-the-counter markets is not particularly reliable. Second, there is no reason to assume the market price is correct. The measure of an option model has nothing to do with the market price of the option. An option model provides a methodology for replicating the terminal payoff of an option. If it is correct, then by following its hedging prescription, the investor will be able to replicate the payoff of the target option, and the cost of doing so will be the model-determined option price.

Thus, rather than being a refutation of the option model, a deviation between the market price and model price may present an investor with an opportunity to make arbitrage profits. If an option model shows a lower price for an option than the price quoted in the market, the option model may still be correct. If it is, the investor can make arbitrage profits by writing the overpriced option available in the marketplace and replicating its payoff by following the hedging prescription of the model. If the model is correct, the replication it dictates will provide the same terminal payoff as the option the investor has written, and will do so for a lower price than that obtained when the option was written.

Option pricing theory itself provides the answer to the best method for evaluating an option model. The construction of an option pricing model begins with the development of a dynamic hedging strategy. This strategy is designed to replicate the payoff of the target option. The option price is the cost of following this hedging strategy; thus, it evolves from the model as a byproduct of the hedging strategy. From a theoretical standpoint, the measure of an option pricing model is whether, when its hedging prescription is followed, it replicates the payoff of the target option for a cost equal to the model price.[3]

---

3. An exposition of the creation of option models as dynamic hedging strategies is presented in Bookstaber, Richard, *Option Pricing and Investment Strategies*, 3rd Edition. Chicago, IL: Probus Publishing, 1991, Ch. 7.

We will illustrate this methodology with tests of the standard Black-Scholes model. Since this model is widely used and easily applied, it will allow a base case for the analysis of other models. Note, however, that our final objective is not to make an evaluation of the Black-Scholes model. Rather, our objective is to illustrate a methodology that can be applied to evaluate any option model, whether it be for fixed income or foreign exchange options, option-based models for mortgage-backed securities, or swaptions.

## A Description of Hedging Methodology

The objective of an option pricing model is to construct a hedge that will give the same payoff as the target option at expiration. The option price given by the model is the cost of executing this hedge. For example, if we wish to replicate a call option with an exercise price of $100 and an expiration date of one year, the objective of the option model is to devise a hedge that will provide a payoff equal to the maximum of zero or the asset price minus $100 in one year. If the option model states that this option costs $5, it means that the hedging procedure will cost a total of $5 to execute. This generally includes the cost of borrowing any assets needed for the hedge, but does not include transaction costs.

A good option model provides the payoff for the stated cost. In order to provide the same payoff as the option at expiration, the hedge mimics the price behavior of the option throughout its life. Every day, the option model determines how much the option should change with a change in the underlying asset. This relative price change is measured by the option's delta; for example, if a $1 change in the asset should lead the option price to change by $.60, then the option's delta is .60. This delta will depend on the price of the underlying asset, as well as on other variables, such as interest rates and price volatility. The delta, and thus the size of the replicating hedge, will also depend on the exercise price and the time remaining to expiration. The delta drops to zero as the option moves far out-of-the-money and moves toward one as the option moves far into the money; thus, the hedging process is dynamic in nature

## An Example of Option Replication

Exhibit 1 presents an example of a replicating hedge. The option in this example is an at-the-money call option with two months (42 business days) to expiration. The underlying security price is initially $100. Based on the time to expiration, exercise price, security price, and other parameter values, the option model gives a delta of .63.[4] Thus, the initial hedge position, shown in column 4 of the table, is long $62.79 of the underlying security. (The hedge position differs slightly from the delta because the latter is rounded in the exhibit.)

The option model gives a price for this option of $2.13. Just as it would take $2.13 to buy this option in the market (assuming the market followed our model), the hedge also requires an initial deposit of this amount, as is shown in the first entry of the "Cumulative Cash Flow" column. While the hedge is begun with this $2.13 in hand, an additional $60.66 must be borrowed to finance the purchase of the $62.79 position. There will be an interest cost for this financing.

The following day, the security price rises from $100 to $101.09. The increase leads to a positive cash flow of $.68 from the hedge position, and the interest cost on the security position borrowed to create the hedge is $.01, leading to a net cash flow for the day of $.67. This is shown in the "Daily Cash Flow" column. The $.67 is added to cumulative cash flow. The cumulative cash flow is the value of the replicating strategy and provides a check on the tracking of the replication. If the model is correct, the cumulative cash flow should closely match the model's option price. On the second day of the hedge, the cumulative cash flow is $2.80, while the theoretical option price is $2.84. The hedging error is thus $.04.

The delta calculated by the option model also rises with the increase in the security price, moving from .63 to .73. This leads to an increase in the hedge position to $73.92. On the next day, with 40 days remaining to expiration, the security price rises again to

---

4. This example uses the Black-Scholes model. The volatility used in this example is the actual volatility of the sample path, .11, and the interest rate is assumed to be 10%.

## Exhibit 1.   Option Replication Simulation

| Days to Expiration | Current Security Price | Option Delta | Hedge Position | Daily Cash Flow | Cumulative Cash Flow | Theoretical Option Price | Hedging Error (Model- Simulation) |
|---|---|---|---|---|---|---|---|
| 42 | 100.00 | 0.63 | 62.79 | 0.00 | 2.13* | 2.13 | 0.00 |
| 41 | 101.09 | 0.73 | 73.92 | 0.67 | 2.80 | 2.84 | 0.04 |
| 40 | 102.14 | 0.82 | 83.28 | 0.74 | 3.54 | 3.61 | 0.07 |
| 39 | 99.94 | 0.62 | 61.67 | -1.81 | 1.73 | 1.99 | 0.26 |
| 38 | 98.93 | 0.50 | 49.73 | -0.64 | 1.08 | 1.39 | 0.30 |
| 37 | 98.56 | 0.46 | 45.13 | -0.20 | 0.89 | 1.18 | 0.29 |
| 36 | 96.76 | 0.26 | 24.96 | -0.84 | 0.05 | 0.51 | 0.46 |
| 35 | 98.63 | 0.46 | 45.17 | 0.48 | 0.53 | 1.15 | 0.62 |
| 34 | 98.44 | 0.43 | 42.44 | -0.10 | 0.43 | 1.03 | 0.61 |
| 33 | 98.40 | 0.42 | 41.46 | -0.03 | 0.39 | 0.98 | 0.59 |
| 32 | 97.99 | 0.37 | 36.10 | -0.18 | 0.21 | 0.80 | 0.58 |
| 31 | 97.49 | 0.31 | 29.75 | -0.19 | 0.02 | 0.60 | 0.58 |
| 30 | 97.45 | 0.29 | 28.72 | -0.02 | 0.00 | 0.56 | 0.56 |
| 29 | 97.12 | 0.25 | 24.40 | -0.11 | -0.11 | 0.45 | 0.55 |
| 28 | 96.91 | 0.22 | 21.63 | -0.06 | -0.17 | 0.38 | 0.54 |
| 27 | 96.87 | 0.21 | 20.56 | -0.01 | -0.18 | 0.35 | 0.53 |
| 26 | 97.10 | 0.23 | 22.19 | 0.04 | -0.14 | 0.37 | 0.51 |
| 25 | 97.28 | 0.24 | 23.42 | 0.04 | -0.10 | 0.39 | 0.50 |
| 24 | 97.32 | 0.24 | 23.12 | 0.00 | -0.10 | 0.38 | 0.48 |
| 23 | 97.49 | 0.25 | 24.33 | 0.03 | -0.06 | 0.40 | 0.46 |
| 22 | 97.23 | 0.21 | 20.61 | -0.07 | -0.14 | 0.31 | 0.45 |
| 21 | 97.41 | 0.22 | 21.70 | 0.03 | -0.11 | 0.33 | 0.43 |
| 20 | 97.10 | 0.18 | 17.54 | -0.07 | -0.18 | 0.24 | 0.42 |
| 19 | 97.15 | 0.18 | 17.07 | 0.00 | -0.18 | 0.23 | 0.40 |
| 18 | 97.54 | 0.21 | 20.52 | 0.06 | -0.11 | 0.28 | 0.39 |
| 17 | 98.04 | 0.27 | 26.08 | 0.10 | -0.01 | 0.37 | 0.39 |
| 16 | 98.68 | 0.35 | 34.89 | 0.16 | 0.15 | 0.54 | 0.39 |
| 15 | 98.86 | 0.38 | 37.08 | 0.05 | 0.21 | 0.57 | 0.36 |
| 14 | 97.93 | 0.22 | 21.25 | -0.36 | -0.15 | 0.26 | 0.41 |
| 13 | 97.92 | 0.20 | 20.00 | -0.01 | -0.16 | 0.23 | 0.39 |
| 12 | 98.52 | 0.28 | 28.03 | 0.12 | -0.04 | 0.35 | 0.39 |
| 11 | 99.12 | 0.38 | 38.06 | 0.16 | 0.12 | 0.50 | 0.39 |
| 10 | 99.71 | 0.50 | 49.75 | 0.21 | 0.33 | 0.72 | 0.38 |
| 9 | 100.30 | 0.63 | 62.95 | 0.28 | 0.62 | 1.00 | 0.38 |
| 8 | 100.81 | 0.74 | 74.33 | 0.30 | 0.92 | 1.29 | 0.37 |
| 7 | 100.55 | 0.69 | 69.26 | -0.21 | 0.71 | 1.05 | 0.34 |
| 6 | 100.95 | 0.79 | 79.33 | 0.26 | 0.96 | 1.29 | 0.33 |
| 5 | 101.34 | 0.87 | 88.58 | 0.29 | 1.25 | 0.56 | 0.31 |
| 4 | 101.42 | 0.91 | 91.98 | 0.04 | 1.29 | 1.58 | 0.29 |
| 3 | 101.10 | 0.88 | 89.10 | -0.32 | 0.98 | 1.24 | 0.26 |
| 2 | 101.07 | 0.91 | 92.46 | -0.05 | 0.93 | 1.15 | 0.23 |
| 1 | 100.95 | 0.95 | 96.34 | -0.13 | 0.79 | 0.99 | 0.19 |
| 0 | 100.80 | 1.00 | 100.80 | -0.17 | 0.62 | 0.80 | 0.18 |

*Initial option value

$102.14. With the higher delta, the cash flow is $.74.[5] The cumulative cash flow rises to $3.54, but this fails to keep up with the rise in the theoretical value of the option, and the replication error increases to $.07.

The $102.14 price is the highest realized for this price path. The security price drops quickly over time, to a low of $96.87, 27 days before expiration. The delta also drops—to .21. The quick decline in price leads the replication error to increase. With 27 days to expiration, the cumulative cash flow from the strategy is -$.18, while the option price is $.35, leading to a hedging error of $.53. The maximum hedging error over the course of the hedge is even greater than this: with 35 days left to expiration, seven days into the hedge, the error is $.62.

By expiration, the security price recovers to land the option $.80 in the money. The hedging error of the replicating strategy also recovers. The payoff for the replication is $.62, leaving an ending error of $.18.

### The Use of Replication in Simulations

Exhibit 1 illustrates the result of the replication for one price path. We can get a more complete picture of the effectiveness of the model by repeating the same procedure over many paths. In doing so, it is important to select paths that are representative of the actual price behavior of the market.

One way to generate paths is to draw samples from a return distribution. For example, because security returns are conventionally assumed to be lognormally distributed, we could generate a lognormal distribution with a particular mean and variance, draw daily sample returns, and apply those returns to obtain the day-to-day price changes. Unfortunately, this procedure assumes away much of what the methodology seeks to test. By generating lognormal returns, the price paths are made to be consistent with the distribution assumptions underlying the model, but may not be

---

5. This can be calculated by multiplying the hedge position by the return over the one day, 73.92 × (102.14/101.09) = $.7468, and adjusting for one day's interest expense.

consistent with the distribution underlying the actual prices in the market.

A better way to generate paths is to sample from actual market data. By sampling with replacement from a representative historical time series, we can create price paths that embody the key distributional elements of the market.[6] Exhibit 2 illustrates the results of this procedure by generating 10 sample paths from a bootstrap of daily closing S&P 500 prices. In this report, we will generate price paths based on bootstrapping the market data.

**Exhibit 2.  Examples of Generated Price Paths**

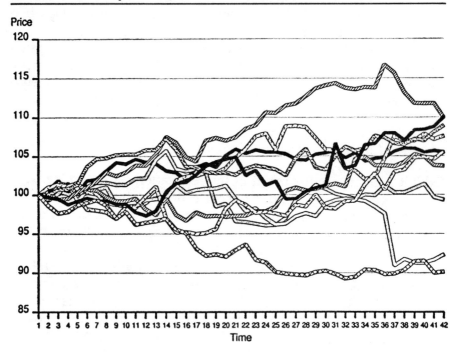

---

6. Given a time series of sample prices, the procedure is to first convert prices into returns. A set of returns is then drawn at random with replacement (so that it is possible to draw the same return more than once), and the starting price, which in our report is set at $100, is multiplied by each return in turn to generate the day-by-day prices.

This methodology, known as bootstrapping, has a strong statistical basis. If the sample is representative of the population and the data points are statistically independent, the paths generated by the bootstrap will maintain the same distributional characteristics as the sample from which they are drawn.

The replication study of Exhibit 1 presents the starting point for using replication in option evaluation. By repeating the replication over many paths, we can evaluate the success of the option model in fulfilling its function. Using this as a starting point, we can also answer more complex option pricing questions. For example, we can compare two option models by looking at their efficiency in replicating on the same set of price paths. Or, we can introduce errors in volatility and interest rate estimation, or impose transaction costs on the hedge. We will look at these sorts of issues in the next two sections of the report.

To illustrate how the base-case replication can be altered, in Exhibit 3 we show the impact of imposing a minimum hedge adjustment size on the replication presented in Exhibit 1. Minimum trigger widths are often used as a filter to prevent unduly frequent hedge adjustment in the face of transaction costs. In Exhibit 3, the option delta is adjusted only when the delta moves by more than 5%. This leads to less frequent hedge adjustments; indeed, there are a number of times during the 42-day hedging period when the hedge remains unchanged for three or more days.

As expected, the hedging error in this case is generally higher than in the case of daily hedging. The maximum error is $.70, compared with a maximum error of $.62 for the case of daily adjustments, and the ending error is $.23, compared with an ending error of $.18 for the daily case. While the error is higher, however, the turnover of the hedge will frequently be lower, so what is lost by less frequent hedging may be gained by having lower transaction costs. We will discuss the tradeoff between replication error and transaction costs in Section V.

## Base Case Results

As a starting point for the tests, we will apply the standard Black-Scholes model in a replication based on a simplified set of parameters: a constant interest rate, no transaction costs, accurate estimates of the average volatility of the path, and hedge adjustments made at the end of each day based on the day's closing

## Exhibit 3.  Option Replication Simulation With 5% Trigger Width

| Days to Expiration | Current Security Price | Option Delta | Hedge Position | Daily Cash Flow | Cumulative Cash Flow | Theoretical Option Price | Hedging Error (Model- Simulation) |
|---|---|---|---|---|---|---|---|
| 42 | 100.00 | 0.63 | 62.79 | 0.00 | 2.13* | 2.13 | 0.00 |
| 41 | 101.09 | 0.73 | 73.92 | 0.67 | 2.80 | 2.84 | 0.04 |
| 40 | 102.14 | 0.82 | 83.28 | 0.74 | 3.54 | 3.61 | 0.07 |
| 39 | 99.94 | 0.62 | 61.67 | -1.81 | 1.73 | 1.99 | 0.26 |
| 38 | 98.93 | 0.50 | 49.73 | -0.64 | 1.08 | 1.39 | 0.30 |
| 37 | 98.56 | 0.50 | 49.28 | -0.20 | 0.89 | 1.18 | 0.29 |
| 36 | 96.76 | 0.26 | 24.96 | -0.92 | -0.03 | 0.51 | 0.54 |
| 35 | 98.63 | 0.46 | 45.17 | 0.48 | 0.45 | 1.15 | 0.70 |
| 34 | 98.44 | 0.46 | 45.28 | -0.10 | 0.35 | 1.03 | 0.69 |
| 33 | 98.40 | 0.46 | 45.26 | -0.03 | 0.32 | 0.98 | 0.67 |
| 32 | 97.99 | 0.37 | 36.10 | -0.20 | 0.12 | 0.80 | 0.68 |
| 31 | 97.49 | 0.31 | 29.75 | -0.19 | -0.08 | 0.60 | 0.68 |
| 30 | 97.45 | 0.31 | 30.21 | -0.02 | -0.10 | 0.56 | 0.66 |
| 29 | 97.12 | 0.25 | 24.40 | -0.11 | -0.21 | 0.45 | 0.66 |
| 28 | 96.91 | 0.25 | 24.23 | -0.06 | -0.27 | 0.38 | 0.64 |
| 27 | 96.87 | 0.25 | 24.22 | -0.02 | -0.28 | 0.35 | 0.63 |
| 26 | 97.10 | 0.25 | 24.27 | 0.05 | -0.23 | 0.37 | 0.61 |
| 25 | 97.28 | 0.25 | 24.32 | 0.04 | -0.20 | 0.39 | 0.59 |
| 24 | 97.32 | 0.25 | 24.33 | 0.00 | -0.19 | 0.38 | 0.57 |
| 23 | 97.49 | 0.25 | 24.33 | 0.04 | -0.16 | 0.40 | 0.55 |
| 22 | 97.23 | 0.25 | 24.31 | -0.07 | -0.23 | 0.31 | 0.54 |
| 21 | 97.41 | 0.25 | 24.35 | 0.04 | -0.19 | 0.33 | 0.52 |
| 20 | 97.10 | 0.18 | 17.54 | -0.08 | -0.27 | 0.24 | 0.52 |
| 19 | 97.15 | 0.18 | 17.07 | 0.00 | -0.27 | 0.23 | 0.50 |
| 18 | 97.54 | 0.18 | 17.56 | 0.06 | -0.21 | 0.28 | 0.49 |
| 17 | 98.04 | 0.27 | 26.08 | 0.09 | -0.12 | 0.37 | 0.49 |
| 16 | 98.68 | 0.35 | 34.89 | 0.16 | 0.04 | 0.54 | 0.50 |
| 15 | 98.86 | 0.35 | 34.60 | 0.05 | 0.10 | 0.57 | 0.47 |
| 14 | 97.93 | 0.22 | 21.25 | -0.34 | -0.24 | 0.26 | 0.50 |
| 13 | 97.92 | 0.22 | 21.54 | -0.01 | -0.25 | 0.23 | 0.48 |
| 12 | 98.52 | 0.28 | 28.03 | 0.13 | -0.12 | 0.35 | 0.47 |
| 11 | 99.12 | 0.38 | 38.06 | 0.16 | 0.04 | 0.50 | 0.46 |
| 10 | 99.71 | 0.50 | 49.75 | 0.21 | 0.26 | 0.72 | 0.46 |
| 9 | 100.30 | 0.63 | 62.95 | 0.28 | 0.54 | 1.00 | 0.46 |
| 8 | 100.81 | 0.74 | 74.33 | 0.30 | 0.84 | 1.29 | 0.45 |
| 7 | 100.55 | 0.69 | 69.26 | -0.21 | 0.63 | 1.05 | 0.42 |
| 6 | 100.95 | 0.79 | 79.33 | 0.26 | 0.89 | 1.29 | 0.40 |
| 5 | 101.34 | 0.89 | 88.58 | 0.29 | 1.17 | 1.56 | 0.39 |
| 4 | 101.42 | 0.87 | 88.24 | 0.04 | 1.22 | 1.58 | 0.36 |
| 3 | 101.10 | 0.87 | 87.96 | -0.30 | 0.92 | 1.24 | 0.33 |
| 2 | 101.07 | 0.87 | 87.93 | -0.05 | 0.86 | 1.15 | 0.29 |
| 1 | 100.95 | 0.95 | 96.34 | -0.13 | 0.74 | 0.99 | 0.25 |
| 0 | 100.80 | 1.00 | 100.80 | -0.17 | 0.57 | 0.80 | 0.23 |

initial option value

price.[7,8] The simulations are done for at-the-money options with three months, six months, and one year to expiration on both the S&P 500 and the 30-year Treasury bond.[9] The starting value of the underlying position is assumed to be $100.

Exhibit 4 shows the results of 100 simulations. In all cases, the average tracking error of the replication strategy is very close to zero, given the standard deviation of the simulations. This suggests that the option model is unbiased; that is, on average the model will provide the predicted payoff, whatever errors may appear on any particular application. The range of the errors, as measured by their standard deviation, is not substantial, approximately $.30 for the S&P 500, and roughly half of that for the Treasury bond.[10]

It is interesting to note that the standard deviation remains fairly constant as the time to expiration of the option being replicated moves from three months to a year. We might expect that greater errors would come into the replication strategy the longer

---

7. The bootstrapping methodology leads to paths that on average will have the same volatility as the sample. However, the volatility will vary from one path to the next. To provide a good estimate of volatility, we estimated the volatility for each path in the simulation individually. Thus, the volatility used for each path will represent the average volatility of that path at the start of the hedge. Since volatility uncertainty is the primary source of option pricing error, specifying the correct average volatility for the hedging period obviously strips the simulation of some realism. As we will show in the next section, however, it is easy to incorporate uncertain volatility into a simulation. We are leaving it out of the base-case analysis to avoid an evaluation of a joint hypothesis of the option model and the volatility estimation (or misestimation, as the case may be).

8. The end-of-day adjustment actually reduces the efficiency of the hedge, since, in practice, adjustments may be made a number of times during the day if the market is extremely volatile. During the days surrounding the crash of October 1987, such intraday adjustments would have certainly improved the hedging accuracy. Further, even on days of moderate volatility, intraday adjustments become important for an option that is near the money as the expiration day approaches. Since effective application of this methodology requires frequent hedge adjustment opportunities, the evaluation of shorter-term options—say, those with one or two months to expiration—may require more than closing prices to be used in the simulation. When only closing prices are available, one technique that can be used is to transform the price sample to have a lower volatility. This can be done by dividing the deviations from mean returns in the sample by a constant. Volatility is related to the square root of time; doubling the volatility is like increasing the time frame fourfold. Thus, if the volatility of the sample is cut into quarters, daily adjustments will be similar to making adjustments four times a day with the original sample.

9. Both data sets covered the 18-month period from November 1987 through April 1989. The Treasury bond prices are based on the phantom on-the-run 30-year Treasury.

10. For a normal distribution, the standard deviation measures the range where approximately 66% of the errors fall. For the three-month S&P 500 option, approximately 66% of the replications gave payoffs within $.30 of the model-predicted replication cost, and for the Treasury bonds approximately 66% of the replications gave payoffs within $.14 of the model's prediction.

**Exhibit 4.   A Comparison of Treasury Bond and S&P 500 Hedging Simulation Results**

**S&P 500**

|  | Time To Expiration | | |
|---|---|---|---|
|  | 3 Months | 6 Months | 12 Months |
| Option Price | 4.76 | 10.04 | 12.35 |
| Ending Error | | | |
| Mean | .03 | -.05 | .01 |
| Standard Deviation | .30 | .29 | .29 |
| Absolute Maximum Error | | | |
| Mean | .40 | .39 | .43 |
| Standard Deviation | .28 | .22 | .28 |
| Error 30 Days Before Expiration | | | |
| Mean | .03 | -0.002 | 0.002 |
| Standard Deviation | .26 | .25 | .30 |

**Treasury Bond**

|  | Time To Expiration | | |
|---|---|---|---|
|  | 3 Months | 6 Months | 12 Months |
| Option Price | 3.55 | 5.98 | 10.45 |
| Ending Error | | | |
| Mean | .02 | -.01 | -.01 |
| Standard Deviation | .14 | .14 | .18 |
| Absolute Maximum Error | | | |
| Mean | .23 | .21 | .25 |
| Standard Deviation | .09 | .11 | .13 |
| Error 30 Days Before Expiration | | | |
| Mean | -.02 | .01 | .01 |
| Standard Deviation | .14 | .11 | .12 |

the hedge is in force. However, two characteristics of option pricing reduce the sensitivity of longer-term options to hedging errors. First, the delta of longer-term options changes more slowly both with changes in the price of the underlying asset and with the passage of time. This means that, if the correct delta hedge is in place, it is less likely to become incorrect. Second, once the longer-term option gets closer to expiration and the sensitivity of the hedge increases, it is likely the underlying asset price will have moved, and the option will have either moved further into or away-from-the-money. This also will reduce the likelihood of hedging error, since the sensitivity of the delta hedge decreases as the asset price moves away from the option's exercise price.

Exhibit 4 also presents two other sets of statistics for each group of the option replication runs. The first, the absolute maximum error, provides a measure of the largest error obtained during the course of the replication. The replication strategy should provide the same payoff as the target option not only at expiration, but throughout the entire period of replication.[11] By comparing the value of the replicating portfolio with the value of the target option we can get a day-by-day reading on the effectiveness of the model and by looking at the largest error during the hedging period, we can get a feel for the intertemporal tracking of the model and a measure of the upside risk potential in executing the strategy.

The absolute maximum error indicates that the replication strategy does at times stray by an average of approximately $.40 from the model value during the course of the hedge for the S&P 500 replication, and by approximately $.25 from the model value for the Treasury bond replication. The standard deviation of these maximum errors is slightly lower than the standard deviation of ending errors. As with the ending errors, the absolute value of the maximum errors is not affected by the time to expiration of the

---

11. Indeed, if the replication strategy gave the same payoff as the target option at the time of expiration, but did not give the same value throughout the time of replication, there would be an immediate arbitrage opportunity. If the replication strategy at some point could be executed with a lower cost, then the strategy would be initiated at that point and the market option written against the position. Since the replicating portfolio and the market option would converge in price at expiration, the investor could pocket the differential.

option.[12] The second set of statistics looks at the hedging errors 30 trading days before expiration. The sensitivity of the hedge can increase substantially as the option approaches expiration, especially if the asset price varies around the option's exercise price.[13] This leads to a potential increase in hedging error during the last days of the option's life. A look at the error 30 days before the expiration provides a check on this source of error. While the mean and standard deviation of the 30-day error is smaller than the ending error, the differences are not substantial.

### Direct Comparisons of Model Performance for the S&P 500 and the U.S. Treasury

It is clear from Exhibit 4 that the fit of the Treasury bond simulation is better than that of the S&P 500. One reason for this is that the volatility of the Treasury bond prices is lower .105 versus .172 for the S&P 500. The lower volatility reduces the possibility of sudden moves, effectively making the hedging period shorter for the Treasury bonds and, therefore, allowing a better fit. By adjusting the path volatility for the S&P 500 to equal that of the Treasury, we can make a direct comparison of the two markets.

Exhibit 5 presents a comparison of the Black-Scholes model performance for the Treasury bond and the volatility adjusted S&P 500.[14] The results indicate that, at least in this base-case test, the Black-Scholes model performs at least as well on Treasury bond options as it does on stock index options. For two of the three option maturities, the standard deviation of the ending error is lower for the Treasury than for the S&P. Furthermore, the Trea-

---

12. The errors tend to revert back from their maximum in the simulations because we use the average volatility over the entire path in the hedging and pricing. Over a portion of the path, the volatility may deviate from the overall average volatility leading to a widening error. By the end of the hedge, the volatility will have recovered to the average level, and the error will have dropped as well.

13. To give an extreme example: just before the option expires, the delta will be very close to 1 if the option is slightly in-the-money, and will be very close to 0 if the option is slightly out-of-the-money. The restriction of once a day hedges in the simulation will exacerbate the errors imposed by this whipsawing.

14. The adjustment is made by multiplying the deviation from the mean in the S&P 500 by .616, the ratio of the Treasury bond volatility to the S&P 500 volatility.

**Exhibit 5.  A Comparison of S&P 500 and Treasury Bond Simulation Results**

**3-Month Option; Option Price = 3.55**

|  | Simulation Results | |
| --- | --- | --- |
|  | Treasury Bond | Adjusted S&P 500 |
| Ending Error |  |  |
| Mean | .02 | -.01 |
| Standard Deviation | .14 | .15 |
| Absolute Maximum Error |  |  |
| Mean | .23 | .21 |
| Standard Deviation | .09 | .15 |
| 30-Day-to-Expiration Error |  |  |
| Mean | -.02 | .01 |
| Standard Deviation | .15 | .16 |

**6-Month Option; Option Price = 5.98**

|  | Treasury Bond | Adjusted S&P 500 |
| --- | --- | --- |
| Ending Error |  |  |
| Mean | -.01 | -.01 |
| Standard Deviation | .14 | .15 |
| Absolute Maximum Error |  |  |
| Mean | .21 | .21 |
| Standard Deviation | .11 | .11 |
| 30-Day-to-Expiration Error |  |  |
| Mean | .01 | .003 |
| Standard Deviation | .14 | .16 |

**1-Year Option; Option Price = 10.45**

|  | Treasury Bond | Adjusted S&P 500 |
| --- | --- | --- |
| Ending Error |  |  |
| Mean | -.01 | -.03 |
| Standard Deviation | .18 | .15 |
| Absolute Maximum Error |  |  |
| Mean | .25 | .18 |
| Standard Deviation | .13 | .13 |
| 30-Day-to-Expiration Error |  |  |
| Mean | .01 | -.02 |
| Standard Deviation | .12 | .13 |

sury bond dominates the S&P replication in both the standard deviation of the maximum error and the standard deviation of the 30-day error. Although obviously preliminary, this result gives some pause for thought, given the immense work that has been done in developing specialized models for fixed income options.[15]

## A Look at Exercise Price Bias

It has been repeatedly reported that Black-Scholes model prices and market option prices consistently differ for options that are far in and far out-of-the-money.[16] A number of explanations can be given for this bias. One is that stocks have return distributions with thick tails, and these tails lead to deviations that are most marked for the "outlier" options. A second explanation is that there is excess demand for writing options near and at the money—thus depressing these option prices—while there is demand for buying out-of-the-money options—so these prices are bid up.[17] The first explanation implies a model misspecification, while the second points to a market effect.

We can test this exercise bias using the replication methodology by extending the simulations reported in Exhibit 5 for options that are in and out-of-the-money. The results for options ranging from 10% in the money to 10% out-of-the-money are presented in Exhibit 6.

---

15. Fixed-income options have at least four special features that make the Black-Scholes model inappropriate. First, the price volatility of the Treasury bond decreases as the bond moves toward maturity. For long-maturity Treasuries, this is not much of a concern. Second, the distribution of Treasury bond returns is not thought to be lognormal, thus violating the distributional assumption of lognormality underlying the Black-Scholes model. Third, Treasury bond prices are correlated with interest rates. In a stochastic interest rate environment, this may cause problems in the cost of carrying the hedge position. Finally, fixed-income instruments pay a known fixed coupon and have a known terminal value.

16. For example, MacBeth and Merville, "An Empirical Examination of the Black-Scholes Call Option Pricing Model," *Journal of Finance*, 1979, shows that the Black-Scholes model underestimates the market price of in-the-money options and overestimates the price of out-of-the-money options.

17. One result of this bias is that the implied volatility of at the money options tends to be lower than the implied volatility of options that are further in or out-of-the-money. A plot of implied volatility as a function of exercise price leads to a convex curve that looks like a smile; thus, this is sometimes referred to as the "smile effect."

## Exhibit 6.   Exercise Bias in Option Replication

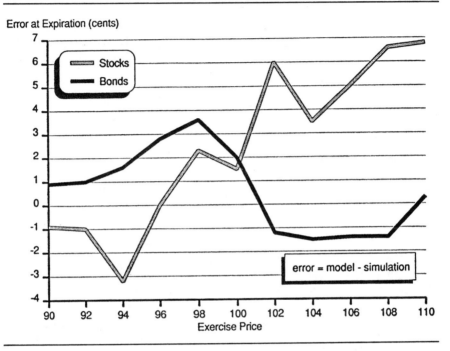

Error at Expiration (cents)

For the options on the S&P 500, there is an upward slope in the ending error as a function of exercise price, suggesting the Black-Scholes model tends to underprice in-the-money options and overprice out-of-the-money options. The same bias is not apparent for the options on the Treasury bond. If anything, there appears to be a tendency for the model to overprice options near-the-money, and to fairly price options that are away-from-the-money in either direction.[18] These differences in bias should not be unexpected, since the S&P 500 index and the Treasury bond are likely to have different distributional characteristics.

---

18. Care should be taken in drawing inferences from the errors for the options with exercise prices that are far-from-the-money—the 90 and 110 exercise prices for the S&P 500, and the 90, 92, 108, and 110 exercise prices for the less volatile Treasury bonds. Given the short time to expiration, the sample size used in the replication, and the volatility of the underlying assets, there will be relatively few cases in which these exercise prices are passed in the simulation.

## The Impact of Volatility and Interest Rate Specification

The model evaluation can be made more rigorous by using more realistic assumptions in the simulation. In this section, we will relax two assumptions from the base-case analysis to provide a better look at the model's performance. First, we will look at the impact on replication of an error in the volatility estimation, and then at the impact of uncertain interest rates.

### The Impact of Volatility Estimation Errors

Exhibit 7 compares the base-case simulations for the S&P 500 options with simulations in which the volatility used in the hedge deviates from the actual price volatility. The table presents the results for options with three months and one year to expiration, and with estimated volatilities that are 20% higher and 20% lower than the actual volatility of the price paths used in the simulations. The starting asset price is assumed to be 100, and the options are at-the-money.

Because the option price changes with a change in volatility, the cost of executing the replication will be different from what is anticipated if there is an error in volatility estimation. The effect of this can be readily calculated simply by comparing the price of the option at the estimated volatility with the price of the option at the realized volatility. Exhibit 7 presents this calculation under the line "Expected Ending Error." For example, the expected ending error for the three-month option with estimated volatility equal to 120% of the realized is .65. The 20% lower realized volatility lowers the model's option price by .65, so even if we replicated the position perfectly in the lower volatility environment, we would expect the hedging cost to be $.65 lower.

A different volatility assumption will not only change the price of the option, it will also change the delta of the option. This will affect the mechanics of the hedge execution, and impose a further error on the replication. If the replication strategy is followed with the incorrect hedge, we may not attain the option payoff, even at the cost implied by the higher realized volatility. In the example above, the $.65 decrease in the option price is correct, assuming the replication is executed properly, given the lower volatility of the market. But if the hedge is based on a volatility estimate that is 20% too high, it will not follow the correct hedging

**Exhibit 7.  The Impact of Volatility Estimation Errors**

| 3-Month Option | Estimated Volatility = Actual | Estimated Volatility = 1.2 x Actual | Estimated Volatility = .8 x Actual |
|---|---|---|---|
| Ending Error | | | |
| Mean | .03 | .58 | -.70 |
| Standard Deviation | .30 | .41 | .50 |
| Absolute Maximum Error | | | |
| Mean | .40 | .75 | .81 |
| Standard Deviation | .28 | .48 | .52 |
| Error 30 Days Before Expiration | | | |
| Mean | .03 | .30 | -.38 |
| Standard Deviation | .26 | .24 | .37 |
| Expected Ending Error | 0 | .65 | -.65 |

| 1-Year Option | Estimated Volatility = Actual | Estimated Volatility = 1.2 x Actual | Estimated Volatility = .8 x Actual |
|---|---|---|---|
| Ending Error | | | |
| Mean | .01 | 1.09 | -.95 |
| Standard Deviation | .29 | .65 | .75 |
| Absolute Maximum Error | | | |
| Mean | .43 | 1.17 | 1.07 |
| Standard Deviation | .28 | .67 | .75 |
| Error 30 Days Before Expiration | | | |
| Mean | -.002 | .98 | -.61 |
| Standard Deviation | .30 | .45 | .64 |
| Expected Ending Error | 0 | 1.13 | -1.05 |

prescription, and will, therefore, not replicate the option as efficiently as possible.

We may find, therefore, that the error of volatility misspecification is more severe than would be suggested by a simple comparison of option prices under the alternative volatilities. This second effect can be seen in the simulation by comparing the standard deviation of the errors. The standard deviations of the errors are higher for the cases of misspecified volatility. For the three-month options, the standard deviations are roughly one and a half times those of the base case, and for the one-year option, the standard deviations of the ending errors are over twice those of the base case. Also, the average absolute maximum error in the three-month option simulations is twice that of the base case, and nearly three times that of the base case for the one year options.[19]

### The Impact of Stochastic Interest Rates

The execution of the option replication requires taking positions in the underlying asset. The carrying cost of these positions, as measured by the interest rate, will affect the option cost. Higher interest rates will increase the cost of a call option, because the underlying asset must be borrowed to replicate a call option. Conversely, higher interest rates will decrease the price of a put option, because the put option replication involves selling (shorting) the underlying asset and lending out the proceeds.

The volatility of interest rates will also affect the cost of the option, for much the same reason that an increase in the volatility of the asset increases the option's cost. The greater interest volatility will lead to greater variation in the delta of the hedge over time, and this, in turn, will lead to greater cumulative costs for the delta adjustments.

Exhibit 8 shows the impact of uncertain interest rates on option replication costs. Both an asset price and interest rate path are generated for each run of this simulation. The interest rates are

---

19. It is also interesting to note that the error imposed by the volatility misspecification increases at a decreasing rate as the time to expiration of the option increases. Volatility misspecification will thus be relatively more of a problem for shorter-term options.

**Exhibit 8.   The Impact of Stochastic Interest Rates**

**A. No Adjustment made to Option Model**

| Time to Expiration (Months) | Hedging Error at Expiration | | |
| --- | --- | --- | --- |
| | Mean Error | Expected Error | Standard Deviation |
| 3 | .09 | .14 | .32 |
| 6 | .21 | .37 | .60 |
| 9 | .61 | .65 | 1.17 |
| 12 | 1.28 | .95 | 2.11 |

**B. Adjustment made for Stochastic Interest Rates**

| Time to Expiration (Months) | Hedging Error at Expiration | | |
| --- | --- | --- | --- |
| | Mean Error | Expected Error | Standard Deviation |
| 3 | -.13 | 0 | .44 |
| 6 | -.24 | 0 | .70 |
| 9 | -.06 | 0 | 1.12 |
| 12 | -.23 | 0 | 1.66 |

drawn for a sample of short-term rates using the same bootstrap-ping methodology that we apply for drawing sample security paths. The hedges are executed on the basis of the mean interest rate; therefore, the interest rate is correct on average for each of the paths in the simulation runs. The carrying cost for the cash flow, however, is based on each particular day's interest rate. The error occurs because of the variance of the interest rates around their mean.

The mean ending error is modest for the three-month option, but in contrast to the impact of uncertainty in volatility, the error here increases at an increasing rate as the time to expiration of the option increases. The standard deviation of the error also increases quickly with an increase in the time to expiration. This suggests that for longer-term options, interest rate uncertainty may pose a greater hedging risk than uncertain volatility.[20]

The second column in Exhibit 8A shows the mean error expected, given the volatility of interest rates.[21] This column is comparable to the "Expected Ending Error" of the volatility analysis of Exhibit 7. As with the volatility results, the errors from the simulation are close to those predicted by the model.

Exhibit 8B employs a modification of the Black-Scholes model that allows for stochastic interest rates. When this model is employed in the hedging simulation, the mean errors drop close to zero, but still retain a noticeable bias. The standard errors also drop compared with those of the unmodified model, but remain high nonetheless, on the order of those observed for the errors under volatility misestimation.

## The Impact of Transaction Costs and Discrete Hedging

Because of the transaction costs of making hedge adjustments, some sort of trigger rule needs to be used in practice, be it carefully constructed or followed ad hoc. Exhibit 3 in Section II illustrated a replication strategy with a minimum trigger level imposed on delta adjustments. In this section, we will expand on that example to look at the effect of discrete delta adjustments on hedging accuracy and hedging cost.

The delta of an option changes continuously with changes in time and in the asset price. Discrete hedge adjustments cause a hedging error because they fail to perfectly match this curvature. In effect, a delta hedge draws out facets of the option payoff curve. The finer the hedge adjustment process, the greater the number of

20. As with any interest-related cost, the carrying cost of maintaining an option hedge will grow exponentially with the time period. Interest rate errors that appear trivial over a three-month holding period can become substantial over a three-year period. For the same reason, the hedging error induced by errors in interest rates increases at an increasing rate with time. By contrast, as mentioned earlier, volatility tends to have decreasing significance as the time to expiration increases.
21. This error was calculated by comparing the Black-Scholes model price assuming constant interest rates with the price given the stochastic interest rates. The model adjustment is based on that suggested by Merton, "Theory of Rational Option Pricing," *Bell Journal of Economics and Management Science* 4 (Spring, 1973): 141-183.

facets, and the better the hedge will match the payoff. On the other hand, finer hedge adjustments generally lead to greater turn-over. Thus, the trade-off in determining the optimal hedge adjust-ment procedure is between the increased hedging error and the decrease in transaction costs.

Exhibit 9 illustrates this trade-off. As this table shows, at expi-ration the standard deviation of the hedging error increases from .39 for a 5% trigger to 1.12 for a 20% trigger. In contrast, the case of daily hedge adjustments shown in Exhibit 1—which itself in-volves discrete hedges—had a standard deviation of .30. The stan-dard deviation of hedging errors 30 days before expiration increases less rapidly with the trigger width, going from .36 for the 5% trigger to .75 for the 20% trigger. The smaller effect is due, in part, to the fact that the option's gamma—which measures the rate of change in delta of the option per dollar change in the underly-ing asset—is lower the longer the time to expiration; thus, wide changes in the delta are less likely.

The last column in Exhibit 9 shows the portfolio turnover as a function of the trigger width. Over the 100 sample paths, the aver-age turnover drops by half as the trigger width increases from 5% to 20%. Once the per-unit transaction costs are specified, the impli-cations of this lower turnover for hedging costs can be easily cal-culated.

**Exhibit 9.   The Effect of Trigger Widths on Hedging Accuracy and Hedging Cost**

| Change in Delta Required for Hedge Adjustment | Standard Deviation of Hedging Error | | Percentage of Portfolio Traded |
|---|---|---|---|
| Trigger Width | At Expiration | 30 Days Before Expiration | |
| .05 | .39 | .36 | 1.67 |
| .10 | .57 | .52 | 1.28 |
| .15 | .85 | .60 | .95 |
| .20 | 1.12 | .75 | .84 |

Exhibit 10 offers a second look at the results of these replication simulations. It presents both the standard deviation of hedging error and the transaction cost of hedging as a function of
trigger width. This case assumed a transaction cost (round trip
commissions and market impact) of $.50 per trade. The number is
obviously only for illustrative purposes; different transaction costs
will cause a parallel shift in the curve.

Exhibit 10 provides an idea of how to determine the optimal
trigger width. By first positing a price of risk to translate the standard deviation of hedging error into a dollar cost, and then adjusting the transaction cost curve to reflect the costs of the particular
market, the cost-minimizing hedge can be computed by choosing
the trigger width that minimizes the sum of these two costs.

**Exhibit 10. Hedging Accuracy and Transaction Costs as a Function of Trigger Width**

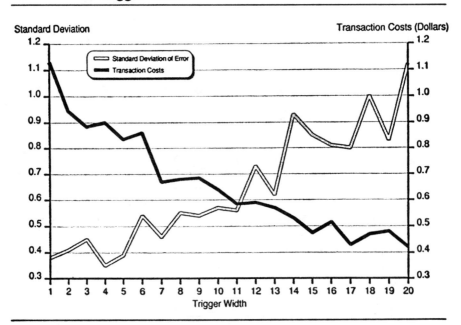

## Conclusion

The purpose of this chapter has been to propose a new option evaluation methodology. This methodology is based on the following proposition: because the key in the development and operation of options models is to construct a dynamic hedge to replicate the target option's payoff, the natural method for evaluating an option model is to test its ability to perform this replication.

This chapter has introduced this evaluation methodology, and has illustrated it using the Black-Scholes option model. The same method can be used for any other model. The only requirement is the ability to access the price and delta of the model for a number of simulated price paths. Thus, even the "black box" option models of computer vendors can be evaluated and compared.

By changing the assumptions of the simulation, the evaluation can also point out the weaknesses and sensitivities of option models. In this chapter, we touched on measuring the impact of interest rate or volatility misspecification. Other areas of concern can also be easily addressed. For equity-related models, it might be interesting to look at the impact of dividend payments. If futures are used in the hedge, cash-futures basis risk can be added to the simulation. For fixed-income instruments, we might want to look at the impact of shifts in the yield curve.

Alternative hedging strategies can also be evaluated using the hedging simulations. In Section V we showed how the methodology can be used to determine the hedging interval that gives the optimal trade-off between transaction costs and delta mistracking. While it makes the simulation more complex, the methodology can also be extended to add options to the set of hedging instruments. The simulations can then look at delta gamma hedging and, thereby, provide a means of determining the value of employing other options in the hedging strategy.

# Chapter 9

# Immunization-Based Duration: A New Concept for Mortgage Securities

Rajiv Sobti
Donaldson, Lufkin, & Jenrette

## Introduction

Since the callability of mortgage-backed securities (MBS) was recognized in 1986, determining a meaningful measure of duration has become an important issue for MBS investors. The limitation of the conventional Macaulay and modified duration measures have become patently clear. Subsequent measures of duration that have been developed are based on some measure of the price volatility of a mortgage-backed security. The immunization properties of these measures of duration are neither clear, nor have they been explored in depth by market participants. Generally, the assumption has been made that the volatility-based measure of duration would serve as an effective immunization measure.

In this chapter, we present and explore a measure of duration for mortgage securities which has true immunization properties. This measure addresses the interaction of price appreciation/depreciation and reinvestment risks which lies at the core of the original measure of duration conceived for noncallable securities.

Given the complicated nature of mortgage securities, a closed-form calculation of duration is not possible. As in the price volatility-based measures of duration, we use numerical techniques to develop an appropriate measure of duration for immunization.

## The Concept

For noncallable bonds, an immunization-based duration measure indicates that point in the future at which the price appreciation/depreciation associated with an interest rate move is offset by the differential impact on reinvestment income.

Strictly speaking, the immunization properties are applicable under the following conditions:

1. The term structure is flat

2. The portfolio is constantly rebalanced after each interest rate shock, and also with the passage of time when the duration of the asset moves at a different rate than the duration of the liability.

While Macaulay duration serves to capture the immunization properties for a noncallable bond, it has little value for a callable security such as a mortgage-backed security. We develop a duration measure below which captures the immunization properties of callable securities.

In this analysis, we examine a series of interest rate shocks which define a path. Several such paths are created and the rate of return is calculated up to each of various points along these paths. We identify that point in the future along each of the various paths where the returns converge and lie in a narrow band. The point represents that time in the future where the rates of return are fairly stable, regardless of the interest rate scenario. We define this point as immunization-based duration.

The following points are worth mentioning in connection with the rate of return calculation.

1. The cash flows received, coupon, and principal (including prepayments) are assumed to be reinvested at the implied forward rate in each period.

2. Future market values are calculated assuming widening or contraction in spreads to the appropriate reference Treasury along with a change in prepayment rates to accommodate the change in interest rates.

3. The total rate of return at each point includes both the sum of reinvested earnings and the market value of the security.

By examining a series of interest rate paths defined by a Monte Carlo simulation, we can calculate

1. Immunization-based duration (IMD)

2. Option-adjusted yield

3. Negative convexity for the security.

This can best be illustrated by the graph in Exhibit 1. The graph represents five sample paths. Path A represents a bullish scenario which begins at a very high return and then gradually declines as the cash flows are reinvested at low reinvestment rates. Path B represents a less bullish scenario which begins at a lower per annum rate of return. Path C represents a stable rate scenario. Finally, paths D and E represent successively bearish scenarios. The initial rates of return in paths D and E are very low and increase over time as higher reinvestment rates come into play. The several paths intersect at a point roughly five years out which defines the *Immunization-based duration* of the security.

The *Option-Adjusted Yield* is the rate of return at the point at which the various paths intersect. This level is generally lower than the static yield and the divergence between the two defines the degree of negative or positive convexity of the security. The smaller the ratio of option-adjusted yield/static yield, the higher the degree of negative convexity.

Negative convexity is characterized by the following:

- A low intersection point relative to the static yield. This is because of adverse selection whereby the cashflows occur at the least advantageous time.

- A relatively wide band at the point of minimum variance of returns.

**Exhibit 1.   Immunizing Duration Analysis**

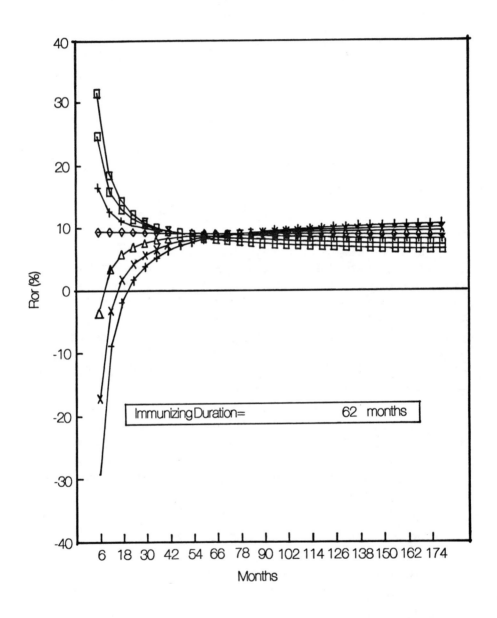

- Paths that tend to diverge relatively quickly outside the minimum variance band.

For a positively convex security, the band of minimum variance is relatively narrow and, furthermore, the paths do not diverge rapidly from the minimum variance point.

We now demonstrate this analysis for four securities, GNMA 8s, GNMA 10s, a PAC (Planned Amortization Class) and a companion bond.

### GNMA 8s and GNMA 10s

We illustrate our comments on negative convexity by comparing GNMA 8s and GNMA 10s. GNMA 10s are more negatively convex and we find the band of minimum variance for GNMA 10s (Exhibit 2) is relatively wider than the band of minimum variance band for GNMA 8s (Exhibit 3).

Further the ratio of option-adjusted yield/static yield is lower for GNMA 10s than for GNMA 8s. The greater the volatility, the wider the band of minimum variance and the lower the ratio of option-adjusted yield/static yield. We will find that GNMA 10s are more heavily affected by increases in volatility than are GNMA 8s.

### PAC Bonds

For purposes of this analysis, we selected Class E from FNMA 1990 Series 73 (Exhibit 4). This is a 5-year PAC with a 9% coupon. We examine the same range of scenarios and estimate the immunization-based duration, option-adjusted yield and the degree of negative convexity for this PAC. The PAC has a much more narrowly contained band and much less divergence after the point of minimum variance, compared to a pass-through security.

### Companion Bonds

We selected Class P from FNMA 1990 Series 73 for this analysis (Exhibit 5). This is a 3-year companion with a 9% coupon. The

**Exhibit 2.   GNMA 10s Immunizing Duration Analysis**

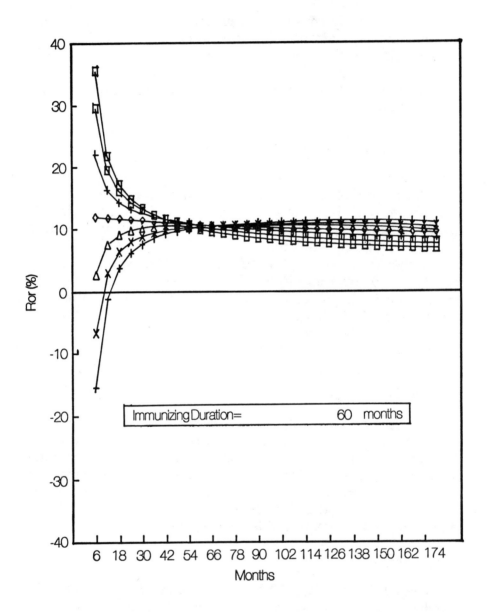

**Exhibit 3.   GNMA 8s Immunizing Duration Analysis**

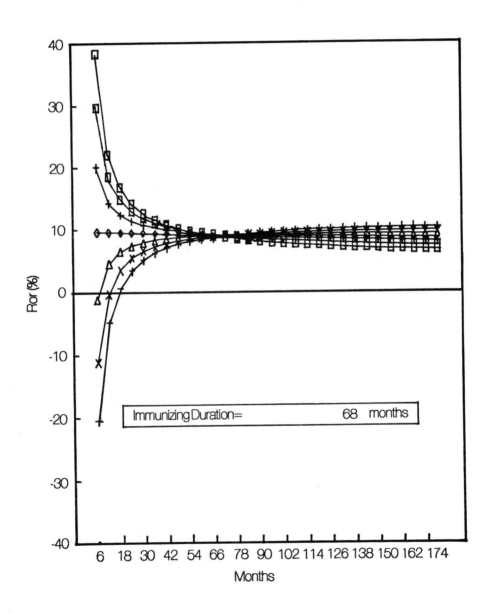

**Exhibit 4.   5-Year PAC**

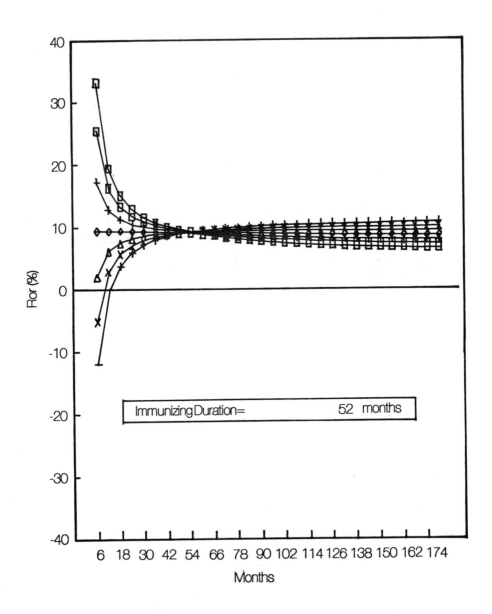

**Exhibit 5.   Companion Bond**

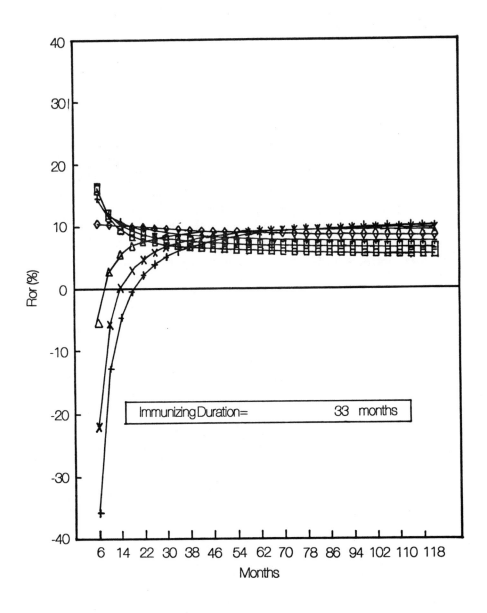

companion has a very wide band at the point of minimum variance and the returns diverge rapidly after this point. In addition, the ratio of option-adjusted yield/static yield is much lower for the companion than for either the GNMA coupons or the PAC bond.

## Conclusion

This measure represents a new way of addressing the immunization properties of callable bonds and defines an appropriate measure of these properties. While the measure is relatively close to the duration measure based on volatility, in certain cases, it provides a more accurate measure than the volatility based measure. Immunization-based duration is a more useful measure for portfolio managers who want to immunize liabilities. It has particular importance for rigorously defined liabilities such as Guaranteed Interest Contracts (GICs) as well as closed-end mutual funds.

# Chapter 10

# The Change in the Cheapest-to-Deliver in Bond and Note Futures (Implicit versus Explicit Option Values)

Stanley Jonas
Lehman Brothers

## Introduction

Bond and note futures are currently in an environment where the combined effects of factor bias,[1] yield spreads,[2] callability bias,[3] and the actual level of yields have produced a major change in the

---

1. Factor bias results from the discounting method used to calculate the conversion factors. Using 8% as the discount rate when market yields are above that level tends to inflate the conversion factors for bonds with distant cashflows (long-term, low coupon bonds) relative to those for bonds with nearby cashflows (short-term, high coupon bonds), favoring the former as cheapest-to-deliver. The reverse occurs at yields below 8%.

2. An upward-sloping yield curve will make lower coupon bonds more attractive to deliver whereas a downward sloping yield curve will make higher coupons more attractive.

3. Conversion factors are biased in that they assume repayment at the earliest call date. Ideally, the call option would be priced in the factor calcuation. In 1985, the U.S. Treasury began to issue 30-year noncallable bonds. Prior to 1985, all 30-year bonds were callable after 25 years. Consequently, newly issued bonds are treated as having at least five years to principal repayment than other callable bonds. Considering that in a yield environment over 8% there is an overvaluation of distant cash flows, this noncallability feature results in very large factors for new bonds and thus biases them to appear cheap relative to futures.

313

cheapest-to-deliver issues (CTD). Factor bias has made the high-coupon callable long bonds the most attractive to deliver. In the Treasury note futures, factor bias, combined with the movements of the yield curve from 6 years to 10 years have recently made the older low coupon 7-year sector of the deliverables the cheapest-to-deliver. These switchovers may provide difficulties for hedgers, but attractive arbitrage opportunities for traders. For both, the current market environment makes clear the necessity to understand the option-like characteristics of basis trading.

Usually, the basis is understood as an option on the level of the market at a given point (e.g., the 10-year or 30-year sector). However, there can be more involved in the basis. The term "sector" refers to a segment of, not a point, on the yield curve; in some instances, such as the September 1989 note contract, the cheapest-to-deliver security may switch between issues of drastically different maturity and duration (on a relative scale). In such instances, the delivery option becomes an option not just on a point on the yield curve, but effectively an option on the slope of the yield curve itself.

## Market Background: The Long Bond Future

The spring rally of 1989 removed the 7¼s of 2016 from the cheapest-to-deliver bond status that it had long held. In July 1989, both the 12s of 2013 and the 10⅜s of 2012 were neck and neck for the title of cheapest to deliver. This new set of bonds had substantially different durations[4] (10.61 years for the 7¼s compared to 8.69 years for the 10⅜s.

---

4. Treasury trades are usually evaluated in terms of risk in one of three ways: duration, yield value of 1/32nd, and volatility. Duration and the yield value of 1/32nd measure a security's risk exposure at any point in time. Duration is an approximate measure of the price sensitivity of a security to changes in its yield to maturity. Modified duration, which is Macaulay's duration divided by $(1+y/2)$, measures the percentage change in the price of a security per unit of change in its yield to maturity.

## Metamorphosis

The duration of the cheapest-to-deliver coupon will determine the duration of the futures[5] contracts. For both the note and the bond contracts, the change in deliverability from the previous cheapest-to-deliver bonds/notes has had a major impact on assumed contract duration[6] and thus on the appropriate hedge ratios for both hedging and basis trading. Both bond and note futures contracts can literally metamorphosize, changing dramatically their effective durations and thus their responses to changes in the level of interest rates. Exhibits 1, 2, and 3 graphically illustrate the changes in duration and convexity that the switchover in bond futures represents. Similar though slightly diminished effects can be seen in the ten-year note futures.

### *The Basis Trade*[7]

Entering into a basis trade would be relatively riskless if one were assured that the cheapest-to-deliver would not change during the term of the trade. Unfortunately, with even moderate movements in yields, there is a distinct possibility that the CTD will change at some stage of the trade. When the CTD is replaced, the future changes its spots, or rather its effective duration. Consequently, a change in yields will no longer cause the same change in the future's price as it did prior to the change in CTD. As a result, the ratio of the price movements of the future to the no-longer-CTD

---

5. Actually this statement represents a substantial oversimplification of the relationship between cash and futures. Avoiding the issue as to whether futures are correctly priced relatively to the forward price and assuming that the futures price is fully arbitraged (i.e., that the futures price acts like the deliverable bond from the futures delivery date to the deliverable's maturity date), then the future price implies a yield to maturity from the delivery date to the maturity date of the delivered contract. To calculate the future's duration, use the forward price plus accrued interest of the cheapest-to-deliver, calculate its implied yield to maturity from the delivery date, and divide by the appropriate conversion factor.

6. In the note futures the shift was from the current 10-year sector to the low coupon and shorter maturity 7-1/4s of '96. This surprising shift was a result of the inversion in the bond market. In an inverted environment, the short maturities lose ground to the longer, i.e., they become cheaper.

7. Basis traders are those that specifically attempt to take advantage of the relative price movements of cash and futures on a factor-weighted basis.

**Exhibit 1.   7 1/4 of '16 versus 10 3/8 of '12**

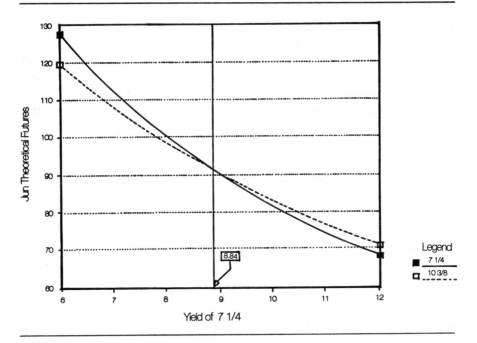

bond will not equal the factor of the bond.[8] At this point, the original basis trade becomes nothing more than an improperly hedged yield spread trade.[9]

## Factor-Weighting versus Duration-Weighting[10]

If the bond or note being hedged is not the cheapest-to-deliver, factor-weighting is inappropriate because if the cheapest-to-deliver

---

8. This is not alchemy. If this phenomenon did not occur (i.e., if factor-weighting were always the appropriate hedge), then there would be no difference in which bond to deliver. The delivery option would be worthless, and there would be no basis traders.

9. By improperly hedged we call attention to the factor that when the cheapest-to-deliver changes, the basis trader's position shifts to a yield spread trade, but the size of the futures position has been set using the conversion factor of the previously cheapest-to-deliver bond. This weighting will produce, by definition, an imbalanced trade at delivery of the newfound cheapest to deliver.

10. While this chapter focuses on the use of duration, the value of a basis point can be equivalently used in designing hedge ratios. The value of a basis point (PVBP) is defined as the change in the quoted price of the bond associated with a change in the yield on the bond of one basis point. The PVBP can be interpreted as the slope of the price-yield line at any given price. That is, the value of a basis point is the derivative of price with respect to yield, evaluated at the quoted price and yield.

**Exhibit 2.   Modified Duration of CTD Bond**

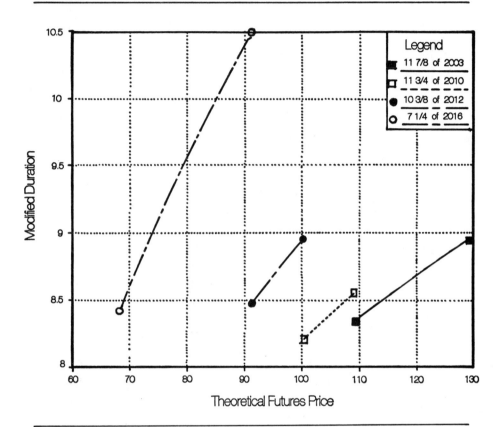

changes, factor-weighting will leave the hedger or the arbitrageur exposed to changes in the absolute level of rates. The correct procedure is to estimate the dollar duration of the bond to be hedged and then the dollar duration of the futures. Though futures obviously have no duration of their own, they can be viewed as sharing the forward duration of the cheapest-to-deliver, divided by its respective factor.[11] The calculation of the appropriate hedge ratio

---

11. For the purposes of this analysis we are totally ignoring the consequences of a change in the implied R.P. This assumption is clearly untenable in the real world, and assumes no correlation between short- and long-term rate movements. It is relatively straightforward, however, to substitute more realistic assumptions of parallel or proportional shifts.

**Exhibit 3.   7 1/4 of '16 versus 10 3/8 of '12**

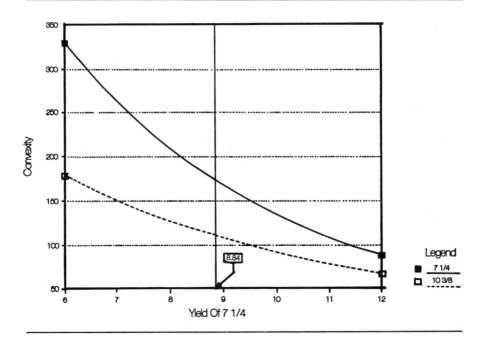

then is a function of matching the two dollar durations. The factor is the appropriate weighting only for the then current cheapest-to-deliver.

### Sample Hedge Trade Calculation[12]

Assume that the cheapest-to-deliver bond on 6/22/89 is 10⅜s of 2012. To determine the hedge ratio to use in a basis (hedge) trade of the 7¼s of 5/15/16 versus the September 89 contract do the following:

1. Calculate the forward dollar duration[13] of a $1,000,000 cash position.

---

12. This calculation utilizes prices as of 6/22/89 and a September 1989 futures price of 95-00/32nds.

13. We are ignoring for the moment the difference between the weighting of a hedge with duration and that of weighting with the value of a basis point. The two techniques will give identical results if the yields on the two bonds are the same.

**Exhibit 4.   7 1/4 of '16 versus 10 3/8 of '12**

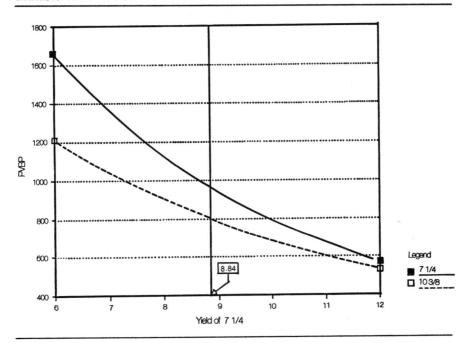

Forward Price = 87-30/32nd
Mod. Duration[14] = 10.61%
Forward Price + Accrued = $900,849
Dollar Duration[15] = .1061 x $900,849 = $95,624.37


2. Calculate the dollar-duration of the futures by dividing the dollar-duration of the cheapest-to-deliver by its conversion factor.

CTD is 10 3/8s of 11/15/2012
Forward Price = 116-20/32nds
Mod. Duration = 8.63%

---

14. Modified duration.
15. Dollar-duration.

Forward Price + Accrued = $119,698 ($100,000 face)
Dollar Duration = .0863 x $119,698 = $10,388.05
Futures Dollar Duration = $10,388.05/1.2245 = $8,442.67

3. Equate the dollar-durations.
$95,624.37 = 's # of contracts x $8,442.67
11.37 = 's # of contracts

Therefore, for each $10,000,000 of the 7¼s one would have an offsetting position of 113 futures contracts. Note that this is substantially different from the factor-weighted hedge.[16] The factor weighted hedge would be approximately 9.2 contracts, a mishedge of 23%.

## The Basis as an Option

Changes in the cheapest-to-deliver and their concomitant duration effects make it clear that any hedge must be considered as a compound trade to be unbundled. Since the 10⅜s of '12 are the CTD into the bond futures, a hedge of the 7¼s against futures can be viewed as a combination of a balanced yield spread trade,[17] long the 7¼s and short the 10⅜s, plus a factor-weighted[18] 10⅜s basis trade. For the hedger and the speculator alike, the basis trade contains within it the following implied optionlike positions. It is important to note that the option the basis represents is a function of where the level of general interest rates are at the iniation of the trade.

---

16. See the next section to explicitly calculate the magnitude of this discrepancy for any given basis and yield level.
17. By balanced we mean duration-weighted, so that the spread is indifferent to parallel shifts in yields.
18. In a factor-weighted trade the number of futures contracts equals the face amount of the cash instrument times its CBOT conversion factor.

| | *Low Yields* | *Very Low Yields* | *High Yields* |
|---|---|---|---|
| Short Basis[19] (short cash/long futures) | Short Put | Short Call and Short Put | Short Call |
| Long Basis (long cash/short futures) | Long Put | Long Call and Long Put | Long Call |

In a low yielding environment (close to 8%) a long basis trade against the then high-coupon cheapest-to-deliver is in the nature of a put and must so be treated by hedger and arbitrageur alike. Conversely, in a high yield environment, the short basis trade (short the cheapest-to-deliver 7¼s and long futures) is similar to a short call position. The reader can determine the other permutations. At relatively low levels of yield, that the cheapest-to-deliver can switch more than once all the way up until older 20-year issues are cheapest-to-deliver, thus the "strangle"-like characteristic in the center box. This path dependency makes hedging and basis trading a dynamic process which is heavily dependent upon the starting point.

## The Switchover Point as Strike Price

If the basis trade can be viewed as an option, what is its strike price?[20] Given today's basis after carry[21] on any two bonds and assuming a parallel shift of the yield curve, we can calculate the point at which they become equally cheap-to-deliver. As this switchover point is approached, the hedger is at risk. Thus, the switchover point is the effective strike price of the change in the cheapest-to-deliver option. The switchover point can be calculated by realizing that the change in price of the 7¼s divided by its conversion factor must offset the price change of the 10⅜s divided by its conversion factor as well as the difference in the basis after carry. The price change of a bond is the change in yield times du-

---

19. We refer here to the basis versus the current cheapest-to-deliver. Essentially, every hedge can be unbundled into a yield curve trade and an accompanying basis trade.

20. We are ignoring, for the time being, the yield curve option inherent in the basis.

21. The BAC (basis after carry) is the difference between the cash bond's price and its invoice price minus the cost of carry in 32nds.

ration times price. To find the cross-over with futures currently at 95-00/32nds, we solve first for $\Delta r$, the change in yield necessary to reach the switchpoint given the following set of prices:

| Coupon | Maturity | Price[22] | C.F. | Duration | BAC |
|--------|----------|-----------|------|----------|-----|
| 7 1/4  | 2016     | 90.0849   | 0.9180 | 10.61  | 24  |
| 10 3/8 | 2012     | 119.6980  | 1.2245 | 8.64   | 9   |

$$90.0849/0.9180 \times 10.61 \; \Delta r = 119.6980/1.2245 \times 8.64 \; \Delta r + (24\text{-}9)/32$$

This yields

$$\Delta r = ((24\text{-}9)/32)/(90.0849/.09180 \times 10.61 \text{ - } 119.6980/1.2245 \times 8.64)$$
$$= 0.25\%$$

or a futures switch price of:

$$F = 95\text{-}00/32 \text{ - } (\Delta r \times 119.6980/1.2245 \times 8.64) = 93.01$$

At this price, the 7¼s overtakes the 10⅜s as the cheapest-to-deliver bond. Next, we must calculate the extent to which the futures price will now move differently due to this change in the underlying cheapest-to-deliver. As yields rise further, the two bond prices will continue to diverge. The extent to which they do so yields a duration-hedge ratio different than that utilizing the 10⅜s as the cheapest-to-deliver bond. The difference in the appropriate hedge ratio may be calculated as follows:

$$\Delta HR = \frac{(90.0849/0.9180 \times 10.61 - 119.6980/1.2245 \times 8.64)}{(119.6980/1.22245 \times 8.64)} = 22.11\%$$

Under our model at the switchover point, the original hedge ratio implemented assuming that the 10⅜s were the cheapest-to-deliver, will be too high by 22%. In a declining price environment

---

22. The forward price plus accrued interest.

we would be overhedged by approximately 22%. What has this "positive convexity" cost us? Essentially, the basis after carry or roughly 9/32nds. How can we evaluate and perhaps recover this cost?

## What's the Fair Price?

To compensate precisely for the potential overhedge at a futures price of 93-01, we could to sell a put on the 7¼s with an expiration date of September 1, 1989 and a strike price of (93-01/32nds × .09180) or exactly 85-13/32nds.[23] As a close approximation, however, we can examine a 93 strike price put on T-bond futures.[24] This option will expire in mid-August, but it will serve to replicate the excess convexity[25] in our trade. The price of a 93 put on the close was 48/64ths or $750 per $100,000 face value. Recall, however, that the hedge ratio will be off by only 22.11%, and thus this is the magnitude of the excess insurance that we must sell.

| | |
|---|---|
| Price of $1,000,000 face value = | $7,500.00 |
| 22.11% necessary | $1,658.57 |
| Cost in 32nds | 5.31/32nds |

Is 5+32nds too little to demand for this option? One quick and accurate way to evaluate the option is to compare the basis after carry with the option premium necessary to achieve convexity-neutrality at the switchover point. From the hedger's perspective, the critical issue is "What will the basis be on my bond at delivery date?" Note that by definition, on delivery day, the basis after carry and the raw basis will converge approximately to zero for the cheapest-to-deliver security. Given the cheapest-to-deliver, it is

---

23. We need a put on the 7 1/4s because, at approximately 93-01/32nds, the bond futures contract beings to trade as though it were a 7 1/4s. It is at this point that we are effectively too short, 7 1/4s or futures.

24. While this strike price does not explicitly exist, can readily be replicated with a combination of 92 and 94 strike price puts.

25. Convexity is here used rather loosely to represent the trade's increasing negative duration in a declining price environment. For option buffs substitute "positive gamma."

relatively simple for any yield curve scenario to determine all other bases on delivery day. The 7¼s hedge as a 10⅜s basis trade.

Ironically, the trader who is attempting to hedge his portfolio of 7¼s, or, for that matter, the arbitrageur who is long the 7¼s basis or any basis is vitally concerned with the path of the 10⅜s basis as well. The hedger is implicitly in two distinct trades: first, he is in a duration-weighted yield spread long the 7¼s and short the 10⅜s; second, he is in a long factor-weighted 10⅜s basis trade versus the September 1989 futures contract. Under the assumption of a parallel shift in the curve, he will be indifferent to the result of his weighted-yield curve trade; thus, his only uncertainty will be the relationship of futures to the current cheapest-to-deliver, here the 10⅜s.

Assuming virtually no change in futures prices and a relatively stable yield curve in September, the following future basis can be projected. At a futures settlement of 95 13/32nd, then[26]

| Coupon | Price | Yield | Raw Basis |
|---|---|---|---|
| 10¾ | 116.29 | 8.525 | 3[27] |
| 7¼ | 88.10 | 8.350 | 23 |

Under the standstill assumption, his loss on the 10 3/8s basis was approximately 6/32nds. (Original BAC of 9/32nds - 3/32nd raw basis at delivery of 3/32nds) More by coincidence than by design, this was almost exactly his income from the sale of the 93 put. It appears that the 10⅜s basis was fairly priced relative to the implied volatility in the T-bond futures option market place.[28]

---

26. For convenience, we assume delivery takes place at the end of the delivery month. For our current purposes, this assumption makes no real difference. In fact, under the current negative yield curve, the approximation of the futures option expiring in the second week of the month preceding delivery becomes more realistic.

27. The raw basis on the 10-3/8s does not converge to zero because the 12s are assumed to become slightly more deliverable.

28. It is paramount to remember that this relative valuation assumes a parallel shift in the curve. Considerations of yield curve shifts can make the value of the implicity appear either cheap or expensive. A basis trade coupled with an explicit option leaves one with a bet on the relative shape of the yield curve.

## A Shift Down in Yields

What could we expect for a relatively large shift in yields? Ultimately, in any rally up until approximately 100-00/32nds on bond futures, the 10⅜s basis will approach zero as it will remain close to the cheapest-to-deliver. At prices above 100 or thereabouts however, it is possible that the 10⅜s basis actually widens to beyond its initial 9/32nds basis after carry and provides incremental profits beyond that covered in this analysis.[29] At a price of 98-26/32nds, the following scenario will unfold:

| Coupon | Price | Yield | Raw Basis |
|--------|-------|-------|-----------|
| 10⅜ | 121.05 | 8.125 | 4 |
| 7¼ | 92.09 | 7.950 | 50 |

## Which Basis Am I In?

Clearly, the results closely approximate our standstill argument, as should be the case remembering our put-like analogy. The sale of the listed option precisely offsets our initial cost.[30] It is important to note that while the 7¼s basis has widened considerably, this presents no excess profit or loss to our hedger, because the duration based hedger is not in the 7¼s basis trade. The 7¼ basis trade would have been initiated with a factor weighted hedge ratio of 92 short futures contracts to $10,000,000 face value of the 7¼s. The extra 22 contracts short while appropriate, obviously prevented one from benefiting from the expansion of the 7¼s basis in a bull market.

---

29. In this case, we can actually look at the 10 3/8s basis as an out-of-the-money put and an out-of-the-money call as well.

30. The hedger has effectively bought the 10 3/8s basis at a net cost after carry of 9/32nds. The final basis value of 4/32nds represents a net loss of 5/32nds per million. This loss is rather coincidentally exactly offset by the sale of the synthetic 93 put for 5+/32nds.

## A Shift Up in Yields

Finally, let us examine a substantial increase in yields from the inception of our original hedge. For a 75 basis points increase in yields, we will see the futures contract at approximately 88-27/32nds:

| Coupon | Price | Yield | Raw Basis |
|---|---|---|---|
| 10⅜ | 109.18 | 9.275 | 24 |
| 7¼ | 81.18 | 9.100 | 0 |

Here, the arithmetic gets slightly more complicated but, hopefully, will produce the same results.

| 7¼ | Position | Price | Profit/Loss |
|---|---|---|---|
| Original Cash Price | $1,000,000 | 87.25 | |
| Final Cash Price | | 81.18 | ($62,187.50) |
| Original Futures Price | 11.37 contracts | 95.00 | |
| Final Futures Price | | 88.27 | $69,978.09 |
| Basis Loss or Gain | | | $7,790.59 |
| Original Opiton Price | 22.11% | 48/64 | |
| Final Option Price | | 4-24/64 | ($7,532.67) |
| Total P/L | | | $257.92 |

We can see that the sum of the P and L from the three components very nearly nets out completely. Given our assumption of a parallel shift in the yield curve, the explicit option has fully replicated the put implied in the 10⅜s basis.

## The Hedge Unbundled

$1,000,000  7¼ Hedge =

Long $1,000,000 7¼ / Short $928,310 10⅜ +

Long $928,310  10⅜ / Short 11.37 September Futures

As the formula above makes clear, we can easily unbundle our 7¼ hedge into two distinct trades; first, a cash market yield spread trade, duration-weighted between the 7¼ and the 10⅜; and, second, a scaled basis trade, replacing the short 10⅜ with the factor-weighed number of September futures contracts. The calculations below will show that net of rounding errors the results are identical.

|  | Position | Price | Profit/Loss |
|---|---|---|---|
| Original Cash Price of 7¼ | $1,000,000 | 87.25 | |
| Final Cash Price | | 81.18 | ($62,187.50) |
| Original 10⅜ Price | $928,310 | 116.17 | |
| Final Cash Price 10⅜ | | 109.18 | $64,691.60 |
| Original Option Price | 22.11% | 48/64 | |
| Final Option Price | | 4-24/64 | ($7,531.22) |
| | | | ($5,027.12) |
| Profit on 10⅜ Basis | $928,310 | (24-9)/32nds | $4,786.60 |
| Approximate P/L | | | ($240.52) |

We can clearly see the three components of the trade. The loss on the cash hedge plus the option position are offset by the gain on the notional 10⅜s basis. Again, note that the size of the 10⅜s basis is not $1,000,000 but slightly less as dictated by the relative price sensitivities of the 7¼s and the 10⅜s. It is clear, assuming a parallel shift, that the basis after carry must be viewed in relation to the implied volatility of the listed option's marketplace. Both give similar but disparate views of the probability that yields will move enough for the cheapest to deliver to change.

### The Free Option

While bond futures traders are by now fully aware of the switch-over option and its effects, the ten-year note futures contract can at times provide an equally attractive opportunity. In spring of 1989, the sharp rally in yields was accompanied by an inversion of the yield curve between 6 and 10 years. This inverting, in effect, cheapened the 7-year sector of the deliverables relative to the 10-year area. This change in yield curve shape, which came at a time when yields were declining, was enough to make the 7¼ of 1996 the cheapest-to-deliver, ten-year note.[31]

Ironically, the marketplace was slow to recognize the importance of this shift, and for a time, the 7¼ of '96 basis was trading near positive cash and carry This gave the trader not only a free put on the level of yields but on the shape of the yield curve itself. If the yield curve steepened, the 7-year sector would gain on the 10-year and the basis of the 7¼ of 96 relative to the September 10-year note future would by definition widen. Appendix A fully outlines the details and the results of this trade.

## Conclusion

The switchover option in bond and note futures can be treated as an explicit option on the level of rates, assuming the presence of a parallel shift in the yield curve. This method of analysis provides a direct and practical method of evaluating the basis after carry relative to other existing options. Care should be taken, however, in examining the impact on the basis trade of shifts in the yield curve and equally as important in the anticipated cost of carry and the risk of the bond in question going special in the basis points marketplace. There are times, however, such as in the 10-year note

31. At June 1989 prices of the September 1989 10-year note future, a yield spread of approximately negative 5 basis points (the 8 7/8s of '98 yielding 5 basis points more than the 7 1/4s of '96) would make both notes equally cheap-to-deliver into the contract.

futures contract where these added complexities can work to the traders' advantage. When the cheapest-to-deliver is near cash and carry, the maximum loss is predetermined, and can be viewed in the way of a premium. Any shifts in the yield curve can only be beneficial to one who is long the then cheapest-to-deliver. Clearly, any movement that makes the cheapest not the cheapest, is a windfall to the arbitrageur. For the hedger and arbitrageur alike, the listed option will provide an indication of changes in the future's duration and convexity and provide a more realistic assumption.

## APPENDIX A

On May 19th the 7¼s of 11/15/96 were the cheapest-to-deliver issue into the ten-year notes futures contract basis September 1989. The implied R.P. was 8.93%, and term R.P. was arrangeable at 9%, approximately full cash and carry (See Basis Chart I, below). As can be seen from the treasury coupon curve chart for that time period, the curve from 7 years to 10 years had inverted dramatically.

In the previously prevailing yield curve environment, the cheapest-to-deliver note had been the 8⅞s of 11/15/98. Because of the difference in maturities between the two notes, the 7¼s will typically trade off of the current 7-year note, while the 8⅞ will tend to rack the then current 10-year maturity.

The existing price structure, in effect, gave the arbitrageur two distinct, though related options. First, an educated basis trader would have known that if the yield spread between the 7¼s and the 8⅞s remained at 9 basis points, the market would only need to trade down to 94-26/32nds on September note futures, from their price of 95-17, for the two issues to become equally cheap-to-deliver. Alternatively, if the yield spread between the two notes became more positive (if the 8⅞s cheapen in relation to the 7¼s) by only 1.2 basis points, then the changeover would occur at the then present price level of 95-17/32nds.

Thus, the two options were a put on the price level of the market, and an option on the yield curve to un-invert, or to go more positive.

| Coupon | Maturity | Price | C.F. | Duration | BAC |
|--------|----------|---------|--------|----------|-----|
| 7¼ | 1996 | 93.4174 | 0.9604 | 5.44 | 4 |
| 8⅞ | 1998 | 104.1574 | 1.0554 | 6.18 | 7 |
| | Switch Point | | 94.26 | | |
| | Delta H.R. | | -12.82% | | |

The free put in this instance can change the effective duration of the hedge by 13% or so in a declining price environment. On the way up, one is appropriately hedged; however, on the way down, one is synthetically short an additional 13% of one's entire position, clearly a valuable option in any portfolio.

## *How Did It Turn Out?*

Looking at the Treasury Coupon Chart for July 12, 1989, we see that by that date the yield curve had uninverted in the 7- to 10-year sector, shifting to a positive 5.6 basis points from its negative 4.5 basis points on the trade's day of inception. The raw basis had gone from -9/32nds to positive 1/32nds or a move of 10/32nds.

On July 12, 1989, the put on the level of the market was far out-of-the-money. But prior to that date, the option could have been traded against dynamically, as in the case of any positively convex security. In the days between May 19 and July 12, 1989, the put's delta effectively changed as market prices moved higher and lower; at these times, the hedge ration could have been rebalanced—buying back more futures as the market fell, selling them out on ensuing rallies.

At termination, however, the final price level of the basis was totally due to the gain on the implicit option on the yield curve. The investor could attribute all of these profits (10/32nds before carry) to the free option that was initially ignored by the marketplace.

**Exhibit A1. Treasury Coupon Yield Curve**

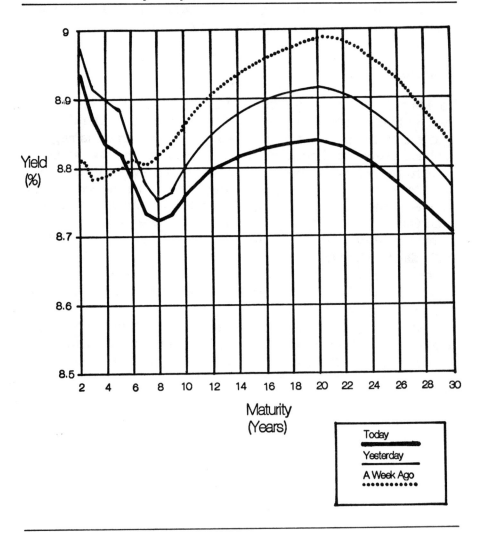

Yield (%)

Maturity (Years)

Today
Yesterday
A Week Ago

## Exhibit A2. CTD Break-even

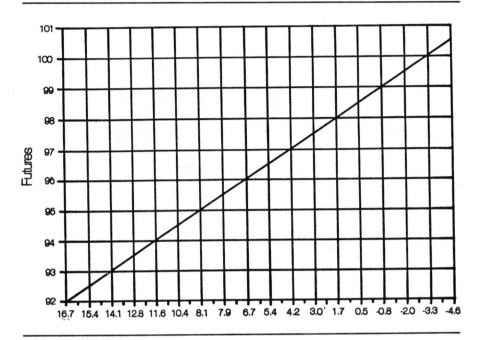

# Exhibit A3. Ten-Year Notes

Prices as of: 5/19/89
Contract: Sep 1989 Price: 95-17

| | Coup/Mat | R.P. | C.F. | Curr P/Yth | | Invoice P/Y | | Forward P/Y | | RB | BAC | IRP | PVBP (F) | DUR(F) | CBAC | D | CYLD |
|---|---|---|---|---|---|---|---|---|---|---|---|---|---|---|---|---|---|
| 9.250 | 1/15/1996 | 9.375 | 1.0603 | 102- 8/ | 8.792 | 101- 9/ | 8.975 | 102-13/ | 8.745 | 31 | 36 | 5.649 | 0.0487972 | 5.080 | 10 | E | 8.77 |
| 8.875 | 2/15/1996 | 9.375 | 1.0422 | 100- 9/ | 8.814 | 99-18/ | 8.965 | 100-16/ | 8.772 | 23 | 30 | 6.162 | 0.0486413 | 5.198 | 10 | E | 8.65 |
| 9.375 | 4/15/1996 | 9.375 | 1.0687 | 103- 6/ | 8.747 | 102- 3/ | 8.946 | 103-11/ | 8.697 | 35 | 40 | 5.134 | 0.0505898 | 5.096 | 10 | E | 9.00 |
| 7.375 | 5/15/1996 | 9.375 | 0.9688 | 92-17/ | 8.830 | 92-18/ | 8.869 | 92-30/ | 8.786 | 0 | 13 | 7.857 | 0.0476576 | 5.379 | 8 | E | 7.96 |
| 7.250 | 11/15/1996 | 9.375 | 0.9604 | 91-14/ | 8.838 | 91-24/ | 8.818 | 91-27/ | 8.796 | -9 | 4 | 8.938 | 0.0498305 | 5.676 | 8 | E | 7.92 |
| 8.500 | 5/15/1997 | 9.375 | 1.0278 | 98- 7/ | 8.815 | 98- 6 | 8.825 | 98-15/ | 8.773 | 1 | 9 | 8.337 | 0.0546334 | 5.787 | 9 | E | 8.64 |
| 8.625 | 8/15/1997 | 9.375 | 1.0354 | 98-29/ | 8.811 | 98-29 | 8.817 | 99- 5/ | 8.774 | 0 | 8 | 8.535 | 0.0560881 | 6.028 | 9 | E | 8.52 |
| 8.875 | 11/15/1997 | 9.375 | 1.0510 | 100-12/ | 8.811 | 100-13 | 8.801 | 100-19/ | 8.770 | 0 | 6 | 8.727 | 0.0578665 | 5.988 | 9 | E | 8.83 |
| 8.125 | 2/15/1998 | 9.375 | 1.0072 | 96- 2/ | 8.776 | 96- 7 | 8.766 | 96-12/ | 8.740 | -4 | 5 | 8.847 | 0.0575068 | 6.343 | 8 | E | 8.27 |
| 9.000 | 5/15/1998 | 9.375 | 1.0608 | 101-16/ | 8.755 | 101-11 | 8.772 | 101-23/ | 8.713 | 5 | 12 | 8.112 | 0.0608151 | 6.212 | 9 | E | 8.85 |
| 9.250 | 8/15/1998 | 9.375 | 1.0774 | 103- 2/ | 8.756 | 102-30 | 8.771 | 103- 8/ | 8.719 | 4 | 10 | 8.293 | 0.0625582 | 6.435 | 11 | E | 8.77 |
| 8.875 | 11/15/1998 | 9.375 | 1.0554 | 100-26/ | 8.747 | 100-26/ | 8.739 | 101- 1/ | 8.706 | 0 | 7 | 8.632 | 0.0628682 | 6.454 | 9 | E | 8.79 |
| 8.875 | 2/15/1999 | 9.000 | 1.0562 | 100-29/ | 8.731 | 100-29/ | 8.732 | 101- 1/ | 8.712 | 0 | 4 | 8.573 | 0.0639385 | 6.709 | 11 | E | 8.59 |
| 9.125 | 5/15/1999 | 9.000 | 1.0739 | 102-25/ | 8.702 | 102-19/ | 8.720 | 102-29/ | 8.673 | 6 | 9 | 8.011 | 0.0659599 | 6.639 | 11 | E | 8.86 |

**Exhibit A4. Treasury Coupon Yield Curve**

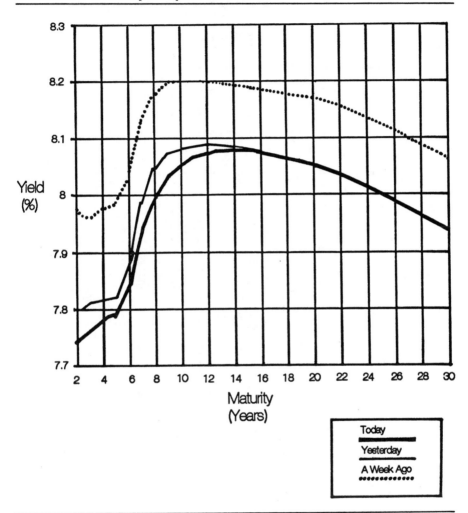

## Exhibit A5. Ten-Year Notes

Prices as of: 7/12/89
Contract: Sep 1989 Price: 99-26

| Coup | Coup/Mat | R.P. | C.F. | Curr P/Yth | | Invoice P/Y | | Forward P/Y | | RB | BAC | IRP | PVBP (F) | DUR(F) | CBAC | D | CYLD |
|---|---|---|---|---|---|---|---|---|---|---|---|---|---|---|---|---|---|
| 9.375 | 4/15/1996 | 9.200 | 1.0687 | 10-13/ | 7.933 | 106-21/ | 8.053 | 107-17/ | 7.890 | 24 | 28 | 3.540 | 0.0531925 | 5.062 | 5 | E | 8.55 |
| 7.375 | 5/15/1996 | 9.200 | 0.9688 | 96-27/ | 7.980 | 96-22/ | 8.018 | 97- 3/ | 7.939 | 5 | 13 | 6.288 | 0.0503027 | 5.349 | 4 | E | 7.52 |
| 7.250 | 11/15/1996 | 9.200 | 0.9604 | 95-28/ | 8.001 | 95-27/ | 8.015 | 96- 4/ | 7.963 | 1 | 9 | 7.188 | 0.0527269 | 5.656 | 4 | E | 7.47 |
| 8.500 | 5/15/1997 | 9.200 | 1.0278 | 102-26/ | 8.007 | 102-19/ | 8.039 | 103- 0/ | 7.970 | 7 | 13 | 6.423 | 0.0578336 | 5.776 | 4 | E | 8.16 |
| 8.625 | 8/15/1997 | 9.200 | 1.0354 | 103-15/ | 8.032 | 103-11/ | 8.047 | 103-20/ | 7.998 | 4 | 9 | 7.255 | 0.0593471 | 6.011 | 4 | E | 8.06 |
| 8.875 | 11/15/1997 | 9.200 | 1.0510 | 104-29/ | 8.053 | 104-29/ | 8.044 | 105- 2/ | 8.018 | 0 | 5 | 8.128 | 0.0611945 | 5.984 | 4 | E | 8.35 |
| 8.125 | 2/15/1998 | 9.200 | 1.0072 | 100-14/ | 8.052 | 100-17/ | 8.035 | 100-20/ | 8.020 | -3 | 3 | 8.548 | 0.0607791 | 6.333 | 4 | E | 7.83 |
| 9.000 | 5/15/1998 | 9.200 | 1.0608 | 105-28/ | 8.055 | 105-28/ | 8.044 | 106- 1/ | 8.022 | 0 | 4 | 8.264 | 0.0641824 | 6.214 | 4 | E | 8.39 |
| 9.250 | 8/15/1998 | 9.200 | 1.0774 | 107-18/ | 8.058 | 107-17/ | 8.052 | 107-22/ | 8.027 | 1 | 5 | 8.165 | 0.0661006 | 6.433 | 5 | E | 8.31 |
| 8.875 | 11/15/1998 | 9.200 | 1.0554 | 105- 9/ | 8.057 | 105-11/ | 8.039 | 105-14/ | 8.025 | -2 | 3 | 8.537 | 0.0664661 | 6.466 | 4 | E | 8.32 |
| 8.875 | 2/15/1999 | 9.000 | 1.0562 | 105-15/ | 8.044 | 105-14/ | 8.044 | 105-19/ | 8.018 | 1 | 5 | 7.871 | 0.0677526 | 6.719 | 5 | E | 8.13 |
| 9.125 | 5/15/1999 | 8.500 | 1.0739 | 107-20/ | 7.989 | 107- 6/ | 8.041 | 107-22/ | 7.971 | 14 | 16 | 5.288 | 0.0700161 | 6.664 | 6 | E | 8.36 |

# Chapter 11

# Multifactor Immunization

Peter D. Noris
Morgan Stanley

## Introduction

An enormous amount of intellect and computer time has been devoted to the development and implementation of duration measures that seek to tell the portfolio manager how much a portfolio's market value will change if interest rates change. Understanding the concept of duration has become a fundamental part of the portfolio manager's training and his job is now largely one of controlling the difference between an institution's asset and liability durations. The manager is continually faced with having to decide whether to match durations and immunize the asset/liability position against interest rate risk, or mismatch durations in an attempt to earn higher returns.

While most of the developmental literature on duration deals with the interest rate risk of default-free and option-free bonds, these techniques are in the process of being extended to encompass virtually any asset or liability that has describable cash flows.[1] But as we try to index the risk of these complicated instru-

---

1. The development of duration measures is addressed by G. Bierwag, G. Kaufman and A. Toeves in "Duration: Its Development and Use in Bond Portfolio Management," Financial Analysts Journal (July/August 1983).

ments, we find that their market value is affected by many factors
in addition to the current level of interest rates. These factors include changes in the probability of future interest rate levels (i.e.,
interest rate volatility) and factors not related to interest rates
(such as the probability of default or changed liquidity).

This chapter develops price sensitivity "durations" for several
different risk factors. After these factors have been measured, we
describe a process of multifactor immunization that will simultaneously control these risks.[2] We also show a method for evaluating
portfolios in which the portfolio manager chooses not to be fully
hedged.

## Multifactor Durations

### A Working Definition of Duration

Duration was first developed as an alternative measure of the life
of a series of known cash flows. Later, the duration of a stream of
fixed cash flows came to be recognized as mathematically equal to
its price sensitivity to interest rate changes. Thereafter, duration
came to have a dual meaning of either length or price sensitivity.
As our generalized definition, we will adopt that which has
proven to be duration's more useful property: duration is a measure of price sensitivity. While the dual meaning can create confusion, the term "duration" has become so entrenched in portfolio
management jargon that we feel compelled to continue its use
when developing other measures of price sensitivity.

The most common usage of duration is to denote a financial
instrument's price sensitivity to changes in the general level of interest rates. We will refer to this duration more specifically as interest rate duration. But, although a change in interest rates is one
of the greatest risks faced by most portfolio managers, many other

2. The process of multifactor immunization is a type of option replication process wherein the goal
for the asset portfolio is to mimic (i.e., replicate) the performance characteristics of the liability portfolio. The purpose of this report is to provide a broad understanding of some risk factors that can
affect the success of this immunization. A more detailed treatment of option replication is given by
Bookstaber, R. in "Understanding Option Replication Technology," *The Handbook of Derivative Instruments*, A. Konishi, Ravi Dattatreya, Eds., (Chicago: Probus Publishing Co.).

factors can affect an instrument's price. Durations can be calculated for any of these factors.

## Interest Rate Duration

Interest rate duration tells the portfolio manager the percentage change in an instrument's price should interest rates change by 100 basis points. This sentence deserves further clarification: first, because duration is a linear estimate, it is accurate only for small changes in whatever risk factor we are measuring (in this case, interest rates). For interest rate duration, the term "convexity" has come to denote a measure for this misestimation risk.[3]

Second, the "100 basis point" change must be clarified in terms of the compounding periodicity of interest rates. The most commonly used interest rate duration, known as Macaulay's duration, is expressed in terms of continuously compounded interest rates. Many portfolio managers use a variant of Macaulay's duration, known as modified duration, that gives price sensitivity for changes in semi-annually compounded interest rates.

Finally, the interest rate "change" must refer to the underlying process governing interest rate movements. Macaulay's duration is based upon an additive shift in a flat term structure of interest rates. Alternative interest rate duration measures can be created that are based upon other processes, including those that incorporate non-flat yield curves and differing interest rate volatilities across the yield curve. Given these caveats, interest-rate duration becomes a most useful tool for the asset/liability manager.

In order to calculate an interest rate duration, a price must be calculated for the instrument in a shifted interest rate environment.[4] The interest rate duration is simply the percentage change

---

3. Duration can be thought of as the first term in a Taylor series approximation of the true interest-rate/price relationship. If the relationship is nonlinear, then calculation of higher order Taylor series terms will help cature this "convex" price relationship.

4. If the price function can be expressed in a closed form, the duration may be calculated directly by taking the first derivative of the function with respect to interest rates and relating it to the beginning price.

in price due to a 100-basis-point rise in interest rates.[5] Convention
dictates that a negative sign be placed in front of this value so that
instruments whose prices decrease when interest rates increase
(such as most bonds) will have positive durations. In addition, interest rate duration is denominated in years because the change
being analyzed is for interest rates that are expressed as a percentage per year.

Exhibit 1 calculates the interest rate duration for a callable
bond. This example separates the callable bond into two components: a long position in a noncallable bond and a short position in
a call option. While the interest rate duration calculation requires
the price change of only the entire callable bond "package," the
separation will become useful as we illustrate other factor durations. By calculating the price change for interest rate environments shifted up and down 100 basis points, the interest rate
duration becomes simply the average percentage change in price.
Note that the call option in this bond has a high, positive duration
but its short position acts to lower the duration of the callable
bond (when compared with the noncallable bond).

## Exhibit 1.   Interest Rate Duration

Bond:  5-year maturity
2 years of call protection
10% coupons

|  | Shift in Interest Rates | | | Interest Rate Duration (Avg. % Change) (yrs.) |
|---|---|---|---|---|
|  | −100 bp | Current | +100 bp |  |
| Noncallable Bond | $105.72 | $101.48 | $ 97.47 | 4.1 |
| Call Option | 2.59 | 1.48 | 0.80 | 58.7 |
| Callable Bond | $103.13 | $100.00 | $ 96.67 | 3.2 |

5. In practice the price changes due to both an "up shift" and a "down shift" in interest rates should
be averaged to better approximate the duration in the current interest rate environment. The interest
rate shifts should be kept as small as possible to avoid picking up price effects caused by convexity.

## Volatility Duration

The assumed volatility of interest rates is integral to the valuation of any instrument whose cash flow is dependent upon interest rates. The call option in a callable bond is an example of such an instrument. If the marketplace's perception of volatility suddenly changes, the callable bond's price should change. This change can occur even though the current level of interest rates has not changed. Obviously, interest rate duration does not tell the whole story of price risk.

Volatility duration will index the price risk of perceived changes in interest rate volatility. It is calculated in a manner similar to interest rate duration, albeit where we analyze shifts in the volatility of future interest rates rather than shifts in the level of current interest rates. We will define volatility duration as the percentage change in price given a 100-basis-point change in interest rate volatility. Since volatility is expressed in terms of percentage change per year, we can calibrate volatility duration in the same units (years) as interest rate duration. Exhibit 2 calculates volatility duration for the callable bond shown previously.

Changes in interest rate volatility should not affect the price of a noncallable bond. Exhibit 2 shows that the noncallable component of the bond has a volatility duration of zero. However, the

## Exhibit 2. Volatility Duration

Bond:  5-year maturity
2 years of call protection
10% coupons

|  | Shift in Interest Rate Volatility | | | Volatility Duration (Avg. % Change) (yrs.) |
|---|---|---|---|---|
|  | −100 bp (14% vol) | Current (15% vol) | +100 bp (16% vol) |  |
| Noncallable Bond | $101.48 | $101.48 | $101.48 | 0.0 |
| Call Option | 1.27 | 1.48 | 1.71 | −14.9 |
| Callable Bond | $100.21 | $100.00 | $ 99.77 | 0.2 |

price of the callable bond must change in order to keep it competitive with a noncallable bond. Exhibit 2 indicates that we could expect the price of the callable bond to change about 0.2% for every 100-basis-point change in interest rate volatility.

The portfolio manager can act to change the portfolio's volatility duration. Assets with negative volatility duration include put bonds and the outright purchase of options (such as puts, calls, caps or floors). Positive volatility duration exists where the portfolio is short an option, as in callable bonds and prepayable mortgage-backed securities. Noncallable fixed rate bonds and fully-indexed floating rate notes trading at par have volatility durations of zero.[6]

A similar concept of volatility duration is used extensively by option traders. The Greek letter kappa denotes the dollar change in an option's price resulting from a 100-basis-point change in volatility. Kappa differs from volatility duration only in that it represents a flat dollar change as opposed to a percentage price change. Kappa (i.e., volatility duration) obviously becomes more important to a portfolio manager as the portfolio's implicit and explicit option positions become a greater proportion of the entire portfolio.

### Spread Duration

The portfolio manager normally thinks of "interest rate risk" in terms of changes in Treasury interest rates. This risk can be due to changes in the current level of Treasury rates (interest rate duration) or the probable levels of future Treasury rates (volatility duration). But, in examining the price of any risky financial instrument, we find that it is dependent not only upon Treasury interest rates but also upon the "spread" that the market demands to compensate for any additional risk. This additional price risk can be measured by a term that we will broadly refer to as "spread duration." In deriving the duration associated with this

---

6. By "fully-indexed floating rate notes," we mean those whose coupons will reset to a fixed spread off the spot rate of interest commensurate with a Treasury instrument having the same maturity as that coupon's payment date.

risk factor, we will make a distinction between credit spread risk and residual spread risk.

**Credit Spread Duration.** The first component of credit spread that we will examine is due to the risk of defaulted or delayed cash flows. The market puts a value on this risk by applying a set of discount rates higher than treasury in the pricing of the instrument's promised cash flow stream. Any shift in the market's required set of discount rates could lead to a price shift. Just as we have calculated an interest rate duration and a volatility duration, so can we calculate a credit spread duration.

For noncallable fixed rate instruments, a shift in credit spread will have the same price effect as a shift in the general level of interest rates. Thus, the credit spread duration of noncallable fixed rate instruments is exactly the same as their interest rate duration. For other types of instruments, the duration relationship is not so direct.

For instruments with cash flows that are interest-sensitive, credit spread duration may differ from interest rate duration. The determining factor is whether a change in credit spread will affect the instrument's "promised" cash flow. For example, let us examine a floating rate note ("FRN") issued at par with a coupon that resets every three months at a spread of 150 basis points above the three-month Treasury rate. The interest rate duration of this FRN is the time to the next coupon reset (e.g., 0.25 years if the coupon has just been reset) because only the first coupon is fixed and any shift in interest rates will cause a commensurate shift in expected future coupons.[7] Thus, shifting Treasury rates will have a relatively small effect on the dollar price of the FRN.

But what if the market suddenly decides that 150 basis points is not fair compensation for the credit risk of the FRN issuer? Even if Treasury rates do not change, the price of the FRN will change, and to a much greater extent than indicated by the low interest rate duration. This larger price change is caused by the market applying the new discount rate to all of the originally promised

---

7. This relationship is true for FRNs trading only at par. Discounted and premium FRNs will have shorter and longer interest rate durations, respectively. Indeed, highly discounted FRNs can have negative interest rate durations.

future coupons and principal, since the changed credit spread will not affect the level of coupons payable by the issuer of the FRN. Therefore, FRNs will have credit spread durations equal to that of a fixed rate bond of the same coupon and maturity (or the duration of a perpetual, if the FRN is a perpetual). Exhibit 3 shows the calculation of a credit spread duration for an FRN with a five-year maturity. Note that credit spread duration is also denominated in years, since the "spread" is expressed in basis points of yearly interest rates.

Not all interest sensitive instruments have credit spread durations that are as intuitively apparent. To the extent that the instrument's contractual cash flow is not affected by a spread change, credit spread duration will equal the Macaulay duration of the expected cash flow stream.[8] But if the change in credit spread affects the contractual cash flow, then the credit spread duration must be calculated in the same manner used to calculate the interest rate duration of a callable bond (i.e., using an option pricing model). For some interest-sensitive instruments, a change in credit spread might have the same cash flow effect as a change in the general level of interest rates. This could be the case for a callable bond for which a change in credit spread would affect the issuer's decision to call the bond (since refinancing costs would also be affected by the credit spread change). In such an instance,

**Exhibit 3.  Credit Spread Duration**

Bond:   5-year maturity
        Noncallable
        Coupons float quarterly at the three-month Treasury plus 150
        basis points

| | Shift in Credit Spreads | | | Credit Spread Duration (Avg. % Change) |
|---|---|---|---|---|
| | −100 bp (50 bp) | Current (150 bp) | +100 bp (250 bp) | |
| Noncallable FRN | $104.19 | $100.00 | $ 96.00 | 4.1 yrs. |

8. Where Macaulay duration is calculated as a present value-weighted average life of the cash flow stream.

the instrument's credit spread duration would be equivalent to its interest rate duration.

**Residual Spread Duration.** Some part of spread is caused by factors other than the risk of defaulted or delayed cash flows. For example, GNMA securities are priced to allow for some spread. Since the GNMA possesses the credit of a United States agency, the spread must be due to some factor other than credit risk. Possible explanations for this spread include lower liquidity than treasuries, supply constraints and maybe even the "nuisance" of processing the cash flows from an amortizing instrument. Notwithstanding the cause of this part of total spread, we will term it "residual spread."

Residual spread duration is calculated in the same manner as credit spread duration and is equal to the percentage price change due to a 100-basis-point change in residual spread while holding all other factors constant. Residual spread duration is also denominated in years. As with credit spread duration, one must assess whether movements in residual spread will affect the instrument's promised cash flow. Indeed, residual spread duration will be equal to credit spread duration in almost every instance.

### The Multifactor Durations of Liabilities

Just as multifactor durations can be calculated for the price of asset cash flows, so too can they be calculated for the present value of a liability. The present value of an insurance liability is the amount of cash that is required to construct an asset portfolio to support the expected stream of benefits, expenses, and profit. Factor durations are calculated by analyzing the change in this present value due solely to a shift in a particular risk factor. The following sections briefly describe the multifactor durations that apply to some insurance liabilities.

**Interest Rate Duration.** The interest rate duration of insurance liabilities, including Single Premium Deferred Annuities (SPDAs) and structured settlement annuities, has been shown to be principally determined by the length of the interest rate guarantee period. However, the duration is modified by features that tend to implicitly change the guarantee period. For example, the interest rate duration of an SPDA will usually increase as interest rates decline because the probability of encountering a minimum interest rate guarantee is increased.[9] Conversely, the duration will decrease after a rise in interest rates since the likelihood of interest-sensitive lapses has increased. In general, the package of features attached to most interest-sensitive life products will cause a product's interest rate duration to be shorter than the Macaulay duration of the product's projected cash flow.

**Volatility Duration.** Most interest-sensitive insurance products have negative volatility durations. Because a significant portion of a product's value consists of volatility-sensitive features such as minimum interest rate guarantees and book-value cash surrender values, an increase in volatility will increase the liability's present value. A product feature that could have a positive volatility duration is the insurance company's option to reset interest rate guarantees. However, most insurance companies do not maximize the value of this option (that is, by adopting a strategy to reset rates aggressively only downward) and the overall product tends to have a negative volatility duration.

**Spread Duration.** Changes in residual spreads will affect the amount of funds necessary to support nonparticipating insurance liabilities. Therefore, nonparticipating products will have non-zero (usually positive) residual spread durations. However, the credit spread duration of nonparticipating insurance products should be zero. Because credit spread is compensation solely for asset default risk, it cannot be used to support a liability payment. If the insurance product is priced correctly, changing credit spreads will not affect the amount of funds needed to support the liability. Participating products should have both non-zero residual spread duration and credit spread duration as a result of their ability to "pass along" investment experience—whether good or bad.

9. If the minimum rate guarantee becomes effective, it can create a lengthy fixed-rate guarantee as long as interest rates stay low. In addition, since most credited rates tend to lag behind market rates of interest, declining interest rates can lead to greater policy persistency, thus increasing the SPDA's duration.

## Multifactor Immunization

When the asset/liability manager has all durations in hand, an attempt can be made to immunize the asset/liability position against changes in any, or all, of the risk factors we have discussed. Matching the multifactor durations of the asset position against the same durations of the liabilities will help to assure that the "excess" residual spread is earned, so long as the match is maintained. Excess spread is, in some sense, the basis point profit that is expected to be earned on the asset position.

Rarely, will any one asset exactly match all the factor durations of an interest-sensitive insurance product. However, a portfolio of diverse assets can be used in combination to match the multifactor durations of the liability. This section illustrates multifactor immunization for some assumed SPDA characteristics. To highlight the non-traditional factor durations (i.e., those other than interest rate duration), we will consider only assets that have the same interest rate duration as the SPDA. We will also ignore credit spread duration since this is a risk that should not affect the SPDA credited rate (and, thus, the amount of assets required to support the SPDA). The residual spread shown are, therefore, net of any credit risk change.

Exhibit 4 shows the characteristics of three hypothetical assets and of the SPDA. All factor durations are expressed in years and indicate the percentage price change for a 100-basis-point move in the risk factor. The residual spread of each asset is also shown. The residual spread of the SPDA is the spread that the assets must earn in order to meet the required SPDA expense and benefit payments. Any positive difference between asset and liability residual spread can be considered to be excess spread, or profit.

Any one asset would immunize the SPDA against movements in the general level of interest rates but would leave the position exposed to changes in interest rate volatility or residual spread. By solving a system of simultaneous equations, we find that allocating 50% of the portfolio to GNMAs and dividing the remainder evenly between noncallable and callable bonds will assure that the portfolio's value changes to the same extent that the SPDA value

**Exhibit 4.   Multifactor Immunization Asset Allocation**

| Instrument | Interest Rate (yrs.) | Residual Spread (yrs.) | Volatility (yrs.) | Residual Spread (bp) | Allocation (%) |
|---|---|---|---|---|---|
| | *Factor Duration* | | | | |
| Noncallable Bond | 3.0 | 3.0 | 0.0 | 100 | 25 |
| Callable Bond | 3.0 | 3.0 | 0.2 | 125 | 25 |
| GNMA | 3.0 | 5.0 | 0.3 | 75 | 50 |
| Asset Portfolio | 3.0 | 4.0 | 0.2 | 94 | |
| SPDA | 3.0 | 4.0 | 0.2 | 75 | |

changes. The difference between the portfolio's residual spread (94 basis points) and the required residual spread of the SPDA (75 basis points) is now immunized against changes in all three risk factors.

In practice, there is obviously a much larger universe of assets from which to select. An "optimization" could be used to select the portfolio of assets that maximizes the portfolio's residual spread, subject to matching all the multifactor durations. Furthermore, if the liability has negative volatility duration (which is typical), it will be necessary to include assets with negative volatility duration (such as caps, floors or options). The next section outlines a method by which an asset/liability manager can decide whether the costs of matching all multifactor durations outweigh the potentially higher residual spread of a mismatched position.

## Risk/Reward of Mismatched Portfolios

Multifactor (or, for that matter, single factor) immunization has its costs. A duration-matched asset portfolio will typically have a lower residual spread and absolute yield than a mismatched portfolio. The asset/liability manager must make an informed decision either to minimize risk through matching or attempt to earn the higher expected return of a mismatched position. A convenient way to summarize the risk/reward inherent in a mismatched position is in terms of confidence intervals.

A confidence interval is a statement about the probability that a result will lie between two extremes. A confidence interval for the residual spread of the GNMA might be that there is a 95% chance that the spread will be between five and 150 basis points at any given time. If the spread is currently 75 basis points, and if the degree of mismatch between the GNMA (asset) and SPDA (liability) residual spread duration is 1 year, the confidence interval can be translated into a 95% chance that the excess spread in the asset/liability position will lie between +18 and -19 basis points. The insurance company risk managers should explicitly define the minimum excess spread they are willing to tolerate for each of the multifactor risks. This minimum spread can be expressed on an asset-by-asset basis or can be in terms of an entire portfolio constraint.

When examining more than one risk parameter, it can be useful to construct tables or graphs that display the current excess residual spread as well as the spread at either end of the confidence interval. Exhibits 5 and 6 show the form of residual spread and interest rate volatility risk/reward analysis that this format will allow. The asset manager can use these types of displays in the asset selection process, keeping in mind that a fully immunized portfolio can also be constructed that has a constant excess residual spread (19 basis points in our example).

## Conclusion

We showed in this chapter that an asset/liability risk manager should examine multiple risks in addition to those due to shifts in the current level of risk-free interest rates. Changes in interest rate volatility and interest rate spread are two other types of risk that should also be considered. When these risks are isolated, the risk manager can compute price sensitivity indexes ("durations"). By

**Exhibit 5.  Excess Residual Spread Risk/Reward**
**(Reflects 95% Confidence Interval around Current Values)**

| | Volatility Risk/Reward | | Residual Spread Risk/Reward | |
|---|---|---|---|---|
| Instrument | Interest Rate Volatility (%) | Excess Residual Spread (bp) | Residual Spread (bp) | Excess Residual Spread (bp) |
| Noncallable Bond | 5 | −25 | 40 | 10 |
| | 15 | 25 | 100 | 25 |
| | 30 | 100 | 200 | 50 |
| Callable Bond | 5 | 50 | 40 | 29 |
| | 15 | 50 | 125 | 50 |
| | 30 | 50 | 200 | 69 |
| GNMA | 5 | 25 | 5 | 18 |
| | 15 | 0 | 75 | 0 |
| | 30 | −38 | 150 | −19 |

using these durations to select a portfolio of assets, it may be possible to immunize the excess spread in the asset/liability position from changes in any—or even all—of these risk factors. Finally, we illustrated a method of using confidence intervals to assist the risk manager (in selecting among less than fully-immunizing asset portfolios).

## Exhibit 6.  Excess Residual Spread Risk/Reward

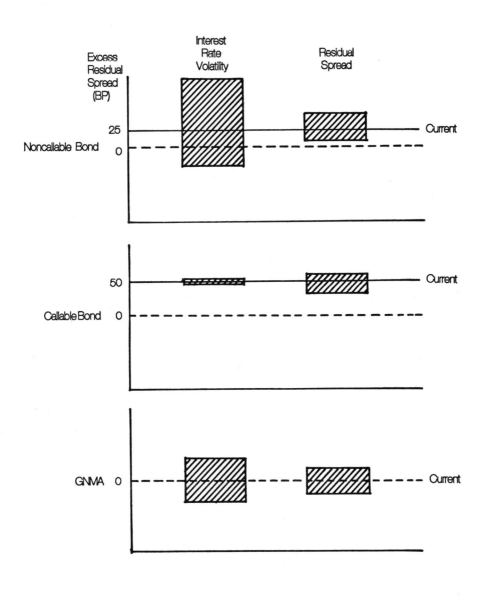

# Chapter 12

# Techniques for Hedging a Future Debt Issuance*

Eileen Baecher
Goldman, Sachs & Co.

Laurie S. Goodman
Goldman, Sachs & Co.

## I. Introduction

What is the best way for a corporate issuer to hedge the interest rate exposure of a proposed debt issuance? Because corporations issue debt for a variety of reasons and under a range of circumstances, there is no single correct answer. A variety of hedging considerations and techniques may be appropriate. The choice of a particular hedge instrument will depend on the size, timing, and nature of the interest rate exposure, the firm's risk tolerance, its interest rate expectations, and the costs of different techniques.

*This chapter is a much condensed version of a Goldman Sachs publication, "The Goldman Sachs Guide to Hedging Corporate Debt Issuance," August 1988. The authors owe special thanks to Andy Duus for initially suggesting this work and for giving helpful and insightful comments from the first to the final draft. We adapted Exhibit 1 from an oral presentation on hedging that he had prepared. Ron Krieger contributed many substantive comments and provided invaluable editorial support. Fischer Black, Bob Kopprasch, Russ Makowski, Jeff Mayer, and Ray Bacon provided useful comments and feedback on earlier drafts. Randall Kau and Bob Nassau of Sullivan & Cromwell reviewed the tax sections, and Robert Waxman of Touche Ross & Co. reviewed the accounting sections. We are also grateful to Kelly Ann LaRosa for her expert typing of numerous drafts of this manuscript.

Most firms allow their expectations for the course of interest rates to point them toward a hedging strategy. The hedge strategy can take three directions. One alternative is to "lock in" or "fix" rates, which would be desirable if the firm expected rates to rise either before the issuance or over the life of the issue. This choice might also be desirable if the firm found current rates acceptable but had no view on the direction of interest rates. Techniques for fixing a rate are discussed in Section II. Another alternative is to set a maximum yield and let the borrowing rate float under that "cap." Techniques for capping a rate are discussed in Section III. The third alternative is not to hedge at all. The firm would select a no-hedge strategy if it had a strong prior view that rates would remain constant or fall before the bond was to be issued. It might also select a no-hedge strategy if its funding needs were uncertain and if it had no idea of the direction of interest rates. In this chapter, we focus on some of the lesser known techniques for hedging, as well as the more common alternatives.

Exhibit 1 summarizes the advantages and disadvantages of each of the hedging alternatives discussed in this chapter. As the table indicates, we divide the specific hedging techniques into two principal types: methods that fix the issuance rate, which we treat in Section II, and strategies that cap interest rates, discussed in Section III. Not included in the table are techniques to fix the credit spread, which are also treated in Section II.

There is one important caveat to keep in mind in hedging an anticipated debt issuance: flexibility is necessary. Over the course of the hedge period, the uncertainties concerning the issuance will be resolved, the firm's outlook on rates will change, or both. As the environment changes, the initial choice of hedge instruments may no longer be appropriate, and the firm may want to adjust its hedge design. For example, it may replace option strategies with techniques that fix the base rate or the spread rate of the issuance.

Moreover, as the market changes, the hedge ratios may have to change if the firm alters its financing plans. The underlying principle of hedging is to match the interest rate sensitivity of a liability (or asset) with an offsetting position that has the same interest rate sensitivity. One way to determine an appropriate hedge

**Exhibit 1. Comparison of Hedging Strategies**

| Type | (A) Prefund Fix (Absolute) | (B) Forward Sale of Treasuries Fix (Treasury) | (C) Short Sale of Treasureis Fix (Treasury) | (D) Sale of Futures Fix (Treasury) | (E) Forward Interest Rate Swap Fix (Treasury) | (F) Rate Hedge Agreement Fix (Treasury) | (G) Purchase Put Option Cap (Treasury) | (H) Purchase Cap Option Cap (LIBOR) |
|---|---|---|---|---|---|---|---|---|
| Avoid Spread Risk | Yes | No | No | No | No | No | No | No |
| Preserve Upside Potential | No | No | No | No | No | No | Yes | Yes |
| Hedge Costs | Medium | Low | Low | Low | Medium | Low | High | High |
| Unwind Spread (bp) | na* | 2–4 | 2–4 | 2–4 | 5–10 | 2–4 | 4–6 | 5–10 |
| Avoid Repo Risk | Yes | Yes | No | Yes | Yes | Yes | Yes | Yes |
| Accounting: Mark to Market | na | Yes | Yes | No | No | No | No | No |
| Gain/Loss at Termination | na | Amortized | Current | Amortized | Amortized | Amortized | Amortized | Amortized |
| Tax: Mark to Market | na | No | No | Yes | No | No if OTC Yes if exchange-traded | No | No |
| Gain/Loss at Termination | na | Capital | Capital | Capital | Ordinary | Ordinary | Capital | Ordinary (IRS guidance expected soon) |
| Maximum Time Period for Hedge: | na | 6 months | 6 months | 18 months | 3 years | 6 months | 9 months | 10 years |
| Credit Exposure | No | Yes | Minimal | Minimal | Yes | Yes | If OTC: yes If exchange-traded: minimal | Yes |

*na = not applicable.

ratio for a debt issuance is to calculate the change in the present value of cash flows of the liability for a one basis point (1 bp) change in interest rates. For a bond that has yet to be issued, this is the present value of a 1 bp change in the coupon rate, as the coupon is determined when the issue is priced. That is, the coupon is generally set such that the bond will initially sell at par, and thus the coupon yield and the yield to maturity are equivalent. One may then calculate the interest rate sensitivity of the hedge instrument and multiply the ratio of these price sensitivities (the "hedge ratio") by the face value of the issuance to determine the required face value of the hedge vehicle.[1] As the expected maturity of the liability changes or as interest rates move, it is important to make sure the hedge ratio is altered properly.

## II. Fixing a Rate

We are now ready to describe the various hedging techniques that an issuer may select to fix or to cap a rate. As we have discussed, one should make the selection only after defining the risks and environment. The flow chart in Exhibit 2 illustrates the decision process and the likely choices. The borrower will usually decide to fix an issuance rate if there is little uncertainty surrounding the need or amount of the funding and if the current level of interest rates is attractive. If it leaves the issuance unhedged, the firm will benefit from a decline in interest rates and will be hurt by an increase in rates before the issue date.

There are two components of a corporate bond's yield: the base Treasury rate and the corporate spread. These components can be hedged jointly or separately. We will first describe techniques that fix the combined rate and then look individually at base rate and spread fixing techniques.

---

1. Tax considerations can, however, make hedge design more difficult. The increase or decrease in coupon payments receives ordinary income treatment, while the price gain or loss on many hedge vehicles is treated as capital gain or loss. A precise hedge would then be one in which the after-tax value of the change in the hedge instrument's price was equal to the after-tax present value of the additional coupon payments. Note that the actual after-tax cost can be determined only if the capital loss carry-forwards and other tax attributes of the firm are known. Firms should bear this in mind when selecting hedge ratios.

## Exhibit 2. Choosing a Hedge Vehicle

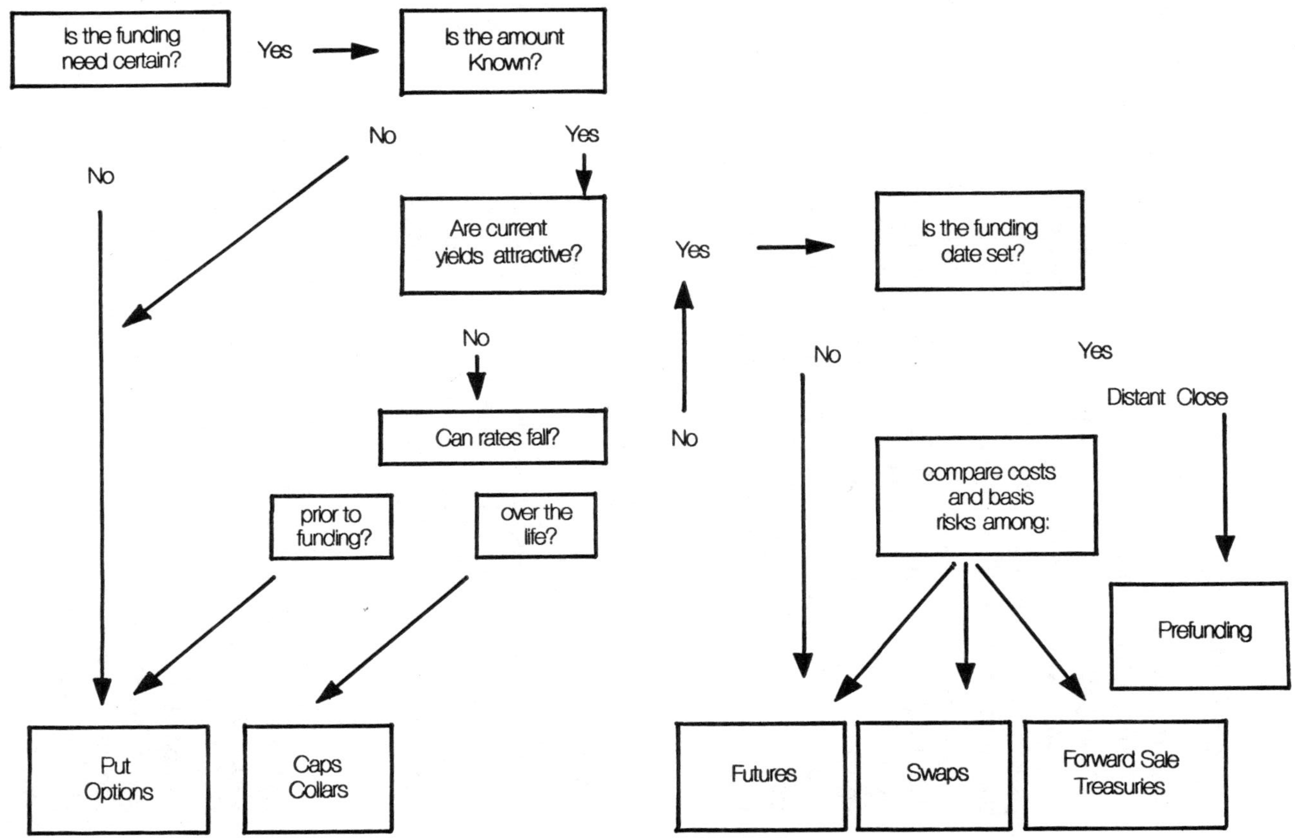

## Full Rate Fix

If a firm wants to fix not only the current rates of interest in the Treasury market but also the current spread of corporate issues off Treasury rates, it will generally opt to prefund. In a prefunding, the borrower brings the issue to market immediately, investing the proceeds at a short-term rate until they are needed. This technique can work very well if the details of the funding, the amount, and the maturity have been established. The cost of a prefunding is the difference between the debt's coupon rate and the short-term rate over the hedge period. Thus, if the yield curve is such that the coupon rate is 10% and the short-term rate is 8%, the cost of the hedge is 200 bp during the hedge period. For a three-month hedge period, this is $0.50 per $100 par, or 8 bp per year for 10 years. If the yield curve is steep or if the hedge period is lengthy, this technique may become expensive.

## Fixing the Base Rate

As Exhibit 1 indicates, there are five techniques (items B through F) available for fixing the base Treasury rate of an issuance: (1) forward sales and (2) short sales of Treasury securities, (3) futures contracts, (4) forward interest rate swaps, and (5) rate hedge agreements.

The most direct method of fixing a base rate is through the sale of Treasury securities of a similar maturity and price sensitivity to the funding. One can do this either as a forward sale or a short sale. The forward sale is an agreement between two parties to sell a security at a date in the future at a price agreed upon today. A short sale requires that the security be delivered immediately, which means that the security must be borrowed through the repurchase (repo) market. Forward and short sales will have similar net costs. They differ in their execution and credit concerns.

## Forward Sales

A forward sale is fairly simple to execute. The firm just asks for a forward bid from a Treasury dealer. No securities or money will change hands until the forward settlement date, even though the ownership of the securities has been exchanged. The dealer (buyer) takes on the security's price risk over the forward period and in return receives only the firm's promise to deliver at the end of the period. Essentially, the forward sale is an uncollateralized credit agreement between the dealer and the firm.

The forward settlement date generally is set on or just after the planned issuance date.[2] On the settlement date, the hedger has two alternatives for closing the hedge. One way is to issue debt and use the proceeds to purchase Treasury securities for delivery against the forward settlement. The hedger will then use the funds received on the forward sale just as he would have used the debt proceeds in an unhedged situation. A much simpler way to remove the hedge is to enter into an offsetting forward purchase. To eliminate the need to actually make or take delivery, the hedger could make this forward purchase with the original counterparty for the same settlement date as the original contract.

## Short Sales

The alternative to the forward sale is a short sale in which the issuer hedges by selling Treasury securities at the beginning of the hedge period. To execute a short sale, the hedging firm generally will borrow in the repo market the Treasury security that will determine the base rate of the issuance, such as the current 10-year

---

2. If the forward settlement falls prior to the funding date, that will leave a period in which a change in the issuance yield will not be covered by a change in the value of the hedge instrument. If the date of the financing is postponed and the forward date does come before the issuance date, the forward sale must be offset with a puchase for that date, and a new forward sale must be established.

Treasury for a 10-year issuance.[3] The firm simultaneously sells the security into the market at the best available price and turns over the proceeds of the sale to the counterparty in the repurchase agreement. (The buyer of securities lends money.) At the end of the hedging period the hedging firm buys notes to replace the original collateral and returns the securities, closing the repurchase agreement. The firm uses the money received from returning the collateral to buy the Treasury notes in the marketplace. To reduce the credit risk, the parties must make the exchange of securities and funds simultaneously. The dealer that "counterparts" the repo often handles the open-market sale and purchase of the Treasury securities, as this saves the hedging firm the effort of taking delivery of the borrowed securities and redelivering them for the short sale.

Hedgers should be aware that the repurchase rate can either be fixed or be allowed to float during the hedge period. If the rate is fixed, the arrangement is called a "term repo." A floating rate agreement is called an "open repo." Most hedgers will prefer to use a term rate because it removes uncertainty as to the cost of the hedge. An open repo may be simpler to use if the end of the hedge period is uncertain. An open repo is re-established daily and net interest payments are made daily. The term repo usually has no interim payments.

### Futures Sales

Futures contracts are standardized forward agreements, where the buyer and seller agree to exchange a type of (but not a specific) Treasury security during a future period at a price agreed upon today. Through either the actual delivery of a security or a cash settlement procedure, futures prices are inextricably linked to the underlying cash market prices. Consequently, the sale or purchase of a futures contract can be considered a substitute for the sale or purchase of the underlying security.

---

3. More precisely, the firm will attempt to borrow a security with a maturity equal to the time to maturity of the anticipated bond plus the time to issuance. In practice, it will select the on-the-run Treasury with a maturity most closely matching the anticipated issue.

When the firm is choosing between futures and forward sales as hedge techniques, the major consideration is the strong liquidity and efficiency of the futures versus the ability to customize the specifics of a forward sale. The liquidity of the futures markets allows hedge design and maintenance to be more flexible and generally more cost-efficient than physical Treasury transactions. The bid-offered spreads in futures are usually only one thirty-second of a point as opposed to one-eighth of a point for many Treasuries, making it simple and efficient to adjust the hedge size and close the hedge.

The customization of forwards may be important to issuers who want to minimize basis risk. Most futures contracts are settled on a quarterly cycle, e.g., March, June, September, and December for the U.S. Treasury contracts. Thus, if a firm wants to hedge through mid-February, the futures can be sold, but futures and cash will not necessarily converge. The greatest liquidity is found in the "front" contract, the nearest contract to be delivered against, and the "next" contract, the second contract to be delivered against. Only bond futures have substantial liquidity farther out than two contracts. For long-term hedges, this may require that the hedge be initiated with the front or next contract and then "rolled" into just prior to the delivery period. The cost of rolling is usually one or two thirty-seconds.

Moreover, the risk of non-parallel yield curve shapes is usually greater for futures hedges than for cash hedges, because there are active futures contracts in a limited range of maturity sectors. In the U.S. markets the most active is the long bond sector, including maturities between 15 and 30 years, with the next largest the intermediate 7- to 10-year notes. The 5-year Treasury note contracts were introduced only recently and generally will not be liquid enough for hedges of more than $50,000,000. Clearly, an issue with a different maturity from that of the futures will be less than perfectly hedged with a futures position. For example, if 10-year note futures are used to duration hedge a 7-year issuance, most of the interest exposure is eliminated. But the hedge will not be precise if 7-year yields increase more than 10-year yields do.

A secondary consideration is the relative cheapness or richness of the futures contract. If an issuer is shorting a futures contract, he wants to short a rich contract. The price of a futures contract is determined in roughly the same way as that of any forward contract. The difference between the spot and futures (or forward) prices reflects the amount of carry available over the contract period. In the cash market, the difference is called the "drop." In the futures market, the difference, calculated by subtracting the security's current price from the price used in the delivery process, is called the "basis."[4] At the time of delivery, a future and its underlying security must have the same price, since they are interchangeable at that time. The basis spread must, therefore, "converge" to zero as delivery approaches.

Even though futures and cash prices will converge at the time of delivery, this does not imply that their prices are always in line during the contract's life. For contracts that include delivery options favoring the party with the short futures position,[5] there will be an additional discount of the futures price. The borrower must take these considerations into account when determining the relative value of futures versus cash—and consequently the attractiveness of futures as a hedge vehicle. It should be noted that while richness or cheapness is always important, it is more important for futures contracts that have relatively low volumes, or are in markets where arbitrage between cash and futures is difficult to implement. These contracts will have wider swings in their value relative to cash securities.

### Forward Swaps

Another technique for fixing a base rate is a forward interest rate swap transaction. An interest rate swap is a contractual agreement

---

4. Delivery prices for contracts that require the physical delivery of coupon-bearing bonds are equal to the futures price multiplied by a conversion factor. Factors provide the mechanism for invoicing each of the deliverable securities.
5. Delivery options exist for contracts that are completed by the physical delivery of any one of a variety of securities. These include the popular U.S. Treasury bone and U.S. Treasury not contracts, both traded on the Chicago Board of Trade. A fuller discussion of delivery options can be found in Arak, Goodman, and Ross (1987), Kane and Marcus (1986) and Meisner and Labuszweski (1984).

between two parties to exchange payments, expressed as a percentage of a notional principal value, on a periodic basis for a number of years. There is no exchange of principal. Outstanding swaps are estimated at $500 billion. Both commercial and investment banks position and trade interest rate swaps, and an active market provides reasonable liquidity. The most liquid swaps are those based on exchanging 6-month LIBOR for the yield on a current Treasury note plus a spread. The majority of swaps have terms of three to seven years, but swaps are available to 10 years. There is also a short-dated swap market for terms of less than three years. Pricing of short-dated swaps is closely tied to the 3-month Eurodollar futures. The futures are based on 3-month LIBOR and therefore provide an efficient hedging mechanism for the swap dealers.

Generally, swaps that begin immediately are used to adjust the character of interest payments on existing assets or liabilities. Hedges of anticipated issuances or receipt of assets can be more effectively executed with a forward swap. A forward swap is just a normal interest rate swap transaction, except that the swap begins on a forward date—normally, the date of the bond issuance. A forward swap hedge proceeds as follows:

1. A firm enters a 3-month forward swap in a notional amount equal to the planned debt issuance, agreeing to pay the current 5-year Treasury yield plus 75 bp. In return, the firm will receive 6-month LIBOR.

2. In three months, the firm issues floating rate debt. Six months after issuance, the first payments are exchanged. The firm pays the fixed rate available at the time the swap was entered and receives 6-month LIBOR. The LIBOR payment is used to pay the interest on the floating rate debt.

3. The net cost of the issuance will be the swap's fixed rate level plus the difference between 6-month LIBOR and the floating rate index at which the firm issues. For example, if the firm issues floating rate debt at 6-month LIBOR + 25 bp, its all-in cost of funds is the 5-year Treasury yield plus the

75 bp swap spread plus the 25 bp margin on the floating rate debt. If the firm instead issues floating rate debt at the commercial paper rate, the cost of funds to the firm will be less than the 5-year Treasury yield plus 75 bp, reflecting the fact that the commercial paper rate is below LIBOR. In lieu of issuing floating rate debt, the firm may terminate or assign the swap, recognizing any gain or loss, and issue fixed rate debt.

For hedging purposes the more customized a swap becomes, the more difficult it will be to reverse if the hedging need is changed or eliminated. Entering into a swap costs nothing in the way of fees or commission payments. The cost of any odd payment dates or fluctuation of par amounts will initially be reflected in an increase in the spread over the fixed rate that the firm is obligated to pay. Additionally, a wider than normal bid-offered spread will be an added cost if the swap is reversed. Swaps based on floating rate indexes other than LIBOR are also available, but they tend to be much less liquid than LIBOR-based swaps.

In a swap, the issuer will be exposed to the credit risk of the counterparty. This is usually a financial institution that acts as the intermediary between one final user who wants to pay fixed and receive floating, and another final user who wishes to receive fixed and pay floating. This risk initially appears smaller than that of a forward sale of Treasury securities, in that there is no notional exchange of principal. However, the credit risk on a swap extends throughout the swap's life.

### Rate Hedge Agreements

A final alternative for fixing the base rate is a rate hedge agreement (RHA). An RHA is a customized contract in which a dealer hedges the yield on a Treasury security on behalf of a prospective issuer. The term of the contract is generally limited to six months. Economically, a rate hedge agreement is no different from a Treasury short sale, but it receives far more favorable tax and accounting treatment. For short hedge periods, an RHA is less costly than a forward swap in many cases.

An RHA specifies a base price for a particular Treasury security or other instrument. This base price is derived from the current price, net of carry. When a prospective issuer enters into an RHA with a dealer, the client may terminate the agreement at any time during its life by asking the dealer to quote a "takedown price" on the underlying Treasury security. An excess of the takedown price over the base price would be payable by the prospective issuer to the dealer, a shortfall would be payable by the dealer to the client. Under the RHA there is no right or obligation to make or take delivery of the specified Treasury or any other property. Settlement is completed solely in cash.

### Tax Treatment of Various Alternatives

To compare accurately the costs of using various techniques to fix a rate, the corporation must consider the relevant tax and accounting treatment. From a tax perspective, there are two issues to be considered: whether the gain or loss will be considered as capital or ordinary, and when the gain or loss will be recognized.

It is uncertain whether the Internal Revenue Service will treat gains or losses arising from sales of securities in the spot market— and the closing of forward or futures contracts on securities or interest rate indexes—as capital gains or losses. Until March 1988, many tax specialists had thought that gains or losses on hedging transactions initiated to reduce the risk of interest rate increases on liabilities would give rise to ordinary income or loss, under the doctrine of *Corn Products Refining Co.* In March 1988, however, the decision by the U.S. Supreme court in *Arkansas Best Corporation v. Commissioner* suggested that the only certain situation in which gains and losses would be ordinary was when inventory was being hedged. Liabilities are obviously not inventory, i.e., property held for sale to customers in the ordinary course of business. Thus, it appears that futures, forwards, and short sales receive capital gain or loss treatment. By contrast, RHAs receive ordinary income or expense treatment. This stems from the absence of a formal sale or exchange or securities.

With respect to the timing of income recognition, the gain or loss from a Treasury short sale, forward sale, or RHA is generally recognized when the hedge is lifted. Futures transactions are marked to market, with the gain or loss recognized upon termination or at the close of the firm's taxable year, whichever is earlier, unless the futures are part of a "hedging transaction." Since *Arkansas Best*, however, it is uncertain whether this test can be satisfied.

For tax purposes, swap expenses are treated as offsets to ordinary income. Payments made (received) will be deductible (includable) in the year in which they accrue. When the swap is closed, any gain or loss is recognized at that time and is treated as ordinary income or expense.

### Accounting Treatment

Futures and forwards and RHAs may be subject to different accounting treatment from that accorded short Treasury sales. As part of a designated hedge transaction of an anticipated debt offering, realized gains or losses from closing a futures position can be amortized over the life of the funding, as outlined in Financial Accounting Standards Board (FASB) Statement 80, "Accounting for Futures Contracts." Statement 80 requires that a change in the market value of an open futures contract be recognized in the income statement as a gain or loss in the period of the change, unless the contract qualifies as a hedge under the hedge criteria specified in the statement. If these hedge criteria are met, a change in the market value of the futures contract is usually reported as an adjustment of the carrying amount of the hedged item. While FASB 80 does not explicitly cover other hedging vehicles, most accountants believe that if the forward or the RHA meets the FASB 80 hedge criteria, the hedge should be carried at market, with gains or losses deferred and recognized as an adjustment to the carrying amount of the anticipated debt.

By contrast, in the case of a short sale most accountants maintain that the gain or loss on the disposition of the security should be recognized at the date of sale. However, some accountants argue, by reference to FASB 80, that the gain or loss may be deferred and recognized as an adjustment to the carrying amount of the anticipated debt issuance.

Swaps receive somewhat different accounting treatment. The net amount due to or from the swap counterparty for a particular financial reporting period should be accrued and included in the determination of net income. Any gain or loss on termination of a linked interest rate swap is deferred and amortized over the remaining term of the liability or the remaining term of the original swap, whichever is shorter.

### Fixing a Spread

If a firm expects interest rates to stay steady or decline but expects credit spreads in general or its firm-specific spread to widen before funds are needed, the firm may wish to consider fixing a spread. It can accomplish this in either of two ways—by executing a spread lock to fix the generic spread, or by prefunding and investing the proceeds in Treasury securities of the same maturity to fix the firm-specific spread. Both of these techniques have been used, with a spread lock the more common choice.

### Fixing a Generic Credit Spread

Fixing a generic credit spread is most easily done through the swap market. The fixed rate on a swap of a given maturity is generally quoted as the current Treasury of the same maturity plus a spread. This so-called swap spread tends to narrow and widen in tandem with general corporate spreads. A spread lock allows a firm to fix the credit spread without fixing the base rate. Thus, a spread lock can be viewed as a tool to hedge the general level of corporate spreads. A spread lock is most effective when a firm knows it will have to come to market within a relatively short time—two or three months.

In a spread lock, the firm agrees to enter into a swap deal at a specified spread to Treasuries, but has a period ranging up to two or three months to fix the absolute rate. That is, the firm must fix the absolute rate by the end of the period, but may choose when to fix the rate within the period. When the base rate is fixed, the pre-specified swap spread is added to give the fixed rate payable on the swap. If Treasury rates decline over near term, the firm is able to take advantage of this.

To see how a spread lock would work, assume that a firm wants a spread lock for the next two months. At the end of the two-month period, or earlier if Treasury rates look attractive in the interim, the firm would issue floating rate debt and take down the swap in which it pays fixed and receives floating. Assume the fixed swap spread was 80 bp and its issuing rate was LIBOR + 25 bp. The firm would, on net, pay the Treasury rate prevailing at the time the swap was taken down plus 105 bp (80 + 25).[6]

### Fixing a Firm-Specific Spread

If a firm wants to fix a spread on a specific issue, it can prefund the issue and invest the proceeds in a Treasury security of the same maturity until the funds are needed. Assume a firm is able to fund today for 10 years at $T_{10}$ + 80 bp. If it invests the proceeds at $T_{10}$, the firm's cost is the 80 bp credit spread plus the bid-asked spread on the Treasury purchase and sale. If we neglect the transaction cost on the Treasury issue, paying the 10-year rate at the time of prefunding plus taking the loss or gain on the Treasury is equivalent to paying the 10-year rate at the time the funds are needed. If rates have risen, the firm's borrowing rate will be lower than the currently prevailing rate, but the Treasury investment will have experienced a loss. Similarly, if rates have fallen, the borrowing rate will be higher than the currently prevailing rate, but the Treasury investment will have experienced a gain. In our ex-

---

6. A spread lock is typically offered at a 2 to 4 bp premium over the straight swap. The premium is present because the swap counterparty will short Treasury securities and invest the proceeds in short-term instruments until the swap is taken down. The negative carry during the hedge period is figured into the quoted spread. Thus, 150 bp of negative carry for two months in $0.25 per $100 par, or 2.5 bp for a 7-year issue.

ample, the 80 bp cost for three months is roughly equivalent to an extra 2.2 bp over the life of the 10-year issue. The purchase and subsequent sale of Treasury securities could be executed through a rate hedge agreement as well as through the physical purchase and sale of securities.

This technique differs from a prefunding to fix the entire rate, in that the proceeds are invested differently. The firm invests the proceeds of a prefunding in a short-term money market instrument. In fixing a firm-specific spread, it invests the proceeds of the prefunding in longer-term notes, the price movements of which will offset changes in the interest rates on the bond issuance.

## III. Capping a Rate

As Exhibit 2 indicates, circumstances may arise in which it will be advantageous for the issuer to put a ceiling on its borrowing rate through the purchase of options. There may be uncertainty as to the details of the issuance, or the firm may feel that interest rates are likely to decline either before the issuance date or over the life of the issue. An option hedge allows the issuer to take advantage of a rate decline while protecting himself from an increase in rates above a specific level. If the borrower is not sure of his funding needs, options can guarantee a maximum funding cost. If it turns out that the funding is needed, the protection is helpful. If the funding is not needed and there is a gain on the option, the firm can exercise the option and liquidate. The maximum loss is limited to the option premium.

The benefits of options must, however, be balanced against their costs, which can seem relatively high when compared with the costs of fixed rate hedges. The costs are higher because an option has an asymmetric risk profile. That is, the price gain to a call option from a decline in interest rates is not mirrored by an equal price loss from a rise in interest rates. Exhibit 3 illustrates the difference in the risk profiles of (1) an issuance hedged with the purchase of a put option and (2) an unhedged issuance.

The two most common option hedges are individual Treasury put options and option packages called "caps" or "collars." A less

**Exhibit 3.  Borrowing Costs—Unhedged and Hedged with Put**

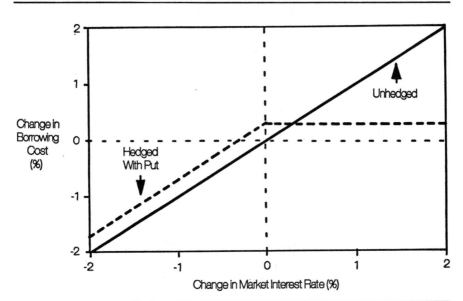

well known alternative is the "caput." We will discuss each of these in turn.

### Buying Put Options

One of the advantages of option products is their flexibility. The firm can choose to cap the cost of the issue at a price level that corresponds to its needs, rather than simply using the current price level in the market. The flexibility to choose a strike level and the known cost (premium) of options are particularly important in the presence of funding uncertainty. Borrowers may be reluctant to buy at-the-money options because of cost considerations, but some level of insurance may be desirable.

Issuers can use either exchange-traded or over-the-counter (OTC) options. Exchange-traded options are available on almost all the major futures contracts. The open interest of options on bond futures traded on the CBT is higher than the open interest on the futures themselves, although the daily volume of options is lower. The advantages and disadvantages of exchange-traded options on futures are the same as those of the futures themselves. One must balance liquidity and lower transaction costs against the limitations of standardization.

OTC options are traded by securities dealers. These dealers stand ready to make markets in the options at a bid-asked spread. The more customized the product, the wider the spread. Options on on-the-run Treasuries have narrower bid-asked spreads than options on off-the-run Treasuries, which in turn have narrower spreads than options on corporates.

An exchange-traded option will hedge movements in particular Treasury rates but cannot hedge the specific characteristics of the corporation's debt. OTC options can be customized to cap borrowing costs at the desired level and eliminate any mismatch between the option term and the borrower's hedging period. A firm that wishes to use an OTC has three choices: (1) purchasing an option on a Treasury security of the same maturity as the anticipated issue, (2) purchasing an option on one of its own outstanding bonds, or (3) purchasing an option on the anticipated issue. Options on Treasury securities would entail a lower bid-asked spread than either of the other two choices. These options, however, require the firm to assume the risk that its credit spread may widen. With options on an outstanding corporate bond or an anticipated issuance, a firm can cap both the base rate and the credit spread for the desired period. The disadvantage to a corporate client of buying an option on the anticipated issuance is that if the issue does not come to market, the firm cannot exercise the option. Before pursuing this alternative, a company should be absolutely sure of its need for funding. If a firm is unsure of the need for funding, buying an option on one of its outstanding issues may be preferred.

The disadvantage of OTC options is the frequently high cost of unwinding them before expiration. Although this applies to both options on Treasuries and options on corporates, it is a more serious problem for options on corporates. If a firm is unsure of exactly when funding may be needed, an exchange-traded option will be preferable. Since most issuers have some degree of funding uncertainty, exchange-traded options are used far more commonly than OTC options. If a firm's credit spread fluctuations are small, it may well prefer to use an exchange-traded option, since it is important to hedge only the base rate. It is unnecessary to pay for a customized product.

In addition to OTC and exchange-traded options, there is a third alternative—synthetic put options—to cap the rate on a new debt issuance. OTC options provide more protection (at a greater cost), but they are expensive to resell prior to maturity. Exchange-traded options have greater liquidity, but their strike prices and maturities are less flexible. If the characteristics of the options desired by the issuer do not match those of an option traded on the exchange, the borrower can create a synthetic option using futures.[7] Synthetic put options allow the borrower to have a customized option, and—if volatility does not increase—they will have lower costs than a typical OTC option. However, synthetic put option positions are rarely used because they require close monitoring and trading of futures.

### Caps and Collars

Occasionally, a firm may have determined a funding need, but either it does not find the prevailing level of interest rates to be attractive or it expects interest rates to move lower prior to the issuance date or over the life of the issue. In these circumstances, Caps and collars, used in conjunction with a floating rather than a fixed rate issuance, are suitable hedge vehicles. Caps and collars are negotiated transactions between the firm and a commercial or investment bank, where the firm pays an initial premium to the bank and in return receives interest payments if the underlying rate moves above an agreed-upon level. For example, if the firm purchases a LIBOR-based cap at 11%, the bank agrees that if LIBOR rises above 11%, the bank will pay the firm for that reset

---

7. See Rubinstein and Leland (1981), and Asay and Edelsburg (1986).

period at a rate equal to the difference between the prevailing rate and 11%.

Thus, if a firm purchases an 11% cap that resets semiannually on $100,000,000, and LIBOR rises to 13%, the firm will receive (.02 × 1/2 × $100,000,000), or $1,000,000. Its net borrowing costs for that period will be:

| | | |
|---|---|---|
| Interest cost | .13 × 1/2 × $100,000,000 = | $6,500,000 |
| Less receipt from cap | -.02 × 1/2 × $100,000,000 = | -$1,000,000 |
| | | $5,500,000 |

Note that the net cost corresponds to an interest rate of 11% (.11 × 1/2 × $100,000,000) = $5,500,000. If LIBOR were 10%, the firm would receive no cap payments, and its floating rate debt would be set at 10% for the period. To compute the maximum all-in borrowing cost with a cap, one must add the amortization of the initial cap premium to the maximum borrowing rate.

Caps are available based on a wide range of money market indexes, including Treasury bills, commercial paper, LIBOR, the prime rate, and the rate on certificates of deposit. LIBOR caps are, by far, the most common. Caps based on other indexes may be arranged but will be slightly more expensive. The firm would select the floating rate index, as well as the maturity of the cap (up to 10 years, but most commonly in the 3-to 7-year range), the ceiling rate, the start date, and the payment frequency (three or six months). An unofficial estimate of the size of the cap market is $300-400 billion of outstanding caps.

A cap can be viewed as a series of options. Consider a 3-year cap that pays every six months. It is actually a series of five options: a 6-month option, a 12-month option, an 18-month option, a 2-year option, and a 2 1/2-year option. There are five rather than six options because payments are determined by the level of LIBOR at the beginning of the period and paid at the end. Thus, the rate for the first six months is determined immediately and hence has no option component. The payment for the period from 6-12 months is determined by LIBOR at the end of month 6, and this option would be exercised if LIBOR exceeded the cap level.

Exhibit 4 gives representative cap costs. These up-front fees will change, of course, as the level of rates changes, volatility changes, or the shape of the yield curve changes.

If an issuer buys a cap and, at the end of three months, decides not to issue the security, it can sell the cap back to the dealer. However, the bid-asked spreads on caps are wider than those on put options; a 25-50 cent bid-asked spread would be typical. This translates into 5-10 bp per year on a 5-year issue. If the bond is to be issued and rates have declined, the buyer can either resell the cap and issue a fixed rate bond, or keep the cap and issue at the lower floating rate. If rates have risen, the issuer can issue floating and keep the now more valuable cap. Alternatively, the issuer can resell the cap at a gain and issue at the then-higher fixed rate.

A variation on the cap is the floating rate collar. The collar market was created for issuers who prefer capped floating rate liabilities but consider caps too expensive. With a collar, a borrower buys a cap and sells a "floor" at the same time. If rates fall below the floor level, the firm is obligated to pay the difference between the floor level and the floating rate index. The income from selling the floor offsets some of the cost of the cap. For example, if the issuer purchased a cap 262.5 bp above current rates and sold a floor 137.5 bp below current rates for 10 years, the cost of the collared position would reduce the up-front fee by close to 30%. Spe-

**Exhibit 4.  Representative Cap Quotes**

**(in decimal, as of July 28, 1988)**
**Current 3-Month LIBOR = 8 3/8%**

| Term (years) | 9% (+62.5 bp) | 10% (+162.5 bp) | 11% (+262.5 bp) | 12% (+362.5 bp) | 13% (+462.5 bp) |
|---|---|---|---|---|---|
| 3 | 2.43 | 1.47 | .90 | .54 | .31 |
| 5 | 4.97 | 3.40 | 2.28 | 1.55 | 1.05 |
| 7 | 8.18 | 6.13 | 4.39 | 3.27 | 2.45 |
| 10 | 12.10 | 9.45 | 7.12 | 5.59 | 4.41 |

cifically, with LIBOR at 8 3/8%, an 11% cap would sell for $7.12; an 11% cap coupled with a 7% floor would sell for $5.07.

Exhibit 5 shows the risk/return profile of a collared position vis-à-vis a capped position and an unhedged position. When rates are low, both the unhedged positions and the capped position are preferable to the collar. As rates rise, the collar looks quite attractive—it is more favorable than either capped debt or unhedged debt.

Another cap product is the forward cap. A firm may use a forward cap if it expects to issue debt in the future and believes that rates will go up by more than the expectations implied by the existing yield curve. If an issuer decides not to issue the debt, it can sell back the cap. This type of transaction requires that a counterparty write one cap (the longer cap) and buy another cap (the shorter cap). Thus, the transaction costs on this type of hedge are greater than on a normal cap.

**Exhibit 5. Borrowing Costs—Unhedged and Hedged with Caps and Floors**

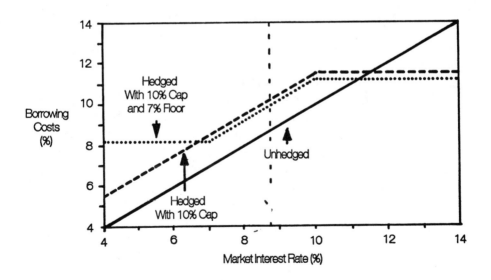

## Caputs

Caps and puts are the two most common devices used to place an upper limit on borrowing costs. Less common but often useful is a "caput"—a call on a put. This gives an issuer the right to purchase a specific put at a given strike price at a particular date in the future. If interest rates rise, the put will increase in value. Thus, the caput, which conveys the right to purchase the put at a preset price, also becomes more valuable. If interest rates decline, the caput will not be exercised. When there is a great deal of uncertainty about the financing, one should consider the caput as an alternative to a cap or a put, as the up-front fee is lower. However, caputs are highly customized products and therefore are hard to resell prior to expiration.

## Tax Treatment

The tax consequences of option buying will depend on whether the option is exchange-traded or OTC. A firm cannot deduct the premium on any option immediately. A gain or loss on the sale or expiration of an OTC option is a capital gain or loss, and is recognized at the time it occurs. Thus, if the option expires worthless, the premium is a capital loss and is recognized at expiration. If a firm sells or exercises the option, the premium is applied against the payoff, with the net amount recognized as a capital gain or loss. For exchange-traded options, changes in the premium are considered gains or losses and are marked to market. Any gain or loss is a capital gain or loss and must be recognized upon termination or at the end of the firm's taxable year, whichever comes first. The tax consequences of cap buying are unclear, although many believe the premium on a cap can be amortized over the term of the cap as an offset to ordinary income. We expect additional guidance from the IRS in the near future.

## Accounting Treatment

Under hedge accounting, the time and intrinsic values of the purchased put option should be split. The time value should be amortized and recognized as an expense over the term of the option. Hedge accounting should be applied to changes in the intrinsic value. For example, assume that a firm purchases a 3-month at-the-money put option (an option with no intrinsic value) to hedge a 10-year debt issue. In this case, the entire premium paid for the option should be recognized as an expense over the 3-month period. If the firm exercises the option, the proceeds on the option would be reflected as an adjustment of the carrying amount of the anticipated debt issue.

The accounting treatment for caps is different. For financial reporting purposes, the cap premium is amortized over the life of the cap instrument. Straight-line amortization is the preferred amortization method in most cases. Any payment made to the cap buyer from the counterparty can be offset against interest payments. If the cap is terminated prior to maturity, any gain or loss from termination is recognized in income immediately.

## IV. Summary

In this chapter, we have described a variety of ways to hedge an anticipated bond issuance. Most of the appropriate hedging solutions will depend on the firm's desired risk profile and the relative importance to the firm of the various hedging criteria, as summarized in Exhibit 1. Clearly, no single technique dominates in all circumstances. Hedge design will depend on the firm's goals and priorities. For example, if an issuer wants a low cost, liquid hedge of the base Treasury rate—and preservation of the upside potential is relatively unimportant—interest rate futures may be the hedging method of choice. If the issuer wants to preserve the upside potential and is willing to spend the money to do so, a put option or a cap is a more appropriate hedge.

Exhibit 2 identifies critical questions that arise in the choice of a hedge. An issuer may well use one hedge technique for one issue and a different hedge technique for another issue at a different time. That is, an issuer may want to fix the base rate for one issue and purchase a cap for another. The firm may even want to change the hedge technique during the course of a single issue.

For example, if the issuer believes interest rates will rise for a short while but is uncertain about their direction thereafter, it may want to initially fix a rate and think about the possibility of capping a rate later. If there is funding uncertainty, fixing a rate may be less desirable than alternatives that preserve upside potential. Once the uncertainty is resolved, fixing a rate may be preferable.

In short, there is no magic key to choosing the best hedge. The appropriate vehicle will vary among issuers, and the decision will be different for a single issuer at different times. The decision may even change for a single issue during the anticipation period. In general, the best hedge in any given situation is the one that largely offsets the price risk of the issuance and most closely meets the firm's own hedge criteria.

## References

Arak, Marcelle, Laurie S. Goodman, and Susan Ross, "The Cheapest to Deliver Bond on the Treasury Bond Futures Contract," *Advances in Futures and Options Research*, Volume 1, Part B, JAI Press, Inc., 1987.

Asay, Michael, and Charles Edelsburg, "Can a Dynamic Strategy Replicate the Returns of an Option?," *The Journal of Futures Markets*, 1986, 6: 63-71.

Kane, Alex, and Alan J. Marcus, "The Quality Option in the Treasury Bond Futures Market: An Empirical Assessment," *The Journal of Futures Markets*, 1986, 6:230-248.

Meisner, James F., and John W. Labuszewski, "Treasury Bond Futures Delivery Bias," *The Journal of Futures Markets*, 1984, 4: 569-573.

Rubinstein, Mark, and Hayne E. Leland, "Replicating Options with Positions in Stock and Cash," *Financial Analysts Journal*, July-August 1981, pp.3-12.

# Index